D0949836

B
Presser, J.   c.1

NEFF.
    MOBBED UP: JACKIE PRESSER'S
HIGH-WIRE LIFE...

B.
Presser, J.   c.1

NEFF.
    MOBBED UP: JACKIE PRESSER'S
HIGH-WIRE LIFE...

1989   22.95   1-90

Alameda Free Library
Alameda, California

Mobbed Up

Mobbed Up

Jackie Presser's High-Wire Life
in the Teamsters, the Mafia,
and the F.B.I.

James Neff

c. 1

THE ATLANTIC MONTHLY PRESS
NEW YORK

ALAMEDA FREE LIBRARY

B
PRESSER, J.

Copyright © 1989 by James Neff

All rights reserved. No part of this book may be reproduced in any form or by any electronic or mechanical means including information storage and retrieval systems without permission in writing from the publisher, except by a reviewer, who may quote brief passages in a review.

Published simultaneously in Canada
Printed in the United States of America
FIRST EDITION

Library of Congress Cataloging-in-Publication Data
Neff, James.
  Mobbed up: Jackie Presser's high-wire life in the Teamsters, the Mafia, and the F.B.I. / James Neff.—1st ed.
    ISBN 0-87113-344-X
    1. Presser, Jackie. 2. Trade-unions—United States—Officials and
employees—Biography. 3. International Brotherhood of Teamsters, Chauffeurs, Warehousemen, and Helpers of America—Biography.
I. Title.
HD6509.P74N44   1989   331.88'11388324'092—dc20   89-15130

The Atlantic Monthly Press
19 Union Square West
New York, NY 10003

FIRST PRINTING

For Maureen and Jameson

Acknowledgments

Writing the life of Jackie Presser posed interesting challenges. Since the three powerful institutions that shaped his life—the Teamsters, the Mob, and the FBI—resist scrutiny, the task was to penetrate these secret societies. Fortunately for me, key figures in each camp—men who were very close to Presser—chose for whatever reasons to cooperate with this project. Some were interviewed a dozen or more times, and I thank them for their patience and assistance. Other central figures such as Labor Department investigators George Simmons and James Thomas cooperated without reservation. I was also able to draw upon two extraordinary resources for this book. The more important was Presser's FBI informant file, some two thousand pages of top-secret information noted and memorialized over the years by his contact agents. The Presser informant file and its companion, the Anthony Hughes informant file, surfaced during pretrial maneuverings in the Teamsters civil RICO lawsuit. Together they provide a rare look into the Cleveland and national underworld from 1969 to 1986. The release of such sensitive FBI files was unprecedented.

Also of tremendous value were transcripts of nearly a decade of high-level union meetings with the Pressers and other Teamster leaders from Ohio. This record of Teamsters Union Local 507 and Joint Council 41 provided a rare look into the workings of one of the most influential Teamsters operations in the country. These transcripts and attached materials—nearly sixteen thousand pages—included financial reports, letters, and related materials.

Names, dates, incidents, and conversations in this book are true. Nothing has been changed. Some conversations have been reconstructed, but only when contemporaneous notes, memos, or reports of the conversations were available. In many cases, the participants were consulted to get the most accurate account. I took into account individual speech patterns of the parties, making the conversations more accurate than paraphrased versions could ever be.

I would especially like to thank Walt Bogdanich, Greg Stricharchuk, Dan Davis, William Scott Malone, and Dan Moldea for generously providing access to their Teamsters and organized crime files. They saved me months of effort. Walt, Greg, and Dan Davis provided critical readings that improved the book. Dan Davis spent many months tracking down elusive references, documents, and facts, for which I am particularly grateful.

Thanks also to the following: Robert Tissing at the Lyndon Baines Johnson Library; Henry Gwiazda at the John F. Kennedy Library; Joan Howard, Fred Grabowske, and the staff at the Nixon Project of the National Archives; and Cable Network News reporter Janet Kolodzy, who searched through presidential papers at the Jimmy Carter Library for me. The John F. Kennedy Foundation provided a research grant for this book.

Also helpful were Christopher Evans, Steve Ryan, William D. Beyer, John Griffith, Henry York, Steve Bell, John Climaco, Randy Mastro, Marla Alhadeff, Mark Helleher, Lilly Grant, Aurora Davis, Cheryl Jeans, Doug Roller, Stephen H. Jigger, Gary Shapiro, Edward P. Kovacic, Bill Lonchar, Mike Malley, Kevin O'Rourke, Thomas G. Rockman, Fred Jurek, Evelyn Theiss, Stephanie Saul, Walter Sheridan, John Sopko, Jean Tussey, Kevin McCoy, and Dan Wasserman.

Special thanks to my editor, Ann Godoff, her assistant, Nancy Lewin, and publisher Carl Navarre, whose wholehearted support of this book made my task easier, and to my agent, Esther Newberg of International Creative Management, who started it all rolling.

Above all, my deepest appreciation goes to my wife, Maureen, for her love, patience, and stamina during this long haul.

—JAMES NEFF,
Cleveland, June 26, 1989

Contents

Cast of Characters

ALLEN, CHARLIE: Hoffa wanted him to kill Frank Fitzsimmons.

ARATARI, LOUIS: Mob hit man

AUIPPA, JOE: boss of the Chicago Mafia

BELL, GEORGE T.: Charles Colson's assistant

BENDER, GEORGE: former U.S. senator from Ohio

BOFFA, EUGENE: mobster who operated sweetheart trucking firms

BOGDANICH, WALT: former *Plain Dealer* reporter

CANFIL, STEVE: former Strike Force prosecutor

CERONE, JACKIE: underboss of the Chicago Mafia

CIVELLA, CARL: lieutenant in the Kansas City Mafia

CIVELLA, NICK: boss of the Kansas City Mafia

CLIMACO, JOHN: former general counsel of the IBT

COFFEY, PAUL: assistant chief of the Justice Department's racketeering section

COLSON, CHARLES: special White House counsel to Nixon

DORFMAN, ALLEN: "consultant" to Central States Pension Fund, Chicago Mafia associate

FELICE, JOHN "SKIPPY": president of Cleveland Teamsters Beverage Drivers Local 293

FOLEY, JAMES PATRICK: Cleveland police detective in charge of labor relations in the forties and fifties

FORAN, PATRICK: Jackie's FBI handler, 1977–81.

FRIEDMAN, ALLEN: Jackie's uncle

FRIEDMAN, HAROLD: Teamsters vice president, president of Warehouse Local 507

FRIEDMAN, HARRY: Jackie's uncle

FRIEDRICK, ROBERT: Jackie's FBI handler, 1981–86

GREENE, DANNY: labor racketeer; rival to the Cleveland Mafia

GRIFFIN, JOE: head of Cleveland FBI office

HALBIN, PETER: Jackie's publicist

HALER, HARRY: California con man and Mafia associate

HOPCRAFT, DAVID: former *Plain Dealer* executive editor

HOOVER, DUKE: owner of a Teamsters PR firm

HUGHES, ANTHONY: Teamster informant; Jackie's close friend

JIGGER, STEVE: Cleveland Strike Force prosecutor

KLEIN, SAM: family friend; owner of Bally Manufacturing

LANCI, TOM: mobster convicted of murder; Hoover-Gorin "employee"

LIBERATORE, ANTHONY: Cleveland Mafia capo; Hoover-Gorin "employee"

LICAVOLI, JAMES T., a.k.a. Jack White: boss, Cleveland family, 1976–1982

LONARDO, ANGELO: underboss of the Cleveland family; informant

MARGOLIS, DAVID: chief of the DOJ's Organized Crime section

MCCANN, MARTIN: Jackie's FBI handler, 1972–77

MCCARTHY, WILLIAM: Teamsters president, 1988–

MOCERI, LEO "LIPS": Cleveland underboss, murdered in 1976

NARDI, JOHN: president of Cleveland Vending Workers Local 410; Presser business partner

NESS, ELIOT: Cleveland Safety Director, 1935–41

OLAH, STEVE: late Cleveland Strike Force chief

PRESSER, BARI: Jackie's daughter by wife Patricia

PRESSER, CARMEN: Jackie's fourth wife, 1971–85

PRESSER, FAYE: Jackie's mother

PRESSER, HERMAN: Jackie's uncle

PROVENZANO, ANTHONY: late New Jersey Teamsters boss

REVELL, OLIVER B.: FBI number-two man behind William Webster

RISPO, BOBBY: bag man and enforcer for sweetheart trucking firms

ROBERTS, DONALD R.: member of 1940s car theft ring

ROCKMAN, MILTON "MAISHE": mob financier; Presser family friend

ROCKMAN, TOM: lawyer son of Maishe

ROLLINS, EDWARD J.: Reagan adviser

ROTATORI, ROBERT: Teamsters lawyer

SCALISH, JOHN: Cleveland godfather, 1944–1976

SCHECTER, SHELDON: friend of Jackie; ran for U.S. Congress
SIMMONS, GEORGE "RED": former Labor Department agent
STOKES, CARL: Cleveland mayor, 1967–71
SYLVESTER, HAROLD: Jackie's friend in the car theft ring
THOMAS, JAMES: former Labor Department agent
TRISCARO, BABE: number-two Ohio Teamster behind Bill Presser, 1951–74
TROTT, STEPHEN: former head of the Justice Department's criminal division
VAIL, THOMAS: Cleveland *Plain Dealer* publisher and editor
WALLS, PAULINE: Jackie's first wife
WEBSTER, WILLIAM: director of the FBI
WILLIAMS, ROY LEE: Teamsters president 1981–83
WHITE, JACK: See Licavoli
WOGE, MAIRY JAYN: *Plain Dealer* reporter and Presser nemesis

Prologue

Jackie Presser read the telegram President Reagan had sent him: "Those of us who care share some measure of your loss and pray that you will be comforted at this difficult time." He was glad the White House had remembered his father. Less than ten months ago, he, Bill Presser, and Reagan had lunch together in Columbus at an Ohio Conference of Teamsters convention. Now it was July 21, 1981; Reagan was president and Jackie's father was being honored at a huge funeral service attended by the Cleveland mayor, the Ohio governor, and dozens of judges and elected officials who owed part of their success to Bill Presser. Even Reagan was in debt to the Pressers. In the fall of 1980, Jackie talked the Teamsters executive board members into throwing the endorsement of the 1.7-million-member union behind the conservative, anti-labor candidate from California.

Several hundred people packed the service at Miller-Deutsch Memorial Chapel in suburban Woodmere. They were a mixed bag: businessmen in expensive suits, rough-hewn truck drivers in out-of-date sport coats, out of town Mob figures. A procession of Cadillacs and shiny cars wove through the suburbs of Cleveland for a dozen miles, tying up traffic and the manpower of a few community police forces. It was a fitting spectacle for a man who secretly ruled as the country's most influential Teamsters official in the decade after Teamsters president Jimmy Hoffa went to federal prison for jury tampering in 1967.

1

A short, obese man whose dark-circled eyes gave him a sad, haunted look, Bill had been dubbed the Fireplug by Hoffa, for obvious reasons. The nickname was shortened to the Plug, only no one ever called Bill this to his face. The men who commonly called him Plug were Mob figures, men who spoke cautiously to each other in code, slang, and broken Italian. Like Hoffa, Presser had known and done business with many of the country's top Mob figures—Nick Civella, boss of Kansas City; Johnny Scalish, Bill's lunch partner and head of the Cleveland crime family; Anthony "Fat Tony" Salerno, the New York City Mafia leader; the list goes on. He had risen to power during the Bloody Thirties, when racketeers gained a toehold in the labor movement by offering strong-arm services to legitimate unions needing muscle to battle company goons on the picket lines. Before he died, he saw the labor movement losing strength and membership by the day, and his name and that of the Teamsters firmly linked to organized crime. His career spanned the birth of modern organized crime and its move to middle-aged respectability in Las Vegas.

Bill Presser rubbed shoulders as a young man with Moe Dalitz and members of the old Cleveland Syndicate, men who went on to build the Desert Inn and other glittery Las Vegas casinos. He was targeted by young Robert Kennedy, counsel for the McClellan rackets committee during the fifties, and in a showdown outside a hearing room, Bill supposedly spit in the future senator's face. Presser also rebelled against his mentor, Jimmy Hoffa, after Hoffa went to prison in 1967. Five years later, Bill helped the Nixon White House compile its shameful Enemies List. Throughout it all, he remained relatively anonymous outside of Ohio. Like his associates in the Mafia, Bill liked it that way. Keep the head down and out of the line of fire of the FBI and the Justice Department.

Four years before Bill Presser's fatal heart attack, he arranged to have his powerful Teamsters vice-president post transferred to his son. The sixteen other Teamsters vice-presidents meekly went along, even though many privately felt Jackie hadn't earned the right to step into his father's shoes. It was a day Bill hadn't expected to see. Jackie had been a bumbler for years, flitting from one failed venture to the next—bowling alleys, a coin shop, a liquor store—getting by on roguish charisma and his father's connections. In the early 1970s, Jackie matured almost overnight, showing a determination to be a Teamsters power and a millionaire like his dad. Curiously, it happened about the same time he began talking to Cleveland FBI supervisor Martin P. McCann, who had an uncanny knack for cultivating underworld informants.

McCann had already developed Jackie's bodyguard and adviser, ex-prizefighter Tony Hughes, into a valuable source. By the early 1970s, the Mob in Cleveland was split into two warring camps, the old-time Mafia crew battling a younger, more ruthless gang led by flamboyant gangster Danny Greene. McCann warned Jackie several times when he picked up intelligence that he and Tony Hughes might be hit. Before long, Jackie decided he needed the protection McCann and the FBI could offer. Soon Jackie was on the road to becoming the FBI's best labor racketeering source. Code-named the Tailor and later ALPRO, Jackie helped the Justice Department build cases against some of the more elusive organized crime figures—Allen Dorfman, Nick Civella, Maishe Rockman, Fat Tony Salerno, Joseph "Joey Doves" Auippa, and others. Two years before his father's funeral, for instance, Jackie had told the FBI that Teamsters vice president Roy Lee Williams of Kansas City, a rival, had taken part in a scheme to bribe Nevada senator Howard Cannon in exchange for holding up proposed trucking legislation harmful to Teamsters. After a massive FBI probe, Williams was indicted. But it didn't stop him from being elected Teamsters president a month before he traveled to Cleveland for the Presser funeral. In brief remarks at the service, Williams called Bill "the consummate trade unionist, a guiding light for the rest of us younger officers. . . . He was a mentor and my friend for thirty-three years." He knew that Jackie, several steps away, didn't like him, but Williams didn't realize how far Jackie had gone to destroy him.

It was a day of mixed feelings for Jackie Presser. He had loved his father. "He was an outstanding parent," he said at the service. "He devoted his life to the betterment of mankind. He was a person of great wisdom, integrity, and compassion." But now Jackie wouldn't have to stand in his father's shadow anymore. He was finally going to be judged on his own. He was in charge. That much was clear on the warm summer morning at his father's interment at Mt. Olive Cemetery. Jackie was center stage, thanking the seven Teamster vice-presidents and dozens of politicians in attendance. Nearly bald with a fringe of gray, Jackie, fifty-five, was slimmer than his usual three hundred pounds, dressed in a dark sport coat and beltless tan trousers.

3

Strangely, many Cleveland Mafia members were absent from the spectacle that day. Jackie had told Milton "Maishe" Rockman, Bill's boyhood friend and the Mob's intermediary with the Pressers, to tell Cleveland Mob figures to stay away. Jackie's reasons for doing so were complicated. Though he was working for the FBI as an underworld source, his informant file indicates he was reluctant to implicate Rockman and the other local mafiosi; much of his intelligence about wrongdoing by the Mob or Teamster officials pertained to men from cities other than Cleveland. He either didn't want to hurt people he knew or felt it too risky to take on ranking Mafia members in his hometown. Some of his intelligence was deadly accurate, such as the worthwhile scoop on Roy Williams. Some of it was misleading, second-hand, or worthless.

FBI agent Robert S. Friedrick, a straight-laced Naval Academy graduate and supervisor of the organized crime squad, was Jackie's new contact agent; he had told Jackie the Bureau wanted to update its intelligence files on the Mob by writing down license-plate numbers and snapping surveillance photos of the wise guys who came to pay respects. It was an opportunity too fruitful to pass up, and two hours before the service the FBI set up its stakeout.

Beneath his rough charm, Jackie Presser was a tangle of complexities, far more so than his close associates at the funeral realized. He allowed the Teamsters, the Mob, and the FBI each to think he was wholeheartedly on its side, but in fact he was carefully balancing the interests of each to protect himself. Publicly, he defended the union, denying accusations by congressional critics and union dissidents that the Mafia influenced union decisions. Preposterous, Jackie would say, noting he knew not one so-called Mob guy. Privately, he told the FBI he had to answer to the boss of the Cleveland family. If he cut them off cold, he'd probably get killed.

Above all, he wanted to be considered a respected citizen and not end up like his father, tarred by collective memory as a racketeer. Jackie knew his father had performed favors for the Mob, putting their relatives on the payroll in no-show jobs and approving Teamsters pension-fund loans to finance Las Vegas gambling casinos. Jackie resented it, feeling his father hadn't been compensated enough for taking these risks. All Bill ever got out of it were some boxes of his favorite imported cigars, Jackie fumed. Of course this wasn't true. His father was too sharp for that.

4

To keep his image clean, Jackie did what corporations do. He hired a public relations firm, unusual at the time in Teamsters circles, to remake his image into one of respectability. He threw out his black shirts and loud sport coats, went on a diet and bought conservative suits. Unlike his father, who didn't care what others thought of him, Jackie was sensitive to public opinion. He wanted to be loved and accepted.

Jackie was at the peak of his power when his father died—welcome in the White House and positioned to take over the Teamsters union from the indicted Williams, who would eventually be convicted for bribing Senator Cannon and forced from union office. Jackie could not have foreseen a new threat to him present at the funeral. Parked outside Miller-Deutsch Funeral Home was a van with smoked glass windows. Inside, two Labor Department investigators, George "Red" Simmons and Jim Thomas were snapping photos from a camera mounted on a tripod and equipped with a telephoto lens. Part of the newly formed organized crime unit of the Labor Department's inspector general's office, the two Labor agents had the same idea as their more powerful and prestigious investigative colleagues at the FBI—see who showed up. "Everybody who was everybody from Cleveland came," Thomas would recall years later. "Mayors, congressmen, all the union leaders, every petty thief in the world. Many attorneys, many accountants, the whole Jewish community."

The FBI agents and the Labor investigators clicked away with their cameras and took notes, each unaware of the other. In theory, the two law enforcement agencies were supposed to work labor racketeering cases together under the supervision of the Justice Department's Strike Force Against Organized Crime. But that was just a theory. Across the country in several cities, the two agencies clashed over their responsibilities. In Cleveland the situation was at its worst, and this would become Jackie's undoing. The chief of the strike force and the head of the FBI field office, two aggressive, stubborn men who liked publicity, were barely on speaking terms. The FBI wanted to protect Presser and the Strike Force wanted to prosecute him, and they couldn't sit down and calmly discuss how to handle the situation.

A tragic collision was inevitable.

1

Early Days

"Jackie was a bully."
JACK KLEINMAN

On August 6, 1926, in Cleveland, Ohio, a frightened eighteen-year-old girl bore a healthy, hefty infant son. It was her first child, and she named him after her brother Jack. Asked at the hospital to fill out a birth certificate, she and the boy's father gave their first names as Fannie and Joseph. They said their surname was Fayf. In careful longhand script, the birth certificate noted that he was a salesman, she a housewife, and that they lived on East Fifty-fifth Street.

None of it was true. There was no Mr. and Mrs. Fayf. The father was William Presser, a nineteen-year-old hatmaker, the mother Faye Friedman, daughter of a bootlegger and gambler. They weren't married and had used false names not only to avoid embarrassment, but also to stick the hospital with the bill.

Their plump infant son, Jackie Presser, just a few hours old, didn't realize he had just played a part in his first scam.

When Jackie was born, Faye Friedman and Bill Presser lived with their parents in Glenville, a middle-class, mostly Jewish neighborhood on Cleveland's east side. Bill's family lived in half of a relatively new two-family frame house, which had small patches of grass in front and in back. Bill, the oldest of Benjamin and Yetta Presser's six children, was short and barrel-shaped, with a quiet, round face marked by dark,

6

brooding eyebrows. Even in lean times, Bill looked well fed; years later Teamsters Union president Jimmy Hoffa would nickname him the Plug.

Faye Friedman lived a few blocks away in a house that seemed huge compared to the three-bedroom home Presser's family squeezed into. Built in 1920, the Friedman home had five bedrooms, two full bathrooms, a finished attic with three gabled windows facing the street, and a full basement complete with hidden compartments and a secret exit for quick escape. The basement was the most important room in the house. Faye's father, Louis, had constructed an illegal distillery there that produced a steady stream of alcohol and income. Louis Friedman told people that he dealt in cattle, but dealing cards and selling booze more accurately described how he supported his five children.

Unlike Bill, the father of her child, Faye Friedman was outgoing and high-strung. Friends said she had a steam engine of a personality, thrusting her voice into laughs or screams, spending her prodigious energy on running the family or on gambling. Born in Austria-Hungary on May 8, 1908, she was sturdy and short, with blue eyes and blond hair. She inherited her father's lust for gambling—horses, cards, gin rummy, anything. Bill Presser hated gambling; he considered it a waste of money, a sign of weakness, a sickness. Eventually, this sickness would help ruin the lives of two of Faye's brothers.

Bill made hats, a hot, smelly, semiskilled trade that brought a steady paycheck to a young man with a new family. "It was hard work, because in those days everything was done by gas," he recalled. "After a while you could pick up the hottest pot and you wouldn't burn your hand—it was all calloused." Hatmakers would heat a pot, or mold, over an open gas flame and then roll and press the unshaped hat around it, constantly brushing the nap of the material. "Oh, it was quite a bit of work and that was under tremendous heat," he said.

The first year or so of Jackie's life, a family member recalls, Jackie lived at a farm for orphans outside of Cleveland; he wasn't reunited with his parents until they secured a place to live, reconciled with their parents, and got married. It was a fancy ceremony, complete with bridal attendants, tuxedoed groomsmen, and Faye dressed in a long white dress. Rabbi S. Goldman performed the service on January 15, 1928, seventeen months after Jackie was born.

7

In 1929, shortly after the stock market crashed, Bill declared bankruptcy and folded up the retail hat shop he operated on West Twenty-fifth Street. Like many other Glenville families during the early Depression, Bill and Faye squeezed by on little money. For a while, they lived with Bill's parents and younger brothers and sisters. Jackie and his brother Marvin, two and a half years younger, slept in the same small bed.

For the next several years, Bill and Faye were often on the run, moving from house to house, apartment to apartment, beating landlords out of rent. They'd put down a month's rent and never make another payment. Two or three months later, a sheriff's deputy would take the streetcar out to the apartment and tack an eviction notice on the door. Between September 1931 and March 1942, Bill and Faye had at least thirteen different addresses. "I grew up in a neighborhood where I can remember where my father used to move into an apartment on the first of the month and on the twenty-ninth of the month we'd have to move out because he couldn't pay the next month's rent," Jackie said. "It was a jungle out there."

In October 1931, a month after enrolling Jackie in public kindergarten, his parents restored his real name by filing an affidavit with Cleveland's bureau of vital statistics. This officially ended his double life, but it wouldn't be the last time Jackie Presser operated under a secret identity.

Before the Depression, Glenville teemed with commerce, mostly small shops—kosher butchers, bakeries, barber shops, candy stores, delis, dry cleaners, drug stores—all clustered along East 105th Street, the crowded, narrow business artery that cut through the heart of the neighborhood. Residents could walk down East 105th and within a few steps hear the Old World sounds of Yiddish, smell fresh-baked rye bread, and, if they listened carefully, detect the clinking payouts of illegal penny-a-pull slot machines tucked in the back of candy stores.

At the time, Glenville was an overwhelmingly Jewish neighborhood, one of three in the city. The suburb of Cleveland Heights was where middle-class Jews lived. The Kinsman area, slightly poorer than Glenville, was the home of trade workers. Glenville was mostly populated by small-business owners, and it was politically less radical than

Kinsman. Glenville's anchor, dominating its social and intellectual affairs, was the Jewish Center. It was an impressive red brick building that contained not only a synagogue, but a swimming pool, a gymnasium with a basketball court, classrooms for the Cleveland Hebrew Schools, and a library. On Sunday mornings, the center's lectures attracted hundreds of people, many from outside the neighborhood, who nourished themselves on speeches about Zionism, the rise of anti-Semitism in Germany, the trade-union movement, and local politics. Afterwards, they stayed around to socialize, cultivate business, and make friends.

Most of Glenville's small shops survived the Depression; after all, people still had to buy bread and repair their shoes. Unemployed workers were in a more desperate situation. In fact, while waiting in lines at the Jewish Social Service Bureau for food handouts, out-of-work Glenville residents rioted after being told that the matzoh for Passover had run out. This was in 1933, the depth of the Depression. "We were growing up at a time when there was nothing, no hope for anything," says Jack Kleinman, who grew up in Glenville and knew Jackie. "As kids, we played kick the can and buck buck, how many fingers up. As far as parents were concerned, it was a lot harder. Having children made your problems even worse. Lot of times, parents were so involved in trying to make a living that they didn't have a handle on what their kids were doing."

The newly married Pressers did frequently pick up and move, but they always stayed within the same few blocks in the heart of Glenville. The moves shouldn't have disrupted young Jackie's schooling at Miles Standish Elementary, but he was a poor student nonetheless. According to family members, Faye didn't encourage Jackie in school, which was unusual for a Glenville parent. Many were the sons and daughters of undereducated immigrants, and as a rule they pushed their children to get an education and get ahead. Teachers were revered. Faye had ended her formal schooling at age seventeen when she dropped out of seventh grade at Miles Standish, just across the street from the Presser home. Bill got halfway through the eleventh grade at Glenville High School before dropping out in 1925.

During the thirties, Glenville High School enjoyed a reputation of academic excellence. Students took their studies seriously, competing for grades and honors. "It was a Jewish neighborhood, and parents held high aspirations for their children," says Abba Schwartz, a retired Cleveland school administrator who grew up in Glenville. "And the teacher was always right. You were expected to perform." Many Glenville graduates won Ivy League scholarships. The school's median IQ, measured in the mid-thirties, was an astoundingly high 117. Years later, in one week in 1977, three Glenville graduates from this era were appointed to U.S. ambassadorships in Austria, Bali, and Costa Rica. It was that sort of student body.

Jackie didn't fit into this culture of education and intellectual achievement. He and his family were outsiders. At age ten, he was still in the slow-learner section of second grade at Miles Standish. For the next five years, he was on the ungraded track at school, meaning that he wasn't promoted from grade to grade each year. Instead, he was moved along as fast or as slow as he was able to learn.

Outside the classroom, on the playgrounds and the streets, Jackie excelled, foreshadowing the leadership he'd display later in life. He was the ringleader of a crew of first- and second-grade boys who roamed Miles Standish and its two huge new playgrounds. They'd enter the school and tear around its giant boiler room, hiding out, playing cowboys and Indians or cops and robbers. Jackie insisted on being the cop. Built like his father—squat, broad-shouldered, heavy—he was the leader, partly because he was the biggest, a friend says. "Jackie was in charge, I was his lieutenant," says Sheldon Schecter, who left the neighborhood and became a successful lawyer, ran for Congress, and kept up ties to Jackie. "He was a husky kid then."

Though he gave a dozen or more in-depth interviews throughout his life, Jackie was extremely secretive and revealed little about his early years. One relative who was close to him says that it's because Jackie's earliest memories were unpleasant. His mother, Faye, has been described as cold and unaffectionate; her younger sister, Millie, became Jackie's surrogate mom, baby-sitting for him for several years. This relative also insists that Jackie eventually learned that he had been left in a foster home as an infant. The news was a shock, embarrassing him and making him unsure of his parents' love.

Many of the Pressers refuse to discuss Jackie or his parents at all, sheltering their extraordinary family history. "The good stories are in my heart, and that's where they're going to stay," Jackie's brother, Marvin, explains. He says he doesn't trust writers and brings up the time a *Cleveland News* reporter called him at home and asked, "Are you the son of William Presser?" "Yes, I am," Marvin said. "I'd like to take you to lunch." "What's your name?" The reporter told him, and Marvin recognized it from the byline on a series of stories about the Teamsters Union that were critical of his father. "You stick that lunch up your ass," Marvin advised.

When Jackie did talk of the old days, he often painted them in rosy hues. "I remember the streets I lived on had front porches and nobody carried a key for their door," Jackie said. "I knew my neighbors. My mother had a swing on the porch, and my grandmother baked her own bread. Friday night was a big night for all of us for homemade soup of meats and stuff." Jackie's childhood friends and acquaintances also tell wistful stories about Depression-era Glenville, stories that clash with the harsher memories of their parents. Jackie and the neighborhood boys would play among the Cultural Gardens, then under construction by Work Projects Administration crews, who sweated with pick, shovel, and shears to grade lawns and mold shrubs and create ceremonial gardens that honored the various ethnic groups of Cleveland. The gardens were located along East Boulevard, which snaked through a narrow valley of woods and a stream that separated Glenville from a Slovakian neighborhood to the west.

In the summers, Jackie and the kids in the neighborhood sometimes watched baseball games between the Glenville ball players and the Catholic players from the Slovakian neighborhood across the boulevard. They played every Sunday afternoon, competing fiercely. "It was between the Jews and the Gentiles, a doubleheader," Jack Kleinman recalls. "Lots of money was bet. When it was all over, there'd be fights. These were guys in their late teens, early twenties. I used to go down and sell them ice cream or cold pop."

Bettors could find many outlets in Glenville. Every few blocks along East 105th Street, they could bet a horse or a ball game with bookies in the back of barbershops or in card rooms. In the established card rooms, you could sit down to a game of poker or *stusch*, a thirteen-card gambling game. Sol Tick ran a place in a room behind a barbershop on East 105th; the Kibbitzer's Club was a few blocks away; the Log Cabin Club, at East 105th and Superior, was tucked into a tiny building that resembled its name. "Everybody knew it was there," Kleinman says. "It was against the law, but anybody could walk in."

11

Jackie's grandfather, Louis Friedman, haunted the card rooms until he died of a heart attack in 1934. He was only forty-eight. His youngest son, Allen, only thirteen, was crushed. Allen was extremely close to his father and wanted to be a gambler and racketeer just like him. Allen's fondest memories include helping his dad make moonshine in the basement still, stirring the hootch and preparing bottles.

Lou Friedman had been born in Hungary, where, according to family legend, he stole horses, painted them to hide characteristic markings, then sold them to unsuspecting customers. Years later in Cleveland, he was kidnapped by a rival bootleg gang while driving two big shipments of whiskey to Chicago. Lou's wife, Theresa, called prominent racketeer Maxie Diamond for help. "All the racket guys loved my mother," Allen says. Within a day, her husband was back, unharmed, his liquor intact, thanks to Maxie. "I had a lot of fun," Lou Friedman said of his adventure.

Big bootleggers risked their lives, but Lou managed to outlive Prohibition. Another notorious Cleveland family, whose fortunes would intermingle with Jackie's over the decades, wasn't so fortunate.

One evening in October 1927, Big Joe Lonardo, the dark, three-hundred-pound don of Cleveland bootlegging, sauntered into a barbershop in the Italian area of Woodland. Big Joe was a flashy dresser who fancied diamond jewelry. This night, he wore diamond rings, cuff links, and a stickpin and carried several hundred dollars in a billfold. He and a younger brother, John, had come to meet the Porellos, newcomers from Sicily who were trying to move in on Lonardo's wholesale corn-sugar cartel. The Lonardos illegally sold corn sugar, a key raw ingredient of bootleg booze, to hundreds of small stills throughout town.

The narrow barbershop served as a social center for the neighborhood, so Big Joe saw no reason for alarm when two men appeared from a back room. The men were on the Porello payroll, but they hadn't come to discuss the corn-sugar market. They pulled out guns and fired a hail of bullets at Big Joe and his brother, stirring up a racket in the busy neighborhood. John Lonardo died instantly in the ambush. Big Joe started to chase his assailants and managed to stagger into the street, blood pumping from his chest. He pulled out a pistol, then collapsed. Cleveland's first Mafia boss was dead.

Angelo, Big Joe's oldest son, was fifteen when his father was murdered. Quickly, he and his cousins and uncles began a campaign of revenge. Soon, the murder of Big Joe had ignited Cleveland's notorious Corn Sugar War. Before the war ended, seven Porello brothers and two more Lonardos were dead.

To take over the corn-sugar cartel from the Lonardos, the politically astute Porello family sought the blessing of the Mafia's ruling council. On December 5, 1928, twenty-four Mafia powers, mostly from Chicago and New York City, met in a Cleveland hotel to discuss important national underworld matters, including, no doubt, the brutal Corn Sugar War. Although this Cleveland meeting never gained the widespread notoriety of the infamous 1957 Mafia convention in Apalachin, New York, it was the first known gathering of the ruling commission of the Mafia. Like the Apalachin convention, this meeting was rousted.

A Cleveland patrolman noticed a suspicious group of men entering the Hotel Statler at half-past four in the morning. "The men looked both ways and pulled their hats down as they entered the hotel," the cop later testified. Police raided the hotel and nabbed twenty-three men and thirteen guns in one room. One of those swept up was Giuseppe Profaci, later known as Joe Profaci, who climbed to boss of the Brooklyn Mafia. Profaci had bad luck with these big Mob meetings—he was the only mafioso who was captured at both the Cleveland and Apalachin meetings.

On July 11, 1929, with Cleveland's Corn Sugar War still raging, teenaged Angelo Lonardo drove a Lincoln sedan to one of the Porellos' sugar warehouses, only a hundred feet from where his father had been slaughtered. In the car was his mother, Concetta, a fat woman in a black widow's dress and thick round eyeglasses. She was the bait. Angelo sent a message to the warehouse manager, Black Sam Todaro, that Concetta wanted to talk to him. Todaro had worked for Big Joe and had arranged the fatal barbershop meeting. Angelo and his family believed that Black Sam had double-crossed them.

As widow of the slain don, Concetta was entitled to respect, so Todaro came out of the warehouse and walked over to the Lincoln. Angelo and a cousin pulled out pistols and fired, killing him with five slugs. Later, near Black Sam's body, police found a playing card—the ace of spades, gangland's calling card of death.

13

More than half a century later, Angelo Lonardo would be called Big Ange and serve as acting boss of the Cleveland Mafia. He would pocket money skimmed from Teamster-financed gambling casinos and would control some Teamsters jobs. He also would give Jackie Presser and the union hierarchy one giant headache after becoming an FBI informant and revealing how he and his Mafia friends had boosted Jackie's career.

Jackie's grandmother Theresa Friedman died a year after her husband Louis, leaving her thirteen-year-old youngest son, Allen, without parents. Allen's sister Faye and her husband Bill Presser took him in, and he and Jackie became close friends. Over the next year, Bill and Faye and the boys wandered through Glenville, moving from Tacoma Avenue to Adams Avenue to East Ninety-ninth Street, all within ten months. Allen resented the moves, his school, his life, and especially the fact that his parents had died. He felt abandoned and angry, and he lashed out with his fists. "I beat up on kids," he admits. "Mothers wouldn't let me hang out with their daughters."

A handsome athletic kid, Allen was soon carrying two hundred pounds on a muscular 5'10" frame. By age nineteen, he had made a career choice. "I wanted to be a crook and racketeer, collect debts for people," he says. He and Jackie, only five years apart, were as close as brothers. Fearless, good-looking Uncle Allen was Jackie's adolescent idol. "He looked up to me like I was the sun, moon, and the stars," Allen says. Big and slow in school, influenced by his increasingly violent uncle, Jackie Presser had turned into a schoolyard bully.

Jack Kleinman, a year older than Jackie, remembers a fight they had at elementary school. "Jackie was a bully," Kleinman affirms. "He was messing around with one of the young girls there or . . . throwing a ball real hard at someone." They squared off on the playground. Kleinman had the advantage of age and height, but Jackie outweighed him substantially. "He ended up with a bloody nose, and I had a chipped tooth or something," Kleinman says. "I don't know if he beat me up or I beat him up. We had some tussles."

† † †

Meanwhile, Bill Presser moved from job to job. He handled cattle, he worked in a window-cleaning company run by his father. By the time Jackie was eight or nine, he ran his own dry-cleaning shop. According to one report, a racketeer tried to shake him down, and Bill picked up a baseball bat and chased him out. Word of the incident got around, and it brought the Plug his first organizing job. A group of small-business owners asked him for help. Presser agreed and ended up persuading the owners and employees of several dozen dry cleaners to band together into an association and to halt a vicious price-cutting war among themselves.

In becoming an organizer, Bill Presser was joining a noble calling in Glenville and in working-class neighborhoods throughout the city. Glenville's Rabbi Abba Hillel Silver, the spellbinding orator and international Zionist leader, advocated trade unions as a way to settle strife and to achieve justice for workers. In fact, at a 1919 address given at Public Square, Cleveland's downtown nerve center, Rabbi Silver savaged the hasty move toward nonunion shops by factories and industrialists right after World War I. A handsome man with a full mouth, thick eyebrows, and dark, intense eyes that flashed behind wire-rimmed spectacles, Rabbi Silver championed the closed shop in sermons and speeches, making it both a religious and social issue.

If his family had been in the habit of going to temple, Bill Presser would have cheered such sermons. His mother, Yetta, had organized garment workers in New York at the turn of the century and, according to family legend, had risked her safety to fight for decent wages and working conditions. Company goons once bashed her in the face during a strike, Bill Presser recalled: "I was one of the very fortunate people who had a mother who had come to this country when she was fifteen years old, by herself, and was an advocate of organization. . . . She had to support herself and became a member of the Ladies Garment Workers of New York City. Several months later, she was one of the women who led a strike, and of course she carried a scar across her head and forehead for the rest of her life. As I grew up, my mother taught me many things by talking to me about the cause of working people and their problems. I listened, and as I grew older, that became a part of my life."

Yetta Presser wasn't alone in her beliefs. Most of her neighbors had come from Poland, Russia, and other parts of Eastern Europe, fleeing czarist Russia and the pogroms. Russia had imposed heavy fines for evading military service and began denying Jews the right to education, a blow to their identity. As a result, these newcomers hated the czar and were sympathetic to the ideas of socialism and collective bargaining.

But Bill Presser, the labor organizer, didn't share the progressive or even liberal beliefs commonly accepted as the bedrock of the labor movement. He was different, a Republican, a small businessman who hated Socialists. If someone interfered with his livelihood or his union position, he felt justified in fighting back with illegal tactics.

Presser told the story of how he and other union officials in the thirties blew up a temporary recruiting shack that the Communist party had erected in the center of town. "Well, there was a time when the Communists had a building on Public Square in Cleveland, many many many years ago, to recruit people to join the Communist party. They searched for members, [people] who had worked and were laid off and they couldn't make a living. The promise to them was that if you join our party we will find you work, we will see that you don't go hungry. Hungry people, if they are hungry enough, will join anything. They were doing a tremendous business. . . . There was a steady stream coming in the front door and walking out the back door. That's how fast they were recruiting. Well, there were a number of labor unions at that time that were being badly hurt by it. We decided to do something about it.

"So this clearing hall for communism . . . just fell down! And we wouldn't help them put it up again. . . . The police and everyone was there, watching it fall down. That was the end of that."

He and his friends had just boldly blown it up. Such tactics would always serve him well.

16

2
The Rackets

*"Bill Presser told them, 'You better do what I say or my
brother-in-law will kill you.'"*

ALLEN FRIEDMAN ON HOW THEY SHOOK DOWN BUSINESSES

William G. Jones, tough and twenty-one, worked at Carley's Dry
Cleaning. It was 1938, and he was happy to have a job, even though
he earned only about ten dollars a week. Cleveland's economy, battered
by the Depression, was still a couple of years away from being kicked
into recovery by the war in Europe.

Bill Jones handled all the chores for owner Ira Carley: he pressed
clothes; he swept floors; he delivered clean laundry from the plant on
busy Carnegie Avenue to the two branch stores in suburban Lakewood
and Cleveland Heights. As Ira Carley got more business, Jones had a
tougher time at work. Carley's success attracted the attention of both
the International Association of Cleaning and Dye Houseworkers and
a stocky, unscrupulous business agent named Bill Presser.

Carley's troubles had started a year or so earlier when he moved
his dry-cleaning business to Cleveland from New York. He boldly cut
prices and began competing fiercely with the seventeen hundred other
dry cleaners in the county. Soon, he was visited by men from the Dry
Cleaners Association who demanded that he join their group, pay dues,
and illegally fix his prices to those set by their association.

It would have been so easy, for all parties, if Carley had just gone
along, but he refused. And the association had to get rough with him.

On Wednesday, December 28, 1938, Bill Jones was unloading
laundry from a truck at the Lakewood shop when he encountered one

of the association's toughs, Ray G. Meyers, who was connected to Bill Presser and the dry-cleaners association. Three of Meyers's men were picketing the front of the cleaner, carrying banners that claimed the store was unfair to organized labor. Ray Meyers, business agent with the International Association of Cleaning and Dye Houseworkers, saw Jones unloading the clean clothes.

"What's the idea? You can't deliver here!" he yelled out.

"Who's going to stop me?" Jones shot back.

Ira Carley came out and helped his delivery man bring the dry cleaning safely inside. As Jones headed back to the truck, Meyers threatened him.

"You're going to get your head opened," the business agent said.

Jones drove off. The next day, the toughs carried through on the threat. It was lunchtime, and Jones and two other Carley workers, Frank Greco and Julia Bejda, went to a diner next door to the main plant on Carnegie. About two dozen men shuffled in and made a point of watching the three eat lunch. Jones recognized some of the men as picketers who had been stationed for days outside the plant.

The gang left the diner a few minutes later. After lunch, as Bill, Frank, and Julia traveled the thirty feet back to the plant, one of the picketers ran up and smashed Jones in the head. Others jumped him and beat him. The three dry-cleaning workers, terrified, ran to the shop.

"Get the girl, too!" yelled one of the thugs.

Just inside the plant, a Cleveland cop, on hand to quell picket-line flare-ups, stepped up. Bill Jones told him what had happened, took him outside, and pointed to the man who had attacked him first. The policeman grabbed the man. Suddenly, from cars parked on the street, dozens of picketers sprang out and surrounded Jones and the cop and his captive. The gang shoved the cop, pulling their friend free. He ran across the street, jumped into a car, and tore off.

This same scene—but with a cast of different workers, unions, and tough guys—was played out repeatedly in the thirties, throughout Cleveland and throughout the country. Window glaziers, dry cleaners, carpenters, and other craftsmen bonded into associations and quasi-unions backed by men who possessed the charisma, cunning, and muscle to persuade others to break laws and bust heads for the promise of a sweeter payday.

Presser and many others, however, ran labor rackets that were simply organizations for extortion and price-fixing. His Dry Cleaners Association was hardly a union. It was made up mostly of owners of small dry-cleaning businesses—Presser himself had owned a shop— who banded together and agreed to fix their prices, often substantially higher than the fair market rate. Then they or their musclemen would approach other dry cleaners and insist they join the association, pay regular dues, and raise their prices. If an owner didn't go along, he'd soon need new windows or first aid. "The labor movement when I started had no rules, no laws, and was a hit-and-miss operation based on jungle tactics," Presser once said.

There's nothing to suggest that Presser and the Dry Cleaners Association were concerned with the wages and working conditions of Carley's employees. Irene Rako, who started working for Carley in November 1938, remembers the young men picketing in front of the plant; she even kidded with them on her way in and out of work. But never did anyone from the association ask her to join a union or sign a pledge card or come to an organizing meeting—even though she was unhappy with her $9.80 weekly wage and was willing to join a union.

Carley fought Presser's harassment. He hired lawyers who sued Bill Presser, the Dry Cleaners Association, its business agents, and its locals. They complained that picketers threatened Carley's customers, falsely claimed a strike was going on, and prevented trucks from delivering coal to the plant. A judge issued a restraining order forbidding Presser, picketers, or anyone in the association from coming too close to Carley's stores. A restraining order is a legal nicety in tough times; it didn't hamper men like Bill Presser. They knew there were other, more creative ways besides a picket line to bring pressure on a balky owner.

Several times during Irene Rako's first year of employment at Carley's Cleveland Heights shop, she came to work and saw shattered glass and boarded windows and inhaled the noxious fumes of home-made stink bombs, which were quickly becoming the popular organizing tool of the day. "The smell was terrible," she says. "People came for their clothes and they stunk. You couldn't get that smell out." She switched to a job at the main plant, met Bill Jones, and married him. The stink bombs kept coming, and Carley eventually gave up. "They drove him out of business," Irene Rako says.

There were some famous veterans of those dry-cleaning battles, Allen Friedman recalls. Not only Bill Presser, but Jimmy "the Weasel" Fratianno and Babe Salupo worked as bombers, he said. Fratianno went on to become a member of the Los Angeles Mafia ten years later, taking on part-time duties as executioner. He personally murdered five men and took part in the slaying of several others. Salupo, arrested numerous times, was convicted of blackmailing prostitutes and imprisoned in Ohio in 1936.

Labor rackets flourished and were even reluctantly tolerated in the thirties. One reason was the ambiguity swirling around labor's bout with management. At the time, many blue-chip corporations were interfering with the legitimate demands of labor unions in ways just as ferocious and unethical as those of the racketeers. In 1936 alone, American corporations spent $80 million on provocateurs, labor spies, and anti-union thugs, as well as millions more for private security forces. Some labor organizers believed this behavior justified their own questionable tactics. In a given conflict, the working public couldn't always figure out whose hands were cleaner.

Bill Presser and the labor racketeers came striding into this gray area. Labor racketeers didn't target steel mills and auto factories and foundries, the giant pools of workers who truly needed the protection of a collective-bargaining agreement. Racketeers picked on small, vulnerable mom-and-pop operations such as dry cleaners, taverns, and bakeries. When a business agent such as Bill Presser made his move, there was little a small-business owner could do to combat the coercion. He or she could complain to the police, but it was usually a waste of time. Police did little to investigate the labor shakedowns and picket-line violence that flared up all over Cleveland.

The situation was made clear to a frustrated Cuyahoga County grand jury seated in 1933 that tried to take a serious look at the problem. The grand jury spent days listening to evidence about various crimes, but none of the presentations pertained to the rash of violence sweeping across the city's businesses. The grand jury, basically a passive body, learned only what an assistant county prosecutor presented. The prosecutor, in turn, depended on police officers for investigation, suspects, and statements. The police, however, were concentrating on other crimes.

In a scathing report, the grand-jury foreman complained that his fellow jurors "had to indict a man who confessed that while 'squirrel drunk' he took off a shoe and smashed four plate-glass windows in a grocery store. Hundreds of windows in Cleveland have been broken by ruthless racketeers this year, but this drunk was the sole window-smasher brought before the grand jury—and he was not a racketeer." It was the perfect climate for Bill Presser's growing operation.

Eliot Ness didn't look like a gangbuster when he arrived in Cleveland. He was slender, six feet tall, and sported fine double-breasted blue suits cut in the current fashion. He made a sharp contrast to the rough-hewn, beefy, working-class Cleveland police force. A graduate of the prestigious University of Chicago, the boyish-looking Ness was only thirty-two years old when he was appointed Cleveland's safety director, put in charge of the police and fire departments, and given sweeping powers to do whatever necessary to keep the city safe. He was a celebrity long before the television series "The Untouchables" made him a national pop hero. In the thirties, people across the country knew how he battled notorious mobster Al Capone with his hand-picked crew of untouchables, honest agents impervious to bribery and corruption. After the repeal of Prohibition, Ness moved to the Treasury Department's Alcohol Tax Unit in Cincinnati to fight backwoods illegal moonshiners. Urbane and ambitious, Ness came to Cleveland in 1935, hired by Mayor Harold H. Burton in a stroke of political genius. Ness was just the right tonic for Cleveland. The city's economy, which relied heavily on steel making and iron casting, was hit harder than most other cities by the Depression. Its police department was reeling from exposés in the city's fiercely competitive newspapers about cops and councilmen on the take who protected open gambling games and illegal nightspots. Hungry for a hero, reporters chronicled Ness's every step, creating a figure of godlike proportions.

Ness and his attractive wife dove into the city's social circuit. They lived alone in a large boathouse on Clifton Lagoon in Lakewood, an older suburb known for its three-mile stretch of elegant homes along the shores of Lake Erie. Ness wasn't a prude. He liked to take a drink and he liked to take late-night boat rides with friends, motoring along the calm, warm summer waters of the lake. His assignment was to take on corrupt cops, syndicate gambling, and labor racketeering—basically clean up the town. As he jumped into the task, the gangsters, Maxie Diamond included, watched warily from the sidelines.

Diamond was close to the Presser family, having rescued Faye Presser's brother Louis after he was kidnapped by the rival gang of bootleggers. Like Faye's father, Diamond had been born in Russia, in 1902. He was slim, about 5'8" and 140 pounds, a flashy dresser, and a graduate of the 105 Gang, named after East 105th Street, the narrow Glenville street with a bookie or a gambling joint on nearly every block. Diamond was described by newspapers as Cleveland's number-one racketeer, but it didn't seem to bother him. Racketeering operated so openly that the label wasn't considered a stigma. In fact, Diamond was helped by the notoriety. It made it easier to shake down shop owners or to prevent rivals from moving in on his illegal operations. Racketeers moved about so boldly and had so much influence with politicians that when passing such gangsters on the sidewalks, many policemen felt obligated to tip their hats.

A few months after Ness took office, Diamond still felt comfortable enough to saunter into the city's central police headquarters and, in an impromptu interview with a reporter, praise Ness for his honesty. Diamond allowed as how he was in the building to see about a real-estate deal. "Dressed like an *Esquire* fashion picture in a well-pressed brown suit, a dark brown snap-brimmed hat, and a dashing checked tan top coat, Diamond puffed on a long black cigar and spoke of Ness," the reporter's story read. "I have never had the pleasure of meeting Mr. Ness, but I'd certainly like to," Diamond said.

Diamond, only thirty-nine, took off his hat and rubbed a temple, showing a few strands of silver among his black hair. "I know Mr. Ness is a swell guy because you can't buy him either for a cigar or any amount of cash," Diamond said. "All I know about him is what I've read, but I know he's an honest man." And how does he like Mayor Burton's administration? Diamond was asked. "It makes no difference to me," he replied. "I've never made a nickel off any of the mayors. . . . Some

22

of the boys have had favors and have made some change by their connections with politicians, but I have never."

"What politicians?" he was asked. Diamond smiled and strolled away.

Diamond was associated with Bill Presser through the laundry rackets. Diamond also operated several large, plush, illegal gambling clubs in and around Cleveland. He was one level down from the top of the Cleveland syndicate, which was dominated by four partners who went on to build Las Vegas: Moe Dalitz, Morris Kleinman, Louis Rothkopf, and Samuel A. Tucker. Together they ran laundries, casinos, and nightclubs.

Ness started his clean-up campaign in earnest in 1936. He targeted the obvious, the gangsters from Little Italy—the Mayfield Road Gang, the newspapers called them—police characters Angelo "Big Ange" Lonardo, George "King" Angersola, Angelo Sciria, and their cohorts in the numbers rackets like Milton "Maishe" Rockman. Like most people, Ness focused his attention on flashy headline grabbers like Maxie Diamond and Shondor Birns, not yet realizing who the secret powers of the underworld really were. Meanwhile, these truly powerful men profited silently, out of sight, grateful for the distraction.

The elusive Moe Dalitz, one of the top four, was called the first among equals of the Cleveland syndicate. His parents owned Varsity Laundry in Detroit, which served University of Michigan students. Early on, Dalitz was connected with Detroit's infamous Purple Gang, which had come into power in the early twenties when laundry owners hired gang members to protect them from labor organizers. "Realizing the possibilities, the gang set up their own racket and forced anyone desiring to operate a laundry to join and pay 'dues' of up to a thousand dollars a week. It became necessary to murder a few holdouts," according to Mob expert Hank Messick.

As he had done in Detroit, Dalitz built a laundry empire in Cleveland. In December 1932, Dalitz, Kleinman, and the others had formed Buckeye Enterprises Company, the first formal arrangement between the Jewish Cleveland syndicate and the Mayfield Road Gang, a group of first- and second-generation Italians who would later be called the Cleveland Mafia—Frank and Anthony Milano, Big Al Polizzi, John Angersola, and others. This innovative arrangement was successful, and there would be many more like it, making it easier for

Bill Presser to coexist with the Mafia in later decades. Over the years, Buckeye split, changed names, and resurfaced as Buckeye Cigarette Service, then as Buckeye Vending, owned by Maishe Rockman, Mafia don John Scalish, and others.

To tackle the Cleveland mobsters, Ness used the techniques that had helped him nail the Capone gang in Chicago. He put together a cadre of supposedly untouchable enforcers, then employed wiretaps and paid informants to gather evidence. In 1939, he and his men had enough evidence to go before a grand jury and get indictments on twenty-three numbers racketeers, including Big Ange Lonardo, Maishe Rockman, John and George Angersola, Chuck Polizzi, and Shondor Birns. The grand jury sealed the indictments so investigators could dig up more evidence.

It had been a long investigation, and Ness had to feel gratified. His top investigator, Lieutenant Ernest Molnar, had worked with him every step of the way. Molnar was part of Ness's Cleveland untouchables, privy to every move and strategy. But Ness had a mysterious blind spot when it came to Molnar. Federal agents remember Molnar coming far outside his city district to interfere with raids on bootleggers and gambling games. With uncannily accurate tips, the lieutenant made impressive arrests as well. But Ness should have recognized that Molnar was going after certain gangsters while protecting their rivals.

Just as the secret indictments were about to be unsealed, the Angersolas, Chuck Polizzi, and several others fled the country aboard the *Wood Duck*, a yacht owned by Mickey McBride, future owner of the Cleveland Browns and the city's Yellow Cab Company. Molnar had tipped them off, and they made their way across Lake Erie, up the St. Lawrence River, and eventually down to Miami Beach. Angelo Lonardo, Maishe Rockman, and others were arrested.

The underworld wise guys had to appreciate the irony: Ness, the college-educated gangbuster, had a bent cop as his right-hand man. Eight years later, a new Cleveland safety director conducted an investigation that nailed Molnar on numerous counts of bribery. He was sentenced to sixty-six years but served only four.

Meanwhile, grand juries were looking into labor racketeering and trying to call as witnesses the victims of shakedowns, blackmail, wide-

24

spread coercion, and violence. It was frustrating. The victims were terrified and wouldn't testify. Of course, the racketeers pleaded the Fifth Amendment and refused to incriminate themselves when called to the top-secret proceedings.

At first, some city leaders thought Ness could make a difference. But it turned out to be wishful thinking. "Mr. Ness and the county prosecutor's office have made a marvelous beginning in this war against rackets," said grand-jury foreman Cyril O'Neil in 1937. But he complained that the public wasn't supporting the crusade strongly enough. "Few people realize the nature of this evil and the damage done by those unprincipled racketeers whose dictatorship is robbing union labor of the right to work and exacting tribute not only from the consumer but from their own organizations as well. No one but a robber has to make a living by threats and coercion, and unless union members want this stigma attached to them, it is their duty to help rid Cleveland of those dishonest business agents and others connected with them who defy all civil and moral codes in their conquest of power."

Indictments were rarely returned.

A few years later, the situation was still the same. After hearing of widespread corruption and racketeering during months of secret proceedings, Arthur J. Cullen, a grand-jury foreman for the September 1941 term, was frustrated and helpless. He lashed out in a report to county judges at the end of his term.

"We seem to be almost helpless in some of the cases of trouble with labor unions, with competing firms, etc. We need laws which will make it possible to deal with modern methods of terrorism, with their professional sluggers, with their unscrupulous lawyers, and with their sub rosa methods of bribery.

"Sometime ago, I was asked to interest myself in a case of intimidation and coercion by collusion between the labor union and a competitor. When it came to a showdown, the complainant was unwilling to testify. Another manufacturer, who seemed to have a clear case of unfair coercion and intimidation and who handed me a digest of the evidence, seemed to merit a hearing before the grand jury. But upon further investigation, I found that he had accepted a large sum of money to call the matter closed."

The Cleveland Police Department's labor-relations bureau was supposed to keep order at strikes and picket lines and remain neutral. But many times police officials sided with the racketeers. Allen Friedman, Jackie Presser's uncle, served as Bill Presser's muscleman on the picket lines. A strapping man full of anger, Friedman threw stink bombs and knocked heads with relish. He also got to know Cleveland police detective James Patrick Foley, who started in the labor bureau in 1938 and eventually became its boss. Foley, a friend of Bill Presser, was on the take. For an envelope of cash, sometimes delivered by Allen Friedman, Foley simply wouldn't see, hear, or stop the union's rough stuff.

By 1939, Bill Presser was known to law enforcers as a police character, a man quick to rustle muscle for a picket line or to swing a chain himself. He was thirty-one and had two sons. The frenetic moving from apartment to rental house to apartment had slowed to a more comforting pace. He had just hooked up with two growing labor unions that needed his organizing talents, the Tobacco and Candy Workers Union and the Music Maintenance Union. This would be a turning point in his career, though he didn't know it yet. In jumping into the booming jukebox and vending-machine business—a field flooded by millions of untraceable, easily skimmed coins—the one-time hatmaker would finally begin to accumulate wealth, more than he ever dreamed he'd possess.

As Bill Presser got into the jukebox business, he also tied up tightly with the Mob. It was inevitable. By the end of the next decade, organized crime would control the vending industry in Cleveland and across the country.

In January 1939, Big Bill joined two Mob racketeers, flashy Maxie Diamond and Samuel "Sammy" Salupo, to form the Cuyahoga Window Cleaning Company. It was a daring move. The window-cleaning business—newspapers referred to it as the window-cleaning racket—was controlled by the Window Cleaning Association. It was a setup familiar to Presser, following a blueprint similar to the one he established with the Dry Cleaners Association: prices were fixed; accounts were frozen with the original contractor; firms didn't compete among themselves, which kept prices and profits high; and newcomers were

26

kept out unless they joined the association, paid healthy dues, and played along. It was peace, protection, prosperity.

If you didn't play along with the Window Cleaning Association, according to the rules set up by Presser and Diamond and Salupo, you chanced a beating or bombing. But the three proprietors of the Cuyahoga Window Cleaning Company were all used to rough stuff. Salupo, three years younger than Bill, had put together an impressive string of arrests, including one for bank robbery, but had escaped conviction and prison until July 1936, when he was sent up for black-mailing prostitutes, demanding three dollars a week in tribute. One of the pimps who oversaw the hookers Salupo was shaking down balked at the arrangement and was killed. The murder was never solved. Shortly thereafter, one of the pimp's prostitutes testified against Salupo, and he was slapped with his first and only prison stint.

Sammy Salupo, twenty-seven, had been released from prison only a few days before becoming a partner with Presser and Diamond in the new venture. He was paroled by the Ohio governor after serving thirty months of his one-to-fifteen-year sentence. Cleveland police and the county prosecutor had bitterly opposed Salupo's parole and were furi-ous with the governor. But Salupo had influential connections with trade unions and political figures; his three brothers worked for dry cleaners and laundry unions affiliated with the International Brother-hood of Teamsters, a union of truck drivers that had begun to grow rapidly after it had successfully organized long-distance freight haulers in 1933. A Democratic ward leader named Anthony "Happy" Hughes (father of boxer Tony Hughes, Jackie Presser's future best friend) wrote to the parole board asking for a break for Sammy. The Metal Trades Council also intervened, and Salupo got an early release.

Salupo was named president of the new company, probably to impress his parole officer; Diamond didn't need the job, and Big Bill had his union titles. The new company shared its offices with those of Euclid Window Cleaning, now run by Presser's brother, Herman, who had taken over the company after his father died. Cleveland detectives, angry that Salupo had been paroled and aware that he had hooked up with labor racketeers Presser and Diamond, set up surveillance on Salupo. He spotted them and, tired of being tailed, called Diamond. The two rushed downtown to city hall and marched up the granite steps, through the five-story lobby, and up the marble-bannistered

27

staircase to the office of Eliot Ness. "I'm a legitimate businessman now," Salupo told Ness. "So have your guys lay off."

But the police kept watching Salupo. He came back to see Ness on several occasions, insisting each time that he had gone straight and wondering why the safety director didn't steer his men to other targets. One reason Ness didn't believe Salupo's claims of innocence, however, was that Presser, Salupo, and Diamond's entry into the window-cleaning field coincided neatly with an outbreak of threats, violence, and cutthroat competition in the once-peaceful and collusive window-washing business. Apparently, the men behind the Window Cleaning Association didn't like their monopoly being disrupted.

On January 30, 1939, Bill Presser, returning home on his usual route down South Boulevard, turned his car in his driveway and stepped out. Suddenly, a passing car slowed, and a gunman fired several shots at close range from the passenger side. Someone was trying to kill Bill Presser. He jumped for cover. Inside the house, Bill's brother, Herman, ran to a third-story window and began firing a .22-caliber target pistol at the car, which quickly accelerated out of sight without being hit.

The police were called. When they showed up, they questioned Presser as to who he thought would want to kill him. Presser dodged their questions. "I have no enemies that I know of. Labor problems, oh no, I'm not involved in anything like that that I know of. Who would want to shoot me? I just don't know." Presser even denied being shot at, but a detective looked at Presser's car and found what appeared to be a bullet hole.

A police report later suggested that someone was retaliating against Presser and Diamond, possibly because of their Cuyahoga Window Cleaning Company. Maybe it was an owner who resented being extorted or, more likely, a muscleman from the Window Cleaning Association.

The trio stayed in business. With their strong-arm experience, Presser, Diamond, and Salupo thought they could break the rules and cut into the window-washing field. There were several attempts to get them to sell their business, but they set their price high and no one in the Window Cleaning Association bought them out. The Cuyahoga Window Cleaning Company continued to operate, acquiring contracts and farming out the cleaning work to subcontractors. Getting the accounts was frighteningly straightforward. A tavern owner explained the industry practice to police. "A solicitor called on me and said I'd better have my window cleaning done by a certain company if I knew what was good for me. He didn't say what would happen, and I didn't wait to find out. I gave him the contract."

A restaurant owner described a different, more creative sales approach. A bunch of men came into his place at mealtime and began quarreling loudly and swearing among themselves. Customers fled the room. After their skit, the hoodlums threatened the owner with a repeat performance unless he gave his window-cleaning contract to the correct company.

At about half-past seven on the morning of August 4, 1939, Sammy Salupo started to drive his fiancée to the Shaker Heights home where she worked as a maid. A few blocks before he got to the house, he honked the car's horn. The car exploded instantly, strewing metal and body parts up to two hundred feet away. Salupo lost both legs. His fiancée—to whom he had given an engagement ring the day before—was killed. Salupo died on the operating table a half hour later, his brother Anthony only a few feet away, his arm stripped and ready to give a blood transfusion. At the bomb scene, the dying Salupo had whispered to police, "My brothers know all about this."

His brother Nick had been a business agent with Bill Presser in the Dry Cleaners and Pressers Union. Alfred "Babe" Salupo was a business agent of the Laundry Workers Union. Anthony worked as a field manager for Triangle Music Company, a jukebox distributor Bill Presser later purchased. Despite their brother's dying declaration, they gave homicide detectives no useful information.

A day after the killing, Cleveland police lieutenant George Zicarelli said that he was convinced the attempted murder of Bill Presser and the murder of Salupo were linked. But how? Who was behind the crimes? Perhaps it was rivalry in the window-cleaning racket, he said. Within days, detectives focused on the theory that racketeers who were getting protection money from independent laundries had killed Salupo because he was trying to break their hold and take over some of the accounts. Cuyahoga Window Cleaning, detectives also learned, had grown out of Euclid Window Cleaning, operated by Herman Presser, an independent who had been frozen out by the association.

Jackie's uncle could only get business by bidding and had decided to take in Maxie Diamond to see if Maxie's muscle could help him acquire customers.

Police Captain Mike Blackwell said that he hoped Salupo's slaying could be solved quickly. He was worried that the killing might touch off a gang war like the Corn Sugar War a decade earlier, during which the rival Lonardo and Porello gangs had littered the streets with bodies while fighting to gain a lucrative monopoly on an important part of the city's economy.

Two weeks after Presser's partner Sam Salupo was blown up, Salupo's sister Carmella was beaten on a sidewalk by two men. She refused to give police any details about her attackers. But Presser and Diamond both realized that they had other, less troublesome business interests. They sold Cuyahoga Window Cleaning later that year.

By now, Bill Presser had perfected the techniques of fixing prices, stifling competition, muscling owners, and, along the way, raising wages for some union workers. He would use these skills repeatedly over the next two decades and make a fortune in the vending business. An artisan proud of his craft, he would try, with varying degrees of success, to hand these lessons on to his son Jackie.

3
Young Jackie

"He seemed torn between two forces."
JACKIE'S FIRST WIFE

In March of 1942, a new pupil was transferred into seventh grade at Glenville's Patrick Henry Junior High School. Looking out over the classroom, the teacher had to notice that the new boy was huge, much bigger than the others, and starting to grow whiskers. This kid could be trouble.

Jackie Presser, five months shy of his sixteenth birthday, had finally finished elementary school and moved up to junior high. By now, he was modeling himself after his uncle, Allen Friedman, who enjoyed the role of mentor. For amusement, Allen and his buddies, including Harold Friedman, the future Teamsters vice president, made the rounds of bars and gambling joints along East 105th and downtown along Short Vincent, a gaudy 485-foot-long street populated by a burlesque hall, beer joints, bookies, bettors, touts, drunkards, and the famous Theatrical Grill—hangout of high-class hookers, mafiosi, politicians, and assorted swells. Jackie was too young to carouse on Short Vincent, and bar owners weren't exactly excited about letting in Uncle Allen and his pals, who weren't yet twenty-one. But Allen got around that. "If you don't let us in, I'll break every window in the place," he would tell them. That usually worked.

By now, Allen was settled in his career as a collector for a loan shark. It didn't carry much prestige in the wise-guy pecking order. You not only had to threaten to hurt one of the poor suckers who got in too deep, but if he failed your deadline, you had to beat him up, to save face as much as to collect the money. Friedman, however, relished being a muscleman and an intimidator; it was a way to vent the anger he felt since the death of his parents. How much of his violent nature rubbed off on Jackie is uncertain. But Jackie clearly was a wild kid, unmanageable and a heartache for his father. He wasn't attending school, and when he did, he failed his studies. School administrators had little choice but to send him to reform school. "I was hard to contain," Jackie once said. "I wanted to grow up faster than my years. I was fast with my hands, and I was fast-tempered." It was also a perfect description of his uncle.

In the fall of 1942, Jackie was sent to the Thomas A. Edison School, known as the bad boys' school, already the breeding ground for future hoodlums like his Uncle Allen, Teamsters leader Babe Triscaro, Mafia hit man Jimmy "the Weasel" Fratianno, and others. Because he was uneducated and unruly, Jackie found himself outside the mainstream of his Jewish peers in the Glenville neighborhood. He had become an example, at least by reputation, of what Glenville parents didn't want their boys to become. "He was a hoodlum when he was a kid," Abba Schwartz says. "He was involved in all kinds of shady dealings and was known as a tough guy." Being the outsider didn't inhibit Jackie. He just barged right in, taking part in the social life whether he was invited or not. "He was what you call the neighborhood bully," Jack Kleinman recalls. "Before the war, girls used to belong to sororities and boys used to belong to clubs. On Friday night, the girls would meet at one of the girl's houses and hold a meeting. Then the boys would come up afterwards and sit around and talk. Jackie would come up around once in a while, and whatever evening we had planned, it was a disaster. He was a pushy person. I don't remember if it was vulgarity or what. You sort of had the sinking feeling after the doorbell rang or a car pulled up that Jackie Presser was coming to visit."

Years later, Kleinman marveled at all the success stories from Glenville but said that he never imagined that Jackie would be one of them. "He was a nothing," Kleinman says. "If you ask did I suspect him to end up in the jug, I say yeah. But to end up with President Reagan and the bigwigs and the intelligentsia, no."

Jackie's strong suit was his outgoing personality and his ability to sway people with charm and gruff argument. "He was a wonderful

32

combination of his mother and his father," says Carmen Presser, an ex-wife. "His mother was just absolutely adorable, with this charisma and this way about her—gregarious, outgoing, very talkative. Could just charm anybody in the world. His father was quiet, caring. Those were the good parts. The bad parts of the two of them, he had those, too." But young Jackie could be petty. Babe Triscaro's son-in-law, Sam Busacca, who became president of the Teamsters Excavation Drivers Local 436 in Cleveland, recalls that Jackie once informed on a friend who had snitched an apple from a cart. The petty thief ended up in juvenile court.

At sixteen and a half, Jackie quit school for good and enlisted in the navy. His uncle Allen had already joined the army and was training to be a paratrooper. On the day Jackie was sent to boot camp, Allen went AWOL to visit him. It was a measure of how close they had become. In the service, Jackie got a look at life outside the intense constrictions of family and neighborhood, something his father had never had at such an impressionable age. It changed Jackie. As part of his service, he worked at night in a food-processing plant, getting his hands dirty and getting a brief taste of boring, blue-collar factory work.

While Jackie served in the Navy, his father branched out into the vending-machine business, hoping to make more money to support his family, especially his wife's gambling habit. As a labor organizer, he had a somewhat limited income, even though he worked on commission. For each person he convinced to sign a union card, he earned ten to twenty-five dollars, whatever fee he had negotiated. It was like selling cars from a lot; the more he sold, the more he made. Presser was selling employees on the merits of various unions—Dry Cleaners, Laundry Drivers, Music Box Workers, and so on. It was a decent living, bouncing from job to job, being a hired gun when it was still legal for a union to buy members.

Presser would work for several unions at once, but he made certain one of them provided a full-time salary and a title. This was his life raft. "I always kept one union for myself for a livelihood," he said, "and that's what led me to the vending-machine business." He handled jukeboxes at first, then cigarette and candy machines, quickly making a small fortune. In 1939, while he and his family were still bouncing around Glenville from apartment to rental house, he organized a group

33

of vending workers into a collective bargaining unit known in the union business as a local. Presser's group was called Local 442 and belonged to the International Brotherhood of Electrical Workers, which had many members who repaired, stocked, and delivered vending machines. He now benefited from a nifty conflict of interest: he not only owned a company that distributed vending machines, but he also controlled the union employees who placed and serviced them. After only seven years in the vending business, Presser was able to state his net worth in a bank application at $223,000. He was wealthy and, with his labor contacts, a behind-the-scenes power, as both jukebox-union boss and owner of jukebox-distributing companies.

With its steady stream of easily skimmed coins and its scattered, vulnerable, mom-and-pop customers, the vending business was a natural place for the Mob to drop anchor during the first wave of postwar prosperity. "Almost every level of the jukebox industry is permeated with hoodlums and the gangster element," said a secret report of the Chicago Crime Commission as late as 1954. "Notwithstanding the inherently legitimate character of the business, in almost every section of the nation it has become a huge racket."

The report, which investigated back to the forties, singled out Bill Presser as one of the prime movers of the racket, the man who organized the Cleveland vending industry into a price-fixing cartel, as he had done a decade before with dry-cleaning shops.

The jukebox industry changed Bill's life. By immersing himself in this field, Presser broadened his contacts throughout the underworld. Instead of associating only with local Jewish gangsters, Presser branched out and incorporated himself with the Italian Mafia. By World War II, the jukebox racket flourished in Cleveland, New York, Chicago, Detroit, and other cities with strong Mob families. The racket was a sophisticated, illicit dance among manufacturer, distributor, and purchaser. Only four jukebox manufacturers existed in America, and they sold only to distributors. Distributors only sold machines to an operator, who was a person or company that owned at least five and up to several hundred machines. The jukeboxes were installed at locations or stops. A string of stops was known as a route.

Presser banded the Cleveland operators into the Phonograph Merchants Association, which cut up the routes among members, setting up a grid of illegal monopolies. The route owners agreed not to

34

raid one another's lucrative jukebox stops. The route-owners association and the union recorded the locations of the jukeboxes on a courtesy list, which was more pernicious than its name suggests. The courtesy list indicated what bar belonged to which route operator and what brand of jukebox was allowed inside. A bar owner unhappy with the jukebox in his place couldn't switch to a different route owner because the route owner, going by the association's rules, would consult the courtesy list and learn that the bar already belonged to someone else. It didn't matter that the barkeeper's jukebox wasn't promptly serviced, that its sound quality was poor or its records outdated. He couldn't bring in a new jukebox unless he wanted trouble.

To enforce the monopolies, Presser used the members of Local 442, who delivered and serviced the machines. In 1951, he asked his members to vote to decertify their local from the Electrical Workers Union and switch over to the much more powerful and fast-growing International Brotherhood of Teamsters (IBT), a catchall trade union that represented not only truck drivers but workers in oil fields, canneries, breweries, bakeries, dairies, and so on. They agreed, and he became president of Teamsters Vending Workers Local 410.

Once a route owner joined the Phonograph Merchants Association, he paid dues of one dollar per jukebox per month. A Teamsters serviceman slapped a sticker on each jukebox to indicate union approval. A worker on a service call would look for the union label. Without it, he refused to make repairs or stock the machine.

Route owners didn't receive services for their healthy association dues, but the captive market was reward enough. Typically, the route owners demanded the first five or ten dollars of the weekly take from their jukeboxes and then split the balance with the different tavern keepers, usually fifty-fifty or sometimes sixty-forty in favor of the route operators. If the bar owner didn't like the arrangement, he had a choice: keep his mouth shut or live without a jukebox.

Incredibly, Presser's union was able to control the giant vending industry with the roughly 250 members of Local 410. If a bar owner installed his own machine, Presser forced him to take it out by having a few of his teamsters throw up a picket line. Beer deliverers were teamsters and honored all such lines. In face of such immense, concentrated economic clout, bar and restaurant owners had little choice but to go along. Enforcing the racket, if need be, were Mob musclemen or guys like Jackie's uncles Allen and Harry. If that didn't work, there were other tactics. Throw in a stink bomb, telephone a death threat, break a window. After that, the bar owner usually changed his position. Basically, the jukebox setup was a clone of the dry-cleaning racket Presser had created in the thirties.

One restaurant owner who tried to test Presser was Clarence Gilles, who ran an all-night diner out on Pearl Road, the busy route that slanted through the west side of Cleveland and down to Cincinnati. Time and time again, his Presser-supplied jukebox wouldn't spin records. Customers complained. Servicemen, trying to fix it, tramped constantly in and out of his small restaurant. Gilles wanted a new machine, but the jukebox distributor refused to replace it. "Take it out," Gilles told him. "I'll get my own jukebox."

"If you take it out, you can't get nobody else in here," the jukebox operator, Andre Allesandro, told him. "This is my stop."

"Well, we're going to get one in here somehow or other, and you're going to get this equipment out," Gilles insisted.

Allesandro's warning didn't faze Gilles, who eventually bought a used machine (he had to go to southern Ohio before he could find someone willing to sell him one) and installed it in his diner. Allesandro quickly dropped by for a chat. He walked in, looked at the intruding jukebox, sat down, and said, "You know you can't do that. You are going to be in trouble. You are going to get bombed."

"Who is going to do this bombing, you?" Gilles asked.

"Oh, no, no. Somebody. The other fellows."

"What other fellows?" Gilles wanted to know.

"Somebody will do it," Allesandro predicted.

Shortly after the bomb threat, Gilles was visited by a Cleveland businessman who distributed the same jukebox model that Gilles had installed himself. "Where'd you get this box?" the distributor asked nervously. Gilles told him about the man downstate. "They think I sold it to you," the distributor complained, referring to Presser's cartel.

Several evenings later, Gilles glanced at a newspaper and noticed a story about the jukebox distributor he had just met. Someone had thrown a stink bomb in his office. The next morning, at quarter to six, Gilles got a telephone call. "Your restaurant has been bombed." He ran over and found the place a mess, reeking of the foul, sickening-sweet stench of the bomb.

The *Cleveland Press,* noting the rash of bombings, wrote about Gilles's plight, giving it full-blown treatment, which put pressure on city hall. The police prosecutor asked detectives to round up likely suspects. At the top of the list was Bill Presser, followed by Joe Fontana, president of Local 410, Andre Allesandro, and others. The prosecutor, a man named Conway, knew the racket and was tired of it. He gathered Presser, Fontana, and the others into a room at the station and demanded, "Who did it?" But Presser and Fontana were old hands at being questioned. They shook their heads and innocently replied, "We didn't do it."

"[I] didn't get off the bus from Painesville this morning," Conway told them, mentioning the nearby farm town. "If this continues, we're going to get an indictment on somebody."

Gilles spent two days at the police station, waiting outside offices, retelling his story. They didn't seem to care. There had been scores of recent bombings of taverns and cafés in disputes over jukeboxes. "Nothing came of it," he complained.

But before Bill Presser left the police station, he took Gilles aside and said, "I am the public-relations man for the Phonograph Operators Association. If you had come to see me, I would have straightened it out." Presser probably would have bent the rules for Gilles. A savvy negotiator, Presser knew that in the long run it was worth it to give in to one pesky customer in order to avoid the gaze of the newspaper and the police.

Gilles was stubborn, however. Nothing Presser could have said would have calmed him. "There was nobody going to come in and dictate any policy of what I could do in my own place," he said later. "My boy had just returned from the service, and we just got through fighting dictators, and we're not going to take anybody here to dictate to us how we can conduct our business."

Once in place, Presser's system worked effectively at each level. George R. Loving could vouch for that. One day, he traveled though Cleveland with a wallet stuffed with cash and a simple mission: to buy a jukebox for his tavern, the Little Harlem. Everywhere he went, he was thwarted by the cartel installed by Presser and the union. First, Loving stopped at the Northern Music Company and talked to the owner about buying a new Wurlitzer. "Are you a member of the Association?" the man asked him. No. "I can't sell to you," the Wurlitzer man said. "If I did, I'd get a bomb through my window."

Loving stopped at the Lake City Amusement Company. "Sell me a jukebox?" he asked. "Are you a union operator with five or more machines?" No, Loving admitted. "Sorry, we won't sell to you." Next stop, the Atlas Company. Same story there. "No, we only sell to operators," Loving was told. "If you want a jukebox for private operation, we can only sell you one without the coin mechanism." "No thanks," Loving said, giving up the search.

"I was quite successful," Bill Presser once said of his jukebox days. "From that I went on to the cigarette vending machines, to the games. . . . Eventually I had all the employees who did service, selection, and maintenance on practically every type of vending there was. And that's where I stayed for many years."

Before long, the newspapers referred to him as "William Presser, Ohio's jukebox czar," as if the name Presser couldn't stand alone in print without the word *jukebox* a few picas away. Five years later, a congressional investigating committee called Presser the creator of a jukebox combine—namely the Phonograph Merchants Association and Teamsters Local 410—that operated "through the threat of picketing, secondary boycotting, bombing, intimidation, and other strong-arm operations."

His father's vending cartel was Jackie's first adult exposure to the business of labor unions. What he saw was a world of blatant conflicts of interest, self-dealing, strong-arming, and deception. It gave him the twisted notion that labor unions were a business, not a calling, to be operated for personal gain, not held in trust for the members. "My teacher taught me, and that's my father," Jackie once said. "I am very fortunate in that . . . I spent my entire life with my father. . . . So I have a big strong arm. I had a good professor."

Bill Presser rationalized the jukebox setup to Jackie as he did years later to Robert Rotatori, his lawyer and confidant. A former Justice Department lawyer, Rotatori forged a friendship with Bill during the seventies when they made many trips together to Columbus, driving 275 miles round-trip, to conduct meetings of the Ohio Conference of Teamsters. On the way back, they'd pull off the interstate and stop at a famous small-town restaurant known for home-cooking because Bill, who was by now obese, worshipped its coconut cream pie. After dinner, he'd buy whole pies and take them home.

During the drives or at dinner, Presser would reminisce, "In order to convince employers to unionize, you had to give them something," he would say. What he gave employers were fixed prices, stability, and higher profits. "Everybody would profit," Presser would continue. "The workers profit. The owners profit. That was the best way, was to get everybody together."

The setup was price-fixing, Rotatori says, adding that "management loved Bill Presser."

When called before a congressional investigating committee several years later, Bill Presser defended Local 410's benefits. "Our contract calls for a forty-four-hour week, time and a half after forty-four hours. Our minimum for the lowest category of any of our people is what we call miscellaneous apprentice help, and it starts at fifty-five dollars [a week]. The collector or record changer starts at a minimum of eighty-five dollars, and mechanics start at $105 a week minimum. Our collectors get this minimum and receive from eighteen to twenty percent of the formal gross. It never can fall below the minimum guarantee. Our employees are covered from one to three weeks vacation, which graduates over a period of years, length of service. We have our welfare plan. All legal holidays are paid for that are not worked. We have our seniority clause in hiring and firing on a department basis. We have union meetings of the membership."

Many workers held a different opinion about the benefits of Local 410. In one documented case, after Presser's union won recognition, jukebox workers were given a weekly raise of $6.34. But after deducting union dues, assessments, and taxes, the result was a loss in take-home pay of a dollar a week.

In the fall of 1944, Presser took his jukebox racket to Detroit, where operators were cutting their prices and jumping one another's stops. Some of them had heard about the smoothly run jukebox cartel in Cleveland; interested in a truce, four operators traveled to Cleveland and called on the jukebox czar.

Presser proposed a peace plan that called for an owners association and a jukebox workers union, both working in concert. Detroit jukebox

distributors Joseph Brilliant, Victor DeSchryver, and others incorporated the Michigan Automatic Phonograph Owners Association, mod-
eled on Presser's Cleveland association. As for the union, they obtained
a charter for a local of the Music Maintenance Workers Union with
the help of rising Teamsters vice president Jimmy Hoffa. Bill was
impressed with the short, stocky, dark-haired Teamsters official. Hoffa
was an intense, charismatic leader who could whip up the troops and
command loyalty. Presser had heard that Hoffa used strikes, violence,
and payoffs to get what he wanted, sometimes for the sole benefit of
union members, but often to line his own pockets. He clearly was going
places in the Teamsters. As a way to get his reward, Hoffa made sure
that one of his Detroit cronies, a pool-hall manager named Eugene C.
James, was made the principal officer of the new jukebox union.

The Detroit version of the Presser jukebox combine soon whipped
up storms of protest. Independent owners loudly complained about
being muscled and forced to pay tribute to the new association; within
two years, a Detroit grand jury began investigating the racket. De-
Schryver, who was either brave or foolish, cooperated, testifying that
he had handed five thousand dollars in cash to Presser for setting up
Local 23814 and for payoffs to Hoffa and his lieutenant, Owen Bert
Brennan.

DeSchryver said that Hoffa evidently wasn't satisfied with the
money Presser had spread around, causing James, the union official, to
plead with the association that he "needed more money to be able to
take care of his obligations" to Hoffa and Brennan. To come up with
the money, DeSchryver and Brilliant raised the weekly dues for association members from fifty cents to seventy cents per jukebox. The cash
was funneled to Hoffa and Brennan, DeSchryver testified, by putting
Josephine Hoffa and Alice Brennan, their wives, on the union payroll.
From September 1945 to April 1946, the women did no work but
hauled in six thousand dollars in kickbacks. Despite his testimony,
neither Hoffa nor any of his associates was charged with crimes.

Besides the five-thousand-dollar fee, Detroit rewarded Presser in
other ways. DeSchryver began talks with Aireon, a jukebox maker, and
arranged to distribute its boxes in Detroit. (Presser, while head of the
Cleveland jukebox local, enjoyed a similar deal with Aireon in Cleveland.) DeSchryver called his new company Marquette Distributing and
quietly issued six percent of its stock to Bill's wife, Faye, and another

six percent to Lillian Nardi, the wife of John Nardi, a Cleveland Mafia associate and Presser friend.

By the time the Detroit grand jury called James, the principal Detroit union officer, it knew enough to grill him effectively. What about the hundred-dollar weekly payments from the local to Jimmy Hoffa? it asked. Just repaying two thousand dollars I borrowed from him, James explained. Then why do your books so far show six thousand dollars in payments on a two-thousand-dollar loan? the grand jury wanted to know. Trapped, James couldn't come up with an explanation. Eventually, he told the grand jury that he continued paying union funds to Hoffa and Brennan because he figured it was good insurance. Besides, James said, Hoffa and Brennan were his friends. "They have been instrumental in helping me in lots of ways."

It was a short-lived friendship. The Mob apparently was disappointed with the pace of its takeover of the Detroit jukebox industry and blamed James. Meanwhile, James griped about being muscled by the Mob. Hoffa's lawyer friend William Bufalino, cousin of an East Coast Mafia boss, forced James out of the union and took over Teamsters Local 985. James was paid off in installments for "selling" the union to Bufalino, who was also a jukebox distributor.

Bufalino was more aggressive than James in establishing racket control. Along with his favored jukebox distributor, Bufalino began visiting tavern owners and demanding that they remove their jukeboxes and replace them with ones from his friend. When they refused, he threw up Teamsters picket lines and pinched off deliveries of food and beer. If this didn't work, the bars were stink-bombed. Echoes of Cleveland.

After Jackie earned his honorable discharge in 1947, he worked in canneries in Modesto and Fresno, California, slicing and pitting peaches. Most of the canning factories were affiliated with the Teamsters. In 1946, he returned home to his family, who were well off by now and living in suburban University Heights. Jackie tried to learn how to repair radios, but he didn't stay with it, and he started driving a truck for Triangle Music Company (years later, Jackie's press release biography always mentioned this job as a badge of honor), a successful vending-machine distributor his father partly owned. Jackie and his uncles Allen and Harry worked for Bill, placing jukeboxes in West Virginia, convincing tavern owners to rent their machines, stocked with records, in exchange for a fifty-fifty split of the gross receipts. The field was booming, and the Appalachian hills near Huntington, West Virginia, on the Ohio River, were virgin territory. There, Jackie Presser met a pretty nursing student named Pauline Walls.

It was evening when Jackie, twenty years old, strolled into Walgreen's Drugstore with a couple of friends. Pauline and her girlfriends were perched at the soda fountain, which was the social center for nursing students. She noticed Jackie right away and pegged him for an outsider. He wore a pin-striped suit, knotted tie, and broad-brimmed fedora; he was a sight. Men in Huntington didn't wear hats, especially ones that made them look like gangsters. "He always wore a suit," Pauline recalls. "And a hat. That big dumb hat."

Jackie walked over, introduced himself confidently, and brought her and her friends back to his table to introduce them to the men he was with, his uncles Allen and Harry. Talk turned to Cleveland, and Pauline was impressed with tales of the big city. "They seemed more worldly than we," she recalls. "I guess this sorta made them interesting. He called the next day, and we had a dinner and movie date."

Pauline was also twenty, just a few months older than Jackie, and living at the school dormitory. She was captivated by Jackie Presser. To her he was exotic, a fat, fun-loving young man who bragged about his family and the importance of his father. "He idolized him," she says. At the same time, Jackie was extremely secretive. He revealed little about his jukebox job and even less about his performance in school; he was already embarrassed that he had never started high school. It was a shortcoming that would haunt him throughout his life.

After several dates, always at the best restaurants Huntington could offer, he disappeared back to Cleveland. After two or three months, Pauline decided she'd never hear from him again. Then one day, he surprised her with a phone call: "I'm in town. Let's get together." Before he came over, he sent roses to her dormitory. This bowled her over; a big-city boy with money to spend on her. She says she quickly fell under his spell.

One time, Jackie arrived at the visiting room of her dorm, decked out in pinstripes, and spotted a piano. He sat down and played a popular song, singing along in a Nat King Cole style. "He had a very good voice," Pauline says. "And he liked to dance." His uncles, Harry or Allen, were usually with him, and sometimes they all double-dated. Pauline and Jackie courted for a year, interrupted by his long trips back to Cleveland. "As things became more serious, Jackie seemed to become quieter, even a little nervous, always looking around him," she says. And no wonder. They were placing jukeboxes in taverns and restaurants, and sometimes it required more than friendly persuasion.

Then, after a long stay in the area, Jackie took Pauline aside and said he had to go back to Cleveland again. But first he had something to ask her. "My father is buying me a new car," he said. "That's nice," she affirmed. "What color do you like? You pick out the color," he insisted. "Light blue. Blue is my favorite color," Pauline answered, curious.

The next time he came to Huntington, he drove out to her school and came inside to pick her up. "I've got a surprise for you," he said. Sitting in the driveway was a light blue Ford sedan. Pauline was impressed. Men her age in Huntington didn't have the money or confidence to pursue her with such flair, tailoring their purchases to her whims. They began an affair. The next spring, Pauline discovered that she was pregnant with Jackie's child. On May 31, 1947, they eloped to Newport, Kentucky, where a couple could get married without waiting for a license. Jackie was living in Beckley, West Virginia, with Uncle Allen, trying to get as many jukeboxes as possible into bars and restaurants.

Pauline kept their marriage a secret, since she'd have had to drop out of nursing school if they found out. Several weeks later, when she had finished her finals, she moved to Beckley to be with Jackie.

For two months they lived in a clean, two-bedroom furnished house in that small central–West Virginia city. Then they received two important visitors: Bill Presser and Jackie's brother, Marvin. So this was the father Jackie bragged so much about, Pauline mused. Fat, egg-shaped, with dark circles under his eyes, Bill was extremely nice to her, smiling and making small talk. Then he took his son outside for a private conversation.

Later Jackie told Pauline, "I've got to go back to Cleveland. My mother's very upset. She says she's going to kill herself unless I leave you." "She doesn't even know me," Pauline insisted. "I know, but she's

43

pushing me to marry someone else—a Jewish girl," Jackie said. In a rush, he packed her clothes and a few belongings. He and Allen drove Pauline, eight months pregnant, to Huntington and left her with her parents. She covered up, telling them that Jackie's mother was sick and he had to return to Cleveland. He swore to her that he'd straighten out the problem with his mom and return right away, she recalls. Months later, after their daughter was born, Jackie returned to Huntington and called his wife. "Come downtown and meet me," he begged her. "We need to talk, but you know where I live," she said. "Come and see me like a man. Quit trying to sneak around." Jackie never came out to see her, which mystifies Pauline to this day.

"He seemed torn between two forces, and I guess he was," she recalls. "But after he deserted and abandoned me in my moment of greatest need, I had lost all respect for him, and if he didn't have enough courage to stand up and be his own man, there probably was no future for us together. Because by then I had given a lot of serious thought and analysis to a strange situation. I began to think he was being groomed to take over for his father. And he was always with his uncles. He would come to town and call but would never come to my house. Why?"

Back in Cleveland, Faye was happy to have her firstborn back. She ran the family, and Jackie was back under her influence again. This maneuver was typical of Faye, says a close relative. "Whoever Jackie married was never good enough for Faye." Jackie began to forget Pauline and freelanced on a couple of picket lines. In connection with this work, he was arrested on August 16, 1947, and charged with contempt of court. He was convicted and fined five dollars.

On September 29, 1947, Pauline gave birth to a healthy baby girl, Jackie Presser's first child, Suzanne. He never once held, talked to, or even looked at her.

"When our daughter was three months old, she had to have minor surgery," Pauline says. "So I sent him a telegram. I don't know if he received it or not. So I decided to go on with my life. I could not depend on a husband who was now a stranger to me. And he let me down during childbirth—one of the greatest moments of a marriage." Two years later, as Jackie was preparing to remarry, their lawyers got together, and Jackie and Pauline got divorced. Jackie was supposed to pay her thirty dollars a week in child support. Pauline was living with her parents in Huntington, rearing her girl, trying to finish nursing

44

school and get a job to support herself. She says Jackie followed the court order for about a year or so, then without a word halted the monthly thirty-dollar support payments.

"That was the end for us," Pauline says. "I didn't want to fight or beg over thirty dollars. I figured a clean break was better." She started to date again, got married, and moved from Huntington. Jackie called a few times after she left, talking briefly to her mother, asking about Pauline. "In the later years, as I watched him climb the ladder, I wondered how we ever ended up together," she says. "He always said, 'It's fate.' He really believed in fate." She remembers that Jackie had another strongly held belief. "He always said, 'There's a sucker born every minute.' "

The partnership between Bill Presser and John Nardi in Triangle Music was significant. It was an extension of a coalition between Jewish and Italian labor racketeers that was first formed in the thirties during the days when unions needed muscle on the lines. Little Italy and the city's boxing gyms served as hiring halls, with tough guys paid a day rate, given temporary union cards, then hauled off to the battlefronts.

Nardi, nine years younger than Bill Presser, was born Giovonni Narcchione on January 21, 1916, in Cleveland's Little Italy. His parents changed their names to Nardi, which John approved, joking that he couldn't pronounce his given name anyway. Dark-haired, with thick black eyebrows, Nardi was a nephew by marriage to Anthony "Old Man" Milano, a bootlegger and gambling-club owner from the prominent Mafia family that ran Cleveland crime in the thirties and early forties. Anthony Milano, underboss in the early forties, gave his nephew a job at the Italian American Brotherhood Club, a social club where mobsters often conspired over card games. Young Nardi soaked it all up while spending hours playing pinochle.

Nardi managed to stay out of serious trouble. In 1939, employed by Vending Workers Local 442, he and two other men were arrested on orders from Eliot Ness. The three had supposedly threatened a bar owner. They told him if he didn't hire a Local 442 union man to service his jukebox, they'd smash it and maybe his face, too. Charges were dropped. By 1946, Tony Milano was living in a Beverly Hills mansion and Nardi, a protégé, worked as a bookmaker in Little Italy with Jimmy "the Weasel" Fratianno, who would soon move to California and make a name for himself as a Mob hit man. Facing a prison term for murder in the late seventies, the Weasel surprised his *compares* by becoming an informer and testifying against Mafia members. Like Bill Presser, Nardi tried to stay in the background and live quietly.

In an impressive flurry of entrepreneurship in the mid-forties, Bill Presser started, participated in, or incorporated at least eight jukebox corporations, all financed by the Bank of Ohio. John Nardi was one of his frequent business partners. Judged by the standards of a straight business deal, Nardi seemed an unusual choice for a partner. He was only thirty years old in 1946, and his most recent job had been as a cook and jack-of-all-trades for a suburban country club. At the time, he asked Bill Presser to sign as comaker on two small notes, one for five hundred dollars, one for three thousand. Nardi defaulted on the five-hundred-dollar loan and a bank took his car as payment. But on paper, Nardi was a jukebox magnate. He and Presser together owned all or part of at least three businesses: Triangle Music Company, founded with a $55,000 loan; Ohio Phonotronic Company; and the Windsor Distribution Company.

In reality, Nardi served as the front man for his relatives in the Milano crime family. Frank and Anthony Milano couldn't put their names on incorporation papers with Bill Presser. It would attract too much heat from law enforcers. Nardi was young, unknown, and didn't have a criminal record. He was perfect for the job.

Nearly a decade later, when Presser gave Nardi the job as secretary-treasurer of Teamsters Vending Workers Local 410, police speculated that Nardi had cemented his role as a liaison between organized crime and the Teamsters. Nardi denied it, saying that Bill had given him the union job simply because he had asked for it.

Presser had many other business associates, some more savory than others. In December 1944, Presser and Leo Dixon of Youngstown spent $122,000 to buy a huge Miami, Florida, vending-machine route, Ja-Mar Music Company. Presser also bought several other jukebox distributorships and routes, including part of the Manhattan Phonograph Company, which borrowed $15,000 from the Bank of Ohio and never made a payment on the loan; Nickel Amusement Company; and City Music and Novelty Company, which he put in Faye Presser's name.

By 1947, Bill Presser had sold Triangle Music to Leo Dixon's sons and began prospecting in virgin territory: cigarette vending. Until then, the field was open; businesses—factories, foundries, hospitals, stores—could select whatever cigarette-vending company they wanted and switch freely to another that would pay more generous commissions.

That changed after Presser and Vending Workers Local 442 moved into the picture. Along with several cigarette and candy distributors or jobbers, Bill formed the Tobacco and Candy Jobbers Association. It was the same old setup: fix prices, apportion exclusive territories, and sit back and watch profits soar. Association members paid Bill a salary. The candy and cigarette jobbers, who enjoyed a $27-million-a-year business in Cleveland, agreed on prices and markups, printed them in a schedule, and distributed it among themselves. Presser's union men in Tobacco and Candy Workers Local 400 enforced the prices, alerting their leaders whenever a jobber or subjobber sold at a discount.

But Presser ran into some opposition. Frank Newman of the Automatic Canteen Corporation of Chicago, a large outfit, had sold cigarettes in Cleveland-area factories for years without a problem. After 1948, he told authorities, Presser showed up and forced companies to dump machines not controlled by him and his cohorts. Newman went to the Chicago Crime Commission and told the director, Virgil W. Peterson, that Automatic Canteen was legitimate and wanted to fight rackets guys like Presser.

Whether this led to the following Justice Department investigation is unclear. However, on June 20, 1951, Presser, the Tobacco and Candy Jobbers Association, Teamsters Local 400 official Michael P. Rini, and various candy jobbers were charged with criminal violations of the Sherman Antitrust Act. Presser was given FBI identification number 707 834-B. Presser's antitrust indictment seemed to have little effect on the cigarette vendors' high-profit cartel. In fact, they became attractive takeover targets, and the Mafia-run Buckeye Cigarette Service started to muscle in on legitimate owners.

Buckeye had been owned since the forties by Frank Embrescia, Maishe Rockman, and Mafia boss John Scalish, a combine of Cleveland's most powerful underworld figures. Rockman, who married Scalish's sister and converted to Roman Catholicism, was a close friend of Bill Presser and an in-law of Big Ange Lonardo. According to raw police intelligence, Buckeye, which had a big string of vending routes, hijacked cigarette shipments for resale, a nifty way to cut its overhead and jack up profits.

Rockman had known Bill Presser since childhood. Convicted of extortion in 1939, Maishe was the financial brains of the Cleveland Mafia. Long before that, he had earned the Mafia's respect as a worker; in the early thirties, he and Big Ange had killed a doctor who they believed had killed Big Ange's cousin during an operation. Maishe was extremely secretive, yet he called attention to himself with the way he dressed: He always wore cowboy garb, with a string tie, boots, and hat. Except when sleeping or eating, he chewed on the end of a thick cigar. The outfit guys called him Cigar Man or Cowboy.

Frank Embrescia, one of his partners, had been in cigarette vending since the Depression. In the early fifties, he visited the office of Louis B. Golden, who, with his brothers, owned Ace Cigarette Service. Golden knew of Embrescia's reputation as a hoodlum.

"I want you to sell me some of your stops," Embrescia told Golden. "My partners and I want to get into the cigarette-vending business in a big way. We'll buy two hundred of your stops. If you don't sell, we'll just take them from you anyway. So save yourself the trouble and sell."

Golden wasn't happy with Embrescia's proposal, but he was realistic. "Let me think about it," he said.

Several months passed, during which Golden avoided Embrescia. Then Embrescia called on him again. "Lou, you've got to make up your mind," Embrescia said. "We've already bought new machines. We're going to make a move on your stops if you don't sell them. You can't win."

Golden met with his brothers. "Should we sell or should we fight?" Sitting at a table, scratching figures on a pad, they worked out a dollar amount of how much it would cost them to compete with Buckeye Cigarette. The Goldens would have to come up with newer machines, hire more solicitors, and pay higher commissions to café and bar owners. Insurance rates would climb. The Goldens stalled for a few more weeks, met with Rockman and Embrescia, then finally decided to sell two hundred of their prime stops to the Mob. Buckeye Cigarette paid the Goldens eighty-five dollars per stop for their machines, goodwill, and inventory—less than one-third the going rate of three hundred dollars per stop.

48

4

Stealing Cars

"The FBI, they went to my sister and Bill and said, 'We know your son Jackie Presser is involved in this.' "

ALLEN FRIEDMAN

In 1948, brawny, prosperous, postwar Cleveland—the nation's sixth-largest city—churned out cars, steel, and a World Series winner. Allen Friedman, back from California and broke, was looking for a place to stay and a way to make money. Like his late father, a bootlegger and a bookie, Friedman found comfort and kinship at card games and cheat spots along the main streets of Glenville. Within days, he met up with a bookmaker he knew who rented a tiny apartment on East 105th and Ashbury. The apartment was used for only a few hours in the afternoons to make and take telephoned bets; the bookie told Allen that he and his wife, Iona, could share it for free. The place was run-down and filthy, but Allen and his wife had little choice. They cleaned and decorated the tiny apartment, making it one of the homiest bookie joints in town.

Several months later, Friedman was visited by a wild young tough who ran around with his nephew Jackie. The friend was trying to impress Allen, who at twenty-seven was older and more experienced. "C'mon downstairs," he said. "I want to show you something."

At the curb sat a new Dodge, gleaming in the cold Cleveland snow. "Where the hell did you get the money to buy this Dodge?" Friedman asked.

"I stole it," the man replied. Friedman gave the joyrider some

49

advice. "Take the car and park it around the building. Leave it. You don't want to go to jail."

Later, walking his dog to a nearby park, Friedman spotted the abandoned Dodge. "I had a Dalmatian, and right behind my building was a park," Friedman recalled. "Every day I'd walk my dog there. And every day I'd see that fucking car there. I saw it there for a week. I saw it there for a month. I saw it there for two months. I saw it there for three months. Why didn't the police pick this car up?" He decided to try to sell it himself. "I went to a few guys I knew who sold cars and asked them how to get rid of it. One guy said the only way to do this is to go down South."

At the time, according to Friedman, a dozen or more states, mostly in the South, didn't require titles in order for car owners to get license plates. A bill of sale was all that was needed to obtain a registration and plates. The trick was to phony up a bill of sale, then use it to sell the car. Friedman explained how he did it. "You go into a used-car dealer and talk to them and steal some of their papers that had their name on it, their letterhead, and write out that they sold you the car, and sign their name. [Then] you go to the clerk of courts and tell them you have to register a car."

He traveled to Tennessee, snitched some letterhead, wrote out a bill of sale using the serial number of the Dodge, which was back in Cleveland, and obtained Tennessee license plates. He says he sold the car for about $2,400. "Everybody was broke," Friedman said. "Jackie's broke. . . . My brother Harry is always broke. And I started hanging around a gambling joint. I started stealing one car a month. At that time, $2,300, $2,400 was a lot of fucking money. My brother Harry said to me, 'What are you doing? Why are you carrying all that money? Where did you get all the money? Where did you steal it?' I said, 'Harry, leave me alone.'"

In the first few months of 1949, Allen himself stole four or five cars, laundered the ownership with phony bills of sale, and then sold the cars. Soon he was swaggering around the gambling joints with a thick roll of cash. "I started building up a bankroll," Friedman said. "I was always carrying six, seven, eight thousand dollars. I didn't trust banks. I still don't. I was carrying the money in my pocket. We were hanging around this card room across the street from the Jewish Center on 105th and Grantwood. My dad used to go there and play cards. Now my brother sees me with my six thousand dollars. Two or three months ago, I was broke. He said, 'Allen, cut me in.' I said, 'Harry, here's a thousand dollars. Leave me alone.'

"I didn't want to tell him it was so easy that I'm stealing one car a month. I was done in a week. Only working a week, stealing the car, registering it, and selling it. I give my brother Harry a thousand dollars. He nagged me, bugged me, 'I'm your brother, cut me in. What are you doing?' So I told him. He said, 'You're a liar.' I said, 'Harry, you want me to give you a thousand a month?' He bugged me and nagged me and said, 'I don't believe you.'" So Allen cut Harry in, his slick little paper shuffle giving another of Jackie's uncles the means to gamble at the neighborhood high-stakes games.

Allen quickly expanded his criminal enterprise after a friend at the car lot told him that any General Motors car could be unlocked by one of sixty-four master keys. "I knew a guy who knew a broad who worked at a key shop," Allen Friedman said. "I went to him and I told him, 'Could I talk to your broad?'" He said yes, and Allen, pouring on the charm, convinced her to make him a duplicate set of the sixty-four master keys.

It became a familiar routine. Friedman would break into a Chevrolet, lie down on the floor or front seat, put the car in neutral, pump the gas pedal a few times, then spin through the sixty-four keys, snaking his arm up to see which one would start the car. Then, he says, he learned that Oldsmobile had one master key; thereafter, he specialized in stealing Oldsmobiles. "I'd go to apartment houses in Pennsylvania, West Virginia, Chicago, Cleveland. Wherever I stole them, I went to another state to sell them," Allen said. "Now that Harry was cut in, I did all the stealing, and he did all the selling. I didn't know he took Jackie along."

Jackie worked as his Uncle Harry's accomplice, Allen said, but didn't get a full cut of the profits. "My brother used to fuck Jackie," Allen said. "Maybe give him three hundred or five hundred dollars. My brother Harry would fuck anybody out of money."

The theft ring continued to expand. "A paratrooper buddy of mine, Steve Roberts, came to Cleveland and looked me up, said he didn't have enough money," Allen said. "He got cut in. Then Jackie said, 'Uncle Allen, how about cutting in Harold Sylvester?' He hung with Jackie. . . . Before I knew it, I was stealing two cars a week, every week. I yelled at my brother Harry. I had it easy and now I'm making just a little bit more money. I'm working every day and night now."

Allen Friedman says he stole twenty-two cars and that Jackie transported and sold six of them. While this was going on, a friend, a tall, broad, dark-haired business agent for the Bakery Workers Union named Harold Friedman (no relation to Allen), observed their illegal operation. Harold Friedman, who later became the world's highest-paid union leader as vice president of the International Brotherhood of Teamsters, saw the money being divided at Allen's apartment and begged to be made a part of the venture. "He said, 'C'mon Allen, Jesus Christ, I'm your friend. How about giving me a piece.' I said, 'Fuck you, you're making money down at the union hall. Us guys don't have anything coming in.' "

On May 26, 1949, Steve Roberts and Harold Sylvester drove to Columbus, Ohio, with new titles and registration papers to sell one of two 1948 Pontiacs Allen had stolen. While trying to unload one of the stolen cars at a used-car lot, one of them pulled out the wrong set of registration papers. Suspicious about the mismatched numbers as well as the sight of two unpolished young men with a shiny new car to sell, the car dealer started asking questions. Roberts and Sylvester got frightened and drove off—but not before the car dealer wrote down their license-plate numbers. Within several miles, two Columbus policemen arrested the pair. After a short interrogation, the two men told the police all about the Cleveland-Tennessee car-theft ring.

Based on this confession, Columbus police quickly notified the FBI, which had jurisdiction over the federal crime of transporting stolen cars across state lines. The bureau was excited and jumped on the case right away.

"Jackie Presser expects us back in Cleveland after selling the one car," one of them told FBI agents. They gave the agents the address of a garage in Glenville where the cars had been stored—9206 Parkgate, right next door to Jackie's grandparents' house. The FBI set up surveillance the next day, but neither Jackie nor Allen ever came by.

On June 2, 1949, FBI agents contacted Jackie, who agreed to be interviewed at the office of Cleveland police detective James Patrick Foley, a good friend of his father's. Jackie admitted that other than a few odd jobs for his father, he had been unemployed since his discharge from the navy three years earlier. But he swore he had no involvement in a car-theft ring. The agents didn't believe him. The bureau had been told that Jackie had been involved, only not as deeply as his uncles.

Curiously, the FBI learned that Harry Friedman was staying at the Fountain Square Hotel in Cincinnati and burst in and arrested him the next day. When he got a chance, Harry frantically telephoned his brother to warn him that the FBI was making arrests. Allen immediately fled from his apartment and hopped a streetcar to a rooming house near downtown. He realized he was in big trouble a day or two later when he read a newspaper story about his friends' arrests. "Smash Seven-State Car Theft Ring," the headline proclaimed. Fond of hyperbole, Hoover's FBI issued press releases and played up its capture of the three men. "The most daring theft ring since the war," said one news story. As a result, Harry got socked with a ten-thousand-dollar bond. His bond papers noted that he used the aliases George E. Graham, Ben Tesler, and Harry Myers.

From his hiding place, Allen learned that the FBI had turned up the heat on the Presser family in trying to find him, the man Roberts and Sylvester had identified as the mastermind behind the theft ring. He slipped out of the rooming house long enough to grab his wife and quietly move to West Virginia, where he found a job selling siding. That lasted for a few months. "Then it all came out," Allen recalled. "Everybody was finking on everybody else. . . . The FBI, they went to my sister and Bill and said, "We know your son Jackie Presser is involved in this.' I was the only one on the lam. They went to my sister and brother-in-law and said, 'We're taking Harry back in jail and raising the bond to $100,000 unless you tell us where Allen is.' " So my sister finked on me and told them what hotel I was in in West Virginia. . . . We got through working that day, canvassing. I walked in my room [and] there were guys with machine guns and shotguns. Coming out of the bathroom!"

Friedman was handcuffed and delivered to the Cuyahoga County Jail in Cleveland, where he languished under a high bond along with his brother Harry and their accomplices Sylvester and Roberts. Of all the defendants, Harry Friedman faced the most severe punishment; he already was a convicted felon. Tragically, his wife had recently died, after a long illness. His gambling left him little time and even less

53

money with which to rear his son and daughter, aged nine and four. This responsibility fell on Jackie's parents and, for several months, Allen Friedman's wife.

The wealthy and powerful Bill Presser decided to pull whatever strings he could to pluck Jackie, who had just gotten married again, from this legal stew. "Bill Presser comes to me, visits me in county jail," Allen recalled. "He says, 'Why are you pleading not guilty?' I said, 'Bill, nobody ever saw me do anything wrong. I'm going to fight this case.' So he said, 'Well, my son's going to get involved if you plead not guilty. There's going to be a big trial.' He said, 'I got it all fixed up where you're going to get two years probation if you plead guilty. And my son won't get involved. I have some higher-up in the government who is going to drop the charges. So please plead guilty.' I said, 'Bill, I'm not going to plead guilty.' "

According to Allen, Bill Presser turned to Harry, the weak link. Bill told Harry he was a loser, a bum who couldn't support his children. Bill promised to adopt Harry's two children, Toby and Ronnie, and give them a good education and a quarter of his estate when he died. For Harry's part of the deal, he had to confess to the crimes and implicate Allen, thereby assuring a tidy uncontested solution for prosecutors.

"So my brother Harry rolled over on me only because of his children," Allen said in an interview last year. "Bill talks Harry into finking on me, saying that I stole these cars and showed them how to do everything."

Harry Friedman wrote out a statement, clearing Jackie and confining blame to himself and the others, and gave it to Bill Presser. The labor boss brought it to the county jail, showed it to Allen, and said, "You plead guilty and I'll still get you two years' probation." Allen agreed, and Jackie was never charged.

Meanwhile, cooperating witnesses Roberts and Sylvester mentioned that Harold Friedman had been with them when they stole a car about a month or so earlier. "I took a ride with three assholes to eat, and they decided to steal a car, the sons of bitches," Friedman recalled recently. He, Jackie, Allen, and one of the others "were playing cards. You know, in those days, there would be card joints all over Cleveland." Afterwards, they went out to eat, and on the way back "they stopped to get out. The next thing I know, they're opening up this car. I said, 'What the hell are you doing?' It ain't their car. Bing, bing, bing, and away they go."

The FBI called Harold to Detective Foley's office. Harold said he remembers the scene vividly.

"Listen, we're looking for Allen Friedman," the agent said.

"I don't know where he's at," Harold replied.

"Well, would you help us find him, locate him, or if you see him would you let us know?"

"What do I look like, some kind of stool pigeon?"

"I'm not asking you to be a stool pigeon."

"You want me to tell you where this guy is at? I don't know where's he's at. I'm not going to tell you."

It was a foolish performance, Friedman recalled years later. He blamed it on being young, foolish, and trying to act like a Hollywood tough guy. "I saw a Humphrey Bogart movie. I'm not going to tell him nothing. I didn't shave, and I give him the whole bit, like James Cagney. . . . I got up and walked out."

To which the FBI agent replied, "I'll send that son of a bitch away if it's the last thing I do."

FBI agents arrested him a few days later and found a handgun in his car. A concealed-weapons charge was added to his auto-theft count. But Harold Friedman had no part in stealing cars, Allen Friedman says today. Roberts and Sylvester told police, "Harold was up at the house and [they] thought he was getting a piece," Allen says. "These guys were five, six years younger than us, and they really didn't know the true story. They assumed that I was giving Harold a piece because Harold and I were very close. He was never involved. He was in the house when we were cutting up the money and talking about how this car was yours and that car was mine. But he never got a penny."

In December 1949, Jackie's two uncles and Sylvester and Roberts plead guilty in federal courts to stealing and transporting cars across state lines. Harry Friedman's confession, entered into the court record, lists without embellishment several cars he stole and in what city he sold them. At the end of his statement, Harry Friedman mentions a final theft that includes a curious extra detail. On May 24, 1949, the statement says, Harry, *while driving his nephew's car*, obtained a title to a stolen 1949 Pontiac and then drove it to Pittsburgh and sold it for $1,700. This incident was apparently the car theft that could be linked to Jackie, and his uncle specifically shouldered the blame for it.

On January 23, 1950, five men—three of whom would eventually become high-ranking Teamsters officials—stood in a line facing U.S. district-court judge E. B. Freed in Ohio's northern district. All of them but Harold Friedman had pleaded guilty to various counts of stealing and selling cars. He had gone to trial five days earlier and was convicted. The judge went down the line, handing out sentences, giving Harry Friedman, Sylvester, and Roberts each three years in prison. When the judge got to Harold, he gave him a two-year sentence. The man who forty years later would be a dark-horse candidate for president of the entire Teamsters Union started crying. Allen Friedman burst out laughing.

"Do you think this is funny?" the judge demanded.

"No sir, when I'm nervous, I laugh," Allen said.

"Well, I'm giving you five years on the first count, five years on the second, five years on the third, and five years on the fourth count," the judge said. "Now, do you think that's funny, young fella?"

"No, Your Honor," Allen said, stunned.

"I'm going to give you a break and run them concurrently," the judge added.

Allen was furious that Bill Presser had lied about getting him probation. Allen had plenty of time to stew about it after he and Harold were shipped to federal prison in Milan, Michigan. "I had a lot of trouble in Milan because of Harold," Allen said. "Because Harold was an SOB. He started beating up dagos. He went in the bakery, and the dagos ran the bakery. He beat the shit out of some of them and they came after me because they thought we were brothers." Harold was paroled after several months and went back to Cleveland and his job with the Bakery Workers Union. "I was very happy to see him go," Allen said. "I lived in a private cell after he left. We had lived in the dormitory. After that, I was the head cook and did more or less what I wanted to do." Without early parole, Allen faced forty months in Milan. His sister Faye pushed her husband to help out, and one day, Allen remembers, he was called into the warden's office to accept a phone call from a U.S. congressman from Ohio. While Faye yelled in the background that she loved him, the congressman told Allen that parole had been arranged.

56

After the car-theft episode, Jackie and his uncle Harry moved apart. Harry didn't think his nephew was grateful enough for his sacrifice, even though Harry would have gone to prison anyway for his part in the ring. "After that, they hated each other with a passion," Allen said. Also, it didn't help matters that Harry, at family gatherings and in front of relatives, would remind Jackie how he once took the fall for him. Jackie didn't contradict him, but he didn't like it either. He sat silently, his resentment building.

Bill Presser and the Mob weren't the only forces strip-mining the resources of the booming vending business. In 1950, the Teamsters hierarchy began promoting vending as a field rich in opportunity. "If Teamsters overlook automatic merchandizing as a field for organization, they are missing one of the biggest bets in modern union organization possibilities," reads an August 1950 article in *International Teamsters* magazine.

"In time to come, such stores as supermarkets, dime stores, drug stores, etc., will be completely automatic. In place of merchandise being in the open for the general public to inspect, it will all be under glass—in rows upon rows of vending machines," the article predicted. "Someone has to service the machines." Bill Presser could have told them this years before.

By 1951, Bill Presser had joined the Teamsters. A year later, he was running Joint Council 41 and the Ohio Conference of Teamsters with the backing of his powerful sponsor, Jimmy Hoffa. Ever the conquistador, Big Bill invaded new territories in his search for more vending-machine workers to organize. He obtained a charter for Teamsters Local 410-A in 1952 and pushed into Akron, Ohio, forty miles south of Cleveland. Soon, Akron police noticed that tavern jukeboxes were being bombed and vandalized all over town.

One victim of Presser's Akron racket was Robert Holland, who owned Leslie's Sandwich Shop, a small storefront, and the popular Sea Gull Restaurant, a larger sit-down place. Presser's Local 410-A insisted that Holland join the union. Holland was also pressured to pay dues to the newly formed Summit County Vending Machine Operators Association, also formed by Presser. Holland refused to do either.

On April 15, 1952, at about one-thirty in the morning, a stink bomb was hurled through the window of Holland's Akron home. Holland realized that the racketeers meant business and notified the police. The assistant chief of the Akron police, John F. Struzenski, assigned detectives to investigate. Within hours, they had linked Presser and his new union to the violence.

Presser's name was familiar to Struzenski. In 1937, he recalled, a Cleveland union had moved into Akron and tried to sign up small dry-cleaning shop owners. Those who refused had been stink-bombed and fire-bombed. Struzenski reexamined the files of the police investigation. "The name William Presser appeared in our records," he said, "indicating that he had some knowledge or was connected with the bombings."

In 1951, Presser also pushed into Toledo with a Teamsters local, designated 410-T. He knew some vending operators from Cleveland who had moved to Toledo and who quickly realized that they could make much more money there if Presser's jukebox cartel was installed. After an October meeting at a downtown hotel, eleven operators agreed to pay Presser a total of twenty-five hundred dollars if he would bring his cartel to town. Each kicked in ninety-one dollars to fund a thousand-dollar retainer to secure Big Bill's services.

But Presser wasn't welcomed by the five existing Teamsters locals in Toledo. Some Toledo Teamsters leaders remembered how he had come to town in 1939 and tried, but failed, to set up his patented jukebox racket.

Once in Toledo, Local 410-T officials decided to picket a bar owned by Mike Yakumithis. They didn't like the idea that Yakumithis had installed a jukebox owned and operated by a man with only two boxes, who stocked and maintained them himself, and didn't kick in dues to Presser's newly formed Tri-State Vending Machines Association. Yakumithis employed one bartender and one waitress, both members of their respective unions. By law, he didn't have a labor dispute. Presser didn't see it that way. However, he picked the wrong guy to intimidate.

Yakumithis decided not to cave in to Presser's strong arm tactics. He hired labor lawyer Daniel McCullough, who wasn't a labor-union hater; several years earlier he had represented a Teamsters taxi-drivers local. But McCullough was outraged at what he learned and decided to take on Presser and his Teamsters. First, he filed for a court order restraining Presser's picketers. At the hearing several days later, court watchers were treated to an unusual sight: officers in the Toledo Teamsters joint council came forward—unsolicited—and testified against Presser. The Toledo Teamsters didn't want a carpetbagging racketeer like Presser moving into their territory.

Next, McCullough subpoenaed records and witnesses. William T. Flynn, executive assistant to Teamsters president Dan Tobin, traveled from Indianapolis to support Presser, but then he had second thoughts. Over the telephone, Tobin ordered Flynn not to testify on Presser's behalf. But in an astounding example of Presser's influence after only one year as a Teamsters official, Flynn ignored his geriatric boss, who would retire a year later. Instead, he aided the up-and-coming Big Bill.

After hearing numerous witnesses and reviewing dozens of exhibits, Judge Hackett, a Democrat who had represented unions as a lawyer, found against Presser and the Teamsters. He explained his ruling:

> There was no misunderstanding, no dispute, legitimate or illegitimate, between the plaintiffs herein and this picketing group, whether it be a union or otherwise, . . . There is ample proof in this case that this union grew out of an unlawful conspiracy between a group of vending-machine operators and a group masquerading under the name of a union which was an appendix to the vending-machine operators. . . .
>
> It couldn't have been a legitimate labor dispute because the object was unlawful. . . . The object was to run this man's business their way instead of his way, and they told him to throw out of his place a jukebox he wanted and put in one that they wanted him to have.

Presser had contended that he just wanted a union man to service the jukebox, but Judge Hackett savaged that claim. "There isn't a scintilla of evidence that anybody belonging to his union, including Presser . . . ever paid a dime to the international organization. There is no evidence that they ever received any charter." Presser was a renegade, claiming to be union but unable to produce official documents that proved he had a union charter. That meant he was pocketing the dues for his own purposes.

Beaten, Presser and his jukebox local left Toledo and instead concentrated on Youngstown, where they had much more success. Presser picked Joseph Blumetti, a Mob associate who had been convicted of running an interstate prostitution ring, to run Teamsters Local 410-Y. Next, Bill dispatched brother-in-law Harry Friedman to Cincinnati, where he relied on the same strong-arm methods that had worked in Cleveland and the other cities. Six or eight Cincinnati restaurants and taverns were promptly bombed, one suffering $4,800 in damage. At first, witnesses to the bombings were afraid to come forward. Then James Luken, an honest Teamsters leader who later became mayor of the city, stepped forward. "We did a little check on him [Harry Friedman] and found that he had just come in from the federal penitentiary and had completed a term for interstate theft of automobiles," Luken said years later. "We objected to that type of people in our movement. . . . There had been some bombings of stores, and we had the local council refuse to take the fellow in or his local in."

Witnesses came forward, and Friedman was charged with blackmail. He beat the case, and headed back to Cleveland. "Harry Friedman," Luken said. "was sort of run out of town."

5
Buying Off Bender

"Everybody has his price."
JIMMY HOFFA

In 1951, Bill Presser reached out beyond his jukebox empire to grab hold of the Consolidated Dump Truck Operators Association, a group of contractors that used trucks to cart earth and debris. His start as the association's chief coincided with a string of bombings, at least thirty-three over the next thirty months. Backhoes, bulldozers, trenching machines—they chugged along fine until a vandal worked his midnight magic. Police in Cleveland and the suburbs didn't solve any of the crimes.

This was the period, 1947 to 1951, when Bill Presser branched into the professional-association business, a time he referred to as having "left the labor movement for a while." Under the guise of the Dump Truck Operators Association, he took cash from construction companies by promising them labor peace and reasonable union contracts in return. He said he was a "labor-relations and public-relations man." Others called it extortion.

He kept busy. In 1951, for example, Presser held influential positions with not only the dump-truck outfit but also with the Phonograph Merchants Association and the Tobacco and Candy Jobbers Association. When asked, Presser admitted to collecting a modest hundred dollars a month, sometimes more, sometimes less, from each of the business groups. However, Presser wasn't a typical businessman; he had no office and didn't meet a payroll. As executive secretary of the

Phonograph Merchants Association, for instance, he mostly settled disputes over violations of its jukebox courtesy list. No one had the job before him, no one after.

It's clear his purpose with the business associations was to get the labor unions to go easy on the companies he promoted when it came time to bargain new contracts. For example, wage increases for members of Vending Workers Local 442, the local he built, plummeted fifty percent after he organized their employers, the tobacco jobbers, into their price-fixing association. During their first year with Presser as head of the tobacco jobbers, union workers received only a five-cents-per-hour raise. For each of the three previous years, the union had come away from the bargaining table with raises of ten cents per hour.

Throughout their careers, the Pressers liked to clap themselves on the back about obtaining top wages for the Teamsters they represented. This episode with the tobacco jobbers was certainly not one Bill would ever talk about. He was more a businessman than a union man, concerned more about wealth than the commonwealth. Unlike his contemporaries in other unions, Bill Presser put his private gain ahead of public service to the members. Like Hoffa, Presser secretly owned parts of companies that hired Teamsters and benefited from sweetheart contracts. But Bill went further. He played both sides of the fence at once.

On June 20, 1951, the Justice Department landed a terrific blow on Presser, just as he stood poised to move into the Teamsters Union and *formally* join forces with Hoffa. Presser and twelve other individuals and companies, including Teamsters Local 400, were indicted for felony criminal violations of the Sherman Antitrust Act. Presser and the others were accused of conspiring to fix prices in Cleveland's $27-million-a-year candy-and-tobacco-jobbers trade. The Justice Department had the case nailed down. The Tobacco and Candy Jobbers Association under Presser, the old hand at setting up economic cartels, had been dumb enough to get caught circulating printed price schedules to which jobbers had to adhere. Teamsters Local 400 and the jobbers spied on each other, watching to make sure each didn't undercut the other's prices or raid customers. If a jobber got out of line and bucked the monopoly, Presser and the Teamsters would force him to comply by picketing his warehouse or his customers.

Presser's federal criminal indictment posed a big problem for him

and the International Brotherhood of Teamsters. He wanted to bring
his Vending Workers Local 442 into the Teamsters. Would the Teamsters grant him a union charter at a time when he stood accused of
committing labor-related crimes in conspiracy with another Teamsters
local?

Dave Beck, head of the Western Conference, and Jimmy Hoffa,
head of the Central Conference, already had moved into Teamster
president Dan Tobin's territory and were flexing their muscles. They
didn't care about a price-fixing case, and gave Presser his charter. He
quickly persuaded members of his old vending workers local to join the
newly created Teamsters Local 410. Bill could see the bright future of
a mass union like the Teamsters, the most strategically powerful union
in the country. He once explained the switch: "If you can't beat 'em,
join 'em." As part of a plea arrangement, Bill pleaded guilty to a
misdemeanor antitrust violation and paid a fine.

Within two years, his friendship with Hoffa paid off handsomely.
With his backing, Presser took over as president of Joint Council 41,
the powerful ruling body of more than a dozen Teamsters locals in the
Cleveland area.

Though president of the joint council, Presser shared power with
a second in command, N. Louis "Babe" Triscaro, a convicted armed
robber, Mafia associate, and good friend of Hoffa's. After years of
scuffling, smacking heads on picket lines, and recruiting strike muscle
from boxing gyms to staff whatever side wanted to pay his squadron,
by 1952, Babe Triscaro had climbed to one step from the top of Ohio
labor circles. He was president of Teamsters Excavating Truck Drivers
Local 436 and could bring any construction company or any development firm to its knees. Once the Teamsters pinched off delivery of
building materials, a contractor faced huge payroll loses as his laborers
and operators and craftsmen stood idle, waiting. So contractors quickly
caved in to whatever Local 436 demanded.

Triscaro was a 1931 Golden Gloves flyweight champ, short, with
quick hands, slick black hair, and olive skin. He held himself ramrod
straight, looking taller, and commanded respect. Triscaro and Presser
worked as partners. When one of them needed to deal with the underworld, Presser handled members of the Jewish syndicate while Triscaro
met with the Mayfield Road Gang, later called the Cleveland Mafia.

It was an unusual alliance. Some of Triscaro's *compares* complained to him about being partners with a Jew, just as Presser's friends questioned his ties to someone connected with the Italians from Mayfield Road. Over the years of their collaboration, rumors circulated, backed up by very convincing stories, that Presser and Triscaro had a falling out, that they hated each other and were battling for power and perquisites. But Robert Rotatori, a lawyer who later represented them both in criminal cases, said it wasn't true. "There was a lot of rumors around that they were enemies," he said. "They were always friends and enjoyed people thinking they were enemies. They were always very close."

Rotatori says that Triscaro's enemies would complain about him to Presser, while Presser's foes in the union would take their gripes to Babe. By playing out the charade, Presser and Triscaro were able to get information on plots against them through back channels. Like partners in a bar fight, standing back to back and facing off against an encircling mob, Triscaro and Presser hung on to power for more than two decades. "I thought it was a game," Rotatori says. "They really worked together. They'd never allow themselves to be split apart."

Not until the seventies, when it was time to pick a successor to Big Bill, did the two powerful allies begin to clash.

Like Presser, Babe Triscaro enjoyed sweetheart deals with businesses that depended on Teamsters labor. His brother, Joseph, ran four companies—three slag-supply companies and one trucking company—that netted more than $90,000 a year in after-tax profits in 1954. Joe Triscaro's partner was Mrs. Babe Triscaro. She was an equal partner in the profits despite investing only $2,900 in the companies. To further increase the Triscaros' profits, some of the companies employed nonunion truck drivers. When asked, Babe said with a straight face that he knew nothing of his wife's business affairs. Her initial investment, he claimed, came from dollars she saved over the years from the weekly household allowance he gave her. "My wife is a very good homekeeper and a wonderful wife, and my wife is a woman that doesn't believe in mink coats or what have you," Triscaro said. "She lives within her means. Now, that money, she finally admitted to me how she got it, was from the allowance I would give her each week. She would save and she just put it away, and that's how she accumulated that money that she loaned to my brother." Being married to a Teamsters power guaranteed Mrs. Triscaro a tremendous return on her investments. Records show that she put five hundred dollars into Eagle Trucking Company in 1953; when the company was sold four years later, she received $54,000.

Perhaps Triscaro's favorite operative was Moose Maxwell, a hulking six-footer weighing in at two hundred solid pounds who had a hefty arrest record. One night, Moose Maxwell carried dynamite and blasting caps to a construction site where an idle bulldozer rested in the dirt. Moose usually sent subtle messages to construction companies that wouldn't knuckle under to Presser's new dump-truck haulers association, which wanted dues, or to Triscaro's Teamsters Excavation Drivers Local 436, which wanted a labor contract. Subtlety meant pouring sand into a crankcase, causing an engine to seize. This night was different. Moose was tired of subtlety.

Dynamiting the bulldozer sent an unequivocal message.

Maxwell's real name was Richard Finley. Uneducated, he once admitted he had been involved in "unlegal" activities for most of his life. He had used thirteen aliases and had an arrest record that went back to 1929. By the fifties, he had hooked up with the Triscaro faction of the Teamsters and found work as a bomber. From 1950 to 1953, Triscaro companies issued fifty-eight checks to him that bore the notations "tires" or "truck hires." In fact, Finley was paid for bombing heavy equipment or selling stolen tires and other goods back to Joe Triscaro, Babe's brother. Finley said that he was often the finger man for hoods from Pittsburgh who came to Cleveland and picked up dynamite and blasting caps from Triscaro. Moose would drive them out to construction sites and point out the machinery to be blown up. It was an effective way to make sure contractors hired union truck drivers, joined the association, and paid their dues.

It wasn't surprising that police detectives didn't solve these bombings. Many times, the explosions occurred in the new, developing suburbs, where the tiny police forces weren't sophisticated enough to handle an investigation, even though they could surmise that the bombings were the result of labor disputes or extortion attempts. In Cleveland, the labor-relations bureau of the police department wasn't much help either. Its chief, Detective James Patrick Foley, was on the take.

† † †

In October 1952, the Teamsters convened in Los Angeles. Bill Presser, now a union officer after two decades of close ties to the brotherhood, decided to drive out with Babe Triscaro and schmooze with their counterparts from across the country. Tagging along and doing the driving was Cleveland police detective Pat Foley, who, with his dark good looks, resembled actor Tyrone Power. Foley ran the department's labor bureau, supposedly the watchdog over union-management disputes. He started in the two-man labor bureau in 1938 and quickly became its head. He reported directly to the police chief, a close friend.

Foley enjoyed tremendous leeway as a bureau head, settling disputes about the number of pickets or deciding when to make arrests on the lines, all the while racking up impressive overtime claims. After fourteen years as a public servant, he submitted claims for 3,996 hours of overtime, or about seven weeks a year in compensatory time off. He "had a little office at Central Police Station, the first office east of the lieutenant's desk," retired lieutenant Jack Delaney recalls. "They reported directly to Chief George Julius Matowitz. They did a hell of a lot of good between labor and management. . . . They'd meet with both sides, try to draw up rules on the assignments of pickets."

On October 2, 1952, the unlikely trio—a Mafia associate, a labor racketeer, and a Cleveland cop—drove out West. For the next couple of weeks, Foley visited Paramount Studios and his schoolyard friend, comedian Bob Hope, and went sightseeing. He let Triscaro and Presser buy him dinner. Teamsters leaders from other cities had to be impressed with the bold guys from Cleveland: their sidekick was not only a cop but the man in charge of the labor-relations bureau.

Then Presser, Triscaro, and Foley got a bad break. Stan Anderson, television critic for the *Cleveland Press,* visited the Paramount Studios lot where Jack Hope, brother of the comedian, introduced him to Foley. Foley told the reporter he was "staying with the Teamsters at Hotel Statler." Anderson wondered why Foley was out in Los Angeles as the guest of Babe Triscaro, who was just the sort of character that the detective was being paid to scrutinize.

After a bit of legwork, the *Cleveland Press* discovered that during the twenty-seven days Foley spent traveling and relaxing on the West Coast, he was signed in at police headquarters and being paid. The

Press launched a page-one exposé. "Why Wasn't Foley Missed?" asked an October 30, 1952, headline. "One of his companions on this junket," the story read, "was Louis (Babe) Triscaro, a well-known hoodlum with a messy police record." Foley should have known better than to talk to the reporter. He had been careful on the trip until then, even signing into the Statler under a phony name.

Chief Matowitz, stinging from the scandal, brought Foley up on departmental charges and fined him 3,996 hours overtime, about two years of salary. Foley was eventually bounced out of the labor bureau, and the Pressers lost a valuable cohort.

Some police officers were surprised that Foley had acted so foolishly and had gotten caught. "Foley was always a sharp guy, always a half step ahead of the other guy as far as looking out for Foley," Delaney says. "He could see a step ahead of the other guy. . . . Furloughs were based on seniority. If a policeman died or retired, he'd be down there trying to grab the furlough. There's nothing wrong with that. He was just ahead of everybody else." The Pressers told much more hair-raising stories about Foley. Allen Friedman says that Foley actually helped him organize dry cleaners, restaurants, and other small businesses by scaring owners into accepting the union's contract terms. Friedman says he would be out on a picket line, putting on a tough act, not letting people come or go into a restaurant or dry-cleaning shop, shoving them around. If uniformed policemen arrived, Friedman would tell them Pat Foley was on his way. The uniformed police were more than happy to fob off the assignment to the labor bureau. "Then [Foley] would let us do whatever we wanted to," Friedman says.

Once on the scene, the smartly dressed Foley would go inside, talk to the boss, then point out burly Allen Friedman. "See that kid out there," Foley would say. "He's a bomber. We call him the Bomber. Give me a few dollars, and I'll threaten him." On cue, Friedman would walk in the shop, and Foley would berate him, tolerate a little back talk, then build into a scream. "I'll put you in jail for life!" Business owners fell for it. Or, depending on the situation, Friedman says, Foley would try another tactic. Foley would point to Friedman and say, "He'll burn your home down with your children in it tonight. Tell him to come in, and I'll make sure you get a good deal." Foley, Allen says, "made a lot of money" with his Teamsters connections.

Cultivating law enforcers—becoming their friends, giving them gifts, ultimately compromising them, then using them to defeat their opponents—was a tactic used by Bill Presser, Triscaro, and other racketeers. This lesson wasn't lost on Jackie. Years later, he applied it to agents of the FBI.

Within the next two years, the Teamsters' brazen jukebox monopoly and bulldozer bombings attracted the attention of Representative Clare Hoffman, a Detroit congressman, conservative Republican, and man with no use for labor unions or Jimmy Hoffa. Complaints about shady Teamsters activities also surfaced in law-enforcement circles in Detroit, Chicago, Minneapolis, and Kansas City. The Mob had infiltrated Teamsters locals and joint councils in these cities almost as effectively as it had in Cleveland.

In 1953, Hoffman held congressional hearings on labor racketeering in Detroit. For the first time, citizens who bothered to read the local papers learned the name Bill Presser and found out how his jukebox monopoly had been exported from Cleveland and installed in Detroit. By 1954, Hoffman wanted to expand the labor-rackets hearings to Cleveland, Minneapolis, and other cities, but a coalition of Democrats and Republicans on the House Committee on Government Operations blocked his plan by a nineteen-to-one vote and tossed the assignment to a special committee chaired by Representative George Bender from Cleveland. Hoffman was enraged. "They want a friend of labor to run the committee," he fumed. "It looks like a whitewash to me." Bender, who knew Bill Presser and had received Teamsters support in the past, insisted he'd be tough. However, he allowed, "I wouldn't know a racketeer if I met one."

Republican county chairman since 1938, Bender had one hobby: politics. He loved campaigning, entertaining, smooching babies, and singing—whether belting out "Happy Birthday" or intoning hymns. Beefy and back-slapping, Bender had a fine baritone and would break into song "at the drop of a hat," said his long-time aide, Saul Stillman. "It was hard to get him to stop sometimes," he added.

At the 1952 Republican National Convention in Philadelphia, Bender made a name for himself as a Robert Taft supporter who, whenever he got the chance, took center stage and hollered Taft's name while loudly clanging a bell. His critics made him out to be a clown. "The impression in many quarters of Ohio is that George Bender is loud and bombastic and a prototype of a musical-comedy salesman, who kisses babies and sings hymns at the drop of an introduction, waves the flag, and thumps his chest," the *Cleveland Plain Dealer* once commented.

Up until the 1954 congressional hearings, the prospering Teamsters Union enjoyed a favorable public image and wielded clout in Cleveland and across the land. Teamsters president Dave Beck of Seattle was welcomed into the Eisenhower White House. Egotistical, always making grand pronouncements, the Republican Beck was embraced by the American business community and promoted as the nation's leading labor figure. Dan Tobin, a Democrat, had been a close friend of President Roosevelt. Tobin clung to the notion of the Teamsters as a narrow craft union, saying that he didn't want to bring "riffraff" such as long-haul truckers into the ranks. But that all changed. Teamsters enrollment swelled dramatically as younger leaders such as Hoffa, the one-time protégé of Socialist Farrell Dobbs, and Presser continued to organize workers into a mass union that embraced a smorgasbord of jobs: not just in-city delivery drivers, but long-haul truckers, cab drivers, jukebox repairers, loading-dock workers, and so on.

In 1933, the Teamsters union numbered seventy-five thousand workers. Two decades later, it boasted nearly 1.2 million members. With this clout, the Teamsters and Presser could influence public officials who, in a nation of checks and balances, were supposed to guard citizens from economic predators like the vending-machine cartel.

Bill Presser and his friends flourished. In spring 1954, just five months before the congressional investigating committee started to tarnish his reputation, Presser was honored at a testimonial dinner by Teamsters president Beck, Jimmy Hoffa, the Cleveland mayor, county judge James Connell, and other politicians. Presser basked in their compliments. His influence would grow over the years, but right now it worked most effectively (and crudely) at lower levels, such as on picket lines. Among other things, he simply directed his brother-in-law,

69

Allen Friedman, or others, to pay off detectives, who in turn let them get away with rough stuff on the picket lines. "I carried a lot of money to people," Allen says.

During the last four days of September 1954, reporters for Cleveland's three newspapers pushed into a downtown hearing room and scribbled notes of an unusual scene. Powerful Mob associates Babe Triscaro, Maishe Rockman, and Bill Presser, under subpoena in a special congressional inquiry, were forced against their wishes to sit still and be peppered with questions about their finances, businesses, and associates—all the shady activities they had kept secret for years.

"Juke Czar Called by Bender Unit," said one headline. "Probe Subpoenas Records in Quiz of Labor Rackets."

Representative George Bender of Cleveland relished his job as chairman of the congressional committee. It meant that he got to ask more questions and snatch wider newspaper exposure just when he was locked into a tough race for a U.S. Senate seat with the incumbent, Senator Thomas A. Burke, the former mayor of Cleveland. The Teamsters had thrown support to Burke since Bender was embarrassing the union with the probe.

Compared to the McClellan committee rackets hearing four years later, the Bender investigation wasn't a hard-hitting probe. But it did expose, for the first time, racketeering by Presser, Triscaro, and the Teamsters. On the first day of the hearings, the committee came out smoking, calling as a witness Richard Finley, a.k.a. Moose Maxwell. With newspaper and radio reporters filling the gallery, Finley detailed his "unlegal" career, including his facility with dynamite and his paychecks from Joe Triscaro. Bender and Representative Clare Hoffman of Detroit dominated the questioning.

HOFFMAN: Tell the chairman how you damaged machinery, if you did.

FINLEY: Well, put sand in the crankshaft.

BENDER: Sand in the crankshaft? How do you do that?

70

FINLEY: Unloosen bolts on the side of the crane and pour sand in. That would stop operation of the crane. Just to let the people know that they was being molested and that other things would happen to them if they didn't come in line.

BENDER: If they didn't come in line? What do you mean by that?

FINLEY: Well, I was on the gravy.

BENDER: Get on the gravy train?

FINLEY: That's right.

BENDER: Well, what is the gravy train?

FINLEY: Well, the gravy train, I guess, doing their operation, they was to come in line, because they wasn't paying off.

Though Bender got in a few good jabs at the witnesses, Hoffman was the star of the show. He demanded answers and sprayed out sarcastic remarks, hoping to provoke a comeback. One area Hoffman and the committee probed was Bill Presser's phantom trade magazine, *Vending News.* The Phonograph Merchants Association supposedly spent $650 a month for advertising in the tabloid, but it was hardly worth it. Presser published the *Vending News* intermittently and with a minuscule press run. It was a pretty slick scam: a seemingly legitimate way to funnel money from the association to Bill Presser.

The Bender committee dredged up an advertising expert who examined issues of the *Vending News,* then came up with the normal industry price for the trade-journal ads for which Presser charged so much. His expert opinion was that the ads, which said "Greetings" or "Best Wishes," were worth about five dollars an issue, not the $650 an issue pocketed by Presser or Local 410.

"The publication actually had very few copies issued," Bender complained at the hearings, "and was not of general circulation, was nothing more than just a device used for the purpose of obtaining money without rendering any service, and obviously it is some kind of a shakedown." Strong stuff for someone who knew the Pressers and had enjoyed Teamsters support in the past. But then Bender was running for office.

The congressional investigation clearly had Presser and his associates on the griddle. More hearings were scheduled for November in Washington. Something had to be done, Presser realized. Could the Teamsters get to one of the national politicians and halt the probe? Bender was the best choice.

He had shown before he could be compromised. Decades before, in 1931, as Cleveland city commissioner for the gigantic new municipal stadium, Bender was indicted for embezzlement and perjury. As stadium commissioner, he had had hundreds of jobs to dole out, bushels of political plums in the depths of the Depression. Bender had hired hordes of unskilled, temporary employees to work at baseball games, expositions, boxing matches, and other events in the eighty-thousand-seat stadium. On July 3, 1931, in the first sports event at Cleveland Stadium, heavyweight Max Schmeling battled William "Young" Stribling. It was a sensation, with tickets going for three to twenty-five dollars a piece. Bender was accused of selling usher jobs for a dollar each to the army of men needed to work the fight. He stood trial and was acquitted.

The Bender hearings were moved to Washington, and on November 9, 1954, Detective Foley was sworn in. He was nervous. He denied staying at the Statler with the Teamsters, admitted that Presser and Triscaro had bought his meals, but claimed that he bought them a meal or two as well.

As for being signed in at work back in Cleveland while vacationing in Los Angeles, well, it was all a mistake, Foley said. He pointed out that he had been severely punished for it, fined nearly four thousand hours of overtime. None of the representatives asked Foley if he had ever taken any bribes—not that he would have answered the question.

As the hearings continued, Representative Hoffman continued to spear Teamsters witnesses; Bender wasn't as inquisitive as he'd been in September. Then Bill Presser, dressed in a conservative suit, wedged his bulk into a chair and was sworn in. He quickly lost his memory and told the committee that his local had lost its financial records. Once again, Presser pleaded the Fifth about questions on his finances. Hoffman asked him many seemingly innocuous question, such as how he had changed Vending Workers Local 442 into Teamsters Local

410. Then, after Presser had locked himself into his answers, Hoffman sprang a trap.

> HOFFMAN: And the Musical Maintenance Union 442, you were still there?
>
> PRESSER: No, the members of 442 were absorbed into 410.
>
> HOFFMAN: And 442, did that go out of existence, and if so, when?
>
> PRESSER: As an active organization, yes.
>
> HOFFMAN: Did it still have officers?
>
> PRESSER: No. It maintained a charter and that is all.
>
> HOFFMAN: But no officers.
>
> PRESSER: No officers.
>
> HOFFMAN: What was your connection with that, with 442, if any, in 1952?
>
> PRESSER: Actually, there is no connection.

After several minutes and a dozen or so questions, Hoffman slyly circled back.

> HOFFMAN: There is something I don't quite understand. You said that the . . . Local Union 442 is out of business. . . . Yet your income-tax return for 1952 shows that that union paid you five thousand dollars—$5059.49. How do you account for that?
>
> PRESSER: I have answered the question, Mr. Hoffman.
>
> HOFFMAN: If they were out of business, what were they paying you $5,059.49 for?
>
> PRESSER: If they paid me in—
>
> HOFFMAN, INTERRUPTING: They did. You put it on your return.

Bill Presser's reputation was sinking. Bank records showed that in 1952, more than $45,000 was deposited into the checking account of

Local 442, the supposedly defunct union, and that $46,829 was then withdrawn. Bill Presser was the only person who was authorized to sign the checks for the union. Hoffman asked Presser to explain this.

"I refuse to answer that question on the grounds it may tend to incriminate me," Bill said.

It was an embarrassing session for Presser. His only consolation was that the committee couldn't get its hands on the books for Local 410, which had been subpoenaed. During remodeling, someone had put them against a wall in a hallway, and garbagemen had picked up the records and hauled them away, or so Presser claimed. "I happened to be out of town at the time," he added.

On November 10, 1954, after two days of hearings in Washington, D.C., a halt was called to the proceedings. "We are about to recess these hearings, subject to the call of the chair. We are not adjourning these hearings," Bender emphasized, "but we are recessing until further call." "Wait a minute," Hoffman said. He wanted to make sure the witnesses would still stay under subpoena. "They are under subpoena," Bender assured him.

Some thought that Bill Presser was in trouble. He certainly opened himself up to contempt and possibly perjury charges with his misleading answers. He lost his memory, his tax returns, and his union records. The dump-truck association's records had supposedly been stolen, and some of Babe Triscaro's Local 436 records were said to have been incinerated in a fire. Clearly, Bill faced possible criminal sanctions. As he would throughout his career, Presser called upon the Teamsters political war chest and sabotaged the committee's efforts.

His maneuver had been foreshadowed a month earlier, October 1954, in the white heat of the Bender-Burke battle for U.S. Senate. Presser's friend, Cleveland Federation of Labor head William Finegan, charged that Bender had offered to drop the labor-rackets probe if the federation supported him over Burke or remained neutral. Bender lashed out, calling Finegan "an unmitigated liar." Finegan also claimed that Bender had a mysterious meeting with some shady characters at the Miami airport. Bender fired back, linking Finegan to the boss of the Cleveland Mafia. "[Finegan] was on the plane with John Scalish, a racketeer who refused to answer a subpoena when our committee was here last week," Bender charged. (Scalish owned Buckeye Vending along with Bill's close friend, Maishe Rockman.)

By the end of the race, the Teamsters' support for Burke dropped off, and he lost to Bender by a narrow margin. Burke asked the Teamsters, supposedly his backers, for help in getting a recount, but the union turned him down.

"Suddenly in the last week of the campaign, the Teamsters poured money and support [to Bender]," James Luken, president of Cincinnati's Joint Council 26, remembered. "We were all told to support Bender. And Bender, ideologically, was anathema." The reasons for this startling switch became clearer on November 13, 1954, three days after the Bender hearings recessed, when Bill Presser drove down to Columbus and convened a meeting of the Ohio Conference of Teamsters. Teamsters officials from across the state attended. They knew Presser had been hammered by Congress all fall and were wondering how he was getting along. Presser stood before them and, speaking forcefully, reassured them.

"Certain Teamsters in the state of Ohio were used [this fall] for political purposes—I was one of them. It was pretty rough and a rotten time. I am happy to say that the hearings—as far as the people involved in the hearings in Washington and Cleveland—are over."

That was a burden lifted.

"Of the people that were involved," Presser went on, "not a single one was indicted for anything—no one was cited for any contempts, no perjuries." Another relief for the Teamsters leaders. But some of them had to wonder how Presser knew that the Bender hearings were over. How was he certain that no one was going to be cited for perjury or contempt? It hadn't been announced.* Then came the surprise.

"We found that during the latter portion of the hearings," Bill said, "that we had a second friend on the congressional committee, a friend that did a fair job for the people concerned, and his name is George Bender." Though Bender had promised otherwise, he never

---

*Before Big Bill answered that question, he shared a lesson he had learned from the hearings. Don't save records, he said, it just gives investigators the rope to hang you. "I am going to stick my neck out by saying this," he said. "There is no federal law on the statute books that states that a labor organization has to keep books and records beyond its audit period. Under the law, it is a misdemeanor if you don't have those books." For what it's worth, boys, only a misdemeanor. Wink, wink.

reconvened the hearings. Suddenly, the rackets investigation was over.

Several weeks later, Presser sent a letter to the Cincinnati-area Joint Council 26 asking for $40,000 to pay the legal bill he and Triscaro had run up during the Bender hearings. It was a huge amount, considering that the two men had appeared before the Bender committee only twice and had mostly pleaded the Fifth. James Luken, Presser's nemesis at the Cincinnati Teamsters, protested, "We already paid their legal fees." George Starling, the Joint Council 26 leader, explained that "other money was spent to pull strings to see that the charges were dropped."

Luken, future Joint Council 26 president and mayor of Cincinnati, described that meeting years later:

> George Starling, who is now deceased, wasn't too bright. One meeting he came in, and he said that he was there seeking money for the Bender affair. The order had come in, we had to make some contributions. . . . I said, "Well, why?" I think this was after the election. "Why does he need money now?"
>
> I was told, in effect, we had bought the politician. I'm not naive enough, and wasn't then, to not know that occasionally politicians are bought. And I think politicians, on the whole, are more honest than businessmen. . . .
>
> But I was rather amazed that somebody should say we should make contributions to replenish the treasury because someone had been bought. It was the kind of thing people don't normally say at an open meeting.

Years later, Bill Presser freely admitted to close friends that he and the union had spent a small fortune buying off Bender. Among other things, Bender "went to Cuba and came back a wealthy man," Bill told a high-ranking Teamsters official. Back then, some of Presser's friends in the Cleveland syndicate had an interest in one of Havana's gambling casinos, before Fidel Castro kicked them out. However, Bender's aide, Stillman, says he doesn't recall that his boss ever traveled to Cuba.

Jimmy Hoffa was fond of saying "Everyone has his price." Bender proved it.

6
Jackie's First Shot

"I was too smart and too flippy, and I didn't know how to act like a man."

JACKIE PRESSER

"Where are you going, Jackie?"

"Out."

"When will you be back?"

"When you see the car come up the driveway."

Elaine Goeble had been married to Jackie Presser only a few months, and things were already on the rocks. A friend had introduced them in fall 1947. Afterwards, he asked her for a date. She said yes. Before long, Jackie had nicknamed her Gypsy because of her striking dark looks—black hair, olive skin, thick-lashed black eyes, and ever-present gold earrings, her trademark. He bought her meals at nice restaurants, sent her flowers—"wined and dined me," she says—and eventually proposed. She accepted, not knowing that he had a wife and infant daughter living in Huntington, West Virginia.

Throughout his life, Jackie Presser would make a habit of leading two different lives at once. In his private life, he would be married while pretending to be single; in his professional life, he would put on an upstanding, businesslike front while actually engaging in labor racketeering. His passion for secrecy and his skill at lying helped him sequester these wildly conflicting personas.

His Uncle Allen could never understand why Jackie acted this way—at least as far as women were concerned. Keeping two unsuspecting women at once was risky and brought unnecessary headaches. "Jackie was a different kind of guy than I was," Allen Friedman says. "I cheated on my wives, but I never led two lives. I'd grab a broad and fuck her and forget about her. I wouldn't be going with another woman or living with another woman when I was married."

In July 1949, less than a month after he divorced his first wife, Jackie and Elaine were married by a rabbi at the Ansel Road Temple. They moved to a four-suite apartment building the family owned in Cleveland Heights, where they shared a two-bedroom place with Allen and his wife. Several months later, Allen, Harry, and Jackie's pal Harold Friedman went to prison for running their interstate car-theft ring. Elaine was stunned, disbelieving. Her husband's closest friends were all locked up. "Were you involved?" she asked him.

"Mind your own business," Jackie told her.

At the start of their marriage, Jackie held, among other union positions, the job of business agent for Local 274 of the Hotel and Restaurant Employees Union. Jackie bragged about how he landed the job. "Ed Miller, the president, was down to nothing in membership, and he wanted somebody with charisma and balls to organize." Actually, Bill Presser knew Miller, the influential secretary-treasurer of Hotel and Restaurant Employees International, and got Miller to give Jackie a job. "It was the Presser name," John Vinegard, an organizer for Local 274, explains. "Why else would he [Jackie] get the job?"

It wasn't unusual. In the labor movement in cities such as Cleveland, Chicago, Detroit, and New York, sons frequently followed fathers into the union business. Problems started when men like the Pressers considered the union a family business rather than a trust in which they served the members whose hard-earned dues paid their salaries.

In 1947, Ed Miller decided to consolidate several Cleveland-area culinary locals and kick off an organizing drive targeting the thousands of unskilled workers in the area's hotels, banquet halls, and restaurants. He easily shuffled the locals, since the Hotel Employees Union's executive board, like the Teamsters' board, enjoyed sweeping powers; for just about any reason, it could take over a local by merging it or by naming trustees to run it. Under a trusteeship, the international union's executive board could appoint local officers, which is just what it did in

78

Cleveland. The executive board dissolved Vinegard's Local 323, an all-black local of cooks, bartenders, and waitresses, and shifted many of the workers into new Local 274.

For giving up his local, Vinegard, an experienced union and civil-rights activist, was appointed to the important job of organizer for the Joint Culinary Board, which included the newly chartered Local 274 and four other locals. His territory included Cleveland and the surrounding suburbs.

"Jackie came in with the charter," Vinegard explains. "I had the whole county. Part of the deal was I had to have a white boy with me. That was Jackie. Shaker Heights, Beachwood, all those suburbs, I couldn't even go to some of those places. I couldn't even get in to talk to people. We were still fighting Jim Crowism."

When he got out of prison in 1951, Allen Friedman joined Local 274 as an organizer. The local had started with several hundred downtown hotel workers—Vinegard's responsibility—and by the mid-fifties, membership was soaring. Miller named Jackie president of the local, which was still under trusteeship. Later, Jackie ran for election as the incumbent and won.

Much of Local 274's success can be attributed to its organizers and to help from Bill Presser's Teamsters, which provided the crack troops that enforced picket lines and halted delivery trucks. Jackie could take credit for some its success. As a leader, Jackie could be charming and persuasive one-on-one, but he wasn't known for rallying the troops. "Jackie wasn't what I consider an organizer," Vinegard says. "If someone wanted to come along and work something out, he'd handle it. . . . Now I think Allen Friedman was one of the best organizers I ever met. He was a good talker and he had personality."

Soon, Jackie took over as president of the Joint Culinary Board, which comprised the Waiters Local 106, Waitresses Local 107, Bartenders Local 108, and Cooks Local 167, all members of the Hotel and Restaurant Employees Union. In August 1956, Jackie Presser, only thirty years old, his raw ambition plain to see, pushed forward. He was elected president of the state council of the Hotel and Restaurant Employees Union, which oversaw more than thirty thousand workers in Ohio. He started getting noticed by community leaders. "I wanted everyone to know about us," Jackie said. "I thought I was Mr. Big Shot."

Wanting to prove his abilities as a labor man to his dad, Jackie now talked about taking over the entire Hotel Employees Union and becoming the successor to Ed Miller, Allen Friedman recalls. "He was worrying about getting to the top. He tried to get to the top of the Hotel and Restaurant Workers Union in the fifties, pushing around real union people. He always wanted to be top dog." Says Vinegard, "Jackie always had ambitions to be like his dad or bigger. He always wanted to go up."

It seemed as if Jackie slammed a door the day after their honeymoon and shut Elaine out of his increasingly mysterious life. It would become a familiar pattern. He would relentlessly pursue a woman, convince her to fall in love with him, and, the minute they were married, punish her by pushing her aside. A close relative theorizes that Jackie treated his wives this way because he felt abandoned by his mother as a boy. With a wife as substitute mother, Jackie captured her love, only to spurn it as a way to get back at Faye.

Whatever his reasons, there was little chance for Jackie's wives to change his behavior since he wouldn't open up, reveal his feelings, or talk about why he was doing what he was doing. Everything had to be a secret. Elaine says she didn't even know where he worked or exactly what he did. It had something to do with unions, she knew that, but was it with the Teamsters or did he work in the jukebox field for his father? Or both? She wasn't sure.

She says Jackie always carried a gun and slept with it under the bed or under his pillow. This terrified her. "You just did not ask about things," she says. "I learned that. You didn't get close. I did not know what his father was in. I knew he was president of a union. I really did not know."

Jackie left her for days on end, sometimes without money. Faye would call and order Elaine around, telling her to come over and baby-sit for Ronnie and Toby. With the children cared for, Faye could run off and gamble at the nearby Pettibone Club, the fabulous illegal casino run by the Cleveland syndicate. "She was a big gambler," says Elaine, now remarried and living in the Midwest. "She'd gamble her jewels one week, and then Bill would go and get them back. She was always having her jewelry pawned." At the Pettibone, "she took hun-

dred-dollar bills and just threw them down! That was the first time I
saw a hundred-dollar bill."

Every Friday night, Jackie and Elaine were supposed to eat dinner
with Faye and Bill and the clan. These were standing orders from Faye.
Jackie, Marvin, Bill Presser, and Harry and Allen Friedman were all big
men, ranging from two hundred to three hundred pounds, and they
wedged in around the long dining-room table as Faye, a good cook,
carried in steaming dishes from the kitchen. "Her word was ultimate,"
Elaine says. "You did what she wanted to do, go where she wanted to
go, ate when she wanted to eat. . . . When she told Jackie to jump,
he asked how high."

Elaine dreaded the big family dinners. It was hard to relax and
enjoy the food. "There was a lot of friction between Jackie and his
father when they sat down to eat," she says. "He wanted to show his
father he could be better than him."

Jackie's second wife liked Bill Presser. He treated her courteously,
in sharp contrast to the demands and deprecation she put up with from
boisterous Faye Presser. Elaine also felt sorry for Bill. She says she never
saw affection displayed between him and Faye.

Elaine says Jackie's father knew from the beginning that her
marriage to his son wouldn't last. At one point, she recalls, Bill Presser
took her aside and advised, "Get the hell out of here, Gypsy. This is
no place for you. You're a fool to stay with my son."

She knew he was right; she should leave Jackie. She couldn't
survive emotionally much longer.

"He wasn't a demonstrative person," she recalls. "You didn't hang
on him." She says he was extremely possessive, possibly out of jealousy,
but most likely because of his need for secrecy. She wasn't allowed to
talk with anyone other than family or Jackie's inner circle: Harold
Friedman and a few cohorts from Glenville or the union.

She says she learned that Jackie was having an affair and decided,
after fourteen months of marriage, to walk out. "I felt after a while I
couldn't confide in him or trust him," she says. "I couldn't take it. I
never grew up in an atmosphere of lying and cheating and stealing and
whoring around." The day she was granted the divorce, Jackie didn't
even show up in court. It was uncontested; she only asked for one thing,
to have her name back. When she moved out of town, she left many
of her belongings—clothes, furnishings, mementos—stored temporar-

ily with her parents. A few days later, Elaine Goeble's mother unpacked her daughter's photo albums and tore out every picture of Jackie she could find.

Jackie Presser was fortunate to start his union climb with the Hotel and Restaurant Employees Union. Several of its locals and international officers were controlled by the Mob, which made the union the perfect launching pad for an ambitious, cocky, impatient local union officer who was willing to break the law and union rules to achieve power.

The Hotel and Restaurant Employees Union represented about four hundred thousand workers nationwide, most of them bartenders, cooks, and catering workers. The union was closely allied to the Teamsters, calling on it for funds and organizing help; it was also one of the four international unions that the U.S. Department of Labor later identified as being under the thumb of organized crime. The other three were the Laborers, the Longshoremen, and the Teamsters unions.

So strong was the Mob's control of the Hotel and Restaurant Employees Union, a congressional investigating committee found, that the Chicago Mafia family, wielding decades of accumulated influence with executive board members, called in its markers and got its candidate installed as union president in 1973. The man, Edward Hanley, became one of Jackie's good friends in the labor movement.

The Mob began infiltrating some of the Chicago and New York City locals of the Hotel and Restaurant Employees Union during Prohibition. By the thirties, the underworld controlled several locals, including Local 16 in New York. At the union's national convention in 1936, Harry Koenig, head of Local 16, was murdered. His killing sparked an investigation by future New York governor Thomas Dewey, who uncovered a collusive association racket similar to the one played out in Cleveland under the direction of Bill Presser and the jukebox industry.

The New York racket worked like this: a hotel union official would demand, for instance, a one-hundred-percent raise from an employer, who of course would refuse. Pickets would promptly be set up outside the restaurant at lunch hour, or perhaps stink bombs would be thrown inside. Afterwards, the New York Restaurant Association's "collector" would call on the restaurant owner and promise to settle the "strike" for a lower wage; the owner in return had to pay fees to the association based on the number of people he employed. Usually, the owner went along. As a result, the Mob pocketed extortion money, the owner enjoyed labor peace, and the workers sweated for low wages.

It worked just as profitably in Chicago. From 1951 to 1957, the Chicago Restaurant Association collected $1.1 million from various eateries. One-third was funneled to two mobbed-up lawyers, one of whom was Abraham Teitelbaum, former mouthpiece for the late Al Capone.

Oscar Zimmerman wouldn't budge.

For months, Jackie's Hotel and Restaurant Employees Union had been trying to push Zimmerman into signing a union contract for the eighty-eight waitresses, cooks, and busboys who worked at his four Dorsel's restaurants. The battle quickly escalated from picket lines to bombs and death threats. These same aggressive, often illegal, tactics had enabled Jackie and Local 274 to build its membership to more than seven thousand by 1957.

The organizing drive at Dorsel's started out peacefully. In mid-May, Jackie contacted Zimmerman, whom he knew from the old neighborhood. They tentatively agreed that the union would represent Dorsel's employees, even though Jackie hadn't obtained sign-up cards or evidence of employee dissatisfaction, Zimmerman recalls. "We had a deal set up," he says. "It wasn't a sweetheart deal. They were just going to give us a little more time." The next day, the union called the deal off and demanded better terms. Zimmerman refused. "You're going to get bombed," Allen Friedman warned him.

At the time, Jackie's local was making a grand push for membership. The union's national headquarters had given $100,000 to Local 274 to organize new restaurants. This was to be Jackie's big chance to prove himself to be a labor leader in the mold of Hoffa or Reuther. Jackie's plan, according to people who observed him at the time, was to conquer Dorsel's, a small restaurant chain, then tackle larger chains such as Clark's, Stouffer's, and Royal Castle. Then he could boast about being a tough, successful organizer and climb up the union ladder. But he ended up moving too fast and making some mistakes.

Zimmerman, only thirty-three, was strong-willed and athletic, and he hated to part with money he earned. He and his brother had owned the restaurants only six weeks before the union trouble started. They had paid $200,000 to buy Dorsel's, which were twenty-four-hour lunch counters that boasted "Everything Cooked in Butter." After his family started getting telephone death threats, he resolved to fight the union even harder. His motto became He conquers who endures.

On June 7, 1955, Allen, Jackie and a couple of Hotel and Restaurant Employees Union organizers were eating dinner at a big round table in the bar at Kohrman's, a popular restaurant on Short Vincent, Cleveland's garish entertainment strip. Billy Weinberger, part owner, returned from catering a party at a Cleveland Indians baseball game. "Sit down, Billy," they urged him.

"I've got to unload the truck."

"Billy, what time is it?" one of them asked.

He looked up, puzzled, and said, "There's a clock on the wall."

Moments later, Allen slipped out the door and was quickly driven to a Dorsel's at East Ninety-third and Euclid Avenue. He slipped into the restaurant, leaned over a counter, dropped a stink bomb, and ran out.

Friedman raced downtown and rejoined Jackie and the crew at the table. It had taken less than half an hour. Thinking they were clever, they had gone around asking everyone what time it was, in case Allen needed an alibi.

Later that night, Friedman revisited the Dorsel's picket lines, where two waitresses recognized him and called the police. Allen was arrested, and police found a can of deodorizer in his car. He'd need that alibi after all. Since Friedman had a felony conviction for auto theft, Bill Presser wanted to make sure his brother-in-law didn't get convicted again. He faced one year in jail. Big Bill enlisted the help of a savvy, politically connected lawyer, Howard Metzenbaum, the future U.S. Senator.

One week later, Zimmerman's lawyers obtained a restraining order that enjoined the union from trespassing on his property or interfering with his customers. The union would have to picket from the sidewalk. This move escalated the warfare. On June 22, in a synchronized attack at eleven o'clock that night, the remaining three Dorsel's were stink-bombed.

Though Cleveland was a strong union town, these attacks began to turn some people against Jackie's local. "We are not responsible for the stench-bombings," Jackie responded. "We know they have hurt us with the public. It's ridiculous to think we would resort to these tactics when we know they result in a public reaction against us."

Zimmerman shot back, "What do they think? That I stench-bombed my own restaurants?"

The boldness of the bombings—the seemingly complete unconcern about being apprehended—also made the police department look bad. Cleveland police chief Frank W. Story finally reacted. "If there is another bombing, every picket and every union official will be picked up for interrogation, no matter where we find you or what time of day," he threatened. "Whom do you think you're fooling with your alibis? I've been in this business too long. You are forcing us to take drastic action. You are not friends of the community or the police department."

Previously, the police's labor-relations department, under Detective James Patrick Foley, had glossed over union transgressions, tilting the playing field in favor of labor. But the Dorsel's bombings whipped up intense publicity, forcing the police department to take action or look foolish.

After the union orchestrated the triple bombings, Zimmerman went to court and got a restraining order further limiting the picketers. So Jackie and Local 274 got creative. On July 7, 1955, they staged a sip-in at the restaurants. They went inside the Dorsel's before lunch, took up all the stools along its counters, and nursed cups of coffee and glasses of iced tea for several hours. This forced customers to eat lunch elsewhere.

Zimmerman brought out a camera and started taking pictures of the sippers. Michael P. Rini, vice president of Teamsters Local 400 and a codefendant with Bill Presser in his price-fixing case, didn't like this development. He rose from his stool and demanded the camera. He and Zimmerman tussled, and the restaurant owner swore out trespassing charges against him. Rini stood trial and was found guilty.

Since Zimmerman wouldn't bend, Jackie's organizers began to intimidate his customers. The picketers started photographing the faces and license plates of customers who crossed the lines. Dorsel's business continued to drop off.

Allen Friedman's trial for bombing Dorsel's demonstrated just how powerful Bill Presser had become. The prosecutor presented two waitresses who identified Allen as the bomber. Metzenbaum put on three alibi witnesses who swore that Friedman was having supper at Kohrman's at the time of the attack. Metzenbaum then called Billy Weinberger, a well-known figure in Cleveland who had left in 1964 to become an executive at Caesar's Palace in Las Vegas and later Atlantic City. Weinberger testified that he saw Allen in the restaurant around the time witnesses said the stink-bombing took place. This was the excuse the judge needed.*

The judge, hearing the case without a jury, found Friedman not guilty. Allen wasn't surprised. "It had been all set up with the judge beforehand," he admits. Later, Allen informed Metzenbaum he wasn't going to pay his legal fee.

"Yes, you are, musclehead," Metzenbaum replied.

"I'm not paying you," he repeated, laughing.

"Well, then I'm going to see your brother-in-law."

Metzenbaum knew who was the real power behind the Hotel and Restaurant Employees Union.

On October 27, 1955, the Ohio Supreme Court handed down a setback to legitimate unions as well as to labor racketeers. The court ruled six to one that it was unlawful for a union to picket when no dispute existed between an employer and his employees. In other words, Jackie would have to get sign-up cards and complaints from workers about wages or working conditions before he could shut down a restaurant with pickets.

On Armistice Day, six months after it had tried to organize the four Dorsel's, Local 274 pulled off its pickets. Jackie's local gave up after trying every trick in the business, including having a bomber—presumably on orders from Jackie or another honcho—throw three

*Later, Weinburger admitted that he was furious that Jackie and Allen had drawn him into the case. "They set me up," he says. For about two years, he wouldn't speak to the Pressers, even though he had known Bill since high school.

dynamite sticks, wired to explode, at Zimmerman's house. The bomb failed to detonate but did succeed in making the headlines: "Dorsel Bomb Plot Laid to Union." "I think it was meant to go off," Zimmerman says. "It was retribution, to tell the other restaurant guys, Hey, we lost but we don't forget!"

The publicity Jackie and Local 274 generated with their attacks became an effective organizing tool. Many times, all Allen Friedman or another business agent had to do was enter a new restaurant, ask the owner if he knew what had happened to Dorsel's, and then threaten the same if he didn't let his workers join the union. Many restaurants wouldn't even bother to have a vote or see if their workers had filled out sign-up cards. They quickly gave Jackie what he wanted.

In January 1957, in the teeth of a cruel Cleveland winter, Jackie packed up and took his family to the warmth and tropical ease of Miami. He had remarried in 1952, and he and Patricia, his third wife, lived in suburban University Heights with their four-year-old daughter, Bari. He timed the trip so that he could appear before the Hotel Workers Union's annual executive board meeting at a Miami hotel. A day or so after he hit town, Jackie appeared before the union hierarchy and pleaded with them, for nearly thirty minutes, for a thousand-dollar-a-month subsidy for his impoverished local.

Long after the brief meeting, long after the union executives had scattered back home, Jackie, Pat, and little Bari stayed on at the hotel, running up a $2,300 hotel and restaurant bill in three weeks. Back in Cleveland, tanned and refreshed, Jackie submitted a $2,300 expense report to his union for reimbursement. He said he spent the money while attending the annual executive board meeting. After all, he dominated the state board of the union. Who was going to say anything?

Jackie continued to splurge. Local 274 only had a net worth of six thousand dollars, but he decided to spend $17,000 on five new cars for himself, Uncle Allen, and three other organizers. They got Pontiacs, he a Chrysler Imperial. He moved a death-benefit fund into the general fund and began spending that. None of the members protested; probably none of them knew what he was doing. By late fall 1957, Jackie's Joint Culinary Board was $4,500 in the red; Local 274's books were incomplete, a shambles. "Jackie had a free hand with everything, because Miller wasn't going to fool with the Teamsters and Bill Presser," says Vinegard, the organizer.

Local 274 should have operated profitably. It took in over $100,000 a year in dues and had $11,000 in the bank when Jackie started as president. By 1957 it was penniless. Where did it go? "Jackie was stealing from the members," says Allen Friedman, who was there every step of the way.

Earlier that year, Miller had decided to make a move on Jackie Presser. This wasn't something he relished, because it was expected that Bill Presser would resist. But given Jackie's financial shenanigans with Local 274, Miller had little choice.

It is also likely that he had heard that Jackie, head of the powerful state council of the Hotel and Restaurant Employees Union, was going to make a play for his job. Miller had been president for only two years, and a power play by Jackie was a serious threat. Bill Presser, through the Teamsters, had tight ties with such mob figures as John "Johnny Dio" Dioguardi in New York, Joey Glimco in Chicago, and Jimmy Hoffa in Detroit—all of whom exerted some control over the Hotel employees locals in their cities. With his father's backing, Jackie had the clout to cause trouble for Miller at the next union election.

Another reason Miller moved on Jackie may have been that he was worried that Bill Presser and the Teamsters would raid the locals under Jackie's control and steal members. Even Jackie admitted, "The International is afraid that because my father is head of the Teamsters here I'll try to take the locals out of the AFL-CIO."

In the fall of 1957, Miller dispatched two trusted aides to clean up the mess with Presser's Joint Culinary Board. Gustava Holohan, a trustee of the International, was to take over Waitresses Local 107 and Marcel Kenney, who arrived later, was to tackle Local 274. As a way to keep unruly locals in line, the International had the authority to remove and replace trustees, approve times to hold elections, and so on.

Jackie was out of town when Holohan arrived in Cleveland, and his burly crew wouldn't let her into the Local 107 office, which was actually his office. When Jackie returned, he called Holohan into his office and unleashed a tirade. "The International tag don't mean a thing in Cleveland!" he said. "I'll guarantee you won't organize any waitresses in Cleveland."

Ed Miller was clever to send a woman as a trustee, Jackie went on, but that wouldn't persuade him to cooperate out of chivalry. "We do things different in Cleveland," he warned her. "We had a woman here before. She was tossed out by one of the men and slapped by one of the waitresses."

Then Jackie threatened her. "Gussie, I want you to know this. You are not going to go into any of the places representing the Waitresses Union because, if you do, we are going to tangle. You will be found lying out in the street. I would hate to see that." She took the threats seriously.

On Christmas Day, 1957, Ed Miller fired Jackie along with Allen Friedman, John Vinegard, Al Tolin, Milton Zepkin, and Chester A. Hughes, all officers of Local 274 or the Joint Culinary Board. But Jackie wouldn't vacate his offices, so the International went to court to force him out. Finally, on March 7, 1958, common pleas judge Samuel Silbert tossed Presser from the union and ordered him to repay several thousand dollars and turn over union records.

Bill Presser, concerned, called his brother-in-law Allen for his assessment of the situation. Allen told him that Jackie had been stealing from the hotel employees union. If it got the books, Jackie would go to jail for embezzling. Allen recommended burning the office to destroy the records. Go ahead, Bill told him.

On a Saturday night, Friedman poured gasoline and chemicals on the third floor of the building at 1458 East Seventeenth Street and left a lighted candle as a fuse. Before fire fighters could extinguish the blaze, the three-story building had been gutted.

Later in court, Jackie told the judge that his local's records had just been destroyed in a freak blaze in his office. The union's lawyer, Thurlow Smoot, shot back, saying that Presser "is using the name plates and machinery which belong to our union, although he tells us they no longer exist," Smoot continued, "We have evidence he was seen carrying away the records he says were burned in the fire." The judge was a friend of Bill Presser, but he also was angered by Jackie's actions. His attitude on the witness stand—"he was a very arrogant, conceited young man," Smoot recalls—made matters worse. "You have hurt unionism more in this court than any fifty propagandists or a hundred propagandists could have done," Judge Silbert lectured Jackie. "And I am going to go through with this and let the chips fall where they may. . . . Evidently Presser feels that he is a law unto himself and he can do whatever he pleases just to suit his fancy."

Later, Bill Presser met with his son and told him he should stay out of the labor movement, at least for a while. "You're causing too much trouble in this town," he said. "I'll set you up in business."

Bill Presser was disappointed. He had handed Jackie a gift-wrapped opportunity to become a labor leader and he had failed. Jackie got kicked out of his own union, and his father, despite his power, could do nothing to prevent it. But Jackie had one thing to be thankful for: he didn't end up in jail on racketeering charges. Years later, he acknowledged his good fortune. "There isn't many things that I haven't done in this labor movement," he admitted. "And I know there were times when [our lawyers] had to get me out of jail and try to keep me out of getting indicted. I was just a loud-mouth, wild kid. . . . I was too smart and too flippy, and I didn't know how to act like a man. I was still a boy trying to absorb a man's responsibility."

7

Roy Williams, the Mob, and Kennedy

"I never knew there were these kinds of people in the world."
ROY WILLIAMS

Unlike Jackie Presser, Roy Lee Williams didn't have a father who was a union boss to present him with his very own local union. Williams, a stocky, crude-mannered man who spoke with a Missouri twang, cut his teeth in the labor movement on his own. Then, in the fifties, he climbed the Teamster ranks with help from a powerful patron of a different sort—Kansas City Mafia boss Nick Civella.

One of thirteen children, Williams grew up on a truck farm in tiny Leeton, Missouri. He finished sixth grade and never went back. Instead, he worked the rocky soil of his father's farm, often on his knees, pulling weeds from onion patches and picking worms off potatoes. He knew there had to be a better way to earn a living and learned to drive a truck. At nineteen, he signed up to haul freight from Sterling, Illinois, to Denver, eleven hundred miles to the west.

In the late thirties, Williams met Jimmy Hoffa. Over the next decade, the two of them labored long hours over the Central States Drivers Council, bargaining trucking contracts for the region. When Hoffa, the ex–dock worker, decided it was time to learn to drive a truck, Roy Williams taught him, the two of them wheeling a diesel rig at night around the parking lot at Soldier Field in Chicago.

In 1952, Williams, then thirty-seven years old, met one of Kansas City's secret powers, Nick Civella, who ran a North Side political club. The strongly Democratic politics of Kansas City were dominated in the fifties by a half dozen or more neighborhood clubs that promoted candidates and secured patronage jobs. Williams, president of the fifty-five-hundred-member Teamsters Local 41, ran the Teamsters political club. When the groups clashed among themselves over a candidate or a patronage hire, an executive committee of Civella, Williams, and two others would settle the dispute. "I met with him every time we had a political problem," Williams recalled.

It wasn't until November 1957, when he noticed Civella's name and photograph splashed across the pages of the Kansas City newspapers, that he knew his friend was a racketeer, Williams says. Civella had been arrested along with fifty-eight of the country's most powerful Mafia figures in Apalachin, a tiny village of three hundred in New York. Its residents had noticed a long stream of shiny new Cadillacs invading their village and had notified the police. State police and federal agents had raided the home of Joseph Barbara, a liquor distributor who had beaten four murder raps. As authorities moved in, they were treated to the sight of Civella and the other Mafia chieftains panicking, then running pell-mell out a back door and scattering into the woods. Most of them were quickly rounded up.

The interruption of this high-level strategy session was an embarrassing, undignified fiasco for the underworld rulers, but it was the nation's first convincing proof that the Mafia was a national network of criminals who cooperated among themselves. At least twenty-two of the Mafia powers arrested that day were convicted labor racketeers.

At his next meeting in Kansas City with Civella, Williams brought up the news stories about Apalachin. "Those people are my friends," Civella told him. The boss explained that the conclave met to set territories and encourage cooperation among the families. "Kansas City is my territory," Civella told him. "We have working relationships with other areas." Later, Civella made an offer to Williams. "If you go into any areas where you might have problems, let me know and I'll get a hold of my friends." He specifically named Cleveland, Chicago, and New Orleans.

By this time, Hoffa was sending Williams around the country to solve stubborn strikes and other volatile labor situations. Williams negotiated skillfully, hiding his shrewdness and thorough knowledge of trucking behind an aw-shucks country-bumpkin facade. He also used muscle to force contracts on unwilling union members. Not long after

92

the Apalachin arrests, Hoffa sent Williams to San Francisco to break up a stubborn strike led by a hard-nosed local union president who didn't want interference from the International. Before he left, Williams said that he told Civella that he might need some help on the West Coast. At the San Francisco meeting, Williams noticed several menacing young men who wouldn't take off their trench coats or sit down, despite plenty of empty seats. He figured they were Civella's friends. The rank and file evidently got the message; Williams asked for a vote to end the strike and promptly got it.

The same scene unfolded a little while later in New Orleans, where Williams and Hoffa were meeting with oil workers who wanted to join the Teamsters. Before leaving, Williams dropped word to Civella, and musclemen again showed up and stood around the room, arms folded grimly, saying nothing. "There were no problems at that meeting," Williams recalled, "except one man that kept coming to the front and arguing. And he got hit in the head with a mallet. Jimmy Hoffa said, 'Sergeant of arms, please remove this object on the floor so we can continue the meeting.' The sergeant of arms come and got him, took him outside. About twenty minutes later, he was back in, and I have to say he acted like a gentleman when he came back in."

In 1957, Williams's Local 41 first began paying modest benefits to its members from their new health and welfare fund. Williams had negotiated this fringe benefit into Kansas City area Teamsters contracts in 1955 (six years after Hoffa introduced hospitalization and death benefits throughout the Michigan locals). The Mafia was drawn to these trust-fund honeypots, which needed insurance companies to underwrite them and agents to manage them and process claims.

Civella, an astute pension-fund pirate, asked Williams to make loans from the burgeoning new fund to some Mob business associates. Williams naively ignored Civella's request. He might cut deals in politics, but, at the time, he drew the line at the workers' funds. This angered the Kansas City boss.

One evening shortly thereafter, Williams was walking from the union hall to his car when two thugs slipped up from behind him, one on each side. They approached his car. "Get in," one ordered, "then park your car over in the other lot." The thugs got in with him. After he ferried the group where he was told, Williams was ordered, "Take your keys. We'll bring you back."

The two men shoved Williams into their car and sped off. Half a block later, one of the kidnappers blindfolded him. He rode in terror for what seemed like twenty minutes. Then the car stopped, and he was led inside a building and across a hard floor. His footsteps echoed off the walls as if he were inside a cavern.

The kidnappers eased Williams into a chair and pulled off the blindfold. A bright spotlight stung his eyes, blinding him for a minute. A few feet away, he saw only blackness.

"We brought you here for a reason," one of the thugs told him, his words booming eerily in the dark. "You're going to have to cooperate better with Mr. Civella."

Williams sat helpless, unable to see his captors. From the dark, a voice slowly recited the names of his daughters, who were twelve and six years old. "If you don't cooperate," the voice threatened, "we're going to kill your children. And your wife. And you. You'll be the last to go. Do you understand?"

"Yes," Williams replied, shaking. The kidnappers replaced the blindfold and took him back to his car.

"I never knew there were these kinds of people in the world," Williams would say years later. "So I didn't say nothing to my family because I didn't want to excite them. I went looking for help."

First, he detailed the threats to one of his confidants in the union, Thomas Flynn, director of the Eastern Conference. "I think you should go talk to Jimmy," Flynn advised.

It was commonly known among the Teamsters brass that Hoffa had the best connections with and the clearest insight into the underworld. Williams met with Hoffa, told him he had turned down Civella's loan requests, and recounted the threats to his family. "What do I do?" he asked.

"Roy, it's a bad situation," Hoffa replied. "You can run, but you can't hide. My advice to you is to cooperate or get your family killed. Roy, these are bad people. And they were here a long time before you and me came. And they'll be here a long time after we're gone. They've infiltrated into every big local union, every conference and pension fund—even the AFL-CIO! I'm tied tight as I can be."

It wasn't the answer Williams had hoped to hear. He wanted someone to help him. He turned for advice to Frank Fitzsimmons,

Hoffa's assistant and vice president of Local 299 in Detroit. "I know the same people Jimmy knows, and I can't help you," Fitz said.

Williams gave in. He met with Civella and said, "I'll try to cooperate with you." So began a lifelong routine in which Roy Williams met with the Kansas City godfather every three or four weeks, taking Civella's requests for jobs or loans. Later on, Civella used Teamsters official Sam Ancona as a messenger. Eventually, Civella would repay Williams with kickbacks and promote him to other crime families as an up-and-coming union leader. Williams, the family-farm boy, was shorn of any remaining innocence.

Nearly twenty-five years later, Williams would become president of the Teamsters. For two years, he would serve not only 1.8 million members but also his threatening Mafia mentor back in Kansas City. "I made no bones about it," Williams admitted not long before he died in 1989. "I was controlled by Nick, and I think everybody knew it. . . . And when he threatened me, why, that's when I became his boy." Before that time, "I took him as a friend. I didn't know what business he was in or anything else until the papers come out with the Apalachin thing."

Roy Williams wasn't the only one who claimed that he didn't know about the Mob. For decades, FBI director J. Edgar Hoover denied the existence of organized crime. Instead of nailing labor racketeers, he poured the bureau's resources into routing the dwindling, toothless Communist party. In the late fifties, in the FBI's New York office alone, some four hundred agents were assigned to infiltrate and keep tabs on Communists. Only four agents were assigned to battle organized crime in the Mafia's concentrated New York stronghold. In hounding left-wing idealists from the labor movement, Hoover destroyed a force that could have helped resist the infiltration of organized crime into the Teamsters, the Hotel Employees and the Longshoremen unions.

In 1957, while Nick Civella introduced Roy Williams to his friends, millions of television viewers watched a parade of mobsters, murderers, shakedown artists, and blackmailers testify before the Senate Select Committee on Improper Activities in the Labor or Management Field—commonly called the Senate rackets committee or the McClellan committee, after its chairman, Senator John L. McClellan, Democrat from Arkansas. The most spectacular and groundbreaking criminal investigation in U.S. history, the Senate rackets hearings revealed for the first time the sinister, pervasive grip exerted by organized crime on businesses and labor unions.

At the Senate hearing room's long witness table, behind a rat's nest of television and radio cables, appeared a Who's Who of the American underworld—John Dioguardi, charged with ordering the blinding of columnist Victor Riesel with acid; Chicago Teamster boss Joey Glimco, twice arrested for murder; Paul "Red" Dorfman, the tough Capone associate whose son, Allen, was making millions selling insurance and processing claims for the Teamsters; and William Bufalino, the Detroit jukebox-rackets enforcer. Each of these edifying characters had business or union dealings with Bill Presser. Faced with tough questions from the committee's chief counsel, they mostly pleaded the Fifth.

The main event at the hearings, however, was the clash of two short, stubborn, hot-tempered men who commanded intense loyalty from their followers: chief counsel Robert F. Kennedy and Jimmy Hoffa. As the din from the hearings clattered off the hearing room's high ceilings and marbled walls, Kennedy, skinny, only thirty-one, sat at the elevated dais, fielding stares of hatred from Hoffa, who strutted cockily, his black, slicked hair gleaming under the lights. Kennedy peppered him with embarrassing, detailed questions based on the legwork of crack investigators Walter Sheridan, Pierre Salinger, Arthur Kaplan, LaVern Duffy, Carmine Bellino, and others. Hoffa, trying to make the point that he had nothing to hide, had said he wouldn't plead the Fifth before the committee. Instead, he lost his memory when it was convenient. After one frustrating session, Kennedy chided him, "You have had the worse case of amnesia in the last two days I have ever heard of."

On December 5, 1957, less than a year into the McClellan hearings, AFL-CIO chairman George Meany convinced the federation's executive board, after a rancorous argument, to expel the rackets-ridden Teamsters. The ouster stung the Teamsters leaders personally, but it ended up making the union more potent, both economically and politically. No longer did Hoffa, Presser, or any other Teamsters official have to abide by the AFL-CIO's no-raiding policy; the entire work force was fair game for Teamster organizers, and the union's ranks swelled. And no longer did the Teamsters have to pay $750,000 a year in dues to support the AFL-CIO.

In the midst of these three-year-long hearings, Hoffa made a public-relations gesture, announcing in August 1958 that he had created his own special committee to investigate and clean up the Teamsters. Its chairman was former Senator George Bender of Cleveland, whom he knew to be Presser and Triscaro's savior at the jukebox-rackets hearings a few years earlier. Kennedy said he "was flabbergasted" at the Bender choice. A figurehead, Bender did little more than collect a princely $250 a day plus expenses. After Kennedy publicized Bender's munificent pay, Hoffa cut his wages in half.

Bill Presser was subpoenaed to testify before the Senate rackets committee in August 1958. He had plenty of company. The committee also subpoenaed the records of sixteen companies and thirteen individuals who did business with the Teamsters, including Bill's childhood friend Maishe Rockman and mafioso Frank Embrescia, two partners in Buckeye Cigarette Service. Presser feared the worst. He had seen Kennedy and his investigators destroy Teamsters president Dave Beck a year earlier. Kennedy and his staff drove Beck from office after piecing together financial records that showed he had taken $370,000 from the Western Conference of Teamsters as well as "loans" from trucking companies.*

On August 28, 1958, at a joint-council meeting, the Cleveland-area Teamster honchos voted to give their president, Bill Presser, a $20,000 severance check if the McClellan committee bounced him from office as it had Dave Beck. A similar maneuver was later pulled off at a meeting of the Ohio Conference of Teamsters. The Plug would face the committee with the comfort of a $40,000 golden parachute.

It turned out to be a wise precaution. On September 9, investigator Walter Sheridan arrived at Presser's joint-council offices to review some subpoenaed records, searching for links between Bender and the Teamsters. Tucked in an envelope labeled "Christmas list," Sheridan

---

*Seeing an opportunity as this unfolded, Hoffa used his friend Edward Cheyfitz, a Washington public-relations man, to give Kennedy's staff leads on Beck, establishing what would become a Teamsters tradition under Jackie Presser: spilling dirt on union rivals to federal investigators. In due course, Beck was convicted of larceny and income-tax evasion.

found an invoice dated December 8, 1955, for eight engraved silver champagne buckets at a hundred dollars each. On the invoice were the names of the eight to whom the fancy gifts were to be delivered: Beck, English, Hoffa, Brennan, Bliss, Connell, Dorfman, and Bender. The first four were Teamsters officials; Raymond Bliss was the Ohio Republican party chairman; James C. Connell was a federal district judge; Paul Dorfman was the ex-Al Capone associate whose son controlled the Central States Pension Fund insurance business; and Bender was the friendly former senator who had abruptly canceled a congressional hearing that was a threat to Presser. Attached to the invoice was a yellow sheet with the eight names and their initials.

Sheridan took notes, put the envelope with two other files he wanted copied, and told Presser he'd like to take the records with him. "I want to photostat them first," Presser said.

Sheridan left, saying that he'd be back in a few days to pick up the records.

After Sheridan left, Presser tore the names off the invoice. He called the champagne-bucket salesman, an old friend, and asked if he could get rid of the original invoice. The salesman had left the company to take another job but tried to obtain the invoice anyway, without success. "Well, that's that," Presser told him.

Four days later, Sheridan was back. The files sat on a television in Bill's office. "Go ahead, I haven't even had a chance to copy them," the Teamsters boss said.

Sheridan looked in the envelope. He saw the ripped invoice and noticed that the yellow sheet that had been attached to the invoice was gone.

"I knew I shouldn't have trusted you," Sheridan said.

"You have your job to do, and I have mine," Presser replied.

It was a dumb move. Sheridan simply obtained the original invoice from the champagne-bucket company, and Presser, who usually operated much more shrewdly, now faced a seemingly airtight case of obstruction of justice for destroying records under subpoena.

Thanks to his staff, Kennedy was well prepared for Presser on September 17. Kennedy had even asked the FBI to review its files and give him a report on Jackie. The innocuous results mentioned Jackie's connection to the bombing of the Dorsel's restaurants and noted—typical of the bureau—"there was no subversive information."

Roy Williams, the Mob, and Kennedy

Kennedy had been briefed on the Ohio jukebox rackets, loans to Presser's brother Milton from the Joint Council 41 retirement fund, and the concealment of Bill's assets in the name of his wife and brother.

> KENNEDY: You have given jobs, have you not, as union officials to three of your brothers-in-law, all of whom have criminal records, is that right?
>
> PRESSER: I respectfully decline to answer the question and assert my privilege under the Fifth Amendment of the United States Constitution not to be a witness against myself.
>
> KENNEDY: That would include Mr. Harry Friedman, Mr. Joseph Friedman, and Mr. Allen Friedman, is that right, who have held union positions under you at various times?
>
> PRESSER: I respectfully decline to answer.
>
> KENNEDY: Is your son Jack also a Teamster official now? He was an official of another union. Is he now with the Teamsters Union?
>
> PRESSER: I respectfully decline to answer.

Minutes laters, investigator Arthur Kaplan, an accountant, explained about Presser's jukebox monopoly to the committee. "The employers form an association and then sign a master contract with the union, and thereby unionize their employees. We have never found a single instance . . . where it is operated in any other way, or where the unionization has taken place as a result of employee pressure to unionize."

> KENNEDY: Could you tell us about that, Mr. Presser, if that is how you operated?
>
> PRESSER: I respectfully decline to answer.
>
> KENNEDY: You are not interested in the employees, Mr. Presser, you are just interested in getting the money in, isn't that correct?

Presser declined to answer, and on it went. Kennedy asked him ninety-three questions, and Bill, sweating in a light-colored suit, took the Fifth eighty-seven times, neither man endearing himself to the other. Kennedy, with blunt sarcasm, brought up Presser's two $20,000 severance plans from the two last-minute meetings of the Ohio and Cleveland-area Teamsters.

KENNEDY: If he went from one meeting to another, it was a profitable trip.

MCCLELLAN: Let's see that. Where?

KENNEDY: He got $40,000 in the two meetings.

MCCLELLAN: . . . Each to pay him twenty?

KENNEDY: Each to pay him twenty.

MCCLELLAN, TO PRESSER: You were kind of getting prepared for any eventuality, weren't you?

PRESSER: Am I under oath?

MCCLELLAN: Yes.

PRESSER: Do you want me to answer that question, sir?

MCCLELLAN: Yes, I would like for you to.

PRESSER: I respectfully decline to answer the question and assert my privilege under the Fifth Amendment.

Later, according to Presser-family legend, Kennedy and Presser ran into each other in a hearing waiting room or a hallway. As Bill Presser explained it, he told Kennedy what he thought of him in trucker's language. When the short-tempered chief counsel fired back, Presser leaned in and spat in his face. Walter Sheridan said that the incident never took place, and even Bill's friends doubt the tale. "I didn't believe it," said Robert Hughes, the Republican party chairman for Cuyahoga County. "I think there was a loud argument in the hallway, and maybe they got close together and spittle was flying."

Babe Triscaro, head of Excavation Drivers Local 436 and Presser's number-two man in the Ohio Teamsters, also took the hot seat that day. Kennedy questioned him about the three gravel companies he and his wife owned—all employing nonunion truck drivers—which brought them $132,000 in 1957. Hoffa was sitting nearby, and his eyes seemed to widen at this bit of news.

> KENNEDY: In 1951, Mr. Triscaro, you were arrested in connection with the shooting of Jack Halbert and refused to answer any questions. Is that correct?
>
> TRISCARO: I respectfully decline to answer the question.
>
> KENNEDY: Was that in connection with Halbert's willingness to sell you three thousand dollars' worth of hot whiskey?
>
> TRISCARO: I respectfully decline to answer.
>
> MCCLELLAN: Is there any difference between hot whiskey and cold whiskey?
>
> TRISCARO: I respectfully decline to answer the question and assert my privilege under the Fifth Amendment of the United States.

And on and on. Sixty times Kennedy hit Babe Triscaro, the former flyweight fighter, with questions, and Triscaro ducked fifty-seven times, pleading the Fifth. Bill and Babe, the *Plain Dealer* noted, "took so many Fifths the suspicion grew that they were stocking a liquor warehouse." Years later, Triscaro's grandson claimed that it was Babe who confronted Kennedy at the hearings and spit in his face. Kennedy may not have swept racketeers from the union, but he certainly inspired their imaginations.

The next day, the committee recessed until after the November 1958 congressional elections. The Teamsters' glossy magazine took a parting shot, calling Kennedy "its chief bullyboy . . . who went off to Massachusetts to help his millionaire brother, Senator John Kennedy, get reelected."

The McClellan committee didn't seem to scare Triscaro and Presser into righteousness. In 1959, Triscaro, several Cleveland businessmen, and Cleveland Mob figure Dominick Bartone were investigated for selling planes and munitions to both sides in the Cuban revolution. The Cleveland owners of the Desert Inn in Las Vegas controlled several casinos in Havana in partnership with other Mob associates. The McClellan investigators determined that the Mafia, wanting to stay in the good graces of both sides, sold planes to both Castro and Batista forces.

The twisted deal started with a Cleveland businessman, Earl T. Benjamin, who bought eleven army-surplus C-74 Globemaster transport planes in 1957 with the idea of reselling or leasing them. He and a partner paid $400,000, and the government released four planes, which were stored in Phoenix. Benjamin had little success selling the planes or getting the money to purchase the remaining seven. Al Naiman, a Cleveland industrialist and boxing manager of a heavy-weight comer, Tony Hughes, took over. Through his friendship with Teamster leader Babe Triscaro and Mob associate Dominick Bartone Naiman got the idea to sell the planes to the new government in Cuba. This was in January 1959, just after Castro overthrew Batista. For the moment, the Mob's plush gambling casinos were still operating. Bartone, a shadowy figure who made a career out of running guns and drugs, said he had the necessary contacts in Cuba. Three times in early 1959, Naiman, with either Bartone or Triscaro, flew to Cuba to try to close a deal for the planes. They brought in one plane to Havana so the Castro government could inspect it. On April 1, the Cuban government said that it would buy at least four planes, maybe more. The sole reconditioned C-74 was stored in Miami in the meantime. Now Naiman and his partners had to get $300,000 to service and transport the other planes.

This was where Hoffa and Presser stepped in. They backed the plan, and through Hoffa's efforts, a $300,000 loan from the Central States Pension Fund was approved two months later. While they waited for the financing, Bartone had put together a side deal. He had the C-74 in Miami loaded with guns and ammunition, obtained a permit to land in Puerto Rico, but instructed his pilot that he'd be faking engine trouble and landing in the Dominican Republic. But U.S. Customs Service agents had been tipped off. They arrested Bartone and his coconspirators on May 22, 1959, and seized the plane and its cargo. Four days later, the Central States loan committee approved the loan for the plane sale to Castro. But Bartone's arrest caught the attention of the McClellan investigators, and on June 15, a lawyer for the fund told Naiman the loan had been rejected on a technicality.

Roy Williams, the Mob, and Kennedy

Bartone later pleaded guilty and was given a $7,500 fine and probation.

In 1960, after three years in session, the spectacular, 1,525-witness Senate rackets hearings came to a close. Kennedy, Senator McClellan, and their thirty-four investigators had, among other accomplishments, ripped the cover off the Teamsters Union, making "Teamster official" synonymous with corruption in the mind of the public. Jimmy Hoffa, who had been little known outside of Michigan, now commanded national attention. And Bobby Kennedy, soon named attorney general by his brother, President John F. Kennedy, used his knowledge of Teamsters corruption to form the Justice Department's "Get Hoffa" squad.

8

Eastgate

"If you know the right people, you can get anything."
JACKIE'S UNCLE, ALLEN FRIEDMAN

After his disaster with the Hotel Employees Union and his brush with jail, Jackie left the labor movement. He had squandered a tailor-made opportunity to establish himself as a union leader, a man operating on his own terms and in a union only somewhat connected with the Teamsters and his influential father. To redeem himself, he wanted to show his father that he could at least be successful in private industry. He'd also be able to support his wife and two young children, pay the mortgage on his suburban ranch home, and not have to humble himself by asking Big Bill for money.

As was customary in his gambling-addicted family and circle of friends, Jackie wanted to get rich as quickly and as easily as possible. He had the option of letting his wealthy and powerful father create business opportunities for him by putting the arm on friends in the vending or trucking fields. But both father and son knew that Jackie, if he was ever going to achieve lasting satisfaction, would have to seize the day and do something on his own. When he ran the hotel-employees locals, Jackie had been annoyed that many members considered him a wiseass, an upstart who didn't deserve their respect because he'd been installed in the top job instead of earning it.

In early 1960, Bill Presser was burdened with matters more serious than finding a job for his oldest son. For the last two years, Bill had endured the heat from Robert F. Kennedy and the McClellan committee. Now he found himself indicted for obstructing justice—tearing up the invoice that showed he gave engraved silver champagne buckets to politicians. Four months later, he took the witness stand and claimed that he didn't destroy the subpoenaed records because he had been in Washington during the days between Sheridan's two visits to Cleveland. The jury didn't buy that explanation, especially after prosecutors introduced person-to-person telephone records of Hoffa calling Presser at his office and at his home during the days in question. They found him guilty of obstructing justice and gave him a one-year sentence.

Despite such distractions, Bill located a venture for Jackie during his exile from the labor movement. Some businessmen he knew wanted to build a bowling alley, and Bill decided that the Pressers would become secret partners. A trustee of the rapidly growing Teamsters Central States Pension Fund, Bill had Jimmy Hoffa's ear. With Hoffa calling the shots, the Teamsters pension fund would eventually finance the Las Vegas casino investments of the Kansas City and Chicago Mafia families, which hid the loans behind corporate fronts. By the seventies, the Teamsters Central States Pension Fund—the nation's richest employee-benefits pool—was known as the Mafia's bank. In 1960, Bill knew that the fund could certainly come up with a $1 million loan for his family. Later that year, trustees of the Central States Pension Fund voted to lend $850,000 at six and one-quarter percent interest to build the bowling alley, which had escalated into an ambitious entertainment complex called the Eastgate Coliseum. The Pressers kept their financial interest in the Eastgate a secret, though years later, Jackie did admit that Hoffa and his father had procured the loans for him.

Eastgate Coliseum was a state-of-the-art sports complex with fifty bowling lanes, an outdoor miniature-golf course, a huge billiards room, a snack bar, an expensive restaurant, a seven-hundred-seat banquet room, and a handsome nightclub. One of the named partners in the venture was Mittie Coen, the owner of a small bowling alley. Coen, ambitious and scheming, was the only one of the group who had experience in the bowling business. He had owned the successful Mayflower Lanes, which, after bowling leagues and the public left for the night, served as a gambling joint and hangout for bookmakers. Jackie and Uncle Allen were familiar with Mittie's place; they could find a high-stakes gin rummy game there any night. "There was a lot of gambling there," Allen said. "A few bookmakers used to hang out there. Guys used to bet. There was chisel bowling. Do you know what chisel bowling is? You bet a hundred dollars or fifty dollars a game. There may have been thirty guys chisel bowling after all the leagues were finished. Stay 'til two, three in the morning, either playing gin rummy or chisel bowling. For a bowling alley, chisel bowling is a very good income. Instead of bowling three games like a league, these guys would bowl twenty games, betting. That's what Mayflower was. It had leagues, and it was a very successful bowling alley. It was more successful because Mittie had chisel bowling and gin rummy."

Coen and the Pressers hoped the Eastgate Coliseum, named by Jackie's wife after the Roman sports arena, would be wildly successful. It was constructed on Mayfield Road, a major route in suburban Mayfield Heights, a far-flung bedroom community of 13,478. The city boasted little industry except for a few savings banks; its two largest employers were a hospital and the local school board. Surrounding the Eastgate Coliseum site were acres of open land waiting for housing developers. Several hundred yards east was the future interchange of Interstate 271.

At first, the venture looked as if it could become a very sweet deal for the Pressers and their partners. Bowling had surged in popularity after World War II, especially in the industrial Midwest. The automatic pinsetter had been invented in 1952, and its precision and quickness had boosted the sport even more. By 1955, ten bowling alleys in the Cleveland area had automatic pinsetters. Eastgate Coliseum, with its fifty lanes, became one of the showcases of the Brunswick Corporation, a big manufacturer of bowling equipment.

At the same time, according to a 1952 Cuyahoga County grand-jury report, Cleveland-area gamblers and numbers racketeers were starting to funnel their profits into legitimate businesses, bowling alleys and drug stores in particular. Bowling alleys attracted investors because once the doors were opened for business, cash flowed in immediately, and the alleys generally prospered as low-maintenance investments thereafter. On a grander scale, the old Cleveland syndicate boys—Dalitz, Morris Kleinman, and others—were sinking their illegal revenues into the Nevada desert, building glittery casinos that seemed to crystalize the wise-guy dream of success: glitz, costumes, Hollywood stars, flashy women, and a flood of untraceable cash.

106

Eastgate Coliseum, two acres under one roof, displayed the ostentatious Las Vegas influence. Opened with fanfare on January 25, 1961, the Coliseum featured around-the-clock dining and entertainment. For its first three nights of operation, world billiards champion Willie Mosconi was paid to demonstrate his wizardry on the Eastgate's eighteen pool tables. Customers could toss horseshoes in three regulation pits or swim in a heated indoor Olympic-sized swimming pool. Another drawing card on opening night featured bowling legend Steve Nagy competing against his brother, Julius. There were female billiards instructors to teach women the traditionally male sport and a nursery staff to baby-sit children. "People came from miles around to see what a fabulous place it was," Allen Friedman said.

Even before the Eastgate opened, Bill Presser made money on the venture. For arranging and pushing the loan through the Central States committee, Presser demanded and got a piece of the $850,000 loan as a kickback, said Allen Friedman, who had been hired to run the complex as Mittie Coen's assistant. "They got their money up front," he said. "The Pressers wanted the place to go, but if it didn't, they didn't lose anything. They made money before the first brick was laid."

Allen Friedman didn't witness the actual payoff—that was the sort of transaction that, even among family members, would be conducted privately. But he knew kickbacks took place, he said, because at the time he was going through a divorce and had been spending a lot of time at Bill and Faye's house. "I knew it from living in the house, listening to him on the phone and him talking to me and Jackie about business," Allen explained. He also attended Faye's mandatory Sunday brunches, which included all the family. These affairs would often stretch into the afternoon. As the women cleared dishes from the table and his grandchildren romped through the house, Bill would ignite a thick cigar and discuss business with Allen and Jackie, talking freely.

Before long, the FBI began to investigate reports of these kickbacks. The probe started on February 20, 1961, when John DeMarco, the Cleveland Mafia's *consigliere,* and two henchmen strolled into the LaMarca Brothers Barbershop, a Mob hangout on Kinsman Road on Cleveland's east side. The FBI had cultivated a snitch who frequently prospected at the barbershop and dutifully returned to his FBI handlers with nuggets of intelligence. DeMarco, along with John Scalish, the don of the Cleveland family, was a partner in Buckeye Cigarette Service, the lucrative vending-machine company known for its strong-arm tactics. Despite their best efforts to live quietly, DeMarco and Scalish were known on sight by many Clevelanders because their mug shots had been displayed in newspapers throughout the world after the two men, along with sixty-five other mafiosi, had been swept up at the notorious crime-syndicate meeting in Apalachin, New York, in 1957.

In the barbershop, DeMarco and the two men turned the conversation to Bill Presser and his friend, Babe Triscaro, president of the Excavation Drivers Union and the second most powerful teamster in the area. The DeMarco crew noted with envy that Bill and Babe, using $1 million in Teamsters money, had just opened a swanky bowling alley. Bill and Babe's partnership rankled many members of Cleveland's underworld. The Italian and Jewish factions of the Mob had competed for control of the rackets since Prohibition, and a quarter of a century later, crosscurrents of hostility still ran strong just beneath the surface. Bill and Babe constantly heard angry remarks from their respective crew members along the lines of "Why are you hanging around with that cocksucker? He's gonna try to take things over."

After overhearing the bowling-alley remarks, the source informed his FBI handler. This snatch of intelligence quickly sizzled through the FBI's interoffice communications channels; it was hot stuff. The FBI and the month-old Kennedy administration wanted Jimmy Hoffa badly after he had defied the Kennedys during the Senate rackets hearings. This new Cleveland tip tied in with previous FBI intelligence that Hoffa had secretly, and maybe fraudulently, invested in bowling alleys in Cleveland and San Diego. Now, with the Teamsters-financing angle, perhaps a solid fraud case could finally be built against Hoffa and maybe Bill Presser as well.

FBI director J. Edgar Hoover and the new attorney general, Robert Kennedy, were given the information, and Hoover sent a memo on March 6, 1961, ordering the supervisor of the Cleveland FBI office to chase this lead immediately, that it was a top priority. Hoover said to put some "experienced and mature personnel" on it and wire him daily reports.

Within weeks, the Cleveland FBI had tracked down the Eastgate Coliseum's interlocking corporations: a major holding company, others for the bowling alley, restaurant, and bar, and a separate investment company. Other than the fact that Teamsters lawyer Arlene Steuer incorporated the companies, agents found nothing to connect Presser or Triscaro to the complex, let alone Hoffa. The Cleveland FBI office sent Hoover a report of its findings and other possible leads to pursue.

The report irritated Hoover. Wanting to impress Kennedy with the bureau's willingness to snare Hoffa, as well as to distract him from his campaign to force the FBI to target the Mafia instead of Communists, Hoover fired a memo back to the Cleveland office: "It does not appear that sufficient investigation has been made or is planned to determine if Hoffa, Presser, or Triscaro are part owners of the Eastgate Investment Company or to ascertain the circumstances surrounding this company's obtaining the loan from the Pension Fund. . . . Prior Bureau communications in this case have stressed the need for conducting a thorough investigation of this matter. It appears these communications have not made a very deep impression on you." Hoover ordered the Cleveland FBI chief to supervise the case personally and ended with a threat. "You will be held personally responsible for any inadequacy in the investigation."

Babe Triscaro had never been an Eastgate partner, and chasing his involvement proved to be a waste of agents' time. The FBI found nothing linking Hoffa to Eastgate, either; Bill Presser, as he had so often in the past, completely eluded the authorities. The FBI didn't uncover his insider scheme, even though it was common knowledge that Bill sat on the board of the pension fund. His family proceeded to make whatever money it could from the Eastgate Coliseum.

Jackie worked at the Eastgate fairly consistently in its first several months, but the novelty wore off, and soon he wasn't around as much to help Allen and Mittie Coen run the place. For a while that first summer, Jackie brought his eight-year-old daughter, Bari, with him to the bowling alley. She had the run of the place, and its employees looked after her. She played on the putt-putt course, fooled around with a bowling ball, and ordered whatever she wanted for lunch in the restaurant or snack bar. "I would have steak, lobster," she recalls. "I was just the little princess there."

At the bowling alley, Bari was impressed with a young, red-headed woman named Phyllis who was hired to be a secretary. Soon, Phyllis began spending the days with Bari at the pool, swimming and baby-sitting. At home one day, Bari innocently told her mother that a nice lady named Phyllis spent the day at the pool with her. At this bit of news, Patricia Presser got mad and started yelling, which confused her, Bari remembers. Later, at the bowling alley, Bari saw her father and Phyllis kissing. When Bari got older, she understood why her mother had been so upset that day. Jackie and Phyllis had been having an affair.

At first, Bari's life on Meadowbrook Boulevard seemed like the perfect world depicted on "Ozzie and Harriet." "We had cookouts, badminton," she says. "Everybody came to our house." She loved Christmas. "We used to have great holidays. Lights, prime roast, the whole bit. The Friedmans, the Pressers, everybody was there."

Her mother and father were not getting along, however. By the late fifties, Patricia Presser's life had been rocked by a series of trage- dies. Her mother, father, and an uncle had died within two years, leaving her without immediate family. Jackie wasn't home much to provide comfort, and she searched for someone to help ease her suffer- ing. "Pat ran into a woman who believed in witchcraft," Allen says. "She took it very seriously. She started drinking because of Jackie's cheating. Jackie had her institutionalized because he thought she was crazy. At that particular time, she went on the left road instead of the right road. She was seeing figures on the dresser. Jackie made her the way she was. She was a wonderful wife. A wonderful, wonderful wife. She had problems. Her mother, father, and uncle, her only family, died within a year and a half. . . . Then drinking and being with this woman with witchcraft, and Jackie never being home."

At work at the Eastgate, Allen didn't care if Jackie slept with the help; he just wished Jackie would listen to his idea to redesign the miniature-golf course, making it tougher. The regulars were already bored with the layout, and customers were dropping off. The fancy restaurant also wasn't getting much business, and Allen wanted to change the menu and lower prices so that Eastgate's mostly working-class customers could afford to eat there. "We lost a lot of money in the restaurant," Allen said. "I beefed, but Jackie wouldn't listen."

Allen was part of the problem, too. In every straight job he held in his life, he tried to figure out a way to scam his bosses. This was his badge of honor, and he talks proudly of how he stole and cheated. At the Eastgate, he needed only a few moments to figure out a scheme to make himself some money. It was crude and simple: he reached into the cash register when no one was looking and pocketed a few of the larger bills. Then he tore up enough of the score sheets turned in by patrons to cover his theft. At his peak, Allen was stealing a couple of hundred dollars a week. "I'd just take more money and rip up the sheets," Friedman said. "It was so loosely run. The Pressers were never business people, and Mittie Coen never came around. He got busy. During the course of the year, Jackie opened up another bowling alley with somebody else and went for a third in Akron. Jackie Presser was never satisfied with one thing, never stuck with one thing."

Mittie Coen, the experienced bowling-alley hand, promised he'd bring leagues to Eastgate, but the poorly located bowling alley was too far ahead of its time. Housing tracts didn't spring up as quickly as the Eastgate owners had hoped, and the gleaming, upscale bowling alley hemorrhaged red ink. Only the pool room and miniature-golf course made money. By 1962, the Eastgate was in desperate financial straits. Jackie took over all the stock in its five corporations, and Bill Presser and Hoffa arranged for the Central States Pension Fund to loan the Eastgate another $250,000, then another $50,000. The new cash couldn't keep the bowling alley going. "That place was unsuccessful because it was built ten years ahead of its time," Allen said.

The NAACP picketed the Eastgate that year, saying that black youths were told they had to buy a costly membership to swim at the Eastgate pool while whites were paying seventy-five cents and were immediately admitted for the day. While the Eastgate slowly sank, Jackie and his uncle Herman Presser decided to try their luck with a bowling alley in Erie, Pennsylvania. Brunswick Corporation did a marketing study, Friedman remembers, that said that Erie was an underserved bowling market. It was a ripe opportunity, and Brunswick, as usual, presented easy terms to the Pressers to get started.

Allen Friedman, who had also left the Eastgate by this time, invested some money with Jackie and Herman, and construction of the Erie Coliseum was underway. "Brunswick would give you anything," Allen said, "All the credit in the world. Jackie learned how to beat Brunswick, get credit, and he started opening up bowling alleys. He'd say how foolish and dumb they were. It's the truth. If you know the right people, you can get anything. You get close to someone, a banker or manufacturer or purchasing agent, if you give them broads or money or gifts, they're going to cheat their bosses. It's the American way. That's the way I was brought up. So Jackie got close to certain guys in Brunswick, and he got what he wanted . . . a kickback from Brunswick. He bragged about it. If the bowling alley went bad, Jackie made his money up front, before it even opened."

Brunswick gave them cash for the incidentals needed to open the alley, and they financed the expensive pinsetting and ball-return equipment. With the Brunswick line of credit, the three men obtained a loan from an Erie bank. Bill Presser, who had seen what had happened with the Eastgate, didn't get involved in this venture. He was occupied with other matters, such as sweating out an appeal to the U.S. Supreme Court of his June 24, 1960, conviction for destroying the incriminating invoice subpoenaed by the McClellan committee.

The appeal wasn't heard, and in January 1963, Bill Presser was shipped to the federal penitentiary in Sandstone, Minnesota, to begin a one-year sentence. Unlike many of his associates, Bill, fifty-six years old, had never been in prison, and he quickly discovered that he couldn't stand confinement. He was family oriented, older than most of the prisoners, and physically soft. Within a few months Faye Presser, in tears, called Jimmy Hoffa and told him that Bill couldn't handle prison and was breaking down. Chauffeured by a sidekick, a felon named Joe Franco, Hoffa quickly came to Cleveland to visit Faye. He reassured her that he would do everything in his power to obtain an early release for her husband.

On the drive back to Detroit, Hoffa told Franco he could never fully trust Bill Presser again, especially with secrets. The Plug wasn't so tough after all. He couldn't do time, not even one year, Hoffa said. He figured that Presser, if faced with prison again in the future, might do anything to avoid it—maybe even become an informant. After this episode, Hoffa never allowed himself to be as close to Bill Presser as he had once been.

Hoffa's instincts proved correct. The next time Presser was confronted by a possible prison term, he turned informant.

Jackie and his uncle Herman let Allen manage the Erie place, and soon the Eastgate pattern was repeated: the bowling alley didn't get leagues; it barely broke even; and Allen "had my salary and whatever I stole." Jackie and Herman would drive to Erie on Friday afternoons to pick up their paychecks then spend the night at the hotel and restaurant next door, trying to acquaint themselves with the women of Erie, and billing their meals and rooms to the bowling alley. Allen told them to cut this out; they'd have to work. But Herman said that he and Jackie were too busy trying to open another bowling alley in Cleveland Heights to work in Erie. Hearing this, Allen became enraged. "We're all supposed to be equal partners!" he yelled. "You're draining the Erie investment, and now you've got another alley competing with it. You can forget about picking up another paycheck here unless you want to find yourself in the hospital."

By the fall, Allen knew that the Erie Coliseum was going to strike out. Weary of taking phone calls from creditors, he moved back to Cleveland. He told the assistant manager of the bowling alley to collect the week's cash receipts each Monday and meet him at a highway restaurant halfway between the two cities. "Don't pay any bills," Allen told the obedient employee. Then Allen stuffed the receipts—a couple of thousand dollars—into his pockets. Later, he told Jackie what he had done and split the cash with him. Allen and Jackie ran this skim operation for several weeks until the bank foreclosed on the bowling alley.

On August 2, 1963, Bill Presser was released from federal prison after serving less than two hundred days of his felony conviction for destroying evidence subpoenaed by the McClellan committee. Bill was tanned and fat, still the Plug. A few days later in Cleveland, Bill stepped out of a small crowd at Burke Lakefront Airport to greet Hoffa, who had come to town for a meeting of the Teamsters Joint Council 41, the ruling body for the seventeen Teamsters locals in northern Ohio.

"Hi, you old wart," Hoffa said, gripping Presser's hand. Hoffa, a fitness buff, took a step back, looked at Presser's girth, pointed, and said, "I know one thing. If you're going to stay in that shape, I'll personally whip you."

At the time, federal law didn't bar a union official convicted of a labor-related felony from holding office. The day after his release from prison, Bill Presser reassumed his duties as president of the Ohio Conference of Teamsters, the ruling body for all the joint councils in the state. "I was president all the time I was gone," he explained to reporters at Hoffa's welcome party. "By the way, I was reelected last month in Dayton to another four-year term—by acclamation."

A rumor had been floating around that Hoffa was going to name

Presser as his assistant at the International's headquarters in Washington, D.C. But Hoffa, wary now of Presser, didn't want him to work closely with him in Washington. As an assistant, Presser would be privy to Hoffa's private business deals and could easily learn something incriminating, something federal authorities might squeeze out of him the next time he faced prison. "I want Bill Presser in Ohio," Hoffa explained to the Cleveland welcome party. "He's doing a good job here." This suited Presser fine. He didn't want to leave Cleveland anyway.

Not long after his return home, Bill became frustrated with his prodigal son. Not only had Jackie failed in the Hotel Employees Union and with the Teamsters-financed bowling alleys, but he was running wild and ignoring his family. Bill Presser, a stay-at-home family man, was angry and turned to a dear family friend, Sam Klein, for assistance. Klein's parents and Faye Presser's parents had booked passage to the United States on the same ship. Klein grew up in Glenville, and as a young man worked as a bookie specializing in horse races. Eventually, through his ties to Bill Presser, Klein became a millionaire in the vending-machine field. In 1963, he gradually started taking over Bally Manufacturing Corporation, the pinball and slot-machine company that locked up the slot-machine market in Las Vegas and Reno casinos. Government records would show years later that Klein's hidden partner in Bally was East Coast Mob figure Jerry Catena.

After complaining that Jackie wouldn't heed his advice, Bill asked Klein if he would help straighten out his son. Klein said he'd try. "His old man was very unhappy with his performance and got me to beat the shit out of him in the early sixties, try to guide him and make him behave," Klein recalled. "We are dear, dear friends."

Back in Cleveland, the bankrupt Eastgate started to inch its way through the courts in 1964, long after J. Edgar Hoover was interested in linking bowling alleys to Teamster officials. The Teamsters Central States Pension Fund sued Jackie Presser for $1.06 million in defaulted loans. Not only Teamsters pension holders, but ninety-three other creditors were stung by the bankruptcy, from the B'nai B'rith Women's Council (fifty dollars) to millionaire shopping-mall developer Dominic Visconsi (three thousand dollars). The Teamsters took possession of the Eastgate Coliseum through foreclosure then leased it at extremely favorable terms to Sam Klein. Two years later, Bill Presser

114

Jackie at three.

Faye and Bill
Presser on their
wedding day,
January 15, 1928,
seventeen months
after Jackie's birth.

Theresa Friedman, with sons Allen (left)
and Jack, circa 1926.

Bootlegger Louis Friedman, Jackie's
grandfather.

A Murray Hill murder scene during the Corn Sugar Wars, summer 1930. One of the Porello brothers, responsible for the hit of Big Ange Lonardo's father, was killed a few steps away. *(Cleveland State University Press Archives)*

Angelo Lonardo, future acting Mafia boss of Cleveland, on trial for murder after he avenged his father's assassination, June 1930. *(CSU Press Archives)*

The Pressers at a family
wedding. Jackie is in the
front row, right. Bill,
standing, is second
from right.

The Presser family,
shortly before Jackie
enlisted. Jackie's brother
Marvin is at right.

Navy boot camp, 1943. Jackie was 17.

After a year in the Navy, Jackie slimmed down.

Milton "Maishe" Rockman in a rare
public pose at the September 1954
congressional jukebox-rackets hearings
in Cleveland. *(CSU Press Archives)*

Teamster boss N. Louis "Babe" Triscaro
swears to tell the truth at the 1954
jukebox-rackets hearings, then tells the
congressmen he knows nothing about
his wife's three slag and trucking companies. *(CSU Press Archives)*

Bill Presser develops a faulty memory
at the jukebox-rackets hearings. Two
months later, the union switches its
campaign support to Senator George
Bender, who promptly adjourns the
investigation. *(CSU Press Archives)*

Jackie at the hotel workers union office
in 1955, before he is kicked out of office
and his uncle Allen burns down the
building. *(CSU Press Archives)*

Bill and Jimmy Hoffa at the McClellan hearings, 1958. Hoffa wants the Plug to carry committee transcripts back to the Teamsters offices. *(UPI Telephoto)*

The don of the Cleveland Mafia for a quarter of a century, John Scalish tries to hide his face at the McClellan hearings, January 1959. His death in 1976 set off a Mob war. *(CSU Press Archives)*

Jackie's bodyguard and confidant Tony Hughes in 1957, on his way to a heavyweight ranking.

Loan shark Pete DiGravio, whose assassination in 1968 helped bring Hughes and eventually Jackie into the FBI fold.

and the Teamsters Central States Pension Fund trustees sold the Eastgate Coliseum to Klein for $1 million—a bargain-basement price, considering that a bank had recently appraised the Coliseum at $1.4 million. Klein profited handsomely. Teamsters pensioners unwittingly took a beating.

9
Carmen

"He makes you feel as if he doesn't take a breath when he doesn't think of you."

CARMEN PRESSER

In the summer of 1963, at a bowling alley called Severance Lanes, Jackie was introduced by a friend to Carmen DeLaportilla. She was beautiful, brown-eyed, headstrong, and several weeks away from a divorce. At twenty-nine, Carmen was ready to meet new men, but she was unimpressed with this thirty-seven-year-old man with the little boy's nickname. He was short, fat, and parted what was left of his hair just above his ear and swept it across his bald head. He wore the standard tough-guy uniform: gray slacks, black-on-black shirt, and a black mohair sweater with gray and white panels.

With studied casualness, a cigarette dangling from his lips, Jackie pulled a thick wad of bills from his pocket. He began to flip through the roll, clearly making a show.

Who is this guy? Carmen thought. When he stopped leering at her and began to talk, he made an even worse impression. He's really a jerk, she told herself.

Within days, Jackie called the woman who introduced them, asking, "Remember that girl? I want to take her out. Please call her and ask her for me." When Jackie's request was relayed, Carmen laughed. "You've got to be kidding," she said. "All he needs is an apple in his mouth."

At the time, Carmen was busy rearing two rambunctious sons on little money. The last thing she needed was to get involved with a guy

116

who tried to act like a gangster. The morning she signed her divorce petition, Carmen stopped at Corky & Lenny's, a popular suburban deli and breakfast spot frequented by everybody from mobsters to millionaires. She was drained and on the brink of tears. Her divorce had turned out to be tougher on her emotions than she had thought it would be. She was crossing the sidewalk in front of Corky & Lenny's when someone said hello. It was Jackie. He walked right in with her and joined her for lunch. Carmen wasn't in any mood for company; even so, she found herself telling Jackie about the divorce, her two sons, and her financial dilemma.

With great concern and courtliness, Jackie murmured reassurances and gently asked what was she going to do. "Are you sure you're OK? Is there anything I can do to help?"

"I don't know," she said.

"What kind of work are you gonna do?" Jackie asked.

"I don't know. I've got my children to take care of."

Jackie told her to give him her phone number and maybe he could find a job for her. She didn't know his father was a powerful union leader and had friends at all the companies in town. The name Presser meant nothing to her. She thought Jackie was just a guy who owned part of a bowling alley with his uncle. Moved by his sympathy, Carmen gave him her phone number. "Maybe I misjudged him," she thought.

Soon after Jackie and Carmen's chance meeting, he called her and they met for lunch, talking about her job prospects and how her divorce was going. Soon the lunches turned to dinner dates. "One thing led to another, and it wasn't long before we were best friends," Carmen said. "Because he's very, very likable. Very charismatic. When he smiles and laughs, no one is cuter, and no one is more adorable. I always said he could charm the birds right out of the trees. He charmed me."

Then she discovered that Jackie was married and had two children. At first Carmen was surprised, then disappointed that he had deceived her. They had been getting along so well, and she was becoming quite attached to him. But Jackie argued that he was separated, free to come and go, and soon he would be getting divorced. "Can't you understand my situation?" he asked. "After all, it's a lot like yours."

She did understand, and now the unpleasant details of their divorces and the flaws of their mates became a topic of conversation during their dates, binding them even closer. By November 22, the day

117

President Kennedy was assassinated, Carmen and Jackie were practically inseparable. She recalls that her mother, born in Cuba, was visiting from Florida and spent that day bolted to the television, stunned. As the nation reeled, Carmen carefully applied makeup and got dressed for a date with Jackie.

"Where are you going—the president has died!" her mother scolded.

"I don't care," Carmen said. "I have a date with Jackie and I'm going out."*

Her mother argued some more, but Carmen ignored her. "I was falling in love," Carmen recalls. "And I had never loved anybody like that. That was the great love of my life."

Just before Christmas, 1963, Carmen was broke and depressed about celebrating a bare-bones holiday with her boys. "Jackie had twenty-five dollars." Carmen recalled. "That's all he had. We went to Gray Drugstore. And we bought twenty-five dollars of toys for the boys. I wrapped them all up. There were plastic soldiers. Plastic railroad tracks and trains. I can't remember everything we bought. Twenty-five dollars' worth of toys back then was a lot. The kids had a wonderful time. When he did that, that was the start of my really falling in love with him. He was most gentle and most loving with me and my children."

To improve Carmen's finances, Jackie used his father's influence to place her as a no-show employee on the payroll of Sportservice, Incorporated. This Buffalo-based concession conglomerate sold hot dogs, peanuts, beer, and souvenirs at Cleveland Stadium and dozens of other arenas, stadiums, racetracks, and bowling alleys across the country. Each week, Carmen received a check for fifty dollars in the mail, even though she never worked a minute for Sportservice. The company could easily afford the favor; by 1972, its new holding company, Emprise, employed seventy thousand workers in thirty-nine states and Puerto Rico, owned parts of nineteen separate racetracks, and ran the

---

*Jimmy Hoffa showed even less respect for the slain president. Hoffa was out of town that day, and his assistants, after learning of the tragedy, ordered the flags at half-mast outside Teamsters headquarters in Washington, D.C., and sent the staff home. When they called Hoffa and told him what they had done, he flew into a rage, saying that everyone knew he hated the Kennedys and lowering the flags would make him look like a hypocrite. Besides, now Bobby Kennedy was just another lawyer, he gloated.

vending machines in the New York City subway system, to name just
a few of its ventures. It wasn't a surprise the Pressers turned to Sportservice for a favor. Its founder, Lou Jacobs, had extensive ties to the
Teamsters, the Mafia, and Cleveland.*

While Jackie showered affection on Carmen and her two sons, his
own family noticed a change. The cookouts and badminton and family
gatherings gradually stopped. Jackie, Pat, and the kids didn't celebrate
Christmas and Hanukkah together as a family, as they had so faithfully
in the past. Before Bari Presser turned ten, she knew her parents were
having difficulties. She noticed that her father was home less and less.
Her parents fought, and her mother was hospitalized for a mental
breakdown. A turning point, Bari remembers, was the summer when
the family didn't celebrate the Fourth of July. There had always been
a big picnic with relatives and neighbors dropping in. "When there was
no Fourth of July picnic, even a child could see something was going
on," Bari said. "I was upset. I knew something was wrong. I had to lie
to my friends about why we didn't celebrate the holidays."

Meanwhile, despite his promises, Jackie hadn't filed for a divorce.
When Carmen learned about this, she became furious and broke off
their affair. A day or so later, Jackie's uncle Harry Friedman came to
her house and pleaded Jackie's case. "He told me what a terrible home
life Jackie had and how he had been trying to get a divorce for years,
that it wasn't his fault and that he had every intention in the world of
getting a divorce," Carmen said.

But whenever she pressed him, Jackie always had a reason why he
couldn't file for a divorce—his wife was in the hospital, his son was
having problems, whatever. This went on for years. Then, Jackie had
a heart attack in 1966. He was only forty years old, but he weighed
three hundred pounds and smoked incessantly. Leading a double life—
trying to keep his relationship with Carmen and her boys a secret from
his family—added to the strain. "He left home after the heart attack,"
Carmen said. "He was not doing real well with his wife and his family.
I have to be honest. I was not very nice about this whole thing. I

*In the fifties, Jacobs arranged lines of credit and loans for racketeer Moe Dalitz when he
bought the Stardust casino and hotel in Las Vegas. Also, Emprise and Jerry Catena, Mafia don
of the Genovese crime family, were major shareholders in Lion Manufacturing, which was
renamed Bally Manufacturing in 1963 when Presser's friend Klein began to take it over.

consciously made the decision that he was not happy at home and that I had every right to take him for myself. To turn him around, away from his wife. At the time I felt very justified because I had the misguided notion that if a man isn't happy at home, a woman has the right to take him away. That's not just. That was a real bad thing for me. After I did that, I realized it was the wrong thing to do. The fact that some-body else had done it to me . . . it was poetic justice."

Jackie in turn bombarded Carmen with attention and affection. He called her during the day to ask what she was doing, to tell her that he loved her. As he had shown in the past, Jackie was a captivating lover, though certainly not because of his looks or the bedroom pyro-technics he generated. In stark contrast with his tough public persona, he was soft and sentimental. "He wasn't a red-hot lover," said Carmen, who had been married twice before. "I had to teach him everything he knew. Sex was the end of it. The leading up was where he excelled. What he said to you and how he touched you. The beginning of the day, he'd wake up and hug you and kiss you, then he'd call you during the day: 'How are you, sweetheart? What are you doing? I miss you. What are you making for dinner?' A couple of hours later, he'd call: 'I love you.' We'd be watching TV for three hours, and he wouldn't take his hands off me, rubbing my back or my neck. Constant affection, never stopping. It was not the sexual end he excelled in but the emo-tional end. You had a real emotional high."

They settled into a routine, almost as if they were married. He supported her and her children; she cooked dinner and afterwards they watched television or went out. The first time he came over for dinner, Carmen broiled a huge steak and set it down on a plate at a table set for two. "We sat down and had salads," she said. "He took his fork and put the steak on his plate and started cutting it, and he looked at me and he said, 'Aren't you going to have anything to eat?' He was serious. I said, 'Oh, nothing.'"

If Jackie was sensitive about being fat, he never let on. Harold Friedman, the Teamsters leader, derisively referred to him as "Humpty Dumpty," sometimes to his face. Allen Friedman and his cohorts couldn't figure out why Jackie, short and fat, always had his pick of attractive women. It helped that he was good-natured about his bulk. Once he was given a huge gift box of chocolates, which he brought home. Carmen put it in a bottom drawer in a hutch in the dining room.

120

"Every once in a while, I looked to see if it was there, and it was, wrapped up in cellophane," she said. "One day I was going to have company, so I thought, Gee, let's get some of that candy out. I picked up that box and I opened it and I laughed so hard. It was empty, and he left a note in there: 'The candy bandit strikes again.' "

Carmen's children loved his comforting size. Her son Maury said that Jackie wasn't fat—just fluffy. The name stuck. The boys started calling their mom's gun-toting boyfriend Fluff. "He had wonderful hands," Carmen said. "Very affectionate. Very touchy. Little kids loved to sit on his lap because he was so comfortable. He'd just rub them and hug and touch and feel. That was one of the things I loved about him. He used to lay on the couch and the kids laid on top of him and he'd rub their backs. They really loved him. Not that he spent a lot of time with them, because he didn't. He was not there for them. But he was always good-natured. There were two little girls visiting one time, and we were playing dress-up. And he let us put makeup on him and a wig. We put on a little lipstick and did his eyebrows and put a wig on him, and he walked around the house like a girl." She laughed. "I loved that fat thing. I'm telling you, he was the most comfortable human being in the world. As far as I'm concerned, you could not get in bed and be as comfortable as with that Jackie. You just fit right in. It was like having a nice mattress all around you."

Carmen added, "We were obsessed with each other for years. Then all of a sudden, he started to go around with Tony and get involved with the Italians. He had always been around Jewish people, then he started hanging around with Italians. And his whole life-style changed."

A couple of years after he met Carmen, Jackie hooked up with a tough ex–professional boxer named Tony Hughes. Hughes's parents were Italian, having changed their name from Uizzi, and they lived on Murray Hill. Tony was big, powerful, and athletic. He took up boxing, turned pro in 1956, and became a protégé of former heavyweight champion Rocky Marciano. Hughes wasn't fast but had great power in both hands, and he had built up a record of twenty-three knockouts and one loss by the time he got his first shot at a contender, Great Britain's top-ranked Henry Cooper, in January 1962. Hughes lost the fight after getting cut under the eye. He dropped out of boxing shortly thereafter.

Repeating the pattern he began with his Uncle Allen, Jackie attached himself to the slugger, to someone who seemed rough, swaggering, and fearless. Hughes was close to James Licavoli, a.k.a Jack White, a prominent, ruthless member of the Cleveland Mafia who took over as boss in 1976. Licavoli, a friend of Bill Presser and Maishe Rockman, controlled illegal gambling and draw-poker vending machines in the Cleveland and Youngstown areas. Under Licavoli's tutelage, Hughes got involved in a loan-shark operation with Pete DiGravio and Curly Montana. Through his Presser connections, Hughes got a job with the Teamsters in 1968. Soon Jackie and Tony were as close as brothers. Jackie was impressed with Hughes's toughness and his knowledge of the Cleveland underworld. For his part, Hughes knew that it didn't hurt to be tight with the son of one of the most powerful Teamsters leaders in the nation. Hooking up with Tony, and Curly Montana to a lesser extent, marked a turning point in Jackie's life. For the first time, he plunged deeply into the wise-guy world and began soaking up the way they thought, talked, dressed, and conducted business. He visited the after-hours joints and gambling rooms on the Hill with Tony, rubbing shoulders with lawyers, boxers, hoodlums, and businessmen who came to gamble and drink. "I saw Presser up there acting like a big shot," said Richie Giachetti, a 1961 Golden Gloves champ who later trained and managed heavyweight champ Larry Holmes. "He always wanted to let you know who he was. 'I'm Jackie Presser with the union.'"

"When I first met Jackie, he was on the streets," Hughes remembers. "He was running a card game, hustling." One of the guys Tony Hughes introduced Jackie to was Rudy Nativio, a slick-dressing, Frankie Avalon look-alike who later found work as a Teamsters business agent. "Rudy was always kind of a cool character, good-looking, a fast dancer," Carmen said. "He was everything Jackie wasn't, and Jackie liked his style in clothes."

Nicknamed Rudy the Cootie, he and Jackie and Tony Hughes went on shopping excursions together; they bought patent-leather shoes, gaudy silk suits with pegged pants and coats with thin lapels. Jackie looked silly in these getups. "He went shopping one time with Rudy the Cootie," Carmen recalls. "He came back and Jackie thought he was so dressed up. Jackie had the worst taste in the world. He came walking in the house and he had on this orange shiny suit. Have you ever seen three hundred pounds of orange shine? With a green shirt and a green tie and rust-colored shoes? I looked and I couldn't help it—it came out of my mouth before I realized what I was saying. I said, 'The Great Pumpkin is here!' He slammed the door and he stormed out and he never wore that suit again. He was mad, because he thought he had looked dashing. He used to come home with patent-leather shoes. I used to hide them in the trunk of my car until he forgot he had them. Then I'd put them in the Salvation Army boxes. A lot of times when he'd go to Florida, he'd get these things. He said his mother got them for him."

As a result of spending time on the Hill with Mafia associates, loan sharks, and dice-game operators, Jackie became extremely secretive. "I didn't know what he was doing," Carmen says. "He would pick and choose what he told me about. He wouldn't tell me his whole day like he used to. He'd say, 'You're better off not knowing.' And I accepted that."

Taking a page from Tony Hughes, Jackie tried to project a tough image. Like his father, Jackie felt comfortable carrying a gun, and he now made sure he had one when he went out. On one of their early dates, he showed Carmen his permit allowing him to carry a concealed weapon. He needed to carry a gun, he told her, since he transported thousands of dollars in cash from the bowling alley to the bank. Jackie's fondness for guns never bothered Carmen. In fact, he gave her a small pearl-handled .25-caliber handgun to carry in her purse when it was inconvenient or inappropriate for him to carry a briefcase with one or two handguns stashed inside.

"I never was uncomfortable with a weapon," Carmen says. "A couple of times he used to like to play with me to scare me to keep things interesting. He'd say, 'They're following us. Get the gun.' I'd open my purse. Then he'd say, 'Don't turn around! Don't turn around!' I turned around one time and there was no car. He said, 'I told you not to turn around!' "

Another time, Carmen recalls, they where enjoying dinner at the Virginian, a restaurant in Shaker Heights, when a burly, dark-haired older man walked from the bar into the dining room, bent down, and spoke quietly to Jackie for a moment. Carmen doesn't remember the conversation, only that Jackie had suddenly and uncharacteristically lost his appetite. After a few minutes, he handed her the keys to his Cadillac and said, "Go home. There's going to be a fight."

"I'm not going to leave," Carmen insisted.

"They have knives."

Out in the parking lot, she climbed into Jackie's Cadillac but couldn't readjust the driver's seat, which he had shoved back to accommodate his three-hundred-pound girth. Carmen, only 5' 3", perched on the edge of the seat, lifted her head above the steering wheel, and threaded the big, boxy car through the parking lot. Suddenly, Jackie and the burly guy and others came out from under the restaurant canopy and into the lot. "I'll run them over," she decided. She pointed the car at Jackie's potential assailants and mashed the accelerator. The men scattered as she slammed to a stop, Jackie jumped behind the wheel, and they spun off. "It was like Bonnie and Clyde," Carmen recalls, roaring with laughter. "This excited him so. This was one of the things he liked about me. These were the things that brought us together."

10

The Local 507 Story

"Jackie Presser couldn't read a labor contract if his life depended on it."

TEAMSTERS LAWYER BOB ROTATORI

Jackie's close friends weren't surprised when he abruptly abandoned his bowling-alley business in the mid-sixties. Other than an occasional rowdy acting up in the alley's lounge, there was little of the confrontation and excitement he thrived on. Cleveland's rich and powerful didn't spend their evenings rolling frames at the Severance Lanes, so Jackie, in his relentless pursuit of respectability, chased new ventures.

In late 1964, he and Al Tolin, a pal from the Hotel and Restaurant Employees Union, decided they could cash in on the notoriously fickle coin-collecting business, which was peaking after a steady rise since the late fifties. Unfortunately, Jackie's timing could have been better. "People in it for investment and fast profit got out after 1964," a successful Cleveland coin dealer explained.

Presser and Tolin began buying bags of coins from Las Vegas and searching through them for rarities—or at least that's what they told people. "They brought money back and forth from Las Vegas," Carmen recalled. On a few occasions, she accompanied her husband to a Cleveland hotel room, where he met briefly with couriers and exited with bags of money, stashing them in the trunk of his car. Carmen now believes Jackie's business may have fronted a questionable enterprise, possibly skim payments to the Pressers from Las Vegas casino owners who had benefited from Teamsters pension-fund loans.

Her suspicions are supported by the basic facts of the coin business

125

in the mid-sixties. It was unusual for a coin dealer such as Presser to concentrate on coins from Las Vegas, since he could buy bags of uninspected silver coins, at face value, from just about any Cleveland bank. By 1965, silver prices had risen to the point where the amount of silver in dimes, quarters, and half-dollars was worth three percent— soon seven percent—more than the face value of the coins. As a result, speculators made quick, sure-fire profits with little effort by simply buying silver coins at face value and reselling them to precious-metal dealers. When the banks ran out, speculators could buy silver coins from vending-machine companies, which charged five percent above face value. They then winnowed out any rare issues before reselling the leftovers to the precious-metal dealers. From the numismatic stand-point, Presser had no reason to procure bags of coins from Las Vegas.

According to authorities, massive illegal skimming of unreported casino cash was taking place in Las Vegas at the time. "Las Vegas was a gold mine for the Mafia from 1963 to 1966," *Time* reported. "In those years, the gangsters, including then Cleveland Mob boss Frank Milano, 'skimmed' some $12 million annually from the gaming rooms at many of the plastic palaces lining the Strip. The money was stolen from the casinos' profits with the aid of crooked owners and divided among leaders of the Cosa Nostra."

During this time, according to Carmen, Jackie still nurtured a plan to get back in the labor movement. His father could set him up with a brand new Teamsters local as easily as a parent might buy an expensive new toy for a child. But Bill Presser was reluctant to do so, even though he dearly wished his son would follow in his footsteps. Bill didn't want his son to fall on his face, as he had done in the late fifties with the Hotel Employees Union. Bill agreed to get a charter for a new local for Jackie, but first he devised what amounted to an insurance policy. He insisted that Jackie get Allen Friedman and Harold Friedman, both solid union hands, to join the new Teamsters venture.

It was a good time to start a new local; the International Brotherhood of Teamsters was increasing its membership and spending at a healthy clip. The IBT's gross operating expenses in 1957 topped $23.3 million. Nine years later, when Jackie sought a charter, the IBT was spending $80.3 million a year. There was plenty of room in the budget for Hoffa to give Bill Presser's kid a $25,000 grant to start organizing a local. Anything to satisfy the Plug, whose Ohio Teamsters empire was

126

at a peak. Under Bill, the state ranked sixth in size, with 88,318 members. His Joint Council 41 had 62,338 members, making it the eighth-largest Teamsters council in the country.

Jackie recruited Harold Friedman easily enough. His Bakery Workers Local 19 was shrinking, and he enjoyed a challenge. Allen was reluctant at first. At the time, he was working at a lousy job at one of the $29.95 auto-painting franchises that were sprouting up across the country and living with his wife Nancy at the modest Clarkwood Garden Apartments complex. Jackie asked his uncle to join him in the new local, and Allen turned him down. "I didn't want any part of Jackie Presser because of what he did to the hotel workers in the fifties," Allen says.

Jackie stopped by to see him the next morning and poured on his "C'mon, Uncle Allen" routine, but Friedman turned him down again, saying that start-up costs would be too high and he had little to contribute.

To which Jackie replied, "We have the money."

"What do you mean by 'We have the money'?" Allen asked.

"Harold Friedman and myself will each put up approximately $12,500 and the International will match that," Jackie said.

"I've got no money," Allen said.

"We could use Harold Friedman's building, Local 19, and we could use their telephone and their secretaries and their business agents and their printer," Jackie said.

Allen wasn't happy about teaming up with Harold Friedman, whom he considered an egomaniac who always insisted on having his way, and who treated his employees at the union hall like vassals. But Jackie, the charming persuader, convinced his uncle to join their venture.

"Fine," Allen said, "but I don't want to be an errand boy for Harold, eating dinner at eight or nine o'clock at night when he wants to, or going to the bank for him, or taking his shoes to get shined. The only way that I will do it is if one of us would be able to veto. If one of us said no, the other two had to go along. And I want it verified by William Presser in the morning." Otherwise, Allen said, he planned on opening his own car-painting franchise.

The next day, he, Jackie, and Harold visited Bill Presser, told him about the veto arrangement, and reached an agreement. Bill called

127

Teamsters president Jimmy Hoffa and obtained the charter and funds. The new Teamsters local was called Local 507 and chartered primarily to organize warehouse workers.

Jackie became secretary-treasurer; he was supposed to cultivate politicians and judges and lobby for union interests in the statehouse and at city hall, relying on his father's contacts. Allen was named vice president; he was in charge of organizing, since he liked to be on the front lines, working the lunch spots and the sidewalks outside the warehouses, trying to convince workers to sign up. Harold became the president; he ran the books and the scheduling, took care of the building, hired and fired office help, and most important, bargained the contracts.

The real genius behind Local 507 was Bill Presser. "Bill created this warehouse local, which really boomed," Robert Rotatori, one of Local 507's lawyers, says. "Warehouses had never really been organized before. He insisted that Harold Friedman be an officer, because Harold Friedman will take care of business. Bill knew he didn't get in crazy schemes. That always stuck in Jackie's craw—that his father viewed Harold as a better union official. He did all the work. Jackie didn't do anything. You can't find one employer who negotiated a contract with Jackie Presser. Jackie Presser couldn't read a labor contract if his life depended on it. He could read the words, but he couldn't understand it. He never negotiated a contract. He never did the things a labor leader did. Harold Friedman ran the union."

Despite the rigors of starting a local from scratch, Jackie rarely put in full days at the union hall. He was too busy wooing Carmen in the afternoons. "He'd sit there and look at me and cry and carry on and kiss my fingers and my toes because he loved me so much," she said. "He had to know every move I made. And every place I was at and whatever I did. And everything I did was fascinating. He was interested in the laundry. Whatever I did was wonderful."

But Harold changed all that, says Jackie's friend Tony Hughes. "The only reason Jackie straightened out was because of Harold Friedman. Harold made a man out of him. Jackie knew he couldn't make it unless he straightened out."

Harold Friedman was built like an oak tree—at least 6'2" tall, with a thick trunk, broad shoulders, and a moon-shaped face marked by a thicket of black eyebrows. He learned the union business at the right

128

hand of his father, Harvey Friedman, a close friend of Bill Presser's. The son of a tailor, Harvey Friedman had emigrated to the United States from Kiev. He joined the Bakery Workers Union in 1917, getting paid $12.50 a week, and eventually rose to be a candidate— although he lost—for the presidency of the Bakery Workers International. For decades, he and his son treated their Local 19 like a family business. In 1961, for instance, when unions were first compelled to disclose officers' salaries to the Labor Department, it was revealed that more than forty percent of Local 19 dues went to Harvey and Harold's excessively high salaries of $35,000 and $28,000, respectively.

Harold ran Local 507's business side with brutal efficiency. He installed elaborate sign-in sheets, work assignment ledgers, and call-in procedures for business agents as they made the rounds from shop to shop. He wouldn't let secretaries smoke at their desks or display pictures of their children. The business agents nicknamed him Genghis Khan, and Harold relished the comparison. He even kept a biography of the Mongol conqueror in his office. After work, which usually meant eight o'clock or later, Harold went to fine restaurants to dine with the business agents, lawyers, and, occasionally, businessmen whose employees were in Local 507.

Even his friends admit that Harold had an obsessive personality. He went overboard insisting on neatness, precision, and control. When he went out to dinner with his business agents, they could drink a glass of wine only if he was having one. Otherwise, they could drink only cherry soda or water. Harold expected secretaries and the clerical staff to perform like automatons. They were required to clear off the top of their desks before leaving at night. Pencils, always sharpened, were to be kept in the right side of the top desk drawers. "Harold knew how much toilet paper was done a day," said a Local 507 insider. "He counted the rolls of toilet paper. I was in the military, and it was worse than in the military. All the supplies on the shelves had to be evenly spaced."

For his part, Harold refused to wear white shirts, saying they were the sign of management. But he insisted on well-cut, expensive suits and Stacy-Adams's Saratoga shoes. When he heard the shoe company might be folding, he ran out and bought two dozen pairs. Allen, Jackie, and his small, handpicked entourage were the only ones inside Local 507 who didn't have to bow before Harold.

Local 507 was a quick success, and in later years its three cofounders each claimed the credit. Jackie bragged about how, with balls and brains, he built the local from the ground up. Allen would pronounce, "I am the father of 507." Harold, more accurately, declared himself the brains that made Local 507 "the best damn union local in America." In fact, paternity belonged to Bill Presser; he used his immense power as the director of the Ohio Conference of Teamsters to gift wrap Local 507 for Jackie. Bill built Local 507 by the easiest and quickest method possible: he raided other Teamsters locals and dumped their workers into his son's fledgling union.

Teamsters Local 197, a Cleveland warehouse workers local chartered in 1938, was the Pressers' first target. When Local 197's president died in 1965, the Teamsters executive board used its powers to put the local under a trustee, Bill Presser. This was part of Bill's well-conceived plan to give Jackie his own Teamsters local someday. Bill promptly appointed Jackie and Harold administrators of Local 197. In 1967, a few months after Local 507 was born, Bill Presser transferred huge blocks of Local 197's 1,440 union members into tiny Local 507, which at the time had only 250 members and $267 in assets. It was like a minnow swallowing a whale.

In January 1967, still under trusteeship, Local 197 had $27,000 in assets. Harold and Jackie began spending these funds for office equipment and a car to be transferred to Local 507. By November, the assets of once-proud Local 197 had sunk to $97.33 in cash and $6,078 in office furniture and equipment. Bill Presser wrote to the International on November 30 to justify his uninvited plundering of Local 197: "About a year ago, because of the lack of cooperation of Local Union No. 197 and the poor quality of its appointed officers, I instructed Local No. 507 to start transferring the members of Local 197 to Local No. 507." Now, with only twenty-five members left in Local 197, Presser asked the International for permission to merge it with Local 507. The International approved the merger within a week. It was a slick maneuver. The members of Local 197 cast no votes and had no say about it, but they were now controlled by three new union officers—Allen and Harold, both ex-cons, and Jackie, kicked out of a union for financial shenanigans.

The Pressers also ravaged Teamsters Local 521, made up of 860 clerical workers. This time they didn't even use a trusteeship as an excuse. On June 14, 1969, in a notice to just thirty-four members of Local 521, Jackie and Harold boldly announced that Local 521 had been merged with Local 507. This was a surprise to the dues-paying members of Local 521, because theirs was a healthy union. In each of the two years before Bill Presser raided it, Local 521 had collected more than $100,000 a year in dues. Jack Fait had been the local's chief officer since 1951. He said that Bill Presser, without discussion, had ordered Local 521 members into Local 507 and then asked him to step down from his position as an officer of Teamsters Joint Council 41, the ruling board for all the Teamsters locals in northern Ohio. Bill said that new blood was needed to bring full union benefits to Local 521 workers and that Fait should step aside for Jackie and his crew. To take the sting out of the forced retirement, Bill Presser promised to give Fait a generous Teamsters pension and help him find a good job in private industry, Fait said, but "Presser did not keep either of these two promises."

By 1971, Local 507 had 4,430 members toiling in such diverse jobs as warehouse workers, forklift operators, receiving and shipping clerks, watchmen, dock workers, packers, checkers, porters, truck drivers, machine operators, loaders, parking-lot attendants—even zoo attendants. Dues payers from companies scattered across northern Ohio were gathered into 121 different bargaining units, all with different wage scales and contract terms. Two-thirds of the units had thirty or fewer members, only three had over two hundred members, and none was larger than four hundred. As a result, Local 507 members were isolated, didn't share working conditions or job concerns, and didn't know one another. There was little excuse or opportunity for them to work together to solve a common labor problem. As a result, they never formed the bonds necessary to challenge any of Jackie and Harold's autocratic rulings.

The Pressers also plucked large numbers of Teamsters from huge, thriving Local 407, composed of truck drivers who made local deliveries. Ken Paff, a Local 407 member and the future head of a dissident Teamsters group, Teamsters for a Democratic Union, says Local 507 "stole" drivers from the Kroger grocery chain and from Seaway Foods, a distributing company. Local 507 was very quickly becoming one of the biggest, most powerful Teamsters locals in the state.

In 1976, as he neared retirement, Bill Presser again boosted his son's local, folding in the city's cab drivers, Teamsters Local 555, which Bill had presided over since 1955.*

Throughout the early seventies, Local 507 continued to spread across northern Ohio like the horror-movie creature the Blob, devouring Teamsters locals in its path: Petroleum Drivers Local 545, Independent Warehouse Workers Local 752, and others. By 1972, with nearly five thousand workers each paying a fifty-dollar initiation fee and eight dollars a month in dues, Local 507 brought in $790,000 a year, a tempting target for greedy labor racketeers.

When they started Local 507, Harold Friedman told Jackie and Allen that he'd show them how to make money legitimately in the labor movement. It was simple: just raise your salary, Harold once explained. He also became a Teamster trendsetter by collecting salaries from several different union positions. In 1972, for example, Harold collected $49,938 as a vice president of Bakery Workers Local 19; two thousand dollars as a business agent for Bakery Workers Local 56; a thousand dollars as an executive board member of the Bakery Workers International; and a cool $122,881 from Local 507. That year, a total of $179,000 in union members' dues was diverted to the bloated salary of Harold Friedman, merely a local union officer little known outside of Cleveland. Calculated in 1988 dollars, Friedman's outrageous annual salary would be $504,000. By comparison, in 1972, Leonard Woodcock, president of the United Auto Workers, made $47,500 for overseeing a union of 1.4 million members. Local 507 represented about five thousand members.

Indeed, the United Auto Workers, the United Steelworkers, and other unions associated with the former Congress of Industrial Unions (CIO) actually barred their officers from holding more than one union post and from collecting multiple paychecks. Furthermore, the Steelworkers have a rule that local officers may not make more than the highest-paid job in the plants they represent. This dedication to union members' money was lost on Harold and Jackie. For years, Harold was

---

*A few years later, Bill Presser would be investigated by the Labor Department for being a secret owner of Yellow Cab Company, the Cleveland taxicab monopoly put together by Mob associate Arthur B. "Mickey" McBride with the help of musclemen from Murray Hill. McBride went on to build the Cleveland Browns football team. Bill "had a deal going for thirty or forty years with McBride," Allen Friedman says. The taxicab probe never got past its early stages.

the highest-paid union boss in the world. In 1981, at number one on the salary parade, he hauled in $426,873 in pay and expenses; Jackie was number two at $353,736. What really shocked critics was that Harold and Jackie took the lion's share of their salaries not from an international union but from just one Teamsters local—Local 507.

Harold's salary at Local 507 was modest during the first few years. But Allen Friedman testified before a 1982 federal grand jury that Harold supplemented his salary then by taking kickbacks from the business agents who owed him their jobs. "Harold would pay you, let's say five hundred dollars a week or seven hundred dollars a week," Allen said. "They'd take out the federal income tax and the Social Security, and then they would kick back one hundred dollars in cash or one-fifty or two hundred. And he'd open up the right side of his drawer," and they'd drop it in. "I didn't find that out until around '69. And I said [to Harold], 'Well, you were telling me how you are going to make money legitimately on salaries, and you got a drawer full of money there from kickbacks.' "

If Allen is to be believed, the well-paid Local 507 business agents put up with it because they were happy to be taking home recession-proof paychecks two or three times as big as the ones they had made working on loading docks or driving trucks. Harold hired some of them simply because they were tall and muscular; that way, they could double as his bodyguards. "It seemed like everyone over there was called Big Willie or Big Terry or Big Something," said a Labor Department investigator.

Local 507 business agents spent their time driving from factory to factory, sometimes visiting as many as a dozen in a workday. Inside, they investigated worker complaints and collected employer contributions to the various pension funds. Harold insisted that the business agents call the union office both when they arrived at a factory and when they left, and one of Local 507's secretaries would chart their time on a grid. If a business agent needed an hour off to see a doctor, he had to obtain Harold's personal approval.

Like many who knew their way around Murray Hill, Jackie was impressed with Piero "Pete" DiGravio, the well-spoken, expensively dressed loan shark. An honors student in high school, a voracious reader, handsome and athletic, DiGravio eschewed the "dese, dem, and dose" expressions favored by his collector, Jackie's pal Tony Hughes. DiGravio didn't smoke, drank moderately, and, long before it was fashionable, ran miles to stay fit. He also sparred occasionally in a gym. Some called Pete the mayor of Little Italy. He was smooth and successful, a marked contrast to Jackie, a roly-poly, forty-year-old former coin dealer still standing in his father's shadow.

Pete DiGravio was considered a class act on Murray Hill and in the outer circles of the wise-guy world. His loan company bought matching Cadillacs with vanity license plates for his key employees, who included John "Curly" Montana, Al Micatrotto, and Dominic Mutillo. Former heavyweight champion Rocky Marciano, who had managed Hughes as a boxer, invested in the business. Marciano liked DiGravio and once invited him on the road to hang out with Frank Sinatra and his crew. DiGravio was drawn to glamour—he owned a plush supper club—but returned home saying that he was unimpressed with the Rat Pack. Everybody seemed like a bunch of phonies, he said.

DiGravio had a very unusual trait for a mobbed-up businessman: he actually talked about how he made his money. He was in the short-term, unsecured loan business, he would tell you. His company, MDM Investment Company, had offices on Mayfield Road, in the heart of Cleveland's Little Italy. You could come in and borrow a couple of hundred dollars, no questions asked, no red tape, nothing sneaky or underhanded. For every five dollars you borrowed, you had to pay back six dollars, within ten weeks. If you missed a payment, you had to pay five percent of the outstanding loan as a penalty. Those were the terms; everybody knew them, DiGravio said. His business was legal in Ohio, and he paid his taxes like any other businessman.

On May 29, 1968, however, Congress passed legislation that closed the loopholes that allowed loan sharks to lend money at high rates and to conduct "extortionate credit transactions." Several days later, DiGravio said that the law had knocked him out of business; he was now just collecting the money owed to him, not making any new loans. He reminisced about his business to *Cleveland Press* reporter Paul Lilley, explaining how his company didn't collect when debtors died but instead sent flowers to their funerals. "We never had a bit of trouble," DiGravio said. "We built up a fine clientele. Any bank would have been happy to have our borrowers." Then he made a remark that

134

raised eyebrows on the Hill. "Just because we may be tough Italians doesn't mean we are Mafia connected," DiGravio said. "We need the Mafia like we need cancer. We bend over backwards to stay away from those people."

Despite his public remarks and the new law, police detectives believed DiGravio still loan-sharked, only more covertly. In mid-June, DiGravio confided to a banking friend that the Cleveland Mafia was muscling in on his business, demanding ten percent of his gross income for the right to continue operating. Throughout the country, loan sharks were typically required to obtain the imprimatur of the ruling Mafia family before being allowed to operate. They were asked to either borrow their money from Mafia higher-ups and return a percentage as interest or simply rake off a cut of the gross and deliver it as tribute.

The Cleveland godfather at the time, John Scalish, was fifty-five years old and in poor health. He relied on his brother-in-law, Maishe Rockman, to take care of certain Mafia matters. Scalish hadn't inducted new members into the Mafia since the fifties, a management mistake that would cause problems later on. DiGravio, with his businesslike techniques, seemed a good recruit. He made money and he had respect. But he did have some drawbacks: he talked too much; he dressed too well; he didn't stay in the background; and he had made insensitive remarks about the family. His biggest problem, however, was that he resisted the Mafia when it started to muscle in.

On June 21, 1968, Pete DiGravio and three friends drove out to Orchard Hills Country Club in rural Chesterland, Ohio, and teed off for eighteen holes of golf. DiGravio, who shot in the low nineties, played at Orchard Hills several times a week. While the foursome worked their way around the lush green fairways, a man hid in the woods near the sixteenth tee and used long-handled clippers to trim tree branches and build a blind less than twenty-five yards from the tee. At the sixteenth hole, a 306-yard dogleg, DiGravio's foursome let two men play through. Having won the previous hole, Pete had honors and was the first to hit. He walked up, carrying a three iron. Before he could tee up the ball and take a swing, his partners heard a sharp crack and DiGravio fell. "I'm shot!" he screamed.

Three more shots snapped out as the golfers frantically ran away. One slug hit the ground. Another plunged into DiGravio's back. A third pierced his skull.

Later that day, Jackie and Carmen were driving downtown, having another argument about when they were going to get married. They had been practically living together for four years, and Carmen was getting tired of waiting for Jackie to get a divorce. She had no sympathy for his family. She wanted him to marry her immediately. "I'll never forget it," Carmen says. "We heard on the radio that Pete DiGravio had been shot, and Jackie turned as white as a ghost. He started sweating."

Tony Hughes, DiGravio's underling, had even more to worry about. His boss was dead, assassinated by a professional sniper with a .30-caliber automatic rifle. Maybe he was next.

A few days later, Hughes and several other men close to DiGravio carried a steel casket draped with an American flag out of a Catholic church in Little Italy and slid it into a black hearse. DiGravio's body was buried at a nearby cemetery, near a budding crabapple tree. Two FBI agents and several Cleveland police detectives, hoping to overhear something that might help them uncover the killer, infiltrated the five hundred or so mourners.

DiGravio's assassination set in motion a chain reaction that would eventually lead Jackie Presser to the top of the International Brotherhood of Teamsters. According to knowledgeable law-enforcement officials, Pete DiGravio's slaying brought Tony Hughes—and finally Jackie Presser—into the eager hands of the FBI.

One can imagine Hughes's position. He was an undereducated tough guy whose boss had just been murdered. DiGravio's hit looked like an inside job, perhaps carried out by one of his business associates. Everyone was a suspect. Who could Tony Hughes trust? At the same time, FBI agents, including Martin P. McCann, Jr., head of the organized-crime squad, had been quizzing him, probing for details.

McCann had actually been cultivating Hughes for several years, but the ex-heavyweight didn't know it. McCann, an avid sports fan, stopped in every so often to watch Tony work out at the Alta House gym and talk to him casually about boxing. Hughes had no idea that McCann worked for the FBI. According to Tony Hughes's FBI file, he was coughing up harmless stuff at first, details anyone remotely connected with the underworld would know. But before long, Hughes was meeting almost weekly with McCann, a special agent of the old school who liked to drink at the Theatrical Grill and mingle with the judges, politicians, and outfit guys. McCann didn't always dance to the baroque rules listed in the FBI operating manual. At first, he kept Hughes in his hip pocket, not opening an official informant file but meeting with the ex-boxer and later writing down casual notes instead.

Tony apparently decided that he needed protection right after Pete DiGravio was murdered, because the first entry in Tony's informant file is dated July 3, 1969, less than two weeks after the assassination. Hughes was designated CV-882-TE, CV for Cleveland, TE for top echelon. The FBI operating manual describes top-echelon informants as "those providing information primarily regarding the highest levels of organized-crime groups of national significance."

It was at this time that Hughes was hired by Jackie as a business agent for Local 507. Soon, McCann realized that some of the information Hughes was providing couldn't have come from him; it had to be coming from someone else in the Teamsters, someone higher up. It was a cinch for McCann to figure out that the information was coming from Jackie, who heard high-level Teamsters and organized-crime intelligence both from his father and from his own contacts. The new source of information was an interesting development for McCann. He would have to see if he could turn Jackie Presser, too.

Dedicated FBI agents were forever combing the underworld in search of possible snitches, but Marty McCann had an enviable gift, the ability to seduce and secure quality informants. He'd place himself in a bar or an airplane seat where he'd "accidentally" run into a potential source. He enjoyed playing cat and mouse, unlike some agents who preferred the nine-to-five life. Each agent, however, knew the consequences of not having snitches. Routinely, each FBI field agent was required to file a report concerning his informants and the intelligence they had recently provided. If an agent didn't have an informant, he not only had to explain why not but also had to detail what he had done that past month to try to develop one. All FBI agents were saddled with this requirement, not just those assigned to the organized crime, drug-trafficking, and labor-racketeering squads.

An agent's career was tied to his informants; the bigger the snitch, the better the cases to which the agent was assigned or which he developed for other agents. If his informant helped obtain the indictment and conviction of a ranking Mob figure, politician, or public figure, an agent could expect a better assignment or a promotion. At its core, an agent's relationship with a key informant was a marriage of convenience; both parties benefited. An agent could boost his career while fighting crime, and the criminal informant could focus the bureau's attention on his rivals. The best informant was someone still wading through the crime world, which meant that he often ended up as the target of police departments and other federal law enforcers. Naturally, he'd then turn to his FBI handler for help or advice. This not-uncommon scenario presented tremendous danger for an FBI agent, tempting him to help a prize informant avoid arrest or incarceration by obstructing the work of other agencies. Handling informants was the second most likely area in which an agent could sidetrack or destroy a career. Only a drug assignment, where an agent might encounter incredible financial temptation, was riskier.

Marty McCann asked Hughes if he could meet Jackie. After getting the message, Jackie agreed. In fact, he had something he wanted the FBI to investigate. A true believer in the Communist menace, Jackie had learned of a Communist group operating a print shop in Cleveland Heights, and he was convinced that the group was trying to destabilize the United Mine Workers in the Ohio region and that the Teamsters would be next. Jackie wanted to unleash the FBI on the group.

McCann met with Jackie, listening attentively to his paranoid theories about a communist takeover of the American labor movement, nodding, appearing to take it seriously. It was all part of his plan to show concern, gain Jackie's trust, then gradually get him to cough up intelligence on organized crime.

After months and months of cultivation, McCann got Jackie to the point where he agreed to help the FBI make organized-crime cases. With great foresight, Jackie insisted that the FBI couldn't designate him an official informant. He also didn't want a file kept. Fine, McCann said. Jackie's code name was the Tailor. McCann said that when he felt it necessary, he included Presser's intelligence in Tony Hughes's FBI file.

So began what the FBI would later call one of the most valuable informant relationships in its history.

† † †

Jackie Presser was a bundle of contradictions. Though he had never completed eighth grade, he believed uneducated workers had no business campaigning for union office or running a local. "There's a lot of poor labor officials," he once said. "Now how does a guy become a business agent or officer of a local union? He runs because he's a truck driver, a dockman, a warehouseman, a steelworker. He has no exposure to really big business. This is big business. So some guy is popular in an auto mill, steel mill, or machine shop—what have you—and he runs for office, and he wins the presidency of the local union, two, three, five, ten thousand members. The day he sits in the chair for the first time he better understand [labor laws]. He better understand bonding and security. . . . Unfortunately, [for] the limited-educated truck driver, warehouseman, and dockman . . . that's an awesome responsibility to assume. If you're going to be a good leader, you better have that whole education system behind you. Many of them get up and say, 'You hire auditors, and you hire accountants, and you hire attorneys.' But it doesn't work that way. When you hire the professionals, they try to run your operation, and then you are really going to get killed."

Presser's elitist attitude may seem strange, coming as it did from a professed labor leader. But Teamsters presidents Hoffa and Beck had set this tone much earlier. The hero of the Teamsters rank and file, Hoffa nevertheless believed that Teamsters locals should be run by professionals. He may have talked about the dignity and wisdom of the common worker in speeches, but he was only paying lip service. As for his predecessor, Dave Beck, he had once declared, "I run this office just like a business—just like an oil company or a railroad. Our business is selling labor."

Not only did Jackie try to keep the Local 507 rank and file from becoming union leaders, but he and Local 507 president Harold Friedman took extra precautions to thwart even the slightest stirrings of dissent. Borrowing a page from Hoffa, they pushed changes in Local 507's constitution through their executive board. The amendments gave them almost dictatorial powers.

From the very start, Harold and Jackie ran Local 507 as an autocracy. Allen was busy out in the field. After a few months of using the

International's constitution and bylaws to run Local 507, these founding fathers decided to write their own constitution and give themselves even greater powers over the local and its funds. These rule changes explain why Local 507 members put up with the abuses of the Pressers over the years and how Harold and Jackie stayed in power and squelched challenges. They were dealing from a stacked deck.

For example, article 13 of the Local 507 constitution said that no officer, not Jackie or Harold or anyone, could spend more than $3,500 in union funds without a vote of the membership at a regular meeting. It sounded like a democratic way to run a labor union. However, article 15 overrode this limitation and gave sweeping spending power to Jackie and Harold by taking away the membership's voice in how much to pay union officers. Jackie, Harold, and Allen were empowered to set their own salaries and allowances, buy cars, and fund pension plans—all paid for by workers' dues—as long as their handpicked executive board approved these actions, which it always did. After being notified of these changes in Local 507's constitution, the International approved them.

Jackie and Harold got even bolder. They proposed a clause in which candidates for union office were limited to those who had served one year on the executive board. This would limit candidates to anyone already a member of the Presser fan club; a potential reformer would have to find a way to sneak onto the executive board and bite his tongue for a year before getting a chance to challenge the autocrats. Not a likely scenario. But this proposal was too dictatorial even for the International, which was generally not known for its democratic leanings. The International wouldn't allow this clause and two other changes Presser proposed: that Local 507 officers could set the amount of union dues without a secret vote of the membership; and that Harold and Jackie could cancel three months of summertime meetings without a membership vote.

Being turned down on a few bylaw changes didn't inhibit Harold and Jackie. In a letter to the International dated August 31, 1970, they announced that they had amended the Local 507 bylaws to require that all nominations for union office be put in writing five days before a nomination meeting. The intent was obvious: a letter would alert Jackie and Harold to potential opposition and give them time to squelch, buy off, or threaten the upstart. Jackie wouldn't have to worry about arriving at a union meeting to find it packed with secretly mobilized opponents and having himself bounced out in a runaway election. To its credit, the International's executive board rejected this proposal, saying that it conflicted with the IBT constitution. Nonetheless, the changes Jackie and Harold tried to pull off revealed their true antidemocratic motives.

One maneuver that Jackie, Harold, and their cohorts did pull off was to raise the local's initiation fee from fifty dollars to a hundred dollars. This plumped the coffers because many of Local 507's unskilled workers were seasonal help—college students hired for the summer on the loading docks, or warehouse stockers temporarily working the winter holidays. Jackie and Harold told the International that this change was approved by a secret ballot at a general meeting of Local 507 members, but their claim was dubious. No minutes exist of such a meeting, even though minutes were required to be kept. Nine general meetings were supposed to be held each year to be attended by all the members; from January 1968 through February 1973, however, minutes exist for only two of the forty-seven required meetings. During the same five-year period, minutes were kept for only nine executive board meetings. This was no surprise, as secrecy was essential to their autocracy. Harold knew exactly what he was doing. "Jackie Presser got all the notoriety, but Harold Friedman is the brains behind all this," Allen Friedman said.

The ranks of Local 507 grew rapidly during the early seventies. Part of its success, Allen testified, came from sweetheart contracts that Jackie and his father had arranged with several companies in northern Ohio. "If another union was going there to organize them, they would run to Mr. Presser," Allen said. "Let's say the Machinists Union, OK. And this employer would know the Presser family and Mr. Presser would call up Jackie and Jackie would talk to the employer and he would tell me, 'Go on out there and chase the other union down the road.'"

Sometimes, the targeted company would slip the Pressers a list of employee names, addresses, and telephone numbers, giving an organizer like Allen Friedman a huge edge over his competition. He visited workers at home after work; in such private, comfortable surroundings, he convinced many of them to sign cards asking the Teamsters to represent them. On some occasions, Allen says, Jackie told him to go to a warehouse or factory and talk to the workers while they were on the docks or the assembly line. This signaled a special deal, because unions had no right to organize inside a company.

Bob Rotatori remembers his client Bill Presser telling him that Jackie tried to cut sweetheart deals. "Jackie once made a business commitment and promised the promoters they'd have no union problems," Rotatori says. "Well, Bill said he had to meet with these guys and tell them there was no way his son could live up to that commitment. The business would have to have a union. . . . The business never got off the ground, but that was after the promoters had spent a lot of seed money."

Or, as Allen Friedman told a 1983 grand jury investigating his nephew, "Sometimes Jackie would say to Harold, 'Go easy on this contract—he's a friend of the family.' Not the Mafia family, the Presser family." In other words, give the company a break by being a softy at the bargaining table. When this occurred, union members took home lower wages and benefits.

Records of the National Labor Relations Board suggest that most of the shops in Local 507 were organized without a challenge by the employer, a tip-off that employers were welcoming Presser's local, preferring it to a tougher, more straight-shooting union. NLRB files in the Cleveland office show that Local 507 rarely got involved in elections in which either the union or the employer contested the process by filing petitions with the labor board. From 1971 to 1976, Local 507 was involved in twelve contested elections. The busy year was 1974, with four; Local 507 won two, gaining fifty-three new members. Over the next seven years, Jackie's local wasn't involved in a single contested election, although many smaller Teamsters locals in the area were involved in several each. "Local 507 grew primarily by stealing members from other Teamster locals and by signing sweetheart contracts with employers who preferred Local 507 to having a real union," commented Teamsters for a Democratic Union, a reform group.

However, NLRB records don't always paint a complete picture of how a union operates. Local 507 could be rough sometimes in ways that didn't leave a paper trail. In Local 507's earliest days, when Allen Friedman was still an organizer, the local used tough tactics to scare employers into accepting the union. These methods were quicker and easier than going through an election tangled in NLRB red tape.

142

Friedman gave an example of how this worked: He once tried to push Local 507 into a small family-owned paint factory that paid low wages but had loyal workers. He hung around outside when the shifts changed or when workers took a break at the lunch truck, then tried to hand out sign-up cards and pro-Teamsters leaflets. But the paint-shop workers just cursed him. Then a woman slipped him a note that said the workers were poorly paid but afraid to sign the cards, thinking they'd be fired. So Friedman and some Local 507 business agents tried a different tactic. They traveled to the paint departments in the big discount chains and pretended to be writing down information. Before long, a manager would come out and ask what they thought they were doing.

"Get the hell out of our way!" one of the business agents would say. "We're seeing if you sell any nonunion paint. If there's any non-union paint sold here, we're going to put an informational picket line in front of all your stores." Of course, the store managers would call the district bosses, and the threat would get passed up the line. In the case of the stubborn paint factory, Friedman says, some of the discount chains called the paint-factory owners, said they didn't want labor problems, and Local 507 quickly was welcomed into the paint factory to enroll the workers in the union. "We got them a good contract, but we really had to force our way in there," Friedman said.

Many times, Local 507 organizers didn't have the patience to apply an economic tourniquet and instead used cheap, effective, old-fashioned thuggery. "On picket lines, if you wanted to go into the shop and the rest of the people stayed out . . . we would cut your tires or—and I'm ashamed to say this—break your windows and [make] threatening phone calls at night and follow you just to frighten you," Allen said.

Local 507 employed plenty of business agents who could cast an intimidating presence when needed. Besides Allen Friedman, there was former heavyweight boxer and loan shark Tony Hughes; Curtis Conley, a drug dealer convicted of using violence to extort company officials during a 1972 Teamsters strike; Everett Oxyer, charged with conspiracy to extort along with Conley; Steve Kapelka, a gun-toting former second lieutenant who had seen action in Vietnam; and Bobby Kavalec, a refugee from the Dirty Dozen biker gang. Conley was later murdered by a rival drug gang.

Under Jackie and Harold's leadership, some of their business agents got out of hand, stirring up trouble and lawsuits. But they always kept their Teamsters jobs, because Harold Friedman wanted his business agents to look tough and act tough, except around him. Local 507 member Renato Cremona, who used to run a restaurant in Little Italy, says he was assaulted by two business agents, John Irby and Rudy "the Cootie" Nativio, in September 1976 while leaving the parking garage of a downtown Cleveland hotel. He sued the union and lost.

In another example, business agent Terry Freeman, a close friend of Allen Friedman, assaulted two engraving-company supervisors during his first two months as a union official. On January 14, 1977, at an engraving company, Freeman and Big Willie Tunstall grabbed a foreman by the shirt. Freeman sucker-punched the foreman in the face, knocking him to the floor. As workers watched, Freeman hit him, again and again. Bloodied and dazed, the foreman was helped up by his friends and taken to a doctor. "The assault was completely unprovoked and unexpected," the company president complained to Harold Friedman. "We don't want Freeman in our shop and will remove him if he shows up," he added.

Three days later, Freeman and two other business agents visited a company that made custom trim moldings for new cars. The business agents were there to negotiate merit raises, but the shop manager told them they'd have to wait, since the company's personnel director couldn't be found. There would be no negotiations without him.

Freeman didn't like this bit of news, so he grabbed the shop manager, punched him in the face, and started choking him. The other two business agents just watched. "He wanted to show Jackie and Harold he was tough," Allen said of his friend. "Jackie called me and said, 'If he don't stop, I'm gonna fire him! We don't need muscle!' "

By 1972 or 1973, the Cleveland office of the Labor Department decided to focus its attention on Local 507 and began an exhaustive audit, which included interviews with Teamsters officials and members. In a December 1973 report, Labor auditors concluded, "Local 507 is a labor organization designed, created, and operated for the specific purpose of converting its funds to the use of Jackie Presser, Harold Friedman, and Allen Friedman. Its implementation became possible only through the power attached to William Presser's position in the Teamster hierarchy. Once a charter was obtained . . . the new local,

144

insignificant in size and assets, began the takeover of the members and funds of captive locals."

Steve Jigger, Cleveland head of the Justice Department's Strike Force Against Organized Crime, echoed this observation years later. "Unionism is a cause, not a business, but the [Pressers] obviously viewed the unions as their private family business," he said. "They thought it was theirs instead of something they handled in trust for someone else."

There are many examples of how the Pressers used members' money for personal benefit or to reward and appease their organized-crime associates. For two decades, Bill funneled one to two thousand dollars a month in Teamsters Joint Council 41 funds to a company owned by his brother, Milton, and his son Marvin. The company, Ajax Cleaning Contractors, was paid handsomely for cleaning the Joint Council 41 offices. However, others such as Carmen Presser said that the hefty payments were Bill's way to make certain that his unambitious son Marvin, Faye's favorite and her gambling crony, could make a living and support his family. In 1972, Ajax collected $1,763 a month from Local 507; in September 1981, Ajax was paid $2,555.

Bill's largesse with union funds wasn't limited to his immediate family. He also rewarded friends, in particular Maishe Rockman, the mob financier and brother-in-law of the Cleveland don. In the early seventies, Teamsters Joint Council 41 paid Rockman $680 a month for office space for the Teamsters credit union, which was housed in a building he owned at 2020 Carnegie Avenue. In later years, Jackie became unhappy with the setup. "Maishe would never put any money back in the building," a Teamsters insider said. "Jackie used to get really mad about it."

By 1972, the triumvirate—Jackie, Harold, and Allen—was falling apart. Allen Friedman had suffered a massive heart attack in 1969 and was still recovering. When he showed up at the hall, he fought constantly with Harold about how to run union business. Jackie, climbing the state's political and social ranks, was content to let Harold take care of the daily operation of Local 507. Harold wanted Allen out. Allen upset the careful, military routine Harold had imposed. He'd find Allen sleeping on a couch in the inner offices after being up all night manning a third-shift picket line. "It was a constant fight with Harold Friedman," Allen says. "Jackie just went along for the ride, and he knew what was going on, don't misunderstand me. It's just that he was worrying about getting to the top."

To appease Harold, Jackie convinced Allen to organize an independent union of small warehouse companies that couldn't afford the wages and benefits Local 507 demanded from the bigger companies. The idea was that Allen's new union, the Independent Warehousemen Local 752, might one day be able to merge with Local 507. With Allen out of the office and Jackie beginning to get involved in outside business ventures, Harold settled back into a long uninterrupted reign as the ruler of Local 507. As secretary-treasurer, Jackie had the top job, but Harold ran the show. He never granted an interview in his life and planned to keep it that way. He liked being anonymous. If someone got in his way or challenged him in the slightest, Harold ruthlessly drove them from the union.

Harold sometimes purged workers who were troublemakers or who irked one of his favored employers, Allen once testified. By the early seventies, it was extremely difficult for an employer to fire a member of Local 507, the leading Teamsters local in the state. "Once a person becomes a member of this organization, we're going to do everything possible to protect him, and we do, and people can get fired two and three times in this local," Harold Friedman once boasted. "In fact, it takes a long time to get fired, where in another union, you'd be fired in a second. Here they get away with a whole lot more because of the strength of our organization."

But that was only if Harold wanted to back the worker. To others he sometimes denied Local 507's strength and protection, Allen Friedman says. A pesky worker, someone who filed several grievances at a shop or warehouse of a favored employer, was no match for Genghis Khan. Allen Friedman explained the maneuver: "[Harold] would make a big show about it, and he told the boss on the phone, 'Don't worry, we'll get rid of this worker, but we will make a big show for the National Labor Relations Board.' He'd get this public stenographer . . . and they'd go out and have a hearing and that hearing meant nothing. They got rid of that member." Allen said Harold conspired with managers to have workers he didn't like fired. "If you wrote out too many grievances on 507, I found out that Harold would tell bosses to fire them, plant

146

nuts or bolts [in their lockers], or if it was a food warehouse, put in some cans of mustard or catsup, and then [they]'d have an inspection and that was pilfering." In some of Local 507's contracts, pilfering was automatic, uncontestable grounds for firing.

Harold Friedman infused this autocratic spirit in his corps of handpicked business agents. And if a Teamster worker claimed that Local 507 hadn't gone to bat for him, he was lying. At a Local 507 executive board meeting, he lectured his troops in clear, unmistakable terms: "Every single case that has been brought against us . . . is bullshit. Nobody can say anything different. These assholes walk in, 'I'm black, and that's why I got fired. I'm Italian, and that's why I got fired. I'm a woman and that's why I got fired. I'm a Puerto Rican and that why I got fired.' Nobody gets fired in this union. They fire themselves. They won't come to work. When they do come to work, they won't work. They're either stealing or something or smacking some boss, or something like that."

Though Harold Friedman was a dictator, many considered him a benevolent dictator. Through his efforts, Local 507 members earned good wages, received superior pensions, and enjoyed unusual fringe benefits. For instance, if you donated blood at the Red Cross blood bank, you had the day off. It said so right in the contract. A worker could sign out for a Friday donation, spend a few minutes in the morning giving a pint of blood, then take a long weekend. For five workdays before Christmas, Local 507 threw a giant Christmas party, costing several hundred thousand dollars, for all the members and their families. They came down and picked up free turkeys and gifts—flashlights, travel bags, coolers, all embossed with the Teamsters symbol. The party bought the loyalty and good feelings of many members who never gave another thought to the officers' huge salaries.

During the five-day-long Christmas party, Harold stayed in his office and worked, while Jackie, if he was in town, worked the crowd. It didn't mean Harold wasn't a supporter of the party, just that he didn't feel comfortable mingling with the masses. He often bragged about the Christmas party when listing Local 507's accomplishments. "Over thirty thousand of our members and their families attended," he once said. "We spent over $400,000 on gifts and food for the party, and it worked out quite well. It was really one of the biggest and nicest parties in the world. In fact, everything we do is the biggest. Our blood bank is the biggest; our Christmas party is the biggest; and all the other things that we do are the biggest. Of course, there's a saying, Big does not make it better. Well, we're better, whether we're big or not, you know. We just do one hell of a job for our people."

Harold loved to boast about Local 507, usually in front of a captive audience of business agents and union accountants at executive board meetings. Not that they needed indoctrination; they'd heard it many times before. To an outsider, it sounded almost like a pep talk. Harold would trumpet the Local 507 contracts, the double time on Sundays, the sick days, the full day off for donating blood, the two roving holidays among the thirteen a year that members received. "We've got the greatest contracts in the world, and we operate the best goddamn local," Friedman said. "Nine million dollars a year we're paying out in health and welfare and surgical benefits. We have a surgical plan, a health and welfare plan second to none. . . . You can't show me a plan anywhere that can compare to ours. Every doctor bill that you have is paid in full. Visitations in the hospital, operations, as long as it's reasonable and customary, it's paid in full. The hospital bill is paid in full. Pregnancy, paid in full. You can't go to the hospital, you, your wife, your kids in this local, and not have everything paid in full. The ambulance is paid in full. If you go in because you're kooky in the head, we pay it in full."

For the obsessive Harold Friedman, everything about Local 507 had to be the biggest and the best—from its parties to his salary to its charitable causes. "The Teamsters had a blood bank for fifteen years, and they never got fifty pints of blood," he said. "Bill Presser told me and Jackie to take that blood bank over, and we've now made it the biggest in the world. The same thing with the picnic. They told us to take it over, and we made it the biggest in the world. We've got a talent. Everybody has a talent—some guys are great artists—and I'm proud and I don't mind bragging about it."

Harold believed he was creating a labor-movement masterpiece with Local 507, a work of grand perfection. The maestro hid in the background with his huge salary, not once giving an interview, while Jackie took all the credit.

148

11

Pardon Me

"Unless you have that political strength, you're not going to be around very much longer."

BILL PRESSER

It was an unusual scene. Bill Presser, Mr. Stay-at-home, was standing under the glittering light of giant chandeliers, his 297 pounds packed into a tuxedo, squeezing hands, slapping backs, and basking in a glow of praise.

On the night of June 24, 1967, a stunning array of the rich and powerful walked into the ballroom of the Cleveland Sheraton Hotel, including acting Teamsters president Frank Fitzsimmons, the governor of Ohio, the mayor of Cleveland, federal judges, millionaire founders of Fortune 500 companies. They kept streaming in: Sam Klein of Bally Manufacturing; Gabe Paul, president of the Cleveland Indians; Julie Kravitz, founder of the Pick-n-Pay supermarket chain; assorted U.S. congressmen; and many other potentates.

They were attending a testimonial dinner honoring Bill Presser for his charitable work with the mentally retarded. To those who knew Presser well, the event seemed odd. He didn't like to put himself in the public eye or be fussed over, even though, as one of the most powerful men in Ohio, he could have commanded such a star-studded event years ago. Another oddity was that Bill, who hated reporters, knew they'd be out in force at the gala. So why was he going through with it?

The uncharacteristic event was a choreographed performance

149

carefully designed to aid Bill's lawyers, who were asking President Johnson to grant Bill a pardon for his 1961 conviction of criminally obstructing the McClellan committee's investigation. Presser's health was deteriorating, and he wanted to refurbish his tarnished reputation before he died.

Faye Presser and Ernie L. Zeve, a family friend, organized the testimonial dinner, selling tickets for fifty or a hundred dollars each. The profits were to go to the Parents Volunteer Association for Retarded Children, which ran two nonprofit homes for mentally handicapped young adults at which Faye occasionally volunteered. Balding, grandfatherly, a seemingly sincere advocate for the handicapped, Zeve actually was one of Bill's more unsavory acquaintances. Born in 1906, Zeve served as the executive director of PVA and two other local charities, all of which raised tens of thousands of dollars through loosely supervised bingo games. It was suspected that Mob associates were skimming the bingo earnings. As a charity fund-raiser, Zeve was connected with local judges and state lawmakers, many of whom sat on the boards of his charities and were unaware of his shadowy background. Zeve owned the Hotel Sterling, a haven for prostitutes and the site of a high-stakes gambling game held in its basement with the blessing of the Mob, according to police intelligence.

Zeve and Faye Presser poured great effort into the dinner, eventually selling fifteen hundred tickets. They also had a printer design a keepsake program for the event, an impressive, well-written valentine to Bill Presser, tastefully engraved on thick, expensive stock. The program described him in near-saintly terms and then quoted him at length:

> In any walk of life, those who do nothing are never targets of criticism by anyone. Those people who believe in what they are doing and fight for the cause—especially those who are trailblazers—have always been a focal-point for criticism by people of limited stature.
>
> Believing in the cause of labor, having spent my entire adult life in working to the best of my ability in behalf of this cause, and taking controversial positions from a political point of view as well as from the standpoint of organized labor, I have many times been confronted with painful personal decisions. But believing as I

have, my position has always been never to run out on myself, my fellow workers, or on the people I represented.

My thinking for the future will be no different than it has been over the past forty-odd years. I shall remain faithful to my principles, to the cause of organized labor, and to over a hundred thousand members in the state of Ohio for whose welfare I am responsible.

The testimonial raised roughly $100,000, according to the union, and Bill Presser benefited from several soft-touch stories in Cleveland newspapers that lauded his charitable work. The reports didn't mention Zeve's background or Bill Presser's lobbying for a presidential pardon. Not long after the fund-raising dinner, Presser's supporters made sure to send the U.S. Pardon Attorney one of the fancy testimonial programs, which featured laudatory letters from Ohio governor James Rhodes and Cleveland mayor Ralph Locher. The program fairly shouted, Here is the most respected citizen of the state and please take note of his work with charities.

It also didn't hurt Presser's chances for a pardon that he humbled himself in his application to President Johnson. "I violated the law and justly deserved the sentence given me by my peers," said his carefully handwritten plea. "I respectfully pray for your consideration so that I may hold my head high for my country, my children and grandchildren. That the burden on my concious [sic] be lifted and I once again can feel free and untainted as an American citizen. No man can have a greater love for country or family, and it is my desire that the remaining years of my life be dedicated in the furtherance of this cause and feeling!"

While Bill Presser tried to erase his prison record, Jimmy Hoffa was adding to his own. Not long before Presser's testimonial dinner, Hoffa surrendered to U.S. Marshals and was shipped to Lewisburg Federal Prison in central Pennsylvania to begin serving a thirteen-year sentence for jury fixing and pension fraud.

In his first hour in prison, Hoffa was fingerprinted, stripped, sprayed for lice, and slapped into an isolation cell for twenty-four hours. He knew the idea was to break him down, show him who was boss, but

151

he wasn't going to submit; he was the president of the Teamsters. At fifty-four, Hoffa was one of Lewisburg's older prisoners, but he could still snap off one hundred push-ups. Except for his mild diabetes, Hoffa felt in good shape. The guards checked him into a seven-and-a-half by ten-foot cell, confiscated his diabetes pills, and flushed them down the toilet. He protested, showing them a letter from his doctor. They tore it up. Welcome to Lewisburg, Mr. Big Shot Labor Boss.

It didn't take long for Hoffa to understand why Bill Presser, at fifty-six, had nearly cracked during his eight months in the federal pen in Minnesota. Prison was tough on men used to being the boss. Hoffa was quickly complaining about the rotten food, the cramped cells, and the capriciously vicious guards. Ever the organizer, he staged a short-lived food strike and demanded to see the warden. The warden appeared at the mess hall and agreed that the food should be improved; it was, for a while. After Hoffa won his release from prison, he wrote, "I spent fifty-eight months in Lewisburg, and I can tell you this on a stack of Bibles: prisons are archaic, brutal, unregenerative, overcrowded hell holes where the inmates are treated like animals with absolutely not one humane thought given to what they are going to do once they are released. You're like an animal in a cage and you're treated like one."

Hoffa had expected to run the Teamsters from his cell block, relaying messages in and out through visitors. That was why he picked Teamsters vice president Frank Fitzsimmons as his stand-in. Hoffa considered him a loyal but weak coat holder who would give up the top job when Hoffa was released from prison in what he figured would be a couple of years. But Hoffa miscalculated. Fitz refused to be his patsy and eventually started working behind the scenes with Bill Presser and the new Nixon administration to keep his mentor imprisoned.

Using his network of supporters in the union, Hoffa learned in frustrating detail which Teamsters leaders across the country had lined up with acting president Fitzsimmons. Bill Presser was one of them. Like most regional and state conference bosses, Presser enjoyed new power and freedom under the hands-off Fitzsimmons regime. He ran the Ohio Teamsters with only the slightest oversight from the once-suffocating IBT board. "They went with Fitz because his style of managing the union appealed to them," says Presser's friend, Robert Hughes, the Republican party chairman of Cuyahoga County. "Fitzsimmons was decentralizing control. He was less a power-driven guy than Hoffa."

It wasn't until August 30, 1967, five months after Hoffa was locked in Lewisburg, that Bill Presser, after nearly two decades of behind-the-scenes service to Hoffa, was chosen by Fitz and the other vice presidents to fill a vacancy on the IBT executive board. The position didn't necessarily give Presser more political power, but it did give him a boost in salary and, to outsiders, more prestige. Presser now took part in the quarterly meetings of the IBT executive board. Under Fitz, vice presidents actually got to hash out national policy at the meetings. Hoffa fumed in prison about reports that his handpicked stand-in was allowing regional Teamsters heads to usurp powers that Hoffa felt belonged to the president. Hoffa was also infuriated when he heard that Fitz was playing a lot of golf and getting accustomed to the soft country-club life. He vowed he'd put a stop to that when he got out of prison.

Meanwhile, Bill worked on his presidential pardon, getting friendly elected officials to intervene with the president, trying to influence what essentially was a political decision by the Justice Department.

U.S. district court judge James Connell, who had received one of Bill's infamous champagne buckets, said he "would be very happy to speak directly to the president or the attorney general on this matter." Ohio governor James Rhodes promised, "I will call the president direct." The Cleveland police chief, the county prosecutor and sheriff, eleven U.S. congressmen, a senator, and fifteen judges all signed a petition asking President Johnson to pardon Bill Presser. Business leaders who had Teamster employees were also eager to lend support. The editor of the *Cleveland Press*, whose delivery trucks were driven by Teamsters, signed the petition. Thomas Vail, editor and publisher of the *Plain Dealer*, the most influential paper in the state, promised to call or write a letter to Johnson.

Presser's political strength stemmed from Ohio DRIVE, a political action committee whose initials stood for Democratic, Republican, Independent Voter Education. Ohio DRIVE made contributions to political campaigns and endorsed candidates. It was part of a national Teamster lobbying network called Teamsters DRIVE, started by Hoffa in 1961 to line up members of Congress who would help him try to blunt future congressional investigations into the Teamsters.

Since federal law prohibited unions from spending members' dues on political candidates, Ohio DRIVE raised its funds from Teamsters who volunteered five dollars a year from their paychecks. Long before he began lobbying for a presidential pardon, Bill Presser realized the tremendous utility of Ohio DRIVE and worked hard to fill its coffers. At first, less than a quarter of Ohio Teamsters members contributed to Ohio DRIVE, which irked Bill Presser. At some locals, such as Jackie's Local 507, nearly all of their members donated five dollars a year. But this was rare. At union meetings, Bill constantly harped to Teamsters leaders from across the state that they had to register their members to vote, enroll them in Ohio DRIVE, and raise money for contributions that, in turn, could influence votes on labor legislation and other matters.

"Unless you have that political strength, you're not going to be around very much longer," Bill lectured. "We need DRIVE because we need the voting power, and without the voting power, we can't reach the politicians, because there's only two ways to reach a politician, an honest one with votes, and the dishonest one with money. It's been many a year since I've seen money. . . . The only way we can keep that asbestos cover around us is for you to supply us the people we need for the votes, and, of course, very importantly the wherewithal to supply the money to keep those people around us."

The Pressers "recognized early on that with all the problems the Teamsters had, it would be well to maintain civic relations in the community," explained Cuyahoga County Republican party chairman Robert Hughes. Ohio DRIVE's funds attracted elected officials willing to return political favors on legislation and appointments. By the seventies, Ohio DRIVE would become a coat of armor for the Pressers. "There is no other state in this union that has anywhere near the operation you've got here," Bill once bragged to a meeting of Teamster officials who worked with Ohio DRIVE. The Cleveland Mob was well aware of the Teamsters political muscle and repeatedly asked the Pressers to intercede with judges and other elected officials for favors. Cleveland Mafia figure James "Jack White" Licavoli noted enviously that the union was "always connected with judges—they always got connections with somebody." They do this by donating money—"you know what I mean," Licavoli said.

Bill pushed Jackie into Ohio DRIVE. "Yes, Jackie will be around to see you," Bill once told a meeting of Ohio Teamster officials. "But he's a nice fellow, and still just a little bit soft, but he's learning fast. We're going to be around to see you, and we want action, fellows. We want that membership, five dollars a year. It's funny, no one wants to throw away five dollars, but that five dollars gives a limitless policy of protection for the people who work under our mantle of membership, and for you folks as officers of those unions, it's a must. We must have it, and you must go out and help us get it. . . . If you don't, I'm going to scheme and connive and find some way of doing it around you."

Even fireball Faye Presser got into the act, starting a Ladies Auxiliary DRIVE in the early sixties. Carl B. Stokes, the first black mayor of a big city, was elected in 1967 with help from Faye and the Presser DRIVE machine. "Bill would be the one to hand you the check," Stokes said. "The person you would have a dialogue with and the person who I think made the decisions who to give the endorsements to was Faye. Faye worked very close to Bill. She knew people who were meaningful to the Teamsters. She had the women's organization. That was really the political arm."

Members of Ladies Auxiliary DRIVE, mostly wives of Teamsters, handed out leaflets and worked phone banks for candidates whom the union supported. "You could always count on your literature getting out," Stokes recalls. "The only person I knew who took responsibility for that and did it was Faye's group. DRIVE would send the ballot out. When you needed people to do the work over and above that, it would be Faye's women. They'd be the ones to give the rally and do mailings for you and circulate literature. In fact, I don't know of any group during that time that did the kind of organized work the women's DRIVE did."

In exchange for Teamsters' backing, Stokes promised Bill that as mayor he'd allow some of the city's unorganized workers to join trade unions. Shortly after the election, Bill telephoned Stokes and held him to the promise.

Bill Presser's political operation reached into the smallest offices. He instructed his Ohio DRIVE operatives to interview candidates for suburban council seats, for the office of village mayor, municipal judge, county sheriff, and so on. Sooner or later, Jackie once explained, these minor officials were called on to return favors, usually when a teamster got into a minor scrape and needed clout with local law enforcers. "We have to go to some of the politicians," Jackie explained in a closed-door meeting of Teamster officials. "Many of [the] membership get arrested. They have kids doing time in institutions, bad-boy schools, federal institutions, state institutions, and we have to go to the politicians. And God only knows how many of our members get arrested for fighting, reckless driving, and driving without a driver's license, having their driver's license revoked."

It was the contacts and goodwill generated by Ohio DRIVE that the Pressers called on repeatedly to try to get Bill a presidential pardon.

The Justice Department's pardon process was slow, partly because the FBI had to conduct a background check on Presser for the Pardon Attorney's Office, making sure he was keeping his nose clean. In the spring of 1968, Bill was diagnosed as having a cancerous tumor on his rectum that required immediate surgery. Ernie Zeve and Faye stepped up their efforts, using the illness as another argument for the pardon. In a report included in the pardon pleadings, Presser's surgeon, Dr. Victor Scharf, noted, "Mr. Presser is an extremely obese patient. This type of extensive surgery may be associated with significant morbidity and mortality. If he survives the operative procedure, he will still have a very guarded prognosis for life." Scharf predicted that he would have to remove Presser's rectum and create a new opening for the colon.

Several days before Presser's surgery, three members of Congress from Ohio, Charles Vanik, Frances Bolton, and Michael Feighan, wrote a letter urging the U.S. Pardon Attorney to recommend immediate clemency for Presser. Another Presser friend, Congressman Michael J. Kirwan, was also asked to sign this letter but refused; in doing so, he tacitly acknowledged Presser's Mob ties. A memo in Presser's pardon file, obtained for this book, recounts a telephone conversation Kirwan expected to remain private. "Bill is an upstanding gentleman," Kirwan explained, "but I'm eighty-two years old. I don't want to have to take a chance and get smeared by the newspapers like I did several years ago."

Kirwan was referring to the headlines he got from the Senate's Kefauver committee's investigations into organized crime in the early fifties. As a congressman from Youngstown, one of the country's most politically corrupt cities, Kirwan had persuaded unsuspecting colleagues in the House to pass a bill delaying the deportation of Frank Cammarata as an undesirable alien. Cammarata was the brother-in-law of powerful Detroit Mafia figure Pete Licavoli, who got his start in that city's notorious Prohibition-era Purple Gang. Newspapers picked up the Kefauver revelation and embarrassed Kirwan throughout the state.

Despite his surgeon's prediction to the Pardon Attorney, Bill Presser didn't need a colostomy. Dr. Scharf stitched him up with extra-gauge silk sutures, and the big labor boss recovered much more quickly than expected.

The Johnson administration, meanwhile, moved so slowly on Presser's pardon that a new president was elected before a decision was made. When Richard Nixon took over the White House in January 1969, the Presser camp stepped up its efforts to paint Big Bill as a humanitarian worthy of special consideration. In May 1969, Bill Presser was honored at yet another black-tie testimonial dinner, this time for convincing—some would say forcing—trustees of the Teamsters pension plans to invest $1.5 million in State of Israel bonds. It took Presser only three weeks to corral Teamsters locals and other unions into buying the bonds for their pension-plan portfolios, even though the bonds only yielded about four percent. Some Teamster officials privately complained about being forced to buy the low-yielding bonds, but they didn't want to cross Bill. As head of the Ohio Conference of Teamsters, he could retaliate by withholding their organizing funds and other favors. At his testimonial dinner, the host read a telegram from Israel Prime Minister Golda Meir, thanking Presser for his efforts.

A final stroke in Presser's campaign for a pardon was a comment entered into the *Congressional Record* by Representative Michael Feighan praising Big Bill. "To each of his duties, he brings a quiet, thoughtful, kindly approach," Feighan's paean read. "A steady succession of problems involving people from all walks of life find their way to his office, where quietly, humbly, and with apparent ease, solutions acceptable to all seem to emanate from this slightly heavy-set fellow who you sometimes think is dozing as you talk to him, only to have him quickly and incisively go to the heart of the problem you have brought him."

The pardon process dragged on, and Presser continued to pile up

157

goodwill, not necessarily out of calculation, but because it was his nature. He seemed to enjoy doing small personal favors for rank-and-file members who petitioned him. Like a political party boss, Presser got jobs for people, loaned them small amounts of money, and, when he had time, enjoyed sitting around and talking to them. He possessed a common touch that his ambitious son would never master.

"Jackie loved power and liked to manipulate and got his rocks off on that," says a Teamster executive who knew both of them well. "Bill liked people and did a lot of favors. If you crossed him, he could be rough. But he was just a popular human being. . . . Even though I knew him in his twilight, I could see it. He'd sit in a hotel lobby and talk to the maid and the bellman. People would drive in for a grievance, and he'd give them money to get back. He was a unique individual. He could have been a good public servant."

One reason Presser's pardon was moving so slowly through the Justice Department was that its Cleveland office of the Strike Force Against Organized Crime was looking into a shakedown operation Bill and a Chicago associate were running in Ohio, particularly Greater Cleveland.

The Cleveland area was a bustling trucking hub, ripe for the picking; two-thirds of the nation's hundred largest trucking companies operated depots there. These depots did a disproportionate amount of middleman hauling, since the city was roughly halfway between Chicago and New York, the two largest suppliers of commercial products. If Bill Presser wanted to punish a certain company, he could use Cleveland as an economic choke point. Into this intensely competitive climate came James A. Franks, an old-time Chicago hoodlum who, with his dark glasses, brimmed hat, and hoarse voice, looked like someone hired from central casting for a Jimmy Cagney movie.

Their venture began in November 1963 when Presser named Franks public-relations consultant to Teamsters Joint Council 41. By the next spring, Franks, sixty-six years old, began touring the state in his Cadillac, visiting trucking-firm owners and managers and working an old shakedown scam similar to the one Bill had used with vending-machine companies a decade earlier. With all the subtlety of a sucker punch, Franks would drop in unannounced at a firm's business office, proclaim he was an emissary of Bill Presser, and pose a series of ominous questions.

158

"You don't have any labor problems here, do you?"

No, the answer would be.

"See, Mr. Presser wanted me to make sure you didn't have any labor problems here."

We have no problems.

"That's good that you don't have any labor problems. You don't want any of them problems, do you?"

Of course not, the owner would say, by now squirming uncomfortably in his seat.

Franks would then tell the trucking executive about the advertising he was selling for the *Ohio Teamster* and that Mr. Presser thought his company would be interested in buying an ad. The trucking execs— some employing teamsters, others nonunion—quickly got the message: Rather than risk costly, potentially ruinous strikes, slowdowns, or organizing drives, they could buy labor peace for several hundred dollars under the guise of purchasing an ad.

Franks was a persistent solicitor. Told that the company owner was out, he'd gruffly tell the secretary he'd wait, and wait he did, slouching down in the big front seat of his Cadillac and peering out for hours at the entrances, waiting for the executive to return. Between 1964 and 1970, at least sixty-three Ohio trucking firms shelled out more than $594,000 to Franks for so-called ads in the *Ohio Teamster.* The Cleveland Browns football team even spent two thousand dollars.

Franks also put the touch on these trucking companies for ads in what he called special editions of the *Journal.* There was going to be a special Labor Day edition, a Christmas edition, even a Bill Presser testimonial edition. However, only two editions of the *Ohio Teamster* were ever run off, in 1966 and 1970, with a few supplemental pages printed in 1968. Even then, only five hundred copies of the newsprint tabloid were printed each time, a job that cost at most a few thousand dollars. The special editions were never published.

So where did all the money go? According to Bill Presser, three-quarters of the more than $594,000 went to Franks for his commissions and expenses, and the rest went into Teamsters Joint Council 41 bank accounts and was spent on unspecified charitable causes. Presser insisted that he personally didn't profit a penny. Jackie told his FBI handler that Hoffa got all the money.

But during its probe in the late sixties, the Labor Department checked out Franks's Chicago life-style and finances and found that he lived quite modestly for someone who was supposedly earning that much cash. Franks had to be kicking back money to Presser, but labor agents couldn't prove it. "If you know anything about labor racketeering and you know about Presser and his dealings with other people, you know he got the money," said one of the Labor Department's most seasoned racketeering investigators. Franks also neglected to file federal tax returns from 1964 to 1970.

Franks and Presser's downfall came about because some of the companies paid for the elusive ads by check. A former Labor Department official said that a routine Interstate Commerce Commission audit revealed that a trucking company had made a payment to Joint Council 41. On face value, this was a misdemeanor violation of the Taft-Hartley Act, which banned companies from giving anything of value to a union. After investigating, Labor Department officials felt they had an even stronger case and expected Presser and Franks to be charged with felony extortion. But a strike-force attorney recommended lesser misdemeanor charges, and Bill was indicted in July 1970.

The indictment killed his pardon. A few weeks later, the pardon Attorney sent Presser a letter, telling him to forget about getting a presidential pardon. It had just been denied.

On January 22, 1971, Presser and Franks pleaded guilty to some of the charges and waited for sentencing by federal judge Thomas Lambros. A few weeks later, Bill showed up in the courtroom, sporting a winter tan but looking glum. He faced up to eight years in prison and $80,000 in fines.

"The court feels that the offense here is serious enough to impose a prison sentence," Lambros intoned, giving the Presser camp a jolt. Then the judge started talking about Bill's age and his operation for cancer and finished up by giving him a suspended sentence and a $12,000 fine, to be paid in one week. The strike-force lawyers and Labor Department investigators were extremely disappointed.

Judge Lambros's decision, however, did put Big Bill in a jolly mood. "No comment," he said jauntily to reporters on his way out of the courtroom, "unless you can give me $12,000."

† † †

Bill was subsequently hit again with more bad news about his health. He was diagnosed as having diabetes then told he had to undergo surgery on his gallbladder. It looked at if he wouldn't live much longer, and it became a burning concern whether Jackie would take over his positions in the union. Both of them had talked about the succession, but it wasn't a simple procedure. Jackie had only been back in the Teamsters for a few years and was clearly unprepared to take over as president of Joint Council 41 or the Ohio Conference of Teamsters. Babe Triscaro, the number-two man in the joint council since 1951 and closely connected to the Cleveland Mafia family, deserved the top spot if Bill Presser died. In fact, Bill remarked in 1970, "When I step down, Babe will take the reins. There is too much between our families for it to be any other way."

Whether Bill truly wanted Babe to take over at that time is unclear. One thing is certain—to have installed Jackie before he possessed enough clout might have ignited a war between the Italian and Jewish factions of the Teamsters as well as their counterparts in the Cleveland underworld. "Bill certainly was going to bring his son along," Carl Stokes says. "No question that Bill wanted to see Jackie succeed him." But Jackie, who craved public approval and who possessed tremendous ambition, wanted to climb higher in the Teamsters than his father had. "Apparently at that time, Jackie was expressing his aspirations to them that he wanted to be the number-one guy," says Stokes.

At the time, the chances of Jackie ever becoming president of the Teamsters were extremely slim, and even Bill and Faye didn't encourage their son in his dangerous, wishful thinking. "Bill's fears were that all the things that were visited on him—what he felt was persecution by the government, wiretapping, bugging, and all that—was something that would be only magnified for the guy who was the head of the union," Stokes recalls. Bill also knew that his son, if he were to become Teamsters president, would have to accommodate the Mob, Stokes says, which brought with it all sorts of tricky problems, everything from obsessive Justice Department scrutiny to Mafia death threats.

As Jackie admitted at the time, "I know that the higher I go in this union, the greater my chances of someone trying to get me, no matter what I do."

12

Courting Nixon

"Teamsters are stand-up guys."
PRESIDENT RICHARD M. NIXON

Bill Presser wasn't able to enjoy the break he got from Judge Lambros. Before he could catch his breath, the Cleveland Strike Force charged back at him, this time investigating oddities in his union expense account—among them, a Teamsters-paid vacation he took to Hot Springs, Arkansas, and a round-trip airline ticket he approved for a woman who visited Faye at their Miami Beach condominium. The Justice Department was never going to stop dogging him, no matter how tiny the supposed infraction, Bill decided. If only there was a way he could get the government to leave him alone.

Unknown to Presser, one reason he and his family were perennial grand-jury targets was his appearance in the Justice Department's Racketeer Profile, a computerized listing of organized-crime figures and suspected labor racketeers. Until he dropped off the Racketeer Profile list, Presser would forever be the target of ambitious prosecutors and federal agents, since the strike force routinely updated the Racketeer Profile and shared it with the FBI and other agencies.

Robert D. Gary was the thirty-year-old strike-force prosecutor supervising the probe into Presser's union expense account. Years later, Gary hinted that Presser may have been unfairly monitored. "There was no special consideration given to the Presser family," Gary explained. "If anything, they were the target of everything. During the time I was at the strike force and we were pursuing these cases, there

162

couldn't have been more aggressive investigation. I learned just how powerful the government was, because it was so vigorous in going after the Pressers."

In early 1971, Bill Presser tried out two new strategies to get the Justice Department off his back.

The first was to call upon the Teamsters' growing influence with the Nixon administration. To put this in motion, Bill complained to Teamsters acting president Frank Fitzsimmons about being hounded by the Justice Department. Fitz tried to see if he could use his power as Teamsters president to keep his powerful ally on the executive board out of trouble.

On April 29, 1971, Fitzsimmons was chauffered down Pennsylvania Avenue to the Old Executive Office Building and escorted into a large suite of offices assigned to his new White House friend, Charles W. Colson, special counsel to President Nixon. Colson, Nixon's ruthless point man for labor unions, had spent the past several months aggressively courting labor leaders for Nixon's 1972 reelection campaign. Winning over the biggest, toughest union, the Teamsters, was a crucial element in his strategy.

A captivating talker and a tough, aggressive ex–marine commander, Colson had intrigued Nixon with the idea of gathering up alienated, blue-collar Democrats from the key industrial states and forging them with Republicans into a new majority. At the time, many of the Democratic party's mainstays—blue collars and Catholics— supported the Vietnam War, were opposed to the growing abortion-rights movement, and found themselves more in tune with Republican sentiments.

Fitzsimmons sat down and hit Colson with a torrent of gripes about the Justice Department: The Feds are harassing us more than in the Kennedy days, he complained. I thought the Teamsters and the president were friends. Why are we being picked on for nickel-and-dime stuff? Other unions do the same thing and the Justice Department ignores it.

As an example of Justice Department harassment, Fitzsimmons brought up Bill Presser. Putting a rosy hue on the shakedown scheme, Fitz said that a public-relations consultant had gotten Presser in trouble by collecting money from trucking firms for ads in Presser's house newspaper. Yet the public-relations man had done the same thing for three other union leaders who weren't investigated. I don't defend what Presser did, Fitz said, but why doesn't the government pick on the other guys?

Colson listened carefully. He had been working intensely for the past eight months to ingratiate Nixon with the Teamsters, which was why Fitzsimmons felt comfortable enough to visit the White House and ask for a favor in the first place. Colson didn't want anything to tear the delicate relationship he had tacked together; in just a few months, the 1972 presidential campaign would be chugging full-steam ahead, and Nixon wanted the Teamsters endorsement. The union had gone with Senator Hubert Humphrey in 1968. This time, Colson was determined to capture the Teamsters' support for Nixon.

After hearing Fitzsimmons's gripes about the supposed harassment of Bill Presser, Colson, through White House counsel John Dean, asked the Justice Department to go easy on some of the administration's powerful labor-union allies who were being charged with corruption. Actually, Colson had started this process in the fall of 1970. On September 14, in a memo to White House chief of staff Bob Haldeman, Colson suggested that the White House try to derail certain Justice Department criminal investigations into labor leaders, who might then swing their unions' support to Nixon. The breadth of Colson's activities have largely been secret until now. If they had been known in detail by the Watergate Special Prosecutor, Colson's actions might have earned him additional charges of obstruction of justice.

One union official Colson wanted to help was Paul Hall, president of the International Seafarers Union, who was charged with improper election activities. "I would like your permission," Colson wrote to Haldeman on September 8, "to have a confidential meeting with the Attorney General to discuss how the Seafarers prosecution is handled. At the moment, Paul Hall does not blame us but rather accuses the 'bureaucrats in the Justice Department' of harassing him. This is potentially very serious because Hall has enormous influence within the Executive Council and is a real possibility as Meany's successor." AFL-CIO executive Lane Kirkland had the inside track, Colson realized, but he was cultivating Hall and other dark-horse candidates just in case.

Colson also tried to get the Justice Department to go easy on Elwood Moffett, president of the Allied Technical Workers. Colson told Haldeman in a memo, "There is also a prospective indictment of

164

the president of the Allied Technical Workers based on the charge that he misused about ten thousand dollars of union funds over a five-year period on various trips. This is nonsense, and I would also like to bring this up with the Attorney General. This union generally endorses Republicans."

Haldeman must have approved the request, because within weeks, Colson and Nixon's White House counsel, John Dean, met with Attorney General John Mitchell and told him that there wasn't a case against Moffett. An indictment was handed up, but Moffett was acquitted. Anticipating a backlash against the Justice Department because of the acquittal, Colson warned Dean in a December 13, 1971, memo, "Remember we talked to the AG . . . and told them there really wasn't a case. I suppose now the zealots will appeal this all the way. Keep me out of this please. You may recall we both were in this rather deeply once before."

Colson also scurried to the aid of Teamsters union associate Daniel Gagliardi, a hoodlum from New York. Gagliardi was being investigated for extortion, and a January 19, 1972, Justice Department memo predicted that he was to be indicted "sometime next month." Gagliardi knew what to do. He called Colson's office, known by now for coddling labor leaders, and ended up speaking to Colson's deputy, George Bell.

"I talked to Gagliardi, who maintained complete ignorance and innocence regarding the Teamsters," Bell wrote to Colson. "[He] asked that he be gotten off the hook."

"Watch for this," Colson instructed him. "Do all possible." Gagliardi was never indicted.

Nixon and his top aides obviously were willing to compromise the Justice Department at its highest levels if it served the president's political purposes.

A second tactic Bill used to try to ward off Justice Department scrutiny was suggested by a Cleveland Mafia figure, Anthony Liberatore. Liberatore said that he had a friend who could pull strings for Bill at the top of the Justice Department. Unknown to Presser and Liberatore, the friend, Harry Haler, was a notorious West Coast confidence man.

Tony Liberatore, a Laborers Union official soon to be inducted into the Mafia, had served twenty years for murdering two Cleveland policemen. He was pardoned by an interim Ohio governor in 1958 and became acquainted with Jackie and his father shortly thereafter. It was Tony's brother, Hadrian John Liberatore, a member of the Los Angeles Mafia, who had first met Harry Haler. Harry dropped names and spun captivating stories of his political contacts in Washington, endearing himself to Hadrian and the Los Angeles family. To them, Justice Department connections were worth more than gold.

A smooth, gray-haired, spectacled, avuncular man, Haler spent six years in a Chicago orphanage in the thirties, where he first learned how to lie convincingly. Later, he took up gambling and white-collar crime. "I get people to loan me money," he once explained. "Then I run. That's all I've ever done."

Haler's specialty was taking money from hoodlums after promising to get their criminal cases dismissed by the Justice Department. In 1962, calling himself a sports promoter, Haler befriended a California boxing official, Truman Gibson, on trial for illegal activities. For $12,000, Haler promised to get him off. To carry through with the charade and snag the hefty payoff, Haler visited William Hundley, the chief of the Justice Department's Organized Crime Section under Attorney General Robert F. Kennedy, and made a case for his new-found friend. According to federal officials, Haler stole Justice Department stationery, or, as Haler claims, he had some Justice Department letterhead printed up. He then forged Hundley's name to a phony letter announcing that Gibson's case was dismissed because of new information provided by Mr. Harry Haler. Haler passed the letter on to Gibson, who paid him $12,000.

There was a problem, however. Before long, Gibson was indicted on the charges Haler said he had convinced the Justice Department to dismiss. To Haler's surprise, the boxing official was so angry and unconcerned about implicating himself that he actually complained to Justice Department prosecutors that he had paid money to Haler to get his case thrown out. Federal agents arrested Haler, who was charged and convicted of forgery and served two years in prison.

Haler's exploits didn't stop there. President Kennedy was assassinated during his prison term, and Haler, learning that Jack Ruby had shot Kennedy assassin Lee Harvey Oswald, offered to set Ruby up for the FBI if it would help get his sentence reduced. For a while in the mid-fifties, Haler had roomed in Dallas with Ruby. Going by the name Harry Sinclair, Jr., Haler had joined Ruby in working bet-and-run swindles in Dallas and Oklahoma City.

On November 30, 1963, Haler told federal agents that he'd be happy to go to Dallas, talk to his old pal Ruby, and uncover the circumstances that led up to Ruby's slaying of Oswald in the basement of the Dallas police headquarters. Possibly Ruby was in on the Kennedy murder from the start, Haler suggested. He mentioned that Ruby had Mob connections, owned numerous guns, was addicted to fried chicken, and even sold it takeout from his Dallas nightclub. Maybe this could account for the chicken remains supposedly found at the spot where Oswald had shot Kennedy, Haler suggested. The FBI turned down his offer to set up Ruby.

After Liberatore told the Pressers of Haler's Justice Department connections, a meeting was arranged. In 1971, Jackie, Carmen, Liberatore, and his wife took a trip to Las Vegas to meet with Haler. Jackie was a bit on edge, anxious to meet the man who might be able to help his father. "On the way there, I remember that Jackie was very excited about meeting him," Carmen Presser says. In Las Vegas, the two couples enjoyed regal treatment. After all, Jackie was an important teamster whose father had helped loan Teamsters money to build Vegas's flashy casinos, and Tony Liberatore was an up-and-coming Mafia power. Though he didn't wager much, Jackie liked the energy and the gaudy around-the-clock action of Las Vegas.

Tony made the introductions, and soon Haler was impressing Jackie with stories of his clout in the Justice Department. In fact, Haler was *persona non grata* there. William Lynch, head of the Organized Crime Section, knew about Haler's slick trick with Bill Hundley's stationery and told his associates that he refused to pursue cases in which Haler was providing information. Haler would put the pope in the Lindbergh kidnapping if he thought it would help him, Lynch complained. Still, over the years, the FBI, the IRS, and various police forces had used Haler as an informer, and according to court records, at least one of Haler's indictments had been dismissed because he had helped police on another, more important case.

Jackie, his father, and Tony Liberatore knew nothing of Haler's colorful past. If they had, they probably wouldn't have gotten involved with him. Jackie, an accomplished liar, had finally met someone more skillful than himself.

Haler spent quite a bit of time in Cleveland, cultivating Bill and socializing with Jackie and his new wife, Carmen. Finally, after years of promises, Jackie had filed for divorce from his third wife, claiming gross neglect. They had been separated for five years. Perhaps in response, Patricia Presser collapsed and was checked into a nursing home, where she was served with divorce papers on February 11, 1971. A month later, without a lawyer to represent her, Pat signed the divorce agreement. Jackie agreed to pay her $125 a week in alimony, plus medical and dental benefits until she died or remarried. She was to receive a late-model car and the profits from the sale of their Meadowbrook Boulevard home. She received the silverware and household goods. Jackie kept all the stocks and bonds listed on a page in the divorce proceedings that, curiously, was missing when the official court records were examined recently. Jackie took custody of his son Gary, who was living at the Bellfaire Home, a Jewish center for emotionally disturbed kids. Jackie retained full visitation rights to his daughter Bari and agreed to pay for her college tuition until she turned twenty-one.

Then Jackie repeated the pattern he would continue throughout his life: after the divorce came through, he immediately remarried. Nineteen days after Pat signed the agreement, Jackie and Carmen drove five hours from Cleveland to Covington, Kentucky, just over the river from Cincinnati, and finally got married. "We took a trip there with Tony Hughes and [his wife] Pat," Carmen said. "They stood up for us. It was the most horrible experience I ever had. Jackie had called a justice of the peace. He had looked it up in the phone book. We drove to Covington. He wanted to get married out of town because he didn't want any publicity. I don't know why. He keeps his life very private. We couldn't find the justice of the peace. We walked in this old building. It was falling apart. There were squeaky floorboards going up the stairs. We walked into this ghastly room with this old man dressed in mismatched clothes. It was awful, awful! The ceremony lasted nothing flat. There was nothing romantic about it at all. It was a very sad thing for me, because I had waited so long. Because I really loved him. That was that. Then we drove back."

168

† † †

Years later, Jackie would be embroiled in controversy because of Harry Haler, and to protect himself, Jackie would portray Haler as a con artist who tried to get close to him, but with whom he had little contact. This was untrue. He and Haler became fast friends in 1972 and 1973; they had dinner together dozens of times, by Carmen's estimation. The personable Haler even charmed Bill Presser, who had just been indicted again, courtesy of the Cleveland Strike Force. He was charged with five counts of misusing Joint Council 41 funds, including selling a $2,700 union car for one dollar to a retiring business agent and spending eighty-three dollars for a rental car he and his brother-in-law Harry Friedman used while on vacation in Hot Springs, Arkansas.

Haler didn't produce any top-level Justice Department administrators or nifty forged letters this time, but he did convince Bill and Jackie to meet with two IRS agents from the criminal-intelligence division who specialized in organized-crime cases. "I'm close with these guys," Haler insisted. "They can help you."

For several years, Haler had been an informant for IRS intelligence agents John Daley and Gabriel Dennis, who uncovered financial schemes and tax frauds for the Los Angeles office of the IRS. As a gambler and con artist, Haler had his hand in the Los Angeles, Las Vegas, and Chicago crime circles and provided valuable raw intelligence to the agents. Being a professional informant for the IRS and other agencies was his insurance policy when he got arrested on his own schemes. Though convicted eight times over the years, Haler had served a total of only five years in prison, less than eight months per conviction, not bad for a repeat offender.

Haler eventually convinced Bill and Jackie that if they provided the IRS with information, federal authorities, out of gratitude, might go easy on Bill in return. Daley and Dennis, he insisted, "would keep the heat off of you." Especially if the Pressers helped the IRS hook some big fish.

In mid-1971, while Teamsters executive officers held a meeting on the West Coast, Haler arranged for his primary handler, Daley, to meet the Pressers and Allen Dorfman at an Anaheim, California, motel. After Daley arrived, accompanied by a young agent, Bill Presser told Haler and Jackie to take a walk. Then Bill and Allen Dorfman, a powerful member of the Chicago Mob, began feeling out the agents, trying to determine how much help the IRS could give them.

It seemed to Daley that Presser and Dorfman were mostly worried that Hoffa would get out of prison and stage a comeback. They wanted to provide damaging information about his allies in the union and in private industry. Then the agents would be compelled to pursue these suspected crimes.

A few weeks later, Daley and Dennis met again with Haler. This time, Harry brought a new snitch, Teamsters president Frank Fitzsimmons. From 1971 to 1974, the two IRS agents met with Fitzsimmons, Jackie, and Bill in Washington, Miami, Las Vegas, Los Angeles, and at the La Costa Resort Hotel and Spa near San Diego. Haler set up the meetings and then left, allowing the agents to talk to the Teamsters leaders alone. Bill did most of the talking. Jackie attended only some of the meetings.

Fitz and Bill pretended to be candid with the two IRS agents about why they were informing. They claimed they wanted to rid the Teamsters Union of mobsters and racketeers, but the only names they coughed up were allies of Jimmy Hoffa. Daley and Dennis weren't fooled by this clumsy artifice, but they still were grateful for the valuable intelligence. The IRS agents told Fitz and the Pressers that they didn't have the authority to call off probes into the Teamsters by the IRS or other agencies. However, if called upon, the agents would tell a judge or prosecutor that Fitz or the Pressers had helped the government in other criminal cases. At the time, Bill Presser was under indictment in Cleveland for expense-account fraud, so this kind of insurance came in handy. "What they wanted to do, actually, what Jackie and his father really wanted to do, was get rid of the Hoffa guys," Haler recalls.

Eventually, according to federal investigators familiar with Daley and Dennis's reports, the Pressers and Fitzsimmons reached an agreement with the IRS in which they would offer up targets of exchange, persons the Justice Department would prosecute instead of Presser and Fitzsimmons supporters in the Teamsters. Three of the targets of exchange mentioned prominently in Daley and Dennis's reports were Hoffa, Teamsters vice president Harold Gibbons of St. Louis, and Jay Sarno, who had built two Las Vegas casino-hotels with loans from the Teamsters Central States Pension Fund. Presser and Fitzsimmons were terrified that Hoffa might return to power and wanted to bounce his friend Gibbons from the Teamsters executive board. Gibbons also wouldn't go along with their plans to endorse President Nixon over his Democratic challenger, Senator George McGovern. Bill and Fitz also tried to aim IRS auditors at Hoffa's allies in private industry, such as Jay Sarno. Eventually, the Pressers and Fitz added ten or twelve names to the White House's shameful enemies list.

Colson played a major part in compiling the enemies list, updating it regularly with memos from his staffer George Bell and others. Eventually, the list included some two hundred people and eighteen organizations. At the same time, as the Watergate investigators later discovered, Nixon and his cronies were pressuring the IRS to target his political enemies and to ignore the transgressions of his friends. John Dean did reveal that Colson asked him to initiate an audit on Harold Gibbons, a liberal Democrat whom Colson called "an all-out enemy." But Bill and Jackie's part in the Teamsters targets-of-exchange arrangement escaped scrutiny.

One reason that the two IRS agents agreed to the targets-of-exchange deal was that they thought they were soon going to be meeting with Jimmy Hoffa, who could give them a set of targets in the Presser-Fitzsimmons camp. This way, Daley and Dennis figured they'd have a pipeline into the entire spectrum of corrupt Teamsters leaders and their underworld associates. Unfortunately, it was Harry Haler who promised to deliver Hoffa. To convince the two agents of his access to Hoffa, Haler let Daley overhear a telephone conversation he had with the ex-Teamsters president. The IRS agents were never able to meet with Hoffa.

In all, Daley and Dennis compiled about five hundred pages of secret reports that detailed their cross-country meetings with the Pressers and Fitzsimmons. Sometimes those meetings turned into social events held right under the noses of the people the Pressers and Fitzsimmons had snitched on. In Miami, after an important Teamsters meeting, John Daley had dinner with Jackie and Bill and a dozen or so Teamsters leaders from Cleveland and across the country. As a cover, Jackie introduced Daley to the table as a Mafia hit man. Daley sat silently through the meal, soaking up the wise-guy gab while the Teamsters tried to impress him with stories of some of their scams.

† † †

By August 1971, after four years in prison, Hoffa was denied parole for the third time. He seethed. Fitz, Presser, all the guys he had brought along and rewarded had abandoned him, he felt. Even more infuriating, Fitzsimmons had removed his wife, Jo, and his son, James P. Hoffa, from Teamsters jobs, and there was nothing Hoffa could do about it. He was accustomed to being in charge, taking action, barking out orders. In Lewisburg, the only way he could vent his rage was by marching around its quarter-mile outdoor track, ten, fifteen, twenty times a day, all the while plotting his revenge.

One of his friends in Lewisburg, Sam Berger, a former Teamsters official and Manhattan booking agent, worried about how Hoffa was holding up. Berger had been convicted in 1969 of taking part in a $150,000 kickback after using his influence to steer a $1.5 million Teamsters pension-fund loan to the Cashmere Corporation, a Cleveland knitting company. By 1971, Berger later explained, Hoffa was "not the same Jimmy. . . . This last four and a half years have been awfully tough for him, and he's vicious. He's walking around like he's an animal, and he's driving me crazy. He's really, really hard."

While Hoffa was going stir-crazy, many of the inmates, guards, and prison officials were kowtowing to him, keenly aware that if he ever got back the Teamsters presidency, as he kept insisting he would, he'd control millions of dollars and thousands of jobs. Not a bad guy to have as a friend. Younger, minor-league Mob associates—Charlie Allen, Joe Franco, and others—flocked to him, offering protection and loyalty.

Allen served as a Hoffa bodyguard at Lewisburg. Before he was imprisoned, he had worked for corrupt Teamsters leader Frank Sheeran, who ran the union in Delaware, and for Genovese family capo Anthony "Tony Pro" Provenzano, who ruled the Teamsters in northern New Jersey through murder and extortion. Hoffa trusted Allen and began telling him about a plan he had to assassinate Frank Fitzsimmons after his release.

Hoffa made a logical choice in recruiting Charlie Allen to help kill Fitzsimmons. Tall, barrel-shaped, and intimidating, Allen had a lot of practice cracking heads for Sheeran's Teamsters Local 326 in Wilmington, Delaware. "When anybody was going to run against him [Sheeran]," Allen said, "myself and a few other guys would go down and give them a lot of trouble, if not beat the hell out of them. And we discouraged them. At union meetings, we would go there and not let anybody talk except for Sheeran, and we let everybody know we were with Frank Sheeran, and if anybody was against him, they would get hurt."

Allen, who later became a protected government witness with a new secret identity and cash-support payments, said he promised Hoffa that he'd help him execute Fitz.

While Hoffa was trying to get out of prison, Fitzsimmons was secretly pressuring Nixon to postpone paroling his former mentor until after the July 1971 Teamsters convention, where Fitz hoped to be elected president. He started locking the door on Hoffa on December 23, 1970, when he met briefly with Nixon. It marked the first time in twenty years that a Teamsters president, albeit an acting one, was welcomed into the White House.

At the meeting, Fitzsimmons said, "I'm not involved in the Free Jimmy Hoffa movement. I'm not pushing that." He added, "I know I am going to be elected president at the convention next summer." He didn't have to say that his plans could be disrupted if Hoffa was paroled before then.

Nixon stroked Fitzsimmons, praising him for trying to clean up the Teamsters. Fitz gushed back, "The Teamsters are very happy with this administration. We appreciate our friends."

Liking what Fitz told him, Nixon dipped into gangster vernacular and replied, "Teamsters are stand-up guys," meaning that the Teamsters would stand by him even if the going got rough.

During 1970 and 1971, while Fitzsimmons and Nixon conducted their mating ritual, Hoffa kept pressing for a presidential parole. His son, lawyer James P. Hoffa, had met with Colson and asked for help. Unbeknownst to both the Hoffa and Fitzsimmons camps, Colson was actually placing Nixon's political bets on both sides until the president learned which Teamsters leader was going to win the top job at the July 1971 convention. It was too early to tell whether Fitz or Hoffa would triumph. Hoffa's high-priced lawyers had several appeals pending. With a little judicial luck, Hoffa could be a free man before the Teamsters convention. Or he could run for Teamsters president from behind bars, so lax were the union's rules regarding official corruption.

In April 1971, Colson's aide George Bell urged his boss to tell Nixon to sit on the fence and see whether Hoffa was going to run for reelection from prison. If Fitz wins, Bell advised, Nixon should show up at the Teamsters convention to "seal the victory and solidify our position with Fitz. On the other hand, if Hoffa should win with or without opposition, there is some question as to whether the president should appear before a convention which has just elected a president serving time in prison."

Nixon didn't have to make this tough decision. On May 4, 1971, a federal judge denied Hoffa's appeal to have his sentences run concurrently, which would have made him eligible for a parole hearing.

The next day, in talking with chief of staff H. R. Haldeman, President Nixon endorsed plans to use Teamsters goons to assault anti-war demonstrators. Their conversation was immortalized on one of the White House tapes made available during the Watergate investigation.

> HALDEMAN: What Colson's gonna do on it, and what I suggested he do, and I think that they can get away with this, do it with the Teamsters. Just ask them to dig up those, their eight thugs.
>
> NIXON: Yeah.
>
> HALDEMAN: Just call, call, uh, what's his name.
>
> NIXON: Fitzsimmons. . . . They've got guys who'll go in and knock their heads off.
>
> HALDEMAN: Sure. Murderers. Guys that really, you know, that's what they really do.

Hoffa said that he learned his appeal was denied because the judge still believed Hoffa was active in the Teamsters, which his sentence had forbidden. As a gesture, he signed a letter of resignation and gave it to Fitzsimmons, thinking this would help him with the judge. But it was all to no avail. Two months later, Fitzsimmons was elected general president of the International Brotherhood of Teamsters, and the Nixon White House now felt free to shower favors on him and his allies without worrying about angering Jimmy Hoffa and his friends. Hoffa was furious, but he still hoped that if he ever got paroled, he could force Fitz to step aside and could retake the throne.

One of Nixon's favors was to get the rough-mannered, poorly educated Teamsters president into an exclusive country club. Nixon and Fitzsimmons both enjoyed golf, and during one of their meetings, the president told the labor leader he'd help get him into Columbia Country Club, to which Fitz's archrival, George Meany, belonged. Colson left the meeting and handed off the task to his deputy.

"Fitz wants Columbia because that's where Meany belongs," Colson told George Bell. "But if he got into Burning Tree, he could be one up on Meany, which would appeal to him—any way you have to, but do it somehow, whatever needs to be done. I suspect the president would write a letter if needed."

On December 23, Nixon provided Fitzsimmons with the biggest favor yet. The President commuted Hoffa's sentence but included a proviso that restricted him from union activities until 1980, when he'd be sixty-seven years old. Hoffa was furious and said that the commutation documents he had signed the day before hadn't included this restriction; if they had, he wouldn't have signed. He would have been out in 1974 without any restrictions, he explained, in plenty of time to challenge Fitzsimmons for the presidency at the 1976 Teamsters convention.

But Fitzsimmons snookered Hoffa. The former head of Teamsters DRIVE, William Carlos Moore, said in a sworn statement to Hoffa's attorneys that he had heard Fitzsimmons call Colson on the phone, greet him as Chuck, and say, "Chuck, Hoffa should be released from prison, but I think it awfully important that a condition be placed on him that he not be free to seek office and to participate in the labor movement until after he has served his full sentence." Hoffa's full sentence ran to 1980. Moore also admitted that "it became a kind of standing rule with the administration—I'm talking about the Fitzsimmons administration—that let's get Hoffa out of jail, let's get the Hoffa people off our back, but let's restrict him so he cannot come back into the labor movement."

Colson denies it. "There were allegations made that I put that on, and that it was part of a bargain, and the Teamsters retained my law firm, and it was all part of a deal—Fitzsimmons traded support for Nixon for keeping Hoffa out of the union. It's all fantasy."

175

† † †

In the summer of 1972, Jackie and his father put together a secret business deal with Fitzsimmons that released a flood of hundreds of thousands of Teamsters dollars into their own pockets and almost certainly into those of Nixon's Committee to Reelect the President (CREEP). Again, Harry Haler was involved.

With the backing of Fitz and the Pressers, the Teamsters awarded a $1.3-million-a-year public-relations contract to a dinky, fly-by-night Las Vegas PR firm partly owned by Haler. In return, Haler funneled some $300,000 in cash to Jackie, Bill, and Fitzsimmons over the next year and a half. The firm, Hoover-Gorin and Associates, was started in spring 1971 by George Arthur "Duke" Hoover, thirty-two, a former disc jockey who worked at a Las Vegas car-rental agency. A chunky version of actor George Hamilton, Hoover looked like a stereotypical Las Vegas lounge lizard with his purple suits, matching patent-leather shoes, pinkie rings, and gold chains. Hoover had met Haler at a wedding reception in Los Angeles and had convinced the confidence man to join him and his mother's boyfriend, Abnor Gorin, in starting a small ad agency in Las Vegas. The three men each put up five thousand dollars and formed a limited partnership.

Hoover, the active partner, had little success with the new company, which grossed less than $20,000 in 1971. He accumulated only $3,506 in taxable income that year. "Hoover was nothing," Haler says. "He was a broken-down guy in Vegas. In fact, he couldn't even get the telephones installed. I had to lend him the money to get the telephones installed."

In the spring of 1972, Haler introduced Duke Hoover to Bill Presser, and the public-relations neophyte pitched Bill Presser on a plan to clean up the Teamsters' soiled image with billboards and by sponsoring antidrug campaigns.

Bill was receptive to the idea. Jackie had been urging him to hire a PR firm to promote Joint Council 41 and the Ohio Conference of Teamsters. Jackie was tired of the bad press the Teamsters had been getting, particularly in Cleveland. In the early seventies, the city's competing newspapers, the *Plain Dealer* and the *Cleveland Press*, reported extensively on his father's two criminal indictments. Jackie also decided that the Teamsters needed a program to counterattack

176

reporters, "jackals in the news media," he called them. It seemed to him a modern, respectable, businesslike thing to do—pay someone to manipulate the press, feed it stories about union benefits and pay raises and the HUD retirement homes the Teamsters sponsored. Bill, who disliked reporters more than Jackie did, always talked about clawing his way to the top by swinging a piece of chain and a bat. Now he was going to battle his enemies with . . . a press release? It took Jackie a while, but he eventually sold his father on the idea. "Jackie was being alert and looking at the world around him," said Peter Halbin, one of Jackie's first publicists.

Into this ripe atmosphere came Duke Hoover and his rudimentary game plan for polishing the Teamsters image. He became a perfect cover story. Bill Presser referred Hoover to Fitzsimmons, who asked him to make a presentation to the IBT executive board. It was just for window dressing, Haler told him, because a deal had already been cut among him, Jackie, Bill, and Fitz. Hoover-Gorin would get a huge Teamsters contract, and Haler, as an employee of the firm, would kick back several hundred thousand dollars to Jackie.

If any organization could have benefited from a better public image in 1972, it was the Teamsters. Bill and Fitz had an easy time getting the executive board on July 9 to approve a huge four-year contract with Hoover-Gorin that paid the firm $1.3 million annually. After Hoover made his presentation, vice president William J. McCarthy from Boston moved for approval of the plan, and board member Joseph Morgan from Miami seconded the motion. It passed unanimously.

Eight days before this windfall, the Hoover-Gorin partnership was dissolved and the firm was incorporated, with Hoover as president. On August 1, 1972, Duke Hoover and Fitzsimmons signed a four-year contract calling for an annual retainer of $350,000 plus certain expenses, $500,000 a year for advertising, and $450,000 a year for promotion. Hoover-Gorin's retainer was gargantuan, roughly the amount a Fortune 100 company would pay for a top-drawer national campaign to change its corporate name. Also on August 1, Hoover executed a contract with Harry Haler, agreeing to pay him $25,000 a month in commissions and two thousand dollars a month in consulting fees.

Haler said he began making monthly cash payments of $16,500 to Jackie Presser in August 1972, with money from his monthly commission checks. Typically, he called a friend, Bert Lydekkers, branch manager of Crocker National Bank in Covina, California, and asked if he had enough cash to negotiate the check. Haler would stop at the bank then deliver the cash to Jackie wherever he might be—Cleveland, Miami, Chicago, San Francisco, Las Vegas, or wherever.

Carmen Presser witnessed one of the payoffs in a Los Angeles hotel room. "There was a whole gang of people there, Harry Haler and me and Jackie and a gray-haired man and a couple of men that came with Harry," she says. "They came in and they gave Jackie a lot of money. They counted it out right in front of me. They also brought a couple of pieces of jewelry. They asked me to pick out anything I wanted. I didn't like any of it. There was a diamond heart with a pear-shaped diamond in the middle. This guy was trying to sell it to Jackie. . . . And then there was a mink stole. Bergdorf-Goodman. Brand new. You know that that was a hot fur. Jackie bought it for me with some of the money they gave him."

Haler also used a variety of bagmen, mostly friends and relatives, to deliver the cash to Jackie. One courier recalled delivering the money to Jackie at the Canyon Hotel Racket and Golf Resort in Palm Springs in late 1972 or 1973. "We went up to his room," the courier said. "He counted the money out. He said, 'It's all here.' . . . He gave me thirty-five dollars to cover my expenses. The man is cheap."

Jackie later told Haler that he was splitting the kickbacks with his father and Frank Fitzsimmons, Haler recalls. According to Hoover-Gorin's financial records, the huge payments to Haler continued for eighteen months. Also bleeding cash from the PR firm was an arrangement to pay Tony Liberatore and his organized-crime associate, Thomas Lanci, two thousand dollars a month in "consulting fees." Neither could point out any consulting work he did for the union. Liberatore simply got a piece of the action because he had introduced Haler to Jackie. According to Liberatore, Lanci took $1,400 out of his monthly two thousand dollars and gave it to Jackie. Lanci kept six hundred dollars for his taxes and trouble.

As a result of the flood of Hoover-Gorin money to the Pressers and the underworld, Duke Hoover had a tough time putting together a program to polish the Teamsters image. He telephoned Jackie to complain about the firm's lack of funds. "Duke Hoover used to call and complain constantly that there wasn't enough money in the business,"

Carmen says. "He'd call three or four times a week, telling me he didn't have any money. I wondered, Why is he calling me? What do you want me to do about it? I felt really sorry for Duke. He was in the middle. This was a company that was formed expressly to funnel money."

Colson said he fired Hoover-Gorin after he began representing the Teamsters. "I believed that the money was not all going for public relations, which is why I had the contract cancelled," he said.

By 1973, Haler had become close to Jackie. He visited him at Jackie and Carmen's home in bucolic Russell Township, thirty miles east of Cleveland, and dined on Jackie's favorite dish, stuffed peppers. Haler and his wife, Bea, met Jackie and Carmen dozens of times in Los Angeles and Las Vegas, going out to dinner, socializing. "I ate many times with Harry Haler, under a hundred times but not much under," Carmen said. "He was always broke. He was a big con. A real con. And he knew everybody. He had a connection with everybody."

Bill Presser also took a liking to the friendly hustler, not realizing the danger he presented. Bill even warned Haler to be careful around Jackie. "He told me Jackie was a pathological liar but was getting better," Haler says.

Sometime later, at least a year after the kickback money started flowing, Haler would have a falling out with Jackie Presser, who had finally figured out that Haler was a con. So Haler retaliated, telling his IRS handlers about the Hoover-Gorin kickback scheme as well as how Teamsters union funds were being funneled to the Nixon reelection campaign. Daley and Dennis filed detailed memos about the charges and passed these allegations on to their superiors for dissemination to the FBI.

Haler, of course, didn't quit scamming and ended up hurting Daley and Dennis. A year or so later, he got his hands on some stolen securities and attempted to use them in 1975 as collateral for a loan from a Chicago bank. Without telling the two agents what was going on, Haler asked Daley and Dennis to check the securities' serial numbers to see if they were stolen. They were, but it didn't stop Haler from trying to get the loan, and he was caught with the stolen goods. Haler said that he later realized that Jackie was the only one who knew the securities had been stolen and that Haler was using them to secure a loan in Chicago. The Justice Department indicted Haler and threatened to indict his two IRS handlers as accomplices, because they had checked the serial numbers. Daley and Dennis fought back. They reminded their Justice Department superiors of the memos they had passed along in 1972 and 1973 about kickbacks to Jackie and Frank Fitzsimmons, donations to the Nixon reelection committee, and other potential crimes that weren't pursued. "If we're charged, we'll subpoena every official who saw those memos," the two agents said.

The Justice Department backed off, and Daley and Dennis ended up taking early retirement.

Bill and Fitz were pleased with Nixon's landslide victory in November, and they felt that their legal problems would diminish. But Presser was still being pursued in Cleveland over supposed expense-account fraud, and other Teamsters leaders also found themselves under federal investigation. Fitzsimmons complained, saying that his friends were still in trouble while his enemies weren't. "If you can't do anything about it, I'll take my case right to the president," he told the IRS agents. "Go right ahead," they told him.

Within a month or two after the election, Fitzsimmons, Jackie, and Bill each bragged to their IRS handlers that Nixon aides Colson, John Ehrlichman, and H. R. Haldeman had arranged a meeting between Fitz and Nixon in one of the private rooms at the White House. Attorney General Richard Kleindienst was summoned to the session and ordered by Nixon to review all the Teamsters investigations at the Justice Department and to make certain that Fitzsimmons and his cronies weren't hurt by the probes.

Acutely aware of the improper, if not illegal, nature of the meeting, Daley and Dennis covered themselves by detailing the accounts given by Fitzsimmons and the Pressers in official memos and passing them along to their IRS superiors. These memos were sent to the Justice Department several months later, just as the Watergate scandal started to break. However, the reports were never shared with the Senate Watergate committee. If they had been, it's possible that additional charges of obstruction of justice could have been brought against Nixon.

In the meantime, Kleindienst was able to help carry out Nixon's wishes and assist Fitzsimmons and his friends. In early March 1973, he refused to approve a twenty-day extension for an FBI wiretap that was threatening to expose Fitzsimmons's complicity in a Mafia kick-back scam involving Teamsters health benefits.

On January 26, 1973, the FBI had begun monitoring the scheme when it installed court-ordered wiretaps on the telephones of People's Industrial Consultants, a Mafia front set up to channel Teamsters health and welfare funds to Los Angeles Mafia figures, some of whom had Cleveland ties. The wiretaps, as well as an FBI informant, revealed that on February 8, 1973, Fitz met with Peter Milano, Sam Sciortino, and Joe Lamandri, all southern California Mafia members, at the Mission Hills Country Club in Palm Springs. The three men pitched Fitzsimmons a scheme to enroll union members working in California, Illinois, and Michigan in a prepaid health plan. Employers' monthly payments to the Teamsters health and welfare plans would then go to a Los Angeles physician, who had agreed to kick back seven percent of the funds to the Mafia-controlled People's Industrial Consultants. PIC would share a slice of the booty with Fitzsimmons and any other Teamsters leaders who assisted in giving the contract to the Los Angeles Mafia.

The next day, an FBI wiretap at PIC offices picked up a conversation between Raymond DeRosa, a Milano muscleman, and a Los Angeles physician chosen to oversee the clinics. DeRosa said that Fitzsimmons had shaken hands with Milano and agreed to the scheme. "The deal with the Teamsters is all set," DeRosa told the doctor.

On February 12, Fitzsimmons, Allen Dorfman, and his aide Alvin Baron met with Lou Rosanova, an envoy of the Chicago Mob, in the bar at the La Costa Country Club. Rosanova wanted to make sure the Chicago outfit got a cut of the take from the Teamsters health-fund scheme. A few hours after the meeting, Fitzsimmons boarded Air Force One with Nixon and jetted back to Washington, D.C.

Before the PIC wiretaps expired on March 6, the FBI asked for approval to extend them and to install additional taps in public pay phones outside PIC's offices on Wilshire Boulevard in Los Angeles. Kleindienst and his assistant, Henry E. Peterson, refused. FBI agents, infuriated that their investigation was being aborted, leaked the story to *New York Times* reporter Denny Walsh, who wrote about it on April 29, 1973. The revelations embarrassed Fitzsimmons and scuttled the giant health-plan scheme. Peterson later said that the wiretaps had been "nonproductive."

Though the Justice Department gave Fitzsimmons a break, it appeared that the Cleveland Strike Force was determined to pursue the expense account ripoff case against Bill Presser. In June 1973, a Justice Department lawyer from Washington, D.C., came to Cleveland to try the case. After a day and a half of presenting witnesses and evidence, the government rested and the presiding federal judge promptly threw the case out, saying that the government's case was the weakest he had ever seen presented at a trial.

Within months, rumors were circulating through Teamsters and law-enforcement circles that, because of Bill Presser's White House connections, the Justice Department had made only a half-hearted effort to try him. In July 1974, as the Watergate scandal raged, the Justice Department's Watergate Special Prosecution Force began investigating allegations that Nixon, through his aide Colson, had pulled strings in the case for Presser.

A secret Watergate memo based on informant sources, discovered while researching this book, had been sent to Deputy Special Prosecutor Henry S. Ruth, Jr., from an assistant, James Doyle. The memo said, in part,

> Attorney General Kleindienst . . . got a call to come to the White House and was left with the impression he would be seeing President Nixon. When he got to the White House, he was ushered in to see Charles Colson, who had with him Mr. Fitzsimmons, the head of the International Teamsters Union. Colson allegedly told Kleindienst that President Nixon wanted him to take care of the Presser case. A few days later, Kleindienst called Colson and told him not to worry about the Presser case. Presser was subsequently acquitted, and part of the allegation transmitted to me is that the effort made by the federal prosecutors in the case was "lukewarm."
>
> The informant says that his sources allege money was paid by the Teamsters to some party, either Colson or some other official, as a direct result of the Colson-Kleindienst-Fitzsimmons meeting.

Though the expense-account case against Bill Presser was weak, there is much evidence that points to White House payoffs by the Pressers.

Carmen Presser says that Jackie secretly delivered Teamsters

182

money to the White House during this time, though she isn't certain whether the cash came from the Hoover-Gorin kickbacks or another source. "I heard the phone calls," she insists, but she can't remember the name of the White House official with whom Jackie supposedly had dealings. "I've racked my brains," she says. "I remember one thing. Jackie came home and he went crazy turning on the radio and the TV because there were TV people taking pictures who caught him talking to the guy at the steps of the White House." She says Jackie paid off the Nixon White House in return for putting restrictions on Hoffa's parole.

In December 1973, a strike force federal grand jury in Manhattan subpoenaed the records of Hoover-Gorin and moved Harry Haler, incarcerated for a fraud case in California's Lompoc Penitentiary, to New York's Metropolitan Correctional Center, where he waited to be called before the grand jury. Duke Hoover had already been interviewed by prosecutors and remembered being asked if cash from his PR firm had ended up in the coffers at CREEP. Before Haler testified, the grand jury was abruptly shut down.

Since its inception, Hoover-Gorin had been linked to the Nixon White House. Duke Hoover's business card was stapled to Colson's personal notes on his legal pad taken during a July 17, 1972, meeting with the Teamsters executive board just after it had endorsed Nixon for president by a sixteen-to-one vote. (Gibbons voted no.) Colson had Presser's name scrawled on the pad but said last summer that he can't remember why.

Funneling Hoover-Gorin kickbacks to CREEP fits a Teamsters pattern of the time. Hoffa admitted in 1973 that he was told that the Teamsters had given $300,000 to the Nixon reelection campaign. Duke Hoover, the fumble-tongued publicist, told reporters that the Teamsters donated $175,000 to Nixon in 1972. But federal election reports only showed $18,000 in DRIVE contributions, and Fitzsimmons angrily denounced Hoover's facts. Presser's Joint Council 41, however, gave $20,000 to Nixon in October 1972 alone.

Furthermore, according to a secret FBI report, the Department of Justice believes that a secret cash fund of $1 million had been raised for Nixon by mobsters connected with Teamsters leaders. The money was intended as a payoff for the administration's help in keeping Hoffa from challenging Fitzsimmons. *Time* magazine, quoting government informers, said that Teamsters vice president Tony Provenzano and his muscleman, Salvatore Briguglio, ordered that $500,000 in cash be delivered to a White House courier in Las Vegas. Provenzano allegedly told an associate he had collected the money at Fitzsimmons's request and that another $500,000 had been provided for Nixon—also on Fitzsimmons's orders—by Allen Dorfman, a convicted Chicago labor racketeer and adviser to the Teamsters Union pension fund. Provenzano was quoted further as saying the cash had been requested by White House Aide Charles Colson, who handled the administration's relations with the Teamsters.

This could explain one of the most mysterious remarks found on the Nixon White House tapes, a remark that was never cleared up by the Watergate investigation. On March 21, 1973, Nixon talked to his counsel, John Dean, about the Watergate burglars' demands for huge sums of hush money. Nixon said, "What I mean is you could get a million dollars . . . and you could get it in cash. I know where it could be gotten. . . . We could get the money. There is no problem in that."

Hoffa vented a lot of energy and anger fighting the restrictions on his presidential commutation by filing lawsuits. But he still wanted to have Fitzsimmons killed, Charles Allen later testified. Starting in 1972, Hoffa met with Allen several times to discuss the Fitzsimmons murder contract. One of their meetings took place in upstate Pennsylvania, where Hoffa was thinking about buying a coal mine. Another took place in Philadelphia, Allen said. Hoffa gave him cash both times, $18,000 the first time, $15,000 the next.

Eventually, Hoffa was so vengeful, angry, and perhaps unhinged by four years in prison that he wanted to kill five men. Allen said that he only knew of the names of two, Fitz and Tony Provenzano. Bill Presser, as Fitzsimmons's strongest ally, was an obstacle to Hoffa's return and may have been on the hit list. In fact, Jackie told the FBI that Hoffa blamed Bill—the one with political savvy and connections—for getting the restrictions put on his parole.

But Allen, strictly an East Coast operator, couldn't recognize or remember the three other targets Hoffa mentioned as part of his bold plan to eliminate competition and retake the Teamsters Union. Hoffa envisioned Allen traveling to Washington, D.C., and setting up an ambush in the dimly lit parking garage underneath Teamsters headquarters on Capitol Hill. Allen would wait for Fitzsimmons, then spring out and shoot him. "I was supposed to kill Frank Fitzsimmons," Allen testified. "Yes sir, right here in Washington."

Allen may have truly intended to carry out the mission, or perhaps he was just humoring Hoffa. But before Allen could take any action, Hoffa disappeared from the parking lot of the Machus Red Fox restaurant outside of Detroit on July 30, 1975, and was never seen again.

13

The Forge

"It was like walking into a Damon Runyon book."

CARMEN PRESSER

"C'mon," Jackie told his wife. "I've got a surprise for you."

He turned their Cadillac down a narrow, dead-end lane to a clearing where two high-rise apartment towers rose up through the woods. Nestled between the towers was a low, square brick building. Jackie escorted Carmen through a pair of thick wooden double doors, made a sweeping gesture, and proudly said, "See this? This is my new restaurant!"

It was news to her. Jackie had never mentioned a restaurant. But there it was, almost ready for business, a two-hundred-seat room with a huge, copper-domed open-hearth grill. Workers were installing stained-glass panels in the ceiling and red-leather banquettes along the walls. The heavy, red-velvet drapes and maroon Naugahyde tablecloths would come later.

He had a partner, Tony Hughes, Jackie told her. He added, "I'm going to put the restaurant in your name." Carmen was excited. "I thought he was doing something nice for me," she says.

The new restaurant demanded Jackie's attention at a time when he was juggling several conflicting activities. At forty-six, Jackie was making his move up the Teamsters ranks, riding his father's coattails while cementing a bond with Teamsters president Fitzsimmons. Jackie was also newly divorced and had settled with Carmen and her two

186

teenaged boys in a four-bedroom ranch house with a pool that sprawled at the end of a five-hundred-foot driveway on a wooded four-acre lot in remote Russell Township. Complicating his home life and his career even further, Jackie was secretly making powerful new friends in the Mob while snitching to FBI supervisor Marty McCann. And, as if all of this wasn't enough, Jackie was also dancing precariously close to prison by pocketing thousands of dollars in kickbacks from Hoover-Gorin.

But that's the way he liked it. Jackie thrived on excitement and the high-charged thrill of risking a spectacular fall. Just when he was about to slip, he always regained his balance. It was his form of gambling. "He thrived on meshugaas," Carmen Presser says, using a Yiddish word meaning absurd madness. "He thrived on commotion. When things were toughest, he got the most excited. He had to be the center of it. He couldn't have lived a boring life."

Jackie and Tony had leased the site for the new restaurant, a small, one-story, unimproved building between two high-rise apartments, from a company owned by millionaire developer Carl Milstein. Presser and Hughes agreed to pay his company $1,333 a month in rent for fifteen years and to spend $130,000 for remodeling. Jackie put his half of the restaurant in Carmen's name to avoid suspicion of a conflict of interest; among other projects, Milstein's company built and managed various HUD-financed high rises for the elderly. By constructing Teamsters-sponsored HUD apartment buildings, Milstein built up goodwill with the Teamsters—a valuable commodity to a developer—and turned a profit. Milstein was controversial. In 1978, at a time when he controlled $144 million in real estate, he got caught bribing a HUD official, was convicted, and served several months in prison.

Jackie and Tony invited 150 friends, politicians, union officials, clergymen, hoodlums, and business leaders to the opening night of the Forge in the summer of 1972. The crowd was having a great time, drinking cocktails, laughing, and toasting—until the huge hearth, from which the restaurant took its name, was stoked to high heat and the chef and his helpers slapped on steaks, chops, and kabobs for the guests. Within moments, the clean new restaurant filled with smoke. The fan over the grill had been installed backwards, and it blew greasy smoke all over the crowd. "Everybody was choking and had to run outside,"

Carmen says. "They opened all the doors. Jackie was very embarrassed. They had to have the party another night because they couldn't cook the steaks."

The Forge was part of Jackie's drive to give himself an image of respectability. He always said of the Forge, "I didn't open it to make money, I opened it to make contacts." The restaurant enjoyed a good location in a residential apartment complex on the border of suburban Gates Mills, a classy bedroom community of 2,236 in the Chagrin River Valley. Gates Mills was known as the home of the exclusive Chagrin Valley Hunt Club, founded in 1908 by a group of industrialists, among them Charles A. Otis, the first Clevelander to buy a seat on the New York Stock Exchange. Its Anglophilic founders were men who fancied riding and jumping horses and sallying out on a traditional British fox hunt. They bought some rolling land near the river, imported English hounds from Canada, and built a kennel. On Sundays, as horns tootled and dogs bayed, the Midwest millionaires dressed up in formal riding attire, mounted their horses, and chased foxes across the countryside.

The fourteen-story apartment buildings flanking the Forge were actually situated in middle-class Mayfield Heights. The Gates Mills mayor was furious that his village's well-respected name was attached to something as gauche as a blocky concrete-and-glass apartment complex. He slammed its developers. "They are misleading people . . . with the indication that they are moving into Gates Mills. The promotion verges on fraud. . . . There will never be any apartments in Gates Mills as long as I am mayor."

Few of Gates Mills's Waspy residents, the country-club set that Jackie dearly wanted to impress, dined at the Forge. They may have visited it once or twice for dinner, but the uneven food and loud decor put them off. Plus there was Tony Hughes and the Forge's notorious clientele. Tony, Jackie's partner and sidekick, had operated the Commodore Hotel and knew the liquor business. He was a natural-born restaurateur from an old Italian neighborhood. A broad-shouldered ex-pug who looked good in a suit, Tony knew scores of judges and suburban councilmen as well as the wise guys from the Hill. He made friends easily and put customers at ease. While Jackie came off as arrogant and boastful, Tony, everyone admitted, was a hell of a nice guy. "Tony Hughes is the kind of guy who knows everybody," Harold

188

Friedman said. "I don't care who it is, from the president of the United States to the goddamn police chief over here and everybody in between. Tony is a very friendly kind of guy."

Soon, a couple of members of the Cleveland family and their associates were visiting the Forge regularly: James "Jack White" Licavoli, Curly Montana, gambler George "Gigi" Argie, Tommy Sinito, and many others. They were tucked away in the big red-leather banquettes in the back and enjoyed special treatment. "I had a friend who said it was like walking into a Damon Runyon book," Carmen says. "Everybody would be there, and it was hysterical because nobody paid. Everybody got free meals."

The country-club crowd wasn't comfortable with the crew of flashy men in gold jewelry and leisure suits who lurked like pilot fish around the Mafia powers who dined at Jackie's restaurant. "The Gates Mills people came for dinner, and when they saw all the wise guys, they quit coming," Carmen recalls.

Jackie introduced her to the gangsters, making sure he displayed the proper fealty and respect. She wasn't allowed to speak to them, nor did she and Jackie join them at their tables. He had drilled her in wise-guy etiquette. "One thing I did learn from Jackie: I wasn't allowed to ask any questions about anything, because it wasn't polite or in case it would embarrass them to answer. For example, say I met someone socially, and he had a woman with him. I couldn't ask if that was his wife, if they had children, what they did for a living, or where they lived. Or anything like that. You couldn't question them on anything social. I knew immediately if I had crossed over the line, because Jackie would interrupt and steer the conversation elsewhere."

Hughes spent lunches and evenings at the Forge, overseeing the staff, greeting customers, buying drinks for friends, all the while collecting a paycheck from Teamsters Local 507 as a business agent. At first, Jackie went to the Forge every evening, but then he lost interest and let Hughes run the show. Whenever prominent Mob figures stopped in, however, Tony and Jackie, if he was there, treated them like kings. Booze and meals were on the house. Curly Montana, the wealthy mobster, took a side of beef out the back door one night. When needed, the maître d'hôtel or Hughes surrounded the mobsters with a zone of privacy, seating customers at least two tables away.

Mobsters weren't the only customers. Many who came were

hangers-on who hoped to see a few of them. Others were the residents of the apartment buildings, friends of the union, and people who knew the convivial Tony Hughes. After the Forge took off, Jackie and Tony expanded their restaurant enterprise and started a catering business in a leased hall called the Forge Party Center. They tried to drum up business catering weddings and big parties but couldn't make a go of it. Before long, they rented the hall two nights a week to a bingo game supposedly run as a charity fund-raiser for a Jewish congregation. The sponsor of the game was JRS Incorporated, which stood for Jewish Religious Services. JRS didn't have a synagogue or school and wasn't listed in the telephone book. It did have two convicted bookmakers, brothers Johnny and Jimmy Blank (short for Blanco), working the games. During this time, the Blank brothers and five others were under indictment for conspiring to run what the FBI called a multimillion-dollar sports-betting operation. When the *Cleveland Press* broke the story in 1977 revealing that the Blanks were running a bingo game at the Forge Party Center and linking Carmen to the scam as an owner, she became furious. "I went nuts," she says. "I never played bingo. It was a humiliation to me. I didn't even know there was bingo there." She blames Tony Hughes for bringing in the rackets guys. The story quickly faded, and there was little, if any, political fallout for Jackie.

The Cleveland FBI soon learned that the Forge was a gangster hangout. Marty McCann, head of the Mob squad, was pleased with the development. Thanks to the Forge, two prize informants, Hughes and Presser, were able to stay on top of what was happening in the underworld. Conversations, business deals, out-of-town trips—Tony and Jackie heard a lot and were able to recall choice chunks when McCann came around asking questions.

They regularly met McCann at the apartment of Lemar Smith, the Forge manager, who lived in one of the Gates Mills Towers high-rise buildings. Tony never told his manager why he needed the apartment. "He thought I had a broad," Hughes recalls. Tony and Jackie would leave the Forge, walk a few steps, ride the elevator to Smith's apartment, turn on the television set to create background noise, and wait for McCann. After the secret meetings, the FBI supervisor left first. Tony would mess up the bed a little, then they'd leave.

Carmen says she suspected at the time that Jackie and Tony were helping the FBI. She recalls that when Jackie was at the Forge, he and

190

Tony "would go from table to table to table. You want to talk about conniving. There is the king of conniving. . . . Jackie'd be picking their little brains out. Finding out what was happening."

It was dangerous work, but then Jackie, like his mother and her brothers, got a thrill out of taking risks. Faye risked money at the card tables. By informing on the Mafia, Jackie was playing with much higher stakes.

Over the years, Bill Presser had said that if anything happened to him, Babe Triscaro would succeed him as the president of Teamsters Joint Council 41. With Presser's poor health in the late sixties and his legal difficulties in the early seventies, it looked as if Triscaro might soon be the leading Teamster in town. But by 1973, Bill Presser had other plans. He felt that his son Jackie had proven himself as a union official over the past five years. He had cultivated the necessary political and business contacts. And with Jackie's new ideas about public relations and political fund-raising, Bill felt that his son was the kind of leader the Teamsters needed to steer the troubled union into the future. The union's membership had peaked at 2.2 million and was starting to slip as the country slowly realigned itself from a self-sufficient giant to an importer of steel, cars, and Middle East oil.

At a Joint Council 41 executive board meeting in March 1973, Bill Presser revealed his plans for Jackie's succession. The move caught Triscaro off guard and angered him. He felt that Bill should have had the decency to inform him of his plans before the low-level officials learned about them at the closed-door meeting.

Triscaro understood about wanting to take care of one's family. He too had positioned his son-in-law, Sam Busacca, to take the reins of Teamsters Local 436 some day. John Felice, Sr., had done the same with his son, Skippy, and Teamsters Local 293. Harvey Friedman had done the same with his son Harold and Bakery Workers Local 19.

However, many of the sixteen heads of Teamsters locals in Joint Council 41 secretly felt that Jackie, with only five years' experience running Local 507, hadn't earned the right to tell them how to operate.

At the March meeting, Bill said: "Now you all know that while I'm gone, I have left more and more of this daily work to Jack, because he's familiar with it. He knows what's going on. All of the fellows work with him. He works with everybody, but actually he doesn't have any authority to do anything in the council when I'm not there. . . . I would like to have Jackie as my executive assistant, with the full authority to operate while I'm not there, in all of the everyday storekeeping business of the council, like he's doing now, but giving him the authority to do it. . . . We talk to each other every day, wherever I'm at. He's got all of the contacts. He's got all of the connections. He's got everything I ever had and more. It can only be for the good of all of us." Then, referring to Jackie's wealth, Bill said, "He needs nothing from us. Thank God, he's got plenty of his own. He's in good shape."

Triscaro was upset, and Bill, probably sensing this as the meeting went on, spoke up in front of the others and told Babe he was sorry that he hadn't discussed this with him before the meeting.

"Anytime Jackie wants cooperation, I cooperate," Triscaro interrupted, "but never, never once has anybody designated anything for me to do. . . . None of these problems have ever been brought to me, not a one."

Bill attempted to soothe him but argued for Jackie's accession anyway. "It's got to help everybody—with the International contacts he is thoroughly familiar with, and has been for a long time. And he knows what to do, and he knows how to reach out as far as I do. . . . This no longer is a business of ten or fifteen years ago. This is a highly concentrated business, and every move you make, you got to figure out. You're always sitting there with lawsuits, damages, and injunctions facing you on every move you make. . . . Our setup today is still a one-man operation, Bill Presser, and I don't want to work on a one-man operation because I'm spread too thin. I can't keep going this way for a long time."

Jackie's high profile as a Teamsters official obscured the little-known but powerful labor position he had held since 1967—president and general manager of Hotel Workers Local 10, a Cleveland local of some eight thousand cooks, bartenders, hotel maids, kitchen helpers, and other low-paid food-service workers. Local 10 was created in the early sixties from the five different restaurant and hotel locals that Jackie had run in the fifties until he was bounced out for misusing funds.

Jackie spent little time with Local 10 and attended few meetings.

Nevertheless, by 1972, Local 10 paid him $19,500 annually as its president plus giving him a generous expense account. He took in $123,981 as secretary-treasurer of Warehouse Workers Local 507, $12,000 as financial secretary of Bakery Workers Local 19, and $1,100 as recording secretary of Joint Council 41. That year, from labor unions alone, Jackie hauled in $191,581, making him the highest or second highest paid union official in the country. And he was only a local officer.

Despite his wealth, Jackie still found ways to nickel and dime the union members by using their dues for his personal benefit. Neil Morrow, a former Teamsters driver, ran a Sunoco service station in a suburb near Jackie's home. "He used to come in there," Morrow says. "All the other union guys came in there too. Jackie used to buy stuff for his wife and kids' cars and charge it to . . . the Bakers Union or the Restaurant Workers union. This was 1970, 1971. I used to have to go over and start his wife's car."

Jackie didn't have to worry about getting in trouble with the Hotel Employees Union hierarchy as he had in the fifties. Edward T. Hanley, an old family friend, took over as president of the four-hundred-thousand-member Hotel and Restaurant Employees Union in 1973. Related by marriage to Chicago Mob figure Frank Calabrese, Hanley had begun his union career at Local 450, founded by Joey "Doves" Auippa, the future boss of the Chicago Mafia. Hanley grabbed the presidency of the international union because of "the power and influence of Auippa and the Chicago Mob," according to an unpublished 1977 Justice Department intelligence report on labor racketeering. "Ed Hanley represents the classic example of an organized-crime takeover of a major labor union."

One of Hanley's first actions as president was to quintuple the ranks of international organizers, a catchall job description, from twenty to more than one hundred. Then he dished out the jobs to relatives, cronies, Mafia members, juice collectors, embezzlers, Mob figures, and their girlfriends. One of the new international organizers, at $11,000 a year, was Jackie Presser, who did little or no work for the money. He was too busy running Local 507, the Forge, Ohio DRIVE, and other ventures.

14

Skimming Vegas

"It would be my choice that you'd never leave this room alive."

NICK CIVELLA

One of the stunning ironies of Bill Presser's stay-at-home life was that he helped to build the Las Vegas casinos that preyed on the gambling sickness afflicting his wife's family. Faye and her brothers, Harry and Allen Friedman, took jaunts to the Strip and spent hours compulsively rolling dice and squandering tens of thousands of dollars. In Cleveland, they ran at the front of a pack of racetrack regulars. All of them, particularly Harry, had to turn to Bill for money. Bill Presser was forever giving his brothers-in-law handouts of five and ten thousand dollars.

Casino developers and Mob front men also turned to the Plug for financing, but hardly in desperation. Bill reigned as the loan-committee chairman of the country's largest private pension pool, the Teamsters Central States Pension Fund.

When Hoffa went to prison in 1967, he designated Chicago mobster Allen Dorfman as his Central States stand-in, saying, "When this man speaks, he speaks for me." Tall, athletic, a decorated World War II marine, Allen Dorfman was a college graduate, a refinement his gutter tongue and family heritage belied. Dorfman's stepfather was racketeer Red Dorfman, a prize-fighter and close friend of Tony Accardo, the Mafia boss who took over the Chicago Mob from Al Capone. Hoffa had rewarded young Allen with the insurance business from

194

Central States, a payoff to Red Dorfman for helping Hoffa get the support of the Chicago outfit.

Like Jackie, Allen Dorfman loved to golf. Unlike Jackie, he had a low handicap and didn't take up an entire golf cart by himself. By the seventies, Dorfman was wealthy, politically connected, and fond of the good life. Silver-haired and handsomely distinguished, he fancied rubdowns and facials at Teamsters-financed La Costa Country Club, where he owned a condominium.

Surveillance, FBI informant reports, and wiretaps showed that Dorfman answered to Chicago Mafia capo Joseph "Joey the Clown" Lombardo, a cunning hit man who had worked his way up the ranks. With his wire-rimmed aviator glasses, thick black hair, and youngish looks, Lombardo, like Dorfman, possessed the smooth veneer of respectability so often sought by second-generation racketeers.

Without Hoffa's tightfisted control, Dorfman ended up sharing power with Presser. They operated the pension fund without the in-house safeguards and rigid controls of a big bank. As a result, they wielded enormous economic clout. After Dorfman went to prison in 1971 for taking kickbacks, Bill alone ruled the fund. Between 1972 and 1976, he approved loans of more than $183 million to Las Vegas casinos. "All he got for helping those guys was a cigar," Jackie would tell his FBI handlers. Events would prove otherwise.

If Las Vegas hadn't been showered with Teamsters loans, the city would be much dimmer today. During Presser's nearly twenty years on the Central States board, the fund loaned money, sometimes with disastrous results, to the neon lords of the Aladdin, Caesar's Palace, Circus Circus, the Desert Inn, the Fremont, the Lodestar, the Stardust, and the Plaza Towers casinos and hotels, all in Las Vegas. In Lake Tahoe, the truck drivers' retirement money was sunk into the King's Castle and the Sierra. Other gambling operations the Teamsters infused with money include the Riverside in Riverside, Nevada, and the Echo Bay casino in Overton, Nevada.

Teamsters vice president Jimmy Hoffa probably didn't have Las Vegas in mind when he created the Central States, Southeast and Southwest Areas Pension Fund in 1955 by consolidating scores of small pension funds in twenty-two states. The concept—a portable pension in which credits accumulated despite job changes—was a progressive and much-needed improvement in an industry known for layoffs, frequent job changes, bankruptcies, and buyouts. Two years later, Hoffa installed his superstar protégé, Bill Presser, on the Central States pension board, which was composed of eight union officials and eight employer representatives. These trustees were supposed to decide how to invest the two dollars a month that employers paid into the fund for each Teamster on their payroll. In reality, the committee was simply a rubber stamp; Hoffa dictated whom to loan money to. In return, Hoffa routinely demanded a finder's fee of up to ten percent of each loan. The trustees went along with it. The union's trustees were his toadies; the employer trustees, usually trucking-company owners, feared strikes and slowdowns if they lifted a finger against Hoffa.

In sharp contrast, the pension fund for the Teamsters' Western States Conference was managed by Prudential, the giant insurance company. Members of the Western States pension board had little to say about how fund assets were invested. Hoffa shunned such hands-off arrangements. His control over retirees' millions made him one of the most powerful private loan officers in the land. He used his position to reward business leaders and politicians who could help him later, shifting the pension millions from one favored bank to the next. "We're in this business to make friends," he crassly admitted.

It was a reckless operation. Over the years, Hoffa, Presser, future Teamsters president Roy Williams, and other powerful trustees approved hundreds of millions of dollars in loans without pestering borrowers to submit formal applications, credit histories, appraisals, or even collateral. Incredible as it may seem, a $4 million loan to the Aladdin Hotel was secured by $9 million in IOUs from the gambling tables. When *Wall Street Journal* reporter Jonathan Kwitny asked several accountants to review stacks of Central States loan records, the independent experts couldn't believe the shoddiness of the operation and the board's lack of prudence. Stumbling across one ludicrous investment after another, the auditors burst out repeatedly, "Hey, look at this one!" They couldn't believe the collection of deadbeats and crazy risk-takers who had profited at the expense of Teamster members.

Daniel Shannon, a Chicago accountant and pal of the late mayor, Richard Daley, was brought in by Bill Presser to manage Central States operations in 1973. He remembers finding loan applications scrawled by hand on pieces of yellow legal paper. Repayment schedules and other records couldn't be located. "They had money sitting in quite a few bank accounts, some of which were not even earning interest," he says. In 1977, more than fifty Central States loans—with an original cost of $200 million—were in default. The fund was losing roughly $15 million a year in annual interest payments. Central States Pension Fund, *Forbes* magazine reported, was "the scandal of trade union history." Despite exposés, indictments, and attempted government reforms, the plundering went on unabated for a quarter of a century. It was perhaps the biggest, longest-running swindle in U.S. history. Half the loans, according to one estimate, went to the Mob or Mob associates, earning Central States a cynical sobriquet—the Mafia's Bank. Teamster retirees still received their pensions, but the fund didn't grow as fast as it could have. Except for a few dissidents, working Teamsters didn't seem to pay much attention to the financial shenanigans of Central States. The rank and file certainly wasn't going to speak up.

It was Bill Presser and Jimmy Hoffa's old friend Moe Dalitz who brought the Central States honeypot and its low-interest loans to Las Vegas. Dalitz, a gambler and ex-member of the Cleveland syndicate, knew Hoffa from the earliest days of labor racketeering.

Dalitz met Hoffa in the mid-thirties through Hoffa's mistress, Sylvia Pagano, who introduced the rising Teamsters official to the Detroit underworld. A member of the ruthless Prohibition outfit the Purple Gang, Dalitz took over his family's laundry after Repeal and built up a string of laundries and dry cleaners throughout the Midwest, including Cleveland's Pioneer Linen Supply Company. In 1949, a Detroit dry-cleaners owners association faced a strike by Teamsters Local 285 drivers who had the cheek to ask for a five-day workweek. The owners' cartel asked Dalitz to use his connections to settle the dispute. According to McClellan-committee testimony, Dalitz met with Hoffa, who, after a short meeting, promptly ordered Local 285 leaders to take the owners' offer. Hoffa pocketed a $17,500 payoff. "They said I knew Dalitz and that he was a big deal in the Mafia," Hoffa once said. "Hell, yes, I knew Dalitz. I've known him since way back when he owned a string of laundries in Detroit and we threatened him with a strike."

In 1949, Dalitz and his partners from the Cleveland syndicate—Morris Kleinman, Sam Tucker, and Thomas McGinty—completed the construction of the Desert Inn on the Vegas Strip. Two years later, the televised Kefauver Senate hearings gave the country some background on these new Las Vegas businessmen. "At the top of Cleveland's bootleggers were Morris Kleinman, Lou Rothkopf, Moe Dalitz, Sam Tucker, and Maxie Diamond," Cleveland safety director Alvin Sutton told the Kefauver committee. "They were at the helm of the board of directors. They had their suppliers of Canadian whiskey and their salesmen and thugs to distribute contraband and to reap the harvest of money. . . . Ruthless beatings, unsolved murders and shakedowns, threats, and bribery came to this community as a result of gangsters' rise to power."

Dalitz, like Jackie, sought social acceptance. In 1957, the casino owner decided to build a new for-profit hospital in Las Vegas. Two years later, he borrowed $1 million from the Central States Pension Fund for this, its first Las Vegas investment. Dalitz's partners in the hospital included the future founders of Lorimar Productions, and, for a while, controversial lawyer Roy Cohn. It was called Sunrise Hospital, and a fancy San Francisco public-relations firm promoted the venture, bestowing do-gooder status on Dalitz and friends. Several years later, Hoffa approved an $8 million pension loan to Dalitz and some investors to buy the Stardust Hotel and Casino.

Meanwhile, the Cleveland Mob maintained strong ties to Las Vegas and worked at making new ones. The Mafia's ruling commission had declared Las Vegas an open city, so each crime family was entitled to stake out different casinos as their exclusive territory. The Cleveland family got in early with the Desert Inn. Its principal owner, Moe Dalitz, served as an informal referee for territorial disputes among the different Mafia crews, as Jackie informed the FBI. His contact agent made this report in 1978: "The individual who oversees the operations for the LCN [La Cosa Nostra] families in Las Vegas is MOE DALITZ. DALITZ makes certain that there is no cheating with regard to the skim money taken out of the casinos and further, that there is no fighting among families for the control of various casinos."

Since the Cleveland family protected the Desert Inn from shakedowns by other Mafia families, Cleveland godfather John Scalish and his capos were rewarded by the casino with unreported, untaxed cash known as skim. A 1965 FBI memo, based on informant reports, said that Scalish and James "Jack White" Licavoli "had a piece in one way or another in the Desert Inn." Gambler George Gordon carried suitcases of skim to the Cleveland Mob until his death in 1973, Jackie informed the FBI. Thereafter, Maishe Rockman served as courier.

In the summer of 1969, the Cleveland family made a big play for Las Vegas power: it sent two Teamsters officials there to try to create a union for the casino dealers. According to federal authorities, the underworld's idea was to organize the city's seven thousand or so dealers into a Mob-controlled union that had the potential to bring casino owners to their knees. Then, with the threat of a strike, the Mob could devastate individual hotels and force owners to sign sweetheart labor contracts or to buy food, liquor, or vending machines from mobbed-up companies. A dealers union was also a way for organized crime to slip its fingers into casino counting rooms.

At the time, Las Vegas dealers were fired on the mere suspicion of stealing. A casino manager knew that given the odds and the house edge, a blackjack dealer couldn't run a table that lost for two weeks in a row. Such a loss was mathematically impossible. Though the casino manager couldn't prove that the dealer was dumping out, steering cards to an outside man, or palming chips, he knew he was cheating. The dealer was fired. With a union to contend with, the casino would have to prove that the dealer was stealing, a tough task.

The two Cleveland men who came to Vegas to organize were Teamsters officials Nick Nardi, John's brother, and Nick Francis. They were joined, behind the scenes, by Pete Milano, the Los Angeles-based mafioso whose uncle ran the Cleveland crime world in the thirties. Nardi and Francis collected fifteen signatures from dealers, then applied for a charter to create Local 711 of the International Office and Professional Employees Union. The union had been trying to organize dealers for years. This time, however, the union's lawyer was approached by Cleveland labor lawyer Robert Duvin, who vouched for Nardi and Francis, calling them legitimate labor organizers. With Duvin's support, Nardi and Francis got their charter. *Time* magazine reporter Sandy Smith, an expert on the Mob, got wind of this and investigated. He talked to Duvin, who admitted that he represented Peter Milano. Because of the publicity, the union immediately revoked Local 711's new charter, stymieing the Mob for the moment.

199

Whenever Jackie or any of the Pressers went to Las Vegas, they were treated regally. "We got tickets to everything," Carmen says. "Anytime we went to see anything, we never had to stand in line. It was very impressive. I wasn't impressed, but anybody else around was."

On one of their trips, she and Jackie were given the best seats in the house to an Elvis Presley concert, a hard ticket to get in Las Vegas. "We were right up front," Carmen says. "I could look up Elvis Presley's nose. All of the sudden, the table rattled around." In the darkened nightclub, a Presley fanatic, an older woman, had burrowed more than a dozen yards on her hands and knees under the tables on the main floor. She was in a frenzy to reach her sequined idol.

"All of the sudden, this head pops up between Jackie's legs, and Jackie jumped and started screaming," Carmen recalls. The woman tried to leap onstage, but ushers pulled her back. Jackie, realizing what was happening, laughed uproariously. Presley didn't miss a beat.

In 1974, despite his recent legal and medical problems, Bill Presser helped put together a Teamsters-financed scheme that put two major Las Vegas casinos into the hands of the Mafia and netted him as much as $600,000 in kickbacks. It was a masterful conspiracy that involved the cooperation of the Kansas City, Chicago, Milwaukee, and Cleveland crime families, and helped the Mafia coil its grip on the Strip even tighter.

About $1 billion was wagered in Nevada that year, much of it at casinos owned by Fortune 500 companies like Howard Hughes's Summa Corporation. But the gambling public—tourists, truck drivers, high rollers, conventioneers—also spent hundreds of millions of dollars at what the government was later to prove were Mob-controlled casinos that secretly skimmed a fortune from counting rooms and funneled it to the underworld.

It started with Allen R. Glick, a short, balding graduate of a Cleveland law school who seemingly came out of nowhere in 1974 and bought the Fremont and Stardust casinos with a $62 million loan from the Central States Pension Fund, making him the biggest casino tycoon after Hughes. Born in 1942, the son of a Pittsburgh scrap dealer, Glick was distinguished by loud sports coats, dark, neatly clipped sideburns, wire-rim glasses, and sausage-like lips. A captain in the army and a Vietnam veteran, he had a spotless record when he settled in San Diego in 1969 and began charging and hustling his way through the southern California real-estate market.

People like Glick were extremely important commodities to Mafia chieftains who wanted to snare glittery gambling halls and their flood of untraceable, easily skimmed cash. The Mafia needed a front man, a Mr. Clean, because mobsters couldn't own casinos outright; the Nevada Gaming Control Board wasn't supposed to allow it. By law, when a casino opened or changed hands, the Gaming Control Board scrutinized its new owners for Mafia ties or whiffs of financial funny business.

Except perhaps for his youth, Glick made a great front man. He first appeared in Vegas in 1972, when he and three partners spent $4 million for a sixty-acre parcel on the Strip, which he wanted to develop as a recreational-vehicle park. The battered and beleaguered Hacienda casino happened to squat on the plot, and the partners eventually bought it, too. According to Glick, the dumpy gambling hall lured him with a Siren's call. "We became intrigued with the casino industry," he said. One of Glick's Hacienda partners was Eugene Fresch, who had known Glick at Ohio State University and had a friend who knew Bill Presser.

Any ambitious businessman in the Las Vegas area would eventually run across the Teamsters, the biggest lender in the state. While trying to buy the troubled King's Castle casino in Lake Tahoe, Glick met Allen Dorfman and his protégé, Alvin Baron. Central States held the King's Castle mortgage and approved its transfer to Glick. But the Nevada Gaming Control Board got wind of the man Glick was told to hire to operate the little casino, Edward "Marty" Buccieri. Marty had been convicted of drugging and attempting to frame a Kentucky sheriff, George Ratterman. The Cleveland syndicate had been upset with Ratterman, a former Cleveland Browns player, for cracking down on the fancy, illegal gambling casinos the syndicate had freely operated for decades in Newport, Kentucky, just over the Ohio River from straight-laced Cincinnati. Buccieri drugged the sheriff, threw him in bed with a stripper, and took suggestive photos.

Glick's King's Castle deal fell through because of Buccieri. But within weeks, Glick and two former San Diego Chargers assumed a $15 million loan the Teamsters pension fund held on an Austin, Texas,

201

ALAMEDA FREE LIBRARY

office building. This ingratiated him to the pension fund's financial honchos. A month or two later, Glick struck gold.

Along with everybody else wired into Nevada financial circles, Glick learned that the Recrion Corporation wanted to sell off its two casino-hotel complexes, the Stardust and the Fremont. In a move that stunned the gambling industry, the thirty-one-year-old Glick put down a $2 million nonrefundable deposit to secure a four-month option to come up with the $62.7 million needed to buy the two casinos. Glick learned that a Milwaukee dinner-theater owner, Frank Balistrieri, could help him get the money.

Though it strains credulity, Glick portrays himself as a naive businessman-investor who plunged into the gambling industry seemingly unaware of the Mob's control of the Teamsters pension fund. He says he didn't know, at first, that Balistrieri was Frank Bal, boss of the Milwaukee Mafia. Frank Bal suggested that to lock up Teamsters financing, Glick put John and Joseph Balistrieri, his sons, on the payroll as lawyers. Also, Glick should agree to purchase the casino's insurance from a company Dorfman owned. Balistrieri also wanted Glick to sell his sons a fifty percent interest in the two casinos for $30,000. "That was something he wanted," Glick said, "and without this option, I perhaps would be precluded from receiving the loan."

Glick agreed to the conditions, and the Mafia sent emissaries around the country to encourage powerful Central States board members to approve Glick's $62.7 million loan. Balistrieri put the arm on Frank Ranney, a retired Milwaukee Teamsters leader. Frank Bal also got in touch with Nick Civella, the Kansas City boss, and asked him to help Glick. Civella told Roy Williams to vote for it. "He told me to follow Bill Presser's line of thinking," Williams recalls. "And Bill Presser was a friend of Allen Glick's, and Allen Glick was the guy that had the Stardust, and he met with Bill all the time."

Civella had already contacted Maishe Rockman and asked him to tell the Plug to approve the huge Stardust-Fremont loan. Rockman mentioned the request to his brother-in-law, the reclusive John Scalish. The Mafia boss replied, "Well, how much money do them guys need? How much money do they want to make? Aren't they satisfied with what they got?"

Rockman pitched him on the venture. "Johnny, let's do this. We can benefit by it. We can make money." Rockman changed Scalish's mind, secured his approval, and then called on Bill Presser and told him to make sure the Glick loan was approved. Presser told him he'd do what he could.

Nine days after he applied, Glick got the $62.7 million loan—without supplying a personal financial statement or an appraisal of the casinos, a giveaway to investigators that he was fronting for other interests.

In August 1974, Glick's new company, Argent Corporation—*A*llen *R.* *G*lick *Ent*ertainment—bought the two casinos. Within days, Balistrieri called and told Glick that Frank "Lefty" Rosenthal was going to be his right-hand man in the executive suite. Rosenthal, also known as Crazy, was an egotistical, domineering bookmaker who bragged of his handicapping skills and had achieved notoriety at the McClellan committee hearings. Glick gave Lefty a cushy $250,000-a-year job as a gambling adviser after Frank Bal explained that Glick didn't have a choice. Unless, of course, Glick wanted to forget about an additional $65-million renovation loan he wanted from Central States.

By now, Glick knew something fishy was unfolding. He hired a private eye to investigate Frank Bal and quickly learned that not only was he a bookie and a gambler, but that he was also the boss of Milwaukee crime. "I realized I just entered into a trap," Glick recalled.

The pugnacious Rosenthal treated Glick like a piece of furniture and began firing employees at the Stardust and Fremont and replacing them with his own loyalists. Soon, the ground had been prepared for a massive skim operation that federal investigators say netted $7 million from Glick-owned casinos from 1974 to 1976.

Meanwhile, Glick, the army captain who had won a Bronze Star in Vietnam, began fortifying his La Jolla, California, mansion. He installed closed-circuit television cameras and electric fences and posted guards and attack dogs around the Norman-style dwelling. He also secured his second-floor executive suite at the Stardust in Las Vegas. Anyone wanting to see Glick had to first pass through the baccarat pit to a locked doorway, fitted with a one-way mirror, that was controlled by an armed, uniformed guard. Once inside the executive offices, one had to pass muster with a receptionist at the entrance to a smaller, private waiting room occupied by Glick's secretary and another employee. (One of the secretaries Glick shared with Rosenthal

203

was the daughter of Nevada U.S. senator Howard W. Cannon.) One had to negotiate yet another locked door to get into Glick's private office.

Then Glick tried to fire Lefty Rosenthal. The Mob would have none of this, and neither would Rosenthal. "I was placed in this position," he told Glick, "not for your benefit but for the benefit of others. And I have been instructed not to tolerate any nonsense from you, nor do I have to listen to what you say, because you are not my boss."

Glick, an intense man, argued back. Rosenthal put it bluntly: "If you interfere with any of the casino operations or try to undermine anything I want to do here, I [guarantee] you that you will never leave this corporation alive."

Glick called Milwaukee to complain to Frank Bal, who responded matter-of-factly, "What Mr. Rosenthal told you is accurate."

It was evident to Vegas insiders, Teamsters officials, the FBI, and wise guys across the land that Crazy Rosenthal was running the Stardust and the Fremont for the Mob. He promoted the Stardust's huge sports book parlor by touting it and his sports picks on the "Frank Rosenthal Show," a tacky television talk show that featured interviews with Hollywood entertainers and sports figures. Soon the Stardust's sports parlor rivaled the big sports betting parlor at Caesar's Palace.

As Glick tells it, he was snared by the Mafia and there was little he could do to escape. Rosenthal even got Glick's secretary to spy on her boss and report back. Mostly Glick ran the casino hotels, giving free rooms to visiting Teamster big shots and high-rolling mobsters. He traveled on the Argent Corporation's jet to his La Jolla fortress, where he spent time with his wife and young boys among the tennis courts, pool, sauna, and guest and servants' quarters, all overlooking the Pacific.

In March 1975, Glick was interrupted at dinner by a telephone call from Kansas City. It was Lefty Rosenthal, and he demanded to see Glick immediately.

"I can't get there before three or four in the morning," said Glick, making excuses.

"We are going to come and get you or you are going to come voluntarily," Rosenthal threatened.

Glick boarded the company jet, took off immediately, and was met by Rosenthal and Civella associate Carl DeLuna. They led Glick to a nearby hotel and pushed him into a dark room. Two chairs faced each other. Behind one, a light on a pole pierced the dark with a blinding beam, aimed interrogation-style at one of the chairs. Nick Civella sat in the shadows, ominous in a dark suit and dark glasses.

Glick offered his hand, and Civella refused to shake it. They moved to the facing chairs and sat down about a foot apart. The light beamed uncomfortably in Glick's face. He complained about it, and Civella threatened to rip out his eyes.

"You don't know me, but it would be my choice that you'd never leave this room alive," Civella said. "However, because of the circumstances, if you listen, you may."

Though some doubt Glick's account—"Civella wouldn't deal with civilians, guys he didn't know," said a lawyer friendly with him—it was clear that the Kansas City Mafia was unhappy with their front man. Civella told the frightened casino operator that he, Glick, apparently didn't understand that the reason he got the Central States loans was because of Civella.

"Now what is your understanding with Mr. Balistrieri?" Civella asked him.

"I have no understanding," Glick said.

Civella told Glick he was lying. Civella said a $1.2 million kickback, or two percent of the Central States loan, was owed for the Mafia's part in arranging it. "You have a commitment to us," Civella warned. "You owe us $1.2 million. I want that paid in cash. In addition to that, we own part of your corporation, and you're to do nothing to interfere."

"I have no knowledge of it nor can I pay it the way you want it paid," Glick said.

"Well, we will let Mr. Rosenthal handle that," Civella said. "We will let Mr. Rosenthal continue with the casinos and you are not to interfere."

Lefty Rosenthal handled it by bringing in Carl Thomas, an expert in a rather small field—skimming cash from gambling-casino counting rooms. Glick, stashed in his high-security office, later told investigators that he wasn't aware of what was going on, that he was the victim. He said that he had tried to thwart Rosenthal's thieving, like the time Lefty had attempted to take over the car-rental agency and ticket sales office for the Stardust's famous Lido floor show of nearly naked dancers.

Either fearless or foolish, Glick also griped about the outrageous insurance fees Allen Dorfman had billed to the Stardust and the Fremont.

Carl Thomas was the Mob's management consultant for skimming, installing his time-tested systems at various casinos during the seventies. An FBI wiretap later picked up an astonishingly detailed conversation in which Thomas gave a three-hour crash course on casino skimming to Kansas City boss Nick Civella, and his associates Carl Civella, Joe Agosto, and Carl DeLuna.

THOMAS: At the Fremont, we had a ball. . . . We had two cashiers, and I got my comptroller plus my security man's fronting it. [He's] outside the door, the cashiers give [him] the key, they go grab the money, the comptroller's upstairs—he's not actually involved, but we take care of him. Where in case they come and say, "These figures are off, your per's off, this is off." Then he tips us off and we pull up. . . .

Okay, the same thing at the Stardust. There's not that many guys involved, but they gotta be key guys. You follow me? Nick, the guy that's on the outside, the security guard, he don't know what's going on. He just knows they're back there.

NICK CIVELLA: Yeah.

THOMAS: He peaks this guy off anywhere from five hundred to a thousand a month, he's your guy.

CIVELLA: Yeah.

THOMAS: You follow me? But he's not actually doin' the work.

CIVELLA: No idea what's going on, except something is—

THOMAS: Something's goin' on, right.

CIVELLA: —happening. He don't know what or what magnitude or anything.

THOMAS: Right, you understand. The guy that gives us the key, the cashier, he's our guy, he won't press that button. He's back there, he just sits there and he knows somethin' is going. He's got no idea what or anything else. These guys want to make a living too, Nick.

206

Another effective skim technique, Thomas explained, was to have crooked casino employees raid the drop boxes. When chips are purchased, a cashier drops the bills through a slot into a locked box. When full, the boxes are removed and stored in a secure room to be tallied later.

THOMAS: These guys go back there, open the box an' snatch the cash. I've used that system for as long as I can recall.

AGOSTO: I understand.

THOMAS: There is no record.

AGOSTO: Yes, I understand.

THOMAS: They take the money, they go in the office, they count it down, boom, boom, boom, boom. Now the bad part of that system: if they tell you they're taking two thousand a day, they could be taking twenty-four hundred.

Agosto suggested stealing from the cashier's cage. "The cashier is our cashier, right?"

THOMAS: That's what we done in the past. Joe, if we can keep doing that, we may have to go to that. But the bad thing about it, it's a messy way of doing it.

AGOSTO: Why?

THOMAS: Because there's a record of the fills.

They paused, sitting around the table, brainstorming other ways to scam the casinos. Then Thomas said, "Some nights I'm sure you sit here and talk about something for four hours, one problem you're trying to solve. Me . . . and my bookkeeper, my comptroller—who is one thousand percent, they're with me for fifteen years—have sat around in my kitchen, thinking for six hours. Thinking of ways to beat these joints. 'Cause I like to take money out of them."

Despite the seemingly good crowds at the Stardust, the take from its slot machines steadily declined. If the trend continued, Glick felt that his casinos wouldn't meet their mortgage payments with Central States.

On May 1976, to his supposed astonishment, Glick learned why his slots weren't making much money. The Nevada Gaming Commission raided the Stardust's counting room and interrupted what authorities said was a $7-million-a-year skimming operation. Officials said workers in the money-processing rooms rigged the scales to short-weight the tons of coins. The thieves skimmed off the difference between the phony short weight and the actual weight, converted it to cash, and pocketed it. George "Jay" Vandermark, the Stardust's slot-machine manager and one of Lefty Rosenthal's first hires, escaped to Mexico right after the raid.

The torrent of untaxed, unreported, illegally skimmed cash flowed out of the Glick-fronted casinos and sluiced along Mafia conduits to the families in Kansas City, Chicago, Cleveland, and Milwaukee. In Cleveland, Maishe Rockman, nicknamed the Deerhunter because he liked to hunt game, was in charge of picking up the monthly packets of cash, usually eight bundles of five thousand dollars each. He'd be notified by a telephone call, during which arrangements were made for him to pick up the skim in either Kansas City or Chicago. He'd return to Cleveland with the $40,000—sometimes it was higher, $60,000, or even $100,000 one month—and meet with Licavoli and Big Ange Lonardo, underboss since 1976. The three would divide the cash, taking the lion's share themselves and distributing smaller chunks to soldiers and associates. Bill Presser, whose influence got the Glick casino venture going in the first place, pocketed only $1,500 a month, the same amount Teamsters vice president Roy Lee Williams later admitted being paid by the Kansas City Mafia. Jackie told the FBI that Maishe got a taste, too.

Several times, Big Ange went with Rockman to Chicago to collect the skim. "Let me keep you company so you won't be alone," he suggested the first time, and Rockman said fine. The two gray-haired Mob leaders, both in their late sixties and friends since their teens, set off along the turnpike in Rockman's Cadillac, fitted with an oversized gas tank and a secret cash compartment.

On one of their Chicago excursions, Maishe and Big Ange arrived at a Chicago restaurant, sat down, ordered lunch, and called their bagman, Civella's cousin Anthony "Stompy" Chiavola, Sr., a retired Chicago police captain. Chiavola walked in a few minutes later.

"Sit down, have something to eat," Rockman said.

"No, I'm not hungry," said Chiavola, anxious to complete his task.

Maishe stood up and walked outside with Chiavola to his parked car. The two men got inside, Chiavola handed him a package containing $40,000, and they chatted for a few minutes. In the meantime, Lonardo finished his meal and came outside and sat in Rockman's Cadillac. A minute or two later, Maishe rejoined Big Ange. "I got the money," Rockman said.

They drove back to Cleveland. The next night, as was the custom, the two men met with Licavoli and discussed how to split up the money. When there were family members on trial, Rockman kept the skim money in a defense fund to pay lawyers. Otherwise, the skim served as seed money for other rackets—loan-sharking, political payoffs, and drug dealing—that multiplied into even greater profits for the Cleveland family.

Things went smoothly during the first couple of years the Mafia skimmed from Glick's casinos. Then the Cleveland family stopped getting calls saying when and where to pick up the skim. Rockman wondered if Las Vegas authorities had put heat on the Glick casinos, making it too hot for Rosenthal and his counting-room loyalists. He asked Big Ange, who was going to Miami, to see if he could find Chicago underboss Jack Cerone and ask why the skim had stopped.

Lonardo called John "Peanuts" Tronolone, a made member of the Cleveland family who ran a Miami travel agency and kept tabs on Mob activities in south Florida. Lonardo asked Peanuts if he knew whether Cerone was in town. Peanuts said to check at Joe Sonkin's restaurant, a Mob hangout and message drop.

"The next day, we went to Joe Sonkin's restaurant and talked to Joe," Lonardo said. "I asked him if Jackie Cerone was in town. He said yes, and I said will you make an appointment for me? He said he would. I went there the next day and he told me, 'Jackie will see you at the Mt. Sinai Hospital in the lobby at ten-thirty tomorrow.' That's where I met Jackie Cerone. We talked about a few things, and Mr. Cerone asked me if I had something to talk to him about. I said I did. I told him that Maishe Rockman asked me to find out through him what was wrong in Vegas. Did the skimmng stop or is the heat on and no money coming in?"

Cerone said, "No, we've been getting our money. You should have been getting your money, too."

"We haven't," Big Ange said.

"As soon as I get back to Chicago, I'll contact Kansas City and find out what's wrong," Cerone said.

What was wrong was Frank Bal and Nick Civella had begun disagreeing about how to split the Argent casino skim. Cerone stepped in and settled it. For his efforts, the Chicago crime family began taking twenty-five percent of the skim.

Years later, Jackie complained that his father was never sufficiently rewarded for the effort he made and risks he took in voting hundreds of millions of dollars in loans for Mob interests. But Big Ange Lonardo knew otherwise. Years later, he said that Frank Bal had told him that Glick had kicked back $600,000 to Bill Presser and Teamsters president Frank Fitzsimmons for their help in arranging the $62.7 million loan.

An unstable egomaniac, Rosenthal was forever mouthing off and had even threatened a Las Vegas politician. This caused Civella, Balistrieri, and Rockman to worry about Rosenthal bringing the heat down on their nifty operation. Finally, after four years of Rosenthal's public domination of the Argent casinos, the Nevada Gaming Control Board decided that Rosenthal's presence was reason enough to pull Glick's casino licenses.

The crime families decided that Rosenthal had to go. But first Glick had to be dealt with. On April 25, 1978, shortly before Argent's licenses were pulled, Glick was called to a meeting at the office of a Las Vegas lawyer. Sitting there was Carl DeLuna, a capo for Civella, who was in jail at the time.

"He informed me he was sent there to deliver one last final message to me from his partners," Glick said. "He said that he and his partners were finally sick of having to deal with me and having me around and that I could no longer be tolerated. He informed me it was their desire to have me sell [the casinos] immediately.

"He said . . . he was certain I wouldn't find my children's lives expendable. With that, he looked down on his piece of paper, and he gave me the names and ages of each of my sons. . . . And the meeting ended with me saying that I was willing to sell."

In late 1979, five years after putting up only $500,000 of his own money to buy the Stardust and Freemont casinos, Glick netted a few million dollars after selling them for $68 million to Allan D. Sachs, former president of the Stardust, and his Trans Sterling Corporation. Glick sauntered off a healthy, wealthy man. Like Jackie Presser, he had successfully walked a high wire between staying alive and staying out of jail.

15
Polishing an Image

"What the hell do they need public relations for?"
ALLEN DORFMAN

Shortly after Labor Day, 1972, the leaders of sixteen Ohio Teamsters locals filtered into a hotel conference room in Cleveland where Bill Presser had anchored his huge, operation-scarred frame in a conference-room chair. Through a gray haze of cigar and cigarette smoke, he made an angry pronouncement, saying he was sick of other unions getting good press for new programs and services that the Teamsters have been offering for years.

"When dialysis came along, we bought three or four machines. . . . All of the work was done by this council. . . . If you read the papers, the AFL-CIO did it all. No one ever mentions us. I could go on and on and on. This gets a bit ridiculous. . . . [Our members] wonder what the hell are we doing as far as this sick world is concerned, and I think we should tell the world and tell the people and tell our membership, 'This is what we are doing, and this is what we are going to do.' Give them all kinds of stories about the [business] agents and what they do for them. Give them meeting halls and then let them gather."

Communicate with the members? Tell them what was going on? Give them meeting halls and let them gather? Presser's words must have startled this band of secretive, closed-mouth labor leaders, men forever protecting their hindsides from authorities, dissidents, and rivals. This sort of talk had always been considered heresy, words the Teamsters bosses came to expect from rabble-rousers and troublemak-

212

ers who didn't appreciate the contracts their leaders had negotiated for them. What was going on with the Plug?

Times were changing, especially in the five years since Hoffa had been locked away in Lewisburg. His autocracy had been transformed into a system of feudal baronies, with president Fitzsimmons as the slack-handed overseer. Fitz spent much of his time golfing and being courted by the Nixon administration. Unlike Hoffa, Fitzsimmons allowed important regional matters to be decided by Teamsters barons like Bill Presser in Ohio, the Provenzano brothers in New Jersey, and Andy Anderson on the West Coast. Furthermore, unions as a whole were losing members. This hard fact softened some of the old-school Teamster chieftains and made them receptive to new strategies to retain power, such as public relations and political lobbying, weapons their adversaries at the bargaining table had wielded for decades.

Still, long-time Teamster bosses like Babe Triscaro had to be surprised that the push to polish their image came from an old-timer like Big Bill. Presser had learned the hard way from the Senate Rackets Hearings and from various grand-jury appearances that the best way to stay out of trouble was to keep your mouth shut and take the Fifth. Their surprise diminished when they learned that it was Jackie who had sold his father on hiring a public-relations firm to promote the Joint Council. It was a tough sell. "Jackie wanted to bring in public relations," Bob Rotatori, the Teamsters lawyer, said. "Bill felt that the more you stay out of the news, the better off you were. I observed many heated debates between them on that. Bill warned him, 'That's going to be your downfall.' "

"Bill was very proud of his son," said Peter Halbin, a partner with the PR firm the Pressers hired in 1972. "He very much wanted for him to succeed and move ahead in organized labor. So he was supportive of a whole range of innovations that Jackie brought. You see, Bill Presser was far more receptive to new ideas and change than he would want anyone to know. He played a role of being the old-time heavy-handed labor leader. But down deep, on more than one occasion in private conversation, he said, 'Boy, the world ain't what it used to be,' or 'I don't know what you boys are doing,' and then he'd wink."

At this September 1972 meeting of Ohio Teamsters leaders, Bill announced, "I took it upon myself last week, with the approval of the trustees, two of them being present, of retaining the services of an

213

advertising company in Cleveland . . . to give us good exposure in every possible way. The operation is for approximately six months, to see how we come out and the cost of it will be a thousand dollars per month. . . . At this time, I am asking for approval for something that I did without approval several days ago." Bill turned to Jackie and asked, "What is the name of this company?"

"Sam Abrams and Associations," Jackie replied, mangling the name.

Without discussion and by a unanimous vote, the Teamsters hired the PR firm. It was owned by Richard Bellamy, Peter Halbin, an ex-aide to Cleveland mayor Carl Stokes, and one of Bill's associates from the jukebox days, Samuel L. Abrams. Abrams had helped Presser operate a scheme in the fifties through which he extracted money from vending companies that depended on Teamsters Local 410 workers to service and stock their machines. Presser took money for ad space in Local 410's *Vending News*, a tiny, rarely published one-sheet tabloid whose six-hundred-copy press run cost forty dollars. Abrams was the middleman. The Ohio Phonograph Merchants Association, a cartel of vending companies, gave Abrams's ad agency, Ohio Advertising Company, $650 a month. Abrams, acting as the cut-out, or buffer, issued a monthly $650 check to Bill Presser under the guise of buying ad space in *Vending News*. A 1954 congressional subcommittee looking into jukebox racketeering asked Presser if he had received money from Ohio Advertising Company. He refused to answer, saying that he didn't want to incriminate himself. "Obviously, it is some kind of shake-down," Senator George Bender replied. Several months after the last edition of *Vending News*, the $650 checks continued to flow from the vending cartel to Abrams to Bill Presser and Local 410. They were never charged with a crime.

The International Brotherhood of Teamsters first employed publicists in 1958 to counter the Senate rackets hearings, which devastated the union's image with its gritty revelations of Mafia control, self-dealing, violence, sweetheart contracts, and betrayal of the rank and file. These televised hearings had a devastating impact on unions in general. A Gallup poll showed that after only six months of hearings, the public's acceptance of unions dropped dramatically, from seventy-six percent to sixty-four percent.

Throughout the sixties the IBT seemed to ignore its public image.

214

Hoffa was busy tangling with Bobby Kennedy and fighting off a prison term.

By the seventies, "the press operation in Washington was very weak," Halbin explains. "And just as Jackie educated his father, he educated Fitz." Jackie convinced him to appear on "Meet the Press" and to sit still for a question-and-answer session with *U.S. News and World Report.* Fitz felt he came off well.

In Ohio, Jackie made *Ohio Teamster* the centerpiece of his campaign to sell himself as a new breed of labor leader. The monthly tabloid was circulated to 180,000 Teamsters, politicians, members of Congress, and reporters. It was filled with one-sided articles attacking Jackie and Bill's enemies and puffing up their friends. For example, *Ohio Teamster* blasted United Farm Workers Union founder Cesar Chavez, who was battling the Teamsters over organizing California migrant workers. "A great con artist," Jackie branded him. Another story—"Fitz Tells Meany Off"—told of Fitzsimmons's reaction to AFL-CIO chairman George Meany, who had supported Chavez and denounced the Teamsters as unfit to be called a labor union. *Ohio Teamster* defended the managers of the Central States Pension Fund during the height of its scandal and promoted the candidacy of Republican Ohio governor James Rhodes, among other things. The journal featured prominent photographs of Jackie in various can-do poses— cutting ribbons for new buildings, mingling with retirees, being honored with civic awards. Rarely did a reader find a picture of Babe Triscaro, Skippy Felice, or any of the rivals who might upset Jackie's plan to assume his father's powerful union positions.

By the standards of a Fortune 500 company, Jackie's PR campaign was unsophisticated. Still, it was radically innovative when compared to those of other Teamster joint councils, most of which didn't have a press office. Many Teamsters leaders, from vice presidents on down to the local level, resented Jackie's move into the national spotlight using promotional sleight-of-hand rather than hard-won experience. They considered press agentry a waste of money, a self-aggrandizing vehicle for Fitzsimmons and his lackey, Jackie. Millions of dollars in union members' dues were spent on image polishing, including the image of the scandal-tarred Central States Pension Fund. Allen Dorfman, the fund "consultant" and Chicago Mafia associate, disagreed strongly with Presser's campaign. "What the hell do they need public relations for? That's all bullshit. Who the fuck cares what the public thinks. The John Jerk-off in the street doesn't pay anything into the fund. Fuck John Doe Jerk-off. The members, they're the ones who count, and they know they get paid their benefits."

Presser's PR push turned out to be a shrewd move because it gave him a springboard to power. With less seniority than other aspiring vice presidents, Jackie was cut off from the normal avenues to power—bargaining the National Master Freight Agreement or running one of the union's trade divisions such as newspaper drivers or warehouse workers. He was incapable of making a name for himself as a rouser of the rank and file, as Hoffa had done; Jackie was uncomfortable around the so-called unwashed. Instead, he presciently tied his advancement to the new, amorphous, imprecise duties referred to as Teamsters communications. "Nobody had any idea you could build power through communications," says Peter Halbin, Jackie's publicist. "They [his rivals] all wanted to be head of one of the divisions." Jackie leaped over them with public relations.

He also built himself up by assaulting one of the Teamsters' big bugbears, the news media, which in many cases was exposing the same corruption that Jackie was secretly revealing to the FBI. Reporters were "unpatriotic," "jackals," "sensationalists," he said with demagogic fury. Privately, Jackie enjoyed sparring with the press and tried to cultivate a few of them as sources. He needed the media to draw attention to himself. Without a seemingly invincible foe to attack, Jackie was like Senator Joe McCarthy without a Communist threat, a prizefighter with only shadows to box.

Jackie took other steps to reshape his image into that of a respectable community leader. First he gave up his trademark black shirts, white ties, and loud shoes—the young wise-guy look that Teamsters business agent Rudy the Cootie could pull off but just enhanced Jackie's huge body and gangster image. *Cleveland* magazine, the upscale monthly, had tweaked Presser about his sleazy attire. Urged by Carmen, he finally began draping himself in conservative suits. She had been trying to refurbish him since long before they married. "I remember when we first met, he came over one time and he smelled," she says. "He stunk. I said, 'Don't you wear deodorant?' He said, 'That's for sissies.'"

Carmen convinced him to use an anti-perspirant. Years later,

216

when Jackie would carry on self-importantly, she would kid him, "Hey, I used to know you when you didn't wear deodorant. You can't fool me."

Jackie refused to smooth all of his rough edges. He didn't give up his acorn-sized diamond pinkie ring or his heavy gold chain bracelet that spelled out *Jackie*. He chafed when Halbin suggested that he attend seminars and workshops at the American Management Association. "See how the other half sells themselves," Halbin urged. "See how they present themselves." Away from school since the eighth grade, Jackie wasn't about to become a middle-aged student. "I'm too busy," he said.

The remaking process went so far that at one point, Halbin suggested to Jackie that he change his name. "Jackie, isn't it time for your name to be Jack?" Halbin asked seriously. "You're a labor leader. What kind of name is Jackie?"

The suggestion irked Presser. "He looked at me like I was the biggest asshole in the world," Halbin recalls. "He said, 'That's the name my parents gave me. It's on my birth certificate.'"

Thinner now, dressing like a banker, more secure with his new image, Jackie started joining civic committees, charity boards, and community groups at astounding speed. Within a few years of hiring the PR firm Bellamy and Halbin, Jackie had built up a massive résumé that listed thirty-seven civic affiliations, twelve former civic affiliations, and nineteen labor-union affiliations. Among his credits were member of the Hunger Task Force; labor chairman of the New Cleveland Campaign; trustee of the Greater Cleveland Sports Hall of Fame Foundation; vice chairman of the Greater Cleveland Roundtable; editor of the *Ohio Teamster;* vice president of the Teamsters Blood Bank; and on and on.

Before meeting him, many community leaders expected Jackie to be a boorish, obese thug. They were quite surprised to discover that one-on-one, Jackie was charming, down-to-earth, a gifted storyteller and a self-deprecating golf partner who whacked the ball a mile. Before speaking to the Cleveland Rotary Club in March 1975, for instance, Jackie stood in a hallway outside the dining room, surveyed the crowd of several hundred businessmen, then joked, "I guess I'll throw in a couple of 'dese, dem, and dose.' I think I'll talk about booze and broads."

217

"When you're with him, you felt real comfortable, just one of the guys," Alvin "Buddy" Krenzler, now a federal judge, remembers. "He never went high hat, Mr. Big Shot. I never saw any change. He was never too busy, like some of these guys you talk to, and you sense they're looking over your head to see who else is in the room they have to go talk to. When he talked to you, you felt important. . . . If he wasn't in the labor movement, he'd have been successful at something else."

In 1974, the *Cleveland Press* announced, "What Presser has right now is a sweeping influence in labor and political spheres that matches or exceeds that of any other Greater Cleveland labor leader—with the possible exception of his father." Along with the respectability came such public displays of affection as awards dinners and recognition banquets. Unlike his father, Jackie "needed recognition," Bob Rotatori, the Teamsters lawyer, recalls. "Bill didn't want recognition. Jackie loved awards. Man of the Year. He fed on all that. He was always very self-conscious that he wasn't educated. He was always self-conscious that he couldn't write well. That was why he hired PR people. It was something I discerned in him."

Under the strain of his busy schedule, Jackie blossomed into a workaholic. Carmen was left to care for the four teenaged children, her two boys from a previous marriage and Jackie's son and college-aged daughter. On Saturdays, Jackie golfed with his friends at various country clubs in the area. Carmen didn't like golf and hated the country-club scene. Instead, she stayed home and read or shopped for antiques and jewelry. Later she opened an antiques store with Jackie's cousin, Trina Miller, in tony Chagrin Falls, Ohio.

They fell into a routine. By five in the morning, sometimes earlier, Jackie would wake up and drag the nail of his big toe along Carmen's calf until she woke up. She got out of bed, made coffee, brought two cups back to bed, and Jackie talked, filling her in, if necessary, on what he did the night or day before. Then he'd climb out of bed, shower, and leave by seven. Carmen fell back to sleep for an hour or two.

The four kids didn't see much of Jackie, Carmen says, and perhaps out of guilt he gave them whatever they wanted—except his time. When they turned sixteen, he gave each a new car. In 1972, his daughter Bari was injured in a late-night car accident coming home

218

from college. She struggled through extensive physical therapy, becoming discouraged and sassy. "Jackie never understood Bari," Carmen says. "He wanted a little mouse who never talked back. If he only gave her fifteen minutes a day instead of buying her."

Jackie also spent time investing in and starting up companies with friends. He hoped to build a fortune as his father had in the vending business. One of Jackie's ventures was a wine and specialty food store in a small, exclusive shopping mall. His partners were the president and the vice president of Cleveland-based Leaseway Transportation Corporation, the nation's third-largest publicly held transportation company, a huge employer of teamsters. They built the store, Pavilion Wine and Spirits, in 1975 in Beachwood, an upper-class Cleveland suburb, and quickly sparked controversy. After calling in a few favors, Jackie and his partners obtained a liquor permit for their store, even though spirits were normally sold only at Ohio's state-owned liquor stores. In rare instances, the state liquor-control board made exceptions, and a private business was permitted to sell hard liquor in underserved, isolated areas and in locations more than three miles from the nearest state liquor outlet. Jackie's was the first private liquor outlet in the Cleveland area.

How Jackie and his partners got around this restriction in the first place is unclear. However, Jackie's partner, Robert Moss, a Leaseway vice president and former treasurer of the Cuyahoga County Democratic party, just so happened to share an office in Columbus with the former liquor-department permit chief. The *Plain Dealer* raised the idea that Jackie had opened himself to conflict of interest by sharing a personal investment with the top officers of a giant employer of teamsters. "I've known Mr. Moss for thirty years, I know his family," Jackie replied when the question came up. "It looked like a good venture." His daughter, Bari, worked at the Pavilion for a while, and Jackie hoped she would eventually take over the store's management. Because of the negative newspaper publicity, the state learned about the unusual exception made for Jackie's store and revoked the hard-liquor permit. The store folded in a couple of years.

A wildly successful business deal was Jackie's eleven-month investment in a theater in the round called the Front Row, located only a hundred yards or so from his Forge restaurant in suburban Cleveland. In January 1975, Jackie bought one-third of the Front Row Theatre for $40,000 and assumed one-third of a $2.5-million mortgage. Less than a year later, Seeburg Industries, Inc., a maker of vending machines and musical instruments, bought the Front Row for $5 million, more than $1.5 above its fair market value. Jackie netted nearly one million dollars on the inflated sale, and bragged to reporter Greg Stricharchuk that the investment had made him a millionaire.

How does someone make so much money over so little time? That's what the Labor Department wanted to know, and it launched a belated investigation in 1982. Some owners in Seeburg Industries and its subsidiaries later received loans from the Central States Pension Fund, according to Labor Departments reports. The government's theory was that Jackie, who sat on the Central States board in 1975, was paid off through the Front Row transaction as a reward for approving the Central States financing. It was never able to prove its case.

Another highly unusual business transaction involving Jackie also was investigated by the Labor Department, this time in 1975. Sam Klein, Bill's boyhood friend and the owner of Bally Manufacturing, the slot machine maker, gave $120,000 in Bally stock to Bill, Jackie, and other Presser family members in February 1972. Jackie alone pocketed $70,000 worth of stock—totally gratis—from the mob-connected company. Two months later, the Central States Pension Fund loaned Bally $6 million at 8 percent. A year and four months later, Klein gave $16,500 worth of free stock to Bill Presser and his family. In January 1974, the Central States pension fund board, of which Bill was an influential member, loaned Bally an additional $12 million at a below-market rate of 6.5 percent interest.

A Labor investigator in the case said he recommended to the Cleveland Strike Force prosecutor at the time that the persons who received the free slot machine stock be called to testify before a grand jury. That was not done. Just on its face, however, it appears the Pressers benefitted handsomely from their powerful positions on the board of Central States, the Mafia's bank.

Jackie's next step, now that he had gained credibility by appearing on assorted charity boards, was to join an exclusive country club. A golfer who clouted long, somewhat erratic drives, Jackie enjoyed the game's pace, company, and appearance of exercise. More importantly, he still craved to be socially accepted; it was a problem in Cleveland, an old-money city known for snobbishly restrictive clubs. Even today, Catholics, Jews, and blacks are not accepted for membership at many

Cleveland country clubs where establishment bankers, lawyers, and industrialists rub shoulders in the locker rooms or talk business in the men's grills.

In the seventies, there were three predominantly Jewish country clubs in Northern Ohio. The most exclusive was Oakwood, full of wealthy men who didn't soil their hands, cut deals, or build their inherited fortunes aggressively. The forebears of these men had emigrated from Germany to Ohio in a wave that started in 1837 and ended in the mid-1870s. The next step down on the social pecking order, but still elite, was Beechmont Country Club, where new members had to pass the scrutiny of the membership committee. Jackie set his sights on Beechmont but didn't want to be embarrassed by being snubbed. A labor leader whose father was publicly linked to the Mob had two strikes against him.

As usual, Jackie turned to friends: developer and state appeals-court judge Alvin Krenzler and multimillionaire Maury Salzman, who had grown up in Bellefaire, a Jewish orphanage, and went on to found and wholly own Bobbie Brooks Incorporated, a women's sportswear company worth $36 million by 1966. Salzman contributed generously to charities, was respected throughout town and influential enough to get just about anyone past the Beechmont membership committee. Krenzler, chief political operative for former Ohio Republican governor C. William O'Neill in the fifties, also went to work. He informally polled Beechmont's admissions committee members about letting Jackie join. "They all told me they had no problem," Krenzler recalls. Krenzler and Salzman solicited letters from every prominent person they could grab. "We put on a presidential campaign," says Krenzler.

In the summer of 1976, the fifteen-man committee met to vote on Jackie's admission to Beechmont. Each member picked up a white and a black ball. A box was passed from voter to voter around the table, and each put in his hand and released a ball. A white ball meant yes, admit him. A black ball, no. If two or more black balls were tallied, the candidate would be turned down. The box slowly rounded the table, the balls plunked in. When the box was emptied, there were two dark balls. Krenzler and Salzman couldn't believe it—their candidate had literally been blackballed.

Krenzler says that he later collared each of his fellow club members on the admissions committee and asked what had happened.

What was it that made them vote no? Someone must have been holding a mistaken notion about Jackie Presser. "Everybody said they voted yes," Krenzler says, disbelieving. "There must have been two black balls in that box before they voted."

Jackie was deeply hurt. He had joined charity boards and hired a public-relations firm to shape his image as a labor statesman, but he continued to be rejected by those he wanted to be his peers. "Inside he hurt," Krenzler says. "He never said, I'm going to get those guys, or anything like that. He took it philosophically." But he hurt.

Feeling slighted by the city's Jewish establishment, Jackie cut back drastically on pressuring Teamsters locals to support Bonds for Israel drives. "He wanted to belong so much," Carmen says. "He wanted to be more social, with more people of wealth and standing in the community. This is why he was so upset when they didn't accept him at Beechmont."

The next notch down was Hawthorne Valley Country Club. It accepted Jackie almost immediately.

16
Sweethearts

"When you deal with a leasing company, you go back to the old plantation days."

In the mid-seventies, the Teamsters ruling powers held a winter meeting in Florida at the Diplomat, a fancy beachfront resort with a PGA championship golf course just north of Miami. On the lush, manicured links, at the swimming pool, and in the Diplomat's seven restaurants one could find hangers-on and hustlers, backslappers and businessmen, all courting the Teamsters powers. These leaders could reward or ruin companies at the bargaining table as well as unlace the purse strings and loan millions from its pension funds, and everyone wanted to be noticed by them.

At this quarterly IBT executive board meeting, Teamsters vice president Roy Lee Williams noticed a dark-haired man acting chummy with Bill Presser, Jackie, and vice president Salvatore "Sammy Pro" Provenzano of New Jersey. Williams was irritated by the way the stranger carried himself. The guy made a big entrance when he came into a room, swinging his shoulders, talking loudly, acting self-important. Williams, nicknamed "the Rancher," was one of the three most powerful Teamsters at the Diplomat, a tough negotiator who knew trucking and was the first Teamsters vice president since Hoffa to win the respect of long-haul truckers. Williams wanted to know the identity of this operator. His rivals, the Pressers, who considered him a Missouri hayseed, weren't about to make the introduction.

Williams asked Sammy Pro about the boisterous stranger, and

223

Provenzano seemed surprised that Williams didn't know the man, Eugene Boffa. He brought Boffa over and introduced him. "This is a labor consultant who works in our area and we found him to be honest and truthful," Sammy Pro said. "And if he ever gets any business in your particular part of the country, why, he's a good fellow that you can deal with and straighten out problems so you don't have to strike."

As Williams and other Teamsters leaders quickly discovered, Eugene R. Boffa, Sr., was an empire builder who operated under the protection of Mafia leaders Russell Bufalino of Scranton, Pennsylvania, and Anthony Provenzano, Sammy's imprisoned brother, of Union City, New Jersey. An accountant by training, Boffa was convicted in 1961 of looting Manufacturers Bank of Edgewater, New Jersey, while serving as its president. Before his conviction, Boffa formed a labor-leasing company that supplied truck drivers to some of the biggest, most prestigious corporations in the nation.

The scheme was almost elegant in its simplicity. Boffa approached a company that relied on truck drivers—various divisions of Continental Can Corporation were big clients—and offered to supply drivers, pay them, and guarantee labor peace. In return, the corporations had to pay him whatever their trucking payroll had been or maybe slightly less. Both parties profited. Corporations enjoyed lower labor costs, didn't have to bother making out a trucking payroll, and didn't lose money because of strikes, slowdowns, or picketing. Boffa's companies, operating under the name Country Wide Personnel, squeezed eight to ten percent from the payroll as a fee. He traveled the country, signing up companies such as Coca-Cola, J. C. Penney, Continental Can, Crown Zellerbach, Crown Cork and Seal, and others.

Most of these corporations' drivers were originally covered by the Teamsters National Master Freight Agreement, which mandated uniform wage rates and benefits. But Boffa got around the Master Freight Agreement easily enough. After a company signed on with him, it fired all of its drivers; Boffa stepped in and rehired them all the next day. Before doing so, however, Boffa first privately negotiated a cheaper, inferior labor contract with the help of conniving local Teamsters officials, who were told to approve such sweetheart deals by regional Teamsters powers like Presser or the Provenzanos. After being rehired by Boffa, the Teamsters drivers—the victims—found their wages at Country Wide shaved by ten percent or more, even though they were

224

supposedly covered by the National Master Freight Agreement. Sometimes the truckers were paid the same wage but lost seniority, pension benefits, holidays, or sick days.

The elected Teamster officials were rewarded with payoffs. For being allowed to operate in eastern Pennsylvania and Delaware, for instance, Boffa gave two percent of his payroll to Frank Sheeran, president of Local 327 in Wilmington and the most powerful Teamster in the state. Sheeran in turn split his take with his overseer, Mafia boss Russell Bufalino. Other times, Boffa bribed Teamster officials with free Lincolns or sports cars owned by his leasing company.

By the middle seventies, Boffa had thirty labor-leasing companies operating in thirty states, and his benefactors included the Provenzanos, the Pressers, Sheeran, Sam Ancona, the mobbed-up leader of the Teamsters joint council in Kansas City, and other officials. But Boffa never managed to get Roy Williams to warm up to him. He once gave Williams a pair of diamond-studded cuff links. The gift might have impressed the Provenzanos back East, but Roy Lee lived on a Missouri farm and had no need for fancy jewelry. He didn't even have a shirt with French cuffs.

Boffa's key employees were also racketeers. One of his most trusted lieutenants was Robert "Bobby" Rispo, a beefy ex-Teamster who says he started working at nineteen as a goon for Teamsters Local 470 in Philadelphia. Around 1969, Rispo was hired to knock heads and rough up drivers and dissidents who complained about how their officials were running Local 470. "Sometimes you had to go out and threaten a guy, sometimes you had to physically hurt him," Rispo said.

A year or so later, after breaking a few legs, he moved to Teamsters Local 107, also in Philadelphia, which was controlled by the Angelo Bruno crime family. Rispo said he operated a freelance organizing scheme with other wise guys under the protection of Bruno. "How the scheme worked," Rispo explained, "is you just pick out a company at random, a small company, ten, fifteen drivers. And you go into the company and you bring them . . . a letter of recognition. You already had the right to use the Teamsters 107 name. So you go in, and you find out who the boss was. And you hand him a letter and you say, 'Sign this or tomorrow morning I'm putting you on strike.' . . . So the guy, you know, naturally wanted to [know], 'Who are you?'

" 'I'm from Teamsters Local 107. I've got the majority of employees signed up, and they want to be in the union.' So naturally the guy wouldn't recognize it. So the next morning, you go down with three or four guys and put up a picket line, and you just hold the company down. Now after three or four days of this, and this guy's running back and forth between the NLRB and the police department and everybody else, the guy would kind of give in."

In one instance, Rispo said he threw up a bogus picket line to shake down a man who owned a fish company. "He handled live lobsters," Rispo recalled. "And he had a truckload of lobsters. He had five thousand lobsters in water tanks. And the guy kept riding around with them. He had no place to put the lobsters, and the lobsters were dying. At that time . . . it was a big joke because I said, 'I hear all these little voices hollering, "I want water." ' He turned around and gave us $15,000 to get away from his place."

Learning of Rispo's skills as a goon, Boffa hired him to help run the various branches of Country Wide Personnel and eventually promoted him to head of personnel. He handled the legions of disgruntled drivers.

Many times the union members, feeling cheated, asked to see the contract. They were shown what looked like a Master Freight Agreement. Actually, it was a sweetheart contract with pages of the Master Freight language on top and then, tucked in the back, a series of provisions that took back many of the standard benefits. This was Boffa's profit margin. "What we would do was put out what they call a white-paper contract," Rispo explained. "And the local union would agree to this white-paper contract. So that if you look on the surface, you would see Teamsters National Master Freight Agreement. . . . But if you looked on the back, then you would see that we took away his clean-up time, we took away the road-drivers' radius, we took away . . . all his rights under the union. He had none."

Sometimes, if the complaining workers stood up for their rights and complained too loudly, Rispo shipped in a goon squad to bark out threats. "That's how you make the whole thing work," Rispo explained. "It was the whole fear theory that if you don't do it, you're going to get hurt. You know, sometimes you might get hurt permanently. I mean, it's that simple."

Boffa's truck drivers had no one to complain to about the corrupt arrangement. Technically, the Fortune 500 corporations weren't their

226

employers anymore, so they couldn't turn to them. Their union had already agreed to the substandard contract, and their corrupt leaders weren't going to give up kickbacks and free cars. The disgruntled truckers could only turn to Boffa and his shell outfit. "When you deal with a leasing company . . . you go back to the old plantation days," Rispo said. For example, if fed-up truckers struck Continental Can "we'd break the strike the same day because it's a secondary boycott so they can't strike Continental Can. Then they go to the local union. The local union is already working with us, so they got no recourse there."

The list of horrors went on. The Master Freight Agreement stipulated that brakes, windshields, mirrors—all safety equipment—had to be working or the driver didn't take the truck from the depot. But the Boffa companies ignored the violations. Drivers were forced to operate unsafe trucks. "With our company, you drove the truck no matter what was going on," Rispo said. "You drove the truck or you didn't work."

Many courageous teamsters, unwilling to be exploited, did organize slowdowns or wildcat strikes. The affected company would alert Boffa, who would allow the company to terminate its contract with his labor-leasing company. Everybody was fired. Then Boffa would bring in another one of his shell companies, one with a different name, and have his henchmen rehire the out-of-work drivers—all except those the company told him were the rabble-rousers. They were purged.

Each time Boffa shifted teamsters from one of his companies to the next, he dropped wages and benefits a notch. In some cases, drivers became so desperate and uncertain about job security that "guys had to pay money to work, to get the right to work," Rispo said.

The labor-leasing scheme required the cooperation of the company, the local union, and Boffa's outfit. Sometimes, even when he'd line up a company client, Boffa couldn't convince a local union to sell out its members. Such was the case in South Carolina, where Bobby Rispo was dispatched in 1975 to set up a labor lease for a truck depot of Crown Cork and Seal, the can and bottle-cap maker with over $1 billion in sales in 1978. Rispo visited the local Teamsters official, Frank H. Wood of Local 28 in Taylors, South Carolina, and explained what he wanted to do.

Wood courageously refused to go along. Not in my jurisdiction, he said. He threw Rispo out of his office. Rispo called Boffa at his

Elmwood Park, New Jersey, headquarters and told him, "This guy isn't going to budge."

"Ok, what you do is go back to the hotel and hang around down there. Let me reach out to Sam and Roy," Boffa said, referring to Sam Ancona, head of the Kansas City Teamsters, and IBT vice president Roy Williams.

Later, Rispo returned to Wood's office at Local 28. The pressure tactic hadn't worked; Wood still refused to sell out. "I don't care if you call Jimmy Hoffa!" he told Rispo. "Get the hell out of my office!"

Boffa called the head of transportation for Crown Cork and Seal and explained the problem. Crown Cork and Seal closed its Taylors, South Carolina, depot and moved it outside the jurisdiction of Wood's local. "Gene meanwhile made the connection with another local a couple of miles down the road, another jurisdiction of the Teamsters, and we just moved the trucks up there," Rispo said. "Everybody was working hand in hand. It went from the union to the corporation to the leasing company, and the end result, bottom line, is the driver gets shafted."

When Boffa wanted to introduce a sweetheart contract in Ohio, he had to get the Pressers' permission. This was easy to arrange. Bill and Jackie weren't in a position to refuse a request from a friend with important Mafia ties. In return, Rispo swore under penalty of perjury in 1985, he and Boffa gave kickbacks to Jackie Presser.

Rispo had to travel to a hotel in Columbus, Ohio, to attend a day of grievance hearings for Country Wide drivers. Rispo and Ed Strickland of Teamster Local 20 in Toledo were to go through the motions, pretending to be adversaries. Before he left for Ohio, Gene Boffa handed Rispo an envelope of cash and said, "I want you to give this to Jackie Presser."

"Fine," Rispo said. "I'm down there anyway." He said he also brought another envelope of cash for Strickland.

Rispo won the grievance, of course, since the union official was in on the sweetheart scheme. The truck drivers who had complained remained out of work. Afterwards, Rispo and Strickland repaired to the hotel bar and ordered drinks. "Well, I beat you again," Rispo said, joking with Strickland.

228

One of the Country Wide drivers, who had just lost his grievance, overheard Rispo's remark to Strickland and blew up. Not only had he lost his job, but he had just traveled across the state for a fixed grievance session. The driver stalked up to Rispo and Strickland, exploded with anger, and began swearing loudly. He threatened to come back with his friends and kick the tar out of the two.

After the trucker stomped out of the bar, Rispo decided it was wise to finish his drink, pack his bag, and leave. Only he hadn't paid Jackie. He found Presser and said, "Gene said to give this to you, Jack." Presser knew the envelope was coming, slipped it into his pocket, and that was that, Rispo recalls.

This apparently wasn't the sort of slick handoff to which Jackie was accustomed. A week later, Rispo said, Boffa chewed him out for upsetting Presser. Rispo, who later became a government witness, said that Boffa told him he made regular payments to Jackie so that Country Wide could do business in Ohio.

Jackie frequently came home with his pockets stuffed with cash, Carmen recalls. Mysterious piles of neatly wrapped bills—she had no idea where they came from—showed up in Jackie's dresser drawer or in his briefcase. He didn't explain where he got the money, and Carmen knew not to ask. He had been keeping secrets from her for several years now, long before their wedding. Their once-intimate relationship had gradually chilled. Whether to protect Carmen or to protect himself, Jackie told her little about his business. By the mid-seventies, he was living a double life at full-tilt, openly and ambitiously pursuing power in the International while covertly meeting with FBI supervisor Marty McCann and feeding him secrets about his enemies and rivals in the Teamsters and the Mob.

"He tried very hard to keep me totally away from anything having to do with the union," Carmen says. "He tried to keep me and the kids away from that. Then he became successful. The more successful he became, the more separated we became. Because his idea of a life-style and my idea of a life-style were totally different."

One time, she said to him, "Jackie, let's go camping." He replied, "What? Are you crazy? Carmen, Jews don't go camping!"

"He liked the club life, the country-club life. I'm not a person like

229

that. That's when our big problems started. He became a member of Hawthorne Valley Country Club. He started to play golf all the time. He wasn't home anymore. Once he married me, he totally lost interest. I was more at home to take care of the family and take care of the house and that was it. Jackie was home less and less. We sold the house and moved to [an apartment]. He put me away there. It was 1976. It was a beautiful apartment. And after that, he hardly came home anymore. He was traveling a lot."

Within two years, Carmen would file for divorce, not because Jackie was never home, but because she believed he was seeing other women. This infuriated her. Out of revenge and perhaps as a cry for attention, she began sneaking cash from his many hiding places. "Many, many times Jackie would come back with an envelope of money," she says. "He'd go in [the bedroom], put something in his briefcase, lock it, and put it right by his bed. . . . Every once in a while, Jackie used to have hundred-dollar bills like this [holds her fingers an inch apart]. By this time, I knew he was cheating on me, and I was aggravated, and I didn't know how else to get even with him. He'd come in and, I tell you, he'd hide that money. He'd hide it in his socks. He'd hide it in his pants. He'd hide it in his closet. He'd hide it wherever he could hide it. He used to hide it between his underwear in the drawer. I'd pretend I was sound asleep when he'd get up to take a shower. As soon as he hit that shower I'd jump out of bed, I'd go through all the drawers looking for the money, and I'd skim it."

Carmen would swipe several hundred dollars, climb back into bed, slip the cash under her pillow, and feign sleep before Jackie stepped out of the shower and padded back into their bedroom to put on one of his conservative suits. He'd retrieve his cash and depart. Carmen says she snitched cash from his hidden stashes so many times that after falling back asleep, she often forgot she had hidden money under her pillow. Their maid would find it when she made the beds and leave it out on a table.

At first, Jackie didn't say anything about the missing money, not wanting to discuss where he got it. Carmen says he knew she was filching the cash but didn't know how she accomplished it, and it was driving him crazy. Eventually, when Jackie came home with a payoff for someone else and wanted to safeguard it, he'd tell her, "Carmen! Don't take that money! It isn't for me."

230

She used the purloined cash to indulge in an expensive habit—stockpiling costly, tasteful jewelry. "I bought bags of jewelry with the money I took from him," Carmen says. "I love jewelry."

Boffa's empire hit a tiny snag the day Jimmy Hoffa disappeared. Police, the FBI, and other investigators discovered that crime boss Russell Bufalino and mob-controlled Teamsters leader Frank Sheeran were in Detroit the same time that Hoffa disappeared. Authorities traced the license plates of their cars to a company owned by Eugene R. Boffa, Sr. Just who was this businessman who was dishing out favors to crime figures like Bufalino and Sheeran?

Authorities learned that Boffa was a close friend of Salvatore Briguglio, alias Sally Bugs, a Provenzano associate and a prime suspect in the Hoffa murder. A $30,000 loan in the name of Boffa's wife was made to Sally Bugs's wife a few days after the New Jersey hoodlum was released after serving time for a counterfeiting conviction. The FBI and other authorities checked out Boffa and stumbled onto his massive sweetheart operation. Agents learned that the cars Sheeran and Bufalino were driving in Detroit the day Hoffa was kidnapped had been given to them as bribes to allow Boffa's outfit to prosper and multiply.

Throughout this time, Rispo said that Jackie continued to help Boffa's companies, once even solving a problem Country Wide had with an Ohio Teamsters official who complained that his bribe wasn't big enough. Robert R. Groves, president of Local 908 in Lima, Ohio, had agreed to let a Boffa company set up a sweetheart contract, so Rispo came to town and laid the groundwork. As was typical in these schemes, the local Teamsters leader had to stamp his foot, argue, yell, and carry on in front of his members about the contract Boffa's company offered. It was all a show to deceive the rank and file, to convince them that their leader was a true-blue union man looking out for their interests. Continental wanted to reduce benefits and cut wages by fifty cents an hour, and Robert Boffa, Gene's son, had gotten the switch approved by Groves.

Boffa fired all the Continental Can drivers by mail. Rispo arrived under the guise of a different company and began trying to rehire the drivers and put them on a weaker contract. "It was supposed to be all down pat," Rispo said. "It was just a matter of putting on a little show for members, and then Mr. Groves was going to go along with it. . . . It looked like the union was arguing. I mean, we would stand around and scream at each other and threaten to close the company down and everything else. Naturally, the union head there would get all kind of credit even though the guys got cheated. They would still think he was fighting like hell for [them]."

But the little show quickly got out of hand. Groves threatened and screamed at Rispo, pouring it on in front of the drivers, getting them riled up, not giving Rispo an inch.

Rispo was perplexed. This was too realistic. If the drivers got any more excited, Groves would never get them to go along with the sweetheart contract later. Rispo called a time out, slipped in the next room, and met privately with Groves.

"What the hell are you doing?" Rispo asked. "You know, you can drag this thing out for two weeks. Let's get this paper signed. . . . I want to go home."

"No, look, get a hold of Robert," Rispo said Groves told him. "Robert was supposed to send me something, but I didn't get all of it."

Now Rispo understood. Robert Boffa had promised Groves a large bribe and hadn't paid it all yet. Rispo called Gene Boffa and told him about the problem. Gene replied, "All right, let me make some calls. I'll reach out and get a hold of Presser."

After that, everything went smoothly, Rispo said. The Continental Can drivers were switched to the other Boffa company and got cheated out of wages and benefits worth about two dollars an hour.

Though Presser's FBI informant files are extensive, Jackie didn't inform his FBI handlers about Boffa's national network of sweetheart contracts and his payoffs to prominent Teamsters. Even after *Wall Street Journal* reporter Jonathan Kwitny broke a story in 1977 that detailed Boffa's racket and his Mafia ties, Jackie was still afflicted with selective memory. He first talked about Boffa to the FBI in June 1980. Boffa was set to be indicted in a couple of weeks, and the FBI's Los Angeles field office, wanting more information, routed a request to FBI headquarters to ask its sources inside the Teamsters what they knew about Boffa. Jackie wasn't any help, which wasn't surprising. If Boffa was hammered by federal prosecutors, he might be forced to fink on his friends in the Teamsters and the Mob, Jackie included.

Many companies were embarrassed by the publicity in the *Wall*

Street Journal and dropped their contracts with Boffa, including International Paper, Crown Zellerbach, and Inland Container. Boffa simply renamed his shell corporations and brought in new front men. Continental Can and other corporations, knowing that it was just a paper shuffle, quickly returned to the labor-leasing fold.

17
The Weasel

"Jackie told me he don't make a move unless Jack White tells him to."

JIMMY "THE WEASEL" FRATIANNO

One day in 1975, Jackie strode into a private meeting on Murray Hill with two leaders of the Cleveland Mafia, James "Jack White" Licavoli and Tony "Dope" Delsanter. They wanted to introduce Presser to a special friend who had flown in from the West Coast, an angular, silver-haired guy with glasses. His name was Jimmy "the Weasel" Fratianno, and he didn't look like the cold-blooded Mafia hit man who had murdered five men and taken part in killing six others.

Fratianno was sitting among loyal friends. He had known Jack White and Tony Dope for more than forty years. In the thirties, he and Tony Dope had pulled off an impressive string of armed robberies; they stuck up illegal gambling joints, which of course couldn't turn to the police for help. Now Fratianno needed his old friends to convince Jackie, Teamsters communications director and head of Local 507, to go to his higher-ups and get permission for Fratianno to scam members of a San Francisco Teamsters local with a dental-insurance plan.

Following Mafia protocol, which said that out-of-town mobsters had to alert the local crime family before contacting Teamsters union leaders in their area, Fratianno had called Jack White long distance and asked him to set up a meeting with Jackie. Maishe Rockman, the Mafia's intermediary with the Pressers, made the arrangements and brought Jackie to the meeting.

When he saw Jackie, Fratianno was repulsed by how fat he was—

234

the guy had to weigh over three hundred pounds. They exchanged pleasantries, and then Jackie said something that warmed the Weasel's larcenous heart: "I don't make a move unless Jack White says it's OK."

At this first meeting, it was clear that Jackie, a student of the Mob, had heard of Fratianno. They shared the same hometown and several acquaintances. Tony Hughes, Jackie's bodyguard, knew of him, since both had grown up on the Hill. The Weasel had a reputation in Mob circles as a worker—someone unafraid to pull off a hit. He started breaking the law as a boy, stealing fruit from sidewalk stands. Once, a policeman chased him. As the neighborhood paused to watch, an old man remarked, "Look at that weasel run." Making a theft report, the policeman wrote down Weasel as a nickname, and it had followed Fratianno ever since.

Fratianno's ties to the Teamsters went back to 1935, when he freelanced for the union in Cleveland. The Teamsters were trying to organize parking-lot employees, but since the union was small, it was having little success. What was needed was muscle. Bill McSweeney, a hulking union head buster, hired Fratianno and a crew of thugs from Murray Hill. For ten or fifteen dollars a day each, Jimmy the Weasel and his wrecking crew raided nonunion parking lots, throwing acid on cars and slashing tires. It was the Teamsters' quickest, most cost-effective way to convince lot operators to meet union demands.

The Weasel kept up his Teamsters ties over the decades. Allen Friedman remembers the Weasel helping Bill Presser organize dry cleaners by throwing stink bombs. Later, Fratianno did chores for the Plug when he presided over Taxi Drivers Local 555. In 1952, Fratianno attended the International Brotherhood of Teamsters convention in Los Angeles and stayed at the Statler Hotel with Babe Triscaro, his reform-school friend from Cleveland. Triscaro had driven cross-country to the convention with Bill Presser and James Patrick Foley, the corrupt Cleveland police detective in charge of the department's labor office.

Jimmy Hoffa was politicking at the 1952 Teamsters convention, making the connections and deals that would help him get elected Teamsters president five years later. Hoffa got excited when he learned that Fratianno was having dinner that night with Joey Glimco, a capo in the Chicago Mafia and president of a Teamsters local there. Hoffa wanted Glimco's vote for his candidate running for the IBT executive

235

board. Hoffa got Triscaro to introduce him to Fratianno, then Hoffa asked the Weasel to introduce him to Glimco and put in a good word for him. Fratianno gladly obliged; he figured that someday he might want to ask Hoffa to return the small favor.

At that first meeting on the Hill with Jackie, Fratianno quickly got down to business and explained the sophisticated racket he had in mind. "I want you to help Rudy Tham," he started out.

Born Rudolph Tham Antonovich, Rudy Tham was a Mob associate who headed Teamsters Local 856 in San Francisco and became a close Presser friend. Tham was feuding with M. E. "Andy" Anderson, the powerful president of the Teamsters Western States Conference. Over dinner with his pal Fratianno, Tham had complained bitterly that Anderson deliberately humiliated him in front of his membership, the second largest in San Francisco. Anderson wouldn't let Tham settle disputes or tackle difficult negotiations; Anderson handled them himself or farmed them out to an underling. In the macho world of the Teamsters, Tham felt castrated. He wasn't being allowed to fight his own fights. So he had been bad-mouthing Anderson in return, and the scuttlebutt traveled to Anderson in Los Angeles, making him dislike Rudy Tham even more.

As he listened to Tham's gripes, Jimmy the Weasel realized that he could use his Cleveland connections to help Tham and possibly enrich himself. "What are you doing with your dental plan?" Fratianno wanted to know.

"Nothing at the moment," Tham said.

"Rudy, I think I can straighten out your problem," he said.

Tham probably didn't believe Fratianno had the clout to influence the seemingly omnipotent Anderson, who ruled the Teamsters in California and eleven other states. But he said he'd appreciate any help the Weasel could deliver. Then Fratianno made it plain. As a reward for straightening out Anderson, he wanted to run Tham's union dental plan. Fine, Tham told Fratianno.

Fratianno, an ex-bookie, was quick with numbers; there were eight thousand members in Tham's local, and the union would pay about twenty-five dollars per member per month for dental care. It had the makings of a sweet deal: about $200,000 a month or $2.4 million a year

236

to skim from. Fratianno lined up a couple of dentists to provide the services. He figured his cut to be a hefty up-front fee, plus a ten-thousand-dollar monthly rake-off for putting together the deal, plus a few other benefits.

Because he was tight with Fitz, Jackie was the key. He would have to ask Fitz to tell Anderson to lay off Rudy Tham, Fratianno figured.

At Fratianno's next meeting with him, Jackie said there might be a problem with Rudy. "Can you control him?" Jackie asked.

"Yes, I can."

"Will you take full responsibility?" Jackie asked.

"Absolutely."

Fratianno knew what this meant. As he later explained the meeting to Los Angeles mobster Johnny Rosselli: "If he [Tham] starts going wild, they're coming to me, he's my man. If I can't handle him, then it's no good. He does the wrong thing, I've got to clip the bastard. I know that's what Jackie's telling me, so we understand each other."

At the meeting, Fratianno told Jackie that if they resolved the Anderson-Tham dispute, Fratianno would run Tham's local's dental plan as a reward. That meant he would pocket ten thousand dollars under the table each month, with the Cleveland family getting a kickback for its assistance. They of course would be grateful to Jackie for his aid.

"What do you think?" he asked Presser.

"I'll talk to Fitz and let you know," he replied.

Fratianno wasn't the first mobster to understand how much money could be made from fleecing the pension funds and health-benefit plans of the nation's unions. Across the country, organized-crime figures seeking quick scores turned with increasing frequency to the supposedly protected assets of the union workers. The federal Employee Retirement Income Security Act, or ERISA, signed into law by President Ford on Labor Day 1974, was supposed to protect 35 million workers covered by more than three thousand pension and health plans. The Labor Department was supposed to enforce the new law, but with few racketeering investigators and limited expertise, the department floundered for at least five years.

A few years later, after Fratianno became a government witness as part of a murder-conspiracy plea, he revealed how easily the Mob

237

plundered union benefit funds. "There are billions of dollars sitting around in trust funds set up by employers and unions," he explained. "All you do is find out who controls the money. Then you go see them and see if you can work out a deal. You do something for them and they do something for you. It works this way.

"One, you can pay a union officer or a trustee some money up front. Two, you can pay him a kickback when you get the favor. Three, you can do him a favor. You can do a favor for a friend of his. Four, if that doesn't work, you can find out who his superior is and put pressure on the man to come through. Five, if this doesn't work, you might try threats of physical violence. Six, finally, if all else fails, you might break the guy's leg or worse."

The chances of someone like Fratianno getting caught were very slim. By 1987, union pension-fund assets climbed to $70 billion. Employers annually contributed $12 billion to some 3,800 health plans. But only ninety-four Labor Department agents and 172 auditors policed the territory. "It's a license to steal," says Raymond Maria, the Labor Department's deputy inspector general.

In 1976, Fratianno and Tony Dope tried to set up a dental clinic for Teamsters in Warren, Ohio. This time, the Weasel decided to work the scheme through labor racketeer Allen Dorfman. Fratianno explained the setup. "You pick a dentist, and the union gives him a contract to do all the dental work for the members of the locals signed up and their families. Dorfman's company, Amalgamated Insurance Agency, processes all the medical claims and authorizes payment, which means he controls the whole thing. So now we can play some games. Number one, the dentists kick back to certain people so many dollars for each member signed up. And number two, Dorfman can submit phony claims, and nobody's the wiser. It's a sweet setup."

But Dorfman and the Pressers weren't getting along at the time. At a meeting in Chicago, Dorfman told the Weasel, "I don't know how much my name will help you."

Fratianno called the Cleveland family and set up a meeting with Jackie. Jimmy made his pitch, and Jackie replied, "Tell Allen Dorfman he has my blessing."

Back in Chicago, Fratianno as a courtesy told Chicago family chieftains Auippa, Jackie Cerone, and Joey Lombardo what he had worked out with their man Dorfman. Auippa, the don, was upset. Why hadn't Fratianno cleared his Dorfman contact with the family beforehand?

"But I went through Presser and the Cleveland guys," Fratianno said. "Jackie's going to help. He's on our side. If you ever need anything from the Teamsters, I'll go see him."

"I don't like Jackie Presser," Auippa said. "We use Roy Williams and Nick Civella if we need a favor."

Several weeks later, Fratianno got a call from Tony Dope telling him it was OK to come to Cleveland to talk to Jackie again about Rudy Tham. Things hadn't changed a bit for Tham in San Francisco. Andy Anderson wasn't giving him assignments, and Tham continued to bad-mouth his boss.

At the sitdown with Presser, Fratianno said, "Andy isn't doing the right thing. He gives all the messages to somebody else instead of Rudy. Rudy is supposed to get them."

Presser said he had tried, but that Fitz didn't want to lean too much on Andy Anderson because the two of them had split up $125,000 on a kickback scheme. If Anderson got angry, he could hurt Fitz with the information. Don't worry, Jackie said. We'll try something else.

A couple of months later at La Costa, the $100 million resort built with Teamsters loans, Jackie arranged a meeting with Tham, Anderson, Fitz, and himself. Later, Presser called Fratianno and reported that everything was going fine for Tham.

By now, Jimmy the Weasel had invested a lot of time and travel trying to solve Tham's problems and was getting impatient waiting for the payoff, setting up the dental clinic. He kept calling Jackie. Although Fratianno felt he knew Jackie pretty well by now, he still followed protocol when he wanted to meet with him, contacting Jack White or Tony Dope, who in turn called Maishe Rockman, who brought Presser to the meetings. Full of grand ideas, Fratianno asked for Jackie's help on two other business projects. One was constructing an apartment complex; the other was buying a small gambling casino in Jackpot, Nevada. Fratianno needed financing and asked

Jackie to help him get loans from the Central States Pension Fund.

"There's a moratorium on loans there," Jackie said. "But I got other connections that might help you out." Nothing came through. Jackie wasn't coming through for Fratianno, but they kept up a friendly relationship. On a trip to the West Coast with Carmen, they all got together for lunch at a restaurant where the Weasel knew the owner. Fratianno went into the kitchen and prepared lunch to show off his cooking skills for his friends. "He made me the best veal-cutlet sandwich I ever had in my life," Carmen recalls.

At the IBT's 1976 convention at Las Vegas's Aladdin Hotel, Fratianno again met with Jackie. Presser said that he couldn't help Fratianno with a Central States Pension Fund loan. Bowing to pressure from the government, the Teamsters had hired Daniel Shannon, supposedly to clean up the fund. Shannon stopped loans for bowling alleys, nightclubs, casinos, and other speculative real-estate ventures. "We're going to get rid of him," Presser promised. "He never cooperates." Soon, Shannon was forced out, and an administrator more friendly to real-estate ventures was installed.

At the time, both Fratianno and Presser were informing to the FBI. They may have even snitched on each other after one of their meetings.

For Fratianno, informing was just a game, another scam. He dished out mostly worthless information about the Los Angeles family—details that his case agent could easily get elsewhere—and took the FBI's money. So far, he had collected $16,000. Informing also let him move about quickly and freely, because the FBI didn't waste time surveilling its snitches; as a result, Fratianno found it easier to put together his scams.

The Weasel also believed that by strategic disclosure of information, he could use the FBI to help him gain control of the San Francisco crime family. He liked the idea; the FBI not only helping him do in his enemies, but paying him as well. And best of all, if he ever got arrested and needed a friend in the government, his relationship with the FBI would be a valuable insurance policy.

As it turned out, Jackie was playing the same game.

240

18
The Mob at War

"He really thought he was going to be killed."
CARMEN PRESSER

Jackie liked to take along bodyguards when he traveled, usually a couple of Local 507's young, burly business agents, clad in suits, who strode ahead of him into meeting rooms, trying to look mean and alert. Jackie enjoyed creating the impression that he was a provocative figure, constantly in danger, along the lines of the pope or the president.

"Jackie loved the show," Carmen says. "He loved to go in a place and have his boys standing around because it made him look bad. If he wanted to be alone or was bothered with them or wanted to do something on his own, he got rid of them real fast. He liked it just for show; it was not always for safety. He loved to pretend he was in a more dangerous situation than he really was. He thought it made him interesting. It made people say, 'Hey, there goes Jackie Presser!'"

By 1976, however, the bodyguards were more than window dressing. Jackie was in danger. First of all, he was informing regularly to FBI supervisor Marty McCann. Jackie was now also the target of nasty rumors gliding through the underworld, vague whisperings that he was a government fink. One source of the rumors was Jackie's former sidekick, Harry Haler. After he was indicted in Chicago in 1975 for using stolen bonds as collateral for a loan, Haler finally turned on Jackie. He insisted that Jackie had set him up, since he was the only person who knew about the securities being used to get a loan in Chicago. If Haler is to be believed, he later wrote a letter to Fat Tony Salerno in

New York, warning him that Jackie Presser was an FBI snitch. There's nothing to suggest that Fat Tony got the letter, but Salerno had heard that Jackie was supposed to be an informer and said he didn't believe it at the time. Rotatori, the Ohio Teamsters lawyer who was close to Bill Presser, also suspected Jackie of being an informant. "The first time I was convinced he was an informant was when he had dealings with Harry Haler involving a case with stolen securities in Chicago," Rotatori says. "Haler's lawyer in the case said to me Presser was the only one who knew about Haler using the securities for the loan." Defense lawyers for Mob associates form a close-knit fraternity, and it doesn't take much for damaging hearsay to swirl through its ranks.

In 1976, Jackie showed up at a San Francisco IBT executive board meeting wrapped in a cocoon of nervous, shifty-eyed thugs, which provoked other Teamsters leaders to complain among themselves about the disruption. As protectors on the road, Jackie mainly used Tony Hughes, the former prize-fighter, and Bobby Kavalec, a tall, broad-shouldered felon who rode with and served as president of the North Coast Dirty Dozen, a Cleveland motorcycle gang. Jackie sometimes brought backup bodyguards as well.

Roy Lee Williams, the only Teamsters leader with as much power as the Pressers, pulled Presser aside and asked him, "What's with all the big bodyguards?" The other vice presidents hadn't brought any along.

"The Mob is split in Cleveland," Jackie told him, "and I think I picked the wrong side."

Williams knew only too well the feeling of being afraid of the Mob. The Kansas City Mafia and its boss, Nick Civella, had terrified Williams ever since Civella's henchmen visited Williams and ordered him to start cooperating or else they'd kill his family and him.

In private, Williams told Jackie, "Look, if they're going to get you, they're going to get you. It doesn't matter how many bodyguards you've got."

Jackie listened, not saying much. Afterwards, at least at national Teamsters functions, he pared down his traveling party to one—either Bobby Kavalec, Tony Hughes, or one of his imposing business agents.

† † †

Jackie and Carmen DeLaportilla during the Camelot days. She became his fourth wife.

Bill Presser greets President Nixon at San Clemente the day the Union endorsed him over George McGovern, July 17, 1972. *(National Archives, Nixon Project)*

Nixon and mob stooge Roy Williams in San Clemente, July 17, 1972. *(National Archives, Nixon Project)*

Richard Nixon and Teamsters president Frank Fitzsimmons on October 9, 1975, Nixon's first public appearance since his exile from the White House. "This is nice," Nixon said of the golf trophy. "Where's the union bug?" There wasn't one.

Jackie and Fitzsimmons. *(CSU Press Archives)*

Jackie in his pre–Brooks Brothers era, wearing an Indian headdress at a Teamsters function, 1975. (*Akron Beacon Journal*)

Tony Hughes, Jackie, and Frank Fitzsimmons, mid-1970s.

John Nardi, Teamster vending workers Local 410 president, killed by a car bomb in May 1977.

The Teamsters Joint Council 41 parking lot, Nardi's murder scene. Nardi's last words were "It didn't hurt." *(CSU Press Archives)*

Racketeer and FBI informant Danny Greene during the height of the Mob wars. His lawyer, left, is Elmer Giuliani. *(CSU Press Archives)*

Danny Greene was killed getting into the car at left when the car in the center exploded, October 1977. *(CSU Press Archives)*

A rare 1976 sit-down of the Chicago outfit. Joseph Lombardo, Allen Dorfman's handler, is standing at right, rear. Soon-to-be boss Joseph "Joey Doves" Auippa is far left. At center front is Anthony J. Accardo, the ailing boss and former Al Capone bodyguard. *(Chicago Crime Commission)*

Angelo Lonardo and Maishe Rockman, center, pick up Las Vegas skim cash from a Chicago courier, right, in 1979; the FBI secretly recorded the crime. *(Courtesy of FBI)*

Cleveland godfather James "Jack White" Licavoli, camera shy but smiling after being acquitted of bribing FBI clerk Geraldine Linhart, July 1980. *(UPI)*

Faye and Bill Presser in Miami shortly before his death.

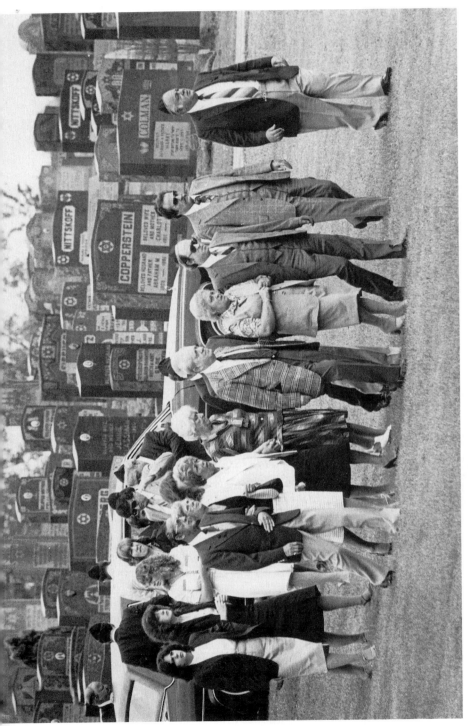

Bill Presser's funeral, July 21, 1981, Mt. Olive Cemetery. (*CSU Press Archives*)

In 1976, the Cleveland crime family was split into two armed camps, each battling the other for control of racketeering in northern Ohio. The preferred method of killing was remote-control car bombs, usually dynamite packed inside a container of nuts and bolts, which burst into a deadly spray of shrapnel. Thirty-seven bombings—placing a package, the gangsters called it—rocked Cuyahoga County that year, twenty-one of them in Cleveland alone. Some were intended to kill, others to send a message. According to national law-enforcement statistics, Cleveland jumped from seventh to first on the list of reported bombings. Cleveland was the bomb capital, and Jackie and his friend Tony Hughes spent a lot of energy trying to stay alive.

Jackie had ties to both of the warring camps and was expected to pick sides. On one side was Cleveland's well-funded Mafia, headed by James "Jack White" Licavoli, the stingy, multimillionaire who still lived modestly in bachelor's quarters on Murray Hill with carpenter Paul Lish. Allied with White were Bill Presser's close friend Maishe Rockman, underboss and former Purple Gang enforcer Leo "Lips" Moceri, Big Ange Lonardo, and assorted lesser mafiosi.

The upstarts were run by Bill Presser's former vending-company partner, Teamsters Local 410 leader John Nardi, the nephew of retired Mafia power Tony Milano. Nardi's partners in crime were a varied crew that included bikers, the Irish Gang from the city's west side, and others.

The war was fought over control of illegal gambling, bookmaking, loan-sharking, and labor rackets, as well as a share of the casino skim money coming from Las Vegas. With its billions from the Central States Pension Fund, its tremendous economic leverage, and its immense patronage, the Teamsters union was the pearl of the Mob's oyster. The union was worth spilling blood over. Whichever side prevailed would continue putting the squeeze on Bill or Jackie Presser for favors and loans. Fred Jurek, one of Jack White's lawyers, once wondered aloud to his client what all the Mob infighting was about. Other than slot machines in bars and several floating gambling games, why were they killing each other?

"What's the matter with you? It's the union," White replied.

† † †

Mob warfare might not have broken out in Cleveland and engulfed Jackie Presser as it did if John Scalish, the silver-haired Mafia boss, had named a successor before he died. A quiet man who briefly flashed into the news after being captured at the Apalachin, New York, crime summit in 1957, Scalish was a low-key crime boss who neglected to induct new members into the Mafia for at least the last half of his thirty-year reign. As a result, the Cleveland Mafia, which numbered as many as sixty made, or officially inducted, members by World War II, dwindled in the mid-seventies to several high-level lieutenants and at most a dozen or so soldiers. Scalish had cancer and lived for years with a colostomy, painfully tending to Mafia matters and his business, now called Buckeye Vending, which he owned with his brother-in-law Maishe Rockman and Mafia figure Frank Embrescia.

On May 26, 1976, a few hours after tricky coronary-artery bypass surgery, John Scalish died. The news hummed quickly through the underworld; within hours, the Cleveland Mafia powers gathered at Scalish's home. By the time Big Ange Lonardo got to his late brother-in-law's residence, he found two ranking mobsters, Jack White and Maishe Rockman, in the basement.

Rockman announced, "Before Johnny had the operation, he told me that he wanted Jack to be the new boss."

Jack White was shocked. He said he truly didn't want the job. He was old, only a few months away from seventy. He was content to sit on his millions, play golf, relax in the steam bath he had installed in his small Murray Hill home, maybe find an afternoon card game at one of the social clubs along the narrow brick streets in the neighborhood. Often he'd just sit on a folding chair outside a nearby café, his favorite cane on his knee, the one with the top that pulled off to reveal a glistening, carefully honed stiletto.

"Angelo is more qualified for the job," White told Rockman at the basement meeting. "He can speak better English and he knows the guys in the other cities."

Big Ange Lonardo wanted to be boss—his father, Big Joe, had been boss during Prohibition, until he'd been gunned down in a barbershop—and he was surprised by Rockman's news. Even so, he urged White to take the job, and after a few minutes of protest, he agreed.

Now they had to break the news to Scalish's underboss, Tony Milano, the Old Man on the Hill, and figure out a way to get him to step aside. Milano was ninety years old, nearly senile but still revered. He was inactive other than holding court at Tuesday-night dinners at the Italian-American Brotherhood Club. When they told the Old Man that White was boss and that he wanted an active underboss, Milano agreed to step aside. But he also was surprised at the choice of boss and stared at Big Ange in disbelief when he was told the news. A couple of years earlier, he had personally recommended to Scalish that Big Ange take over the Cleveland crime family.

Another powerful gangster who had wanted to be Cleveland boss was Tony Milano's nephew, John Nardi, the sixty-one-year-old secretary-treasurer of Teamsters Local 410, the vending local Bill Presser had founded in 1951. Sources inside the Cleveland Mob told the FBI in 1970 that if Scalish were to retire, Nardi was the leading candidate to replace him, based on Milano's standing with the national Mafia and his close friendship with Scalish. John Nardi didn't look like a killer. He was heavy-set, gap-toothed, had thinning black hair, and was utterly devoted to his grandchildren. Most weekdays he worked at the Teamsters Joint Council 41 headquarters, where his small local kept an office. He wore a suit, presenting a low-key, businesslike image. A dozen or so steps from his office was the office of his old business partner, Bill Presser.

Nardi's respectable image dressed up a criminal past that went back to at least 1939, when Cleveland safety director Eliot Ness had Nardi arrested for threatening to smash a jukebox if its owner didn't hire a union man to service it. As the nephew of Tony Milano, Nardi had an entrée into the national underworld. Nardi was smarter and smoother than Frank Milano's two sons—"bums," Jack White called them—and because of this may have been chosen to carry on the Milano-family tradition of running the Mafia in Cleveland. And he was ruthless. In the early sixties, the president of Teamsters Local 416, Pat Catalano, had mysteriously disappeared and presumably had been murdered. Nardi's brother, Nick, took over the local. A few years later, John Nardi was reported to have bragged to underworld figures that he and an Akron Teamsters official "had taken care of" Catalano.

Though Nardi enjoyed the blessing of the Old Man, he had never been officially inducted into the Mafia, had never experienced the blood ritual with a gun and a knife during which one swore to uphold a code of silence and shun drugs and prostitution. He also hadn't carefully built a fortune, as tightfisted White and others had with their loan-sharking and gambling games. Nardi gambled heavily himself, losing huge sums at racetracks and casinos; he was even dragged into court by Caesar's Palace over a ten-thousand-dollar casino debt.

To support his family and his bad habits, Nardi turned to drug smuggling. In 1975, he was indicted for trying to smuggle tons of marijuana from Colombia into the United States. He had some interesting partners—arms dealer Mitchell WerBell III, a onetime CIA operative who sold guns to anti-Communists in South America; a Cleveland insurance executive charged with defrauding and bankrupting Northern Ohio Bank; and Dominick Bartone, the Cleveland mobster who ran planes to anti-Castro forces just after the Cuban revolution. The drug ring's pilot, Kenneth Burnstein, agreed to testify for the government about the smuggling operation. Two weeks before trial, he died when his modified racing plane mysteriously crashed in the Mojave Desert two miles after takeoff. According to a secret FBI source's report, Bartone took credit for the pilot's death.

While Jack White slowly put a new crew in charge of the various rackets, Nardi began to line up allies for what was certain to be a bloody attempt to take over the Cleveland Mafia. White underboss Lips Moceri detected Nardi's plotting and, as Mob informants told the FBI, warned White repeatedly.

If Nardi was going to succeed in taking over the Cleveland Mafia, he needed soldiers. For muscle, he enlisted a fearless, flamboyant gangster named Danny Greene. A former official in the Longshoremens Union, Greene had grown up in Collinwood, the Beirut of Cleveland neighborhoods. Collinwood was clearly demarcated into three zones: the largest was inhabited by Slovenians and others of Eastern European descent; the next mostly by Italians; the third by blacks. Proudly Irish, egotistical, and a killer, Greene hated his criminal competitors, Collinwood's Italian hoodlums—Eugene "the Animal" Ciasullo, Pasquale "Butchie" Cisternino, Allie Calabrese, and others. Nicknamed the Young Turks, they in turn had despised Greene since their days at Collinwood High School, and their battle escalated until, finally, it drew in Nardi, the Teamsters, and Jackie Presser.

Danny Greene called himself the Irishman. He was a captivating, craggily handsome, redheaded labor racketeer who dressed in green, drove a green car, wrote in green ink, and was forever lecturing and quizzing his gang members on points of Irish history. He acted like Robin Hood in his poor neighborhood, delivering turkeys to the needy at Thanksgiving or lending money when someone lost a job. He even paid tuition to send neighbors' children to private Catholic schools. In return, Greene's neighbors protected him by acting as spotters, eavesdroppers, and lookouts. When a stranger or an unfamiliar car was noticed in the neighborhood, Greene's neighbors telephoned to warn him. It might be government agents or rival gangsters trying to kill him.

Born in 1929, Greene had been orphaned as a small child, had grown up in a Catholic children's home, and had joined the marines after high school. There he boxed and became an expert marksman. He returned to Cleveland in the early sixties and took a job working on the docks. He eventually took over the leadership of an International Longshoreman's Union local and used the position to shake down stevedore companies. He ruled with a mailed fist, using union bullies to beat up workers who chafed under his rule. Greene got away with the abuse because he oozed raw charisma. He was a spellbinding speaker at union meetings, and rank-and-file dockworkers admired his ferocity. They treated him like a king. While his men worked the docks, Greene could be seen nearby, sunning himself in a regal pose. Periodically, he would wave over one of his minions and order him to swab him with tanning oil. During cold weather, Greene jogged, lifted weights, or practiced target shooting at the union hall. A vain man, he underwent painful hair transplants and quit smoking and drinking to maintain his looks and physique.

On the docks, it didn't take Greene long to fall in with the wise guys. He met Teamsters power Babe Triscaro, who owned a day-laborer employment service that supplied workers for the stevedore companies. On one of Jimmy Hoffa's visits to Cleveland in the early sixties, Triscaro brought Greene down to meet the legend. Later, Hoffa warned Triscaro, "Stay away from that guy. There's something wrong with him."

Triscaro also introduced Greene to Frank Brancato, a lieutenant of Mafia don John Salish, and Greene found work driving Brancato and collecting overdue juice, or loan-shark loans. Greene also joined forces

247

with Shondor Birns, a sixty-nine-year-old numbers kingpin who needed an enforcer to settle disputes over territories. On one assignment, Greene was supposed to terrorize a freelance numbers operator. While passing his target in a car, Greene ignited a stick of dynamite and threw it. It had an uncommonly quick fuse and detonated just after he let go. The explosion destroyed his car and shattered his right eardrum, but Greene was otherwise unharmed. It was just one of what would become a seemingly endless series of near misses.

In the late sixties, Greene stole a page from Bill Presser's vending-industry cartel and organized the area's trash haulers into the Cleveland Solid Waste Trade Guild. The guild's founders were Byron Sharpe of Ohio Disposal Company, Welden E. Hulligan of the Cleveland Maintenance Company, and Howard B. Bahm of Harry Rock and Company. Bahm was a friend of Cleveland federal judge Frank J. Battisti and J. William Petro, who would be appointed U.S. Attorney for the Northern District of Ohio by President Reagan. For a hefty fee from member companies, Greene fixed prices and awarded monopoly territories. Small independent haulers couldn't afford his extortion and tried to make a living by charging lower tonnage rates. Greene brought them in line by using arson, beatings, and bombings. Many found another line of work. His racket was almost identical to the one in New York City devised by Teamsters official Johnny Dio, who even came to Cleveland in early 1969 to advise Greene how to set up his scheme. By the seventies, Greene's gang included Kevin McTaggert, former boxer Keith Ritson, Brian O'Donnell, and some young members of the Hell's Angels.

For a while, Greene led a charmed life. He was jogging at White City Beach near his home when Michael Frato, an independent garbage hauler who wouldn't knuckle under, and his driver raced up in a car. Frato wedged his three-hundred-pound body out of the window and pointed a loaded carbine at the running target. It was an unusual turn of events; the two men had once been such close friends that Greene had named a son after Frato.

Frato opened fire, and Greene dove to the ground, pulling a gun from his sweat pants and tossing off two shots. "It was the luckiest shot in my life," the marksman said later. He nailed Frato in the right temple, killing him. Greene turned himself in, argued that he had shot in self-defense, and was acquitted by a jury of manslaughter charges.

248

Danny Greene seemed to pick his enemies recklessly, a self-destructive trait that enhanced his reputation as a fearless killer. For instance, Greene capriciously went to war with his old ally, numbers boss Shondor Birns, who had loaned Greene $75,000 to open an after-hours cheat spot. Despite Birns's efforts, Greene refused to repay his former mentor. A short time later, Greene found a bomb on the axle of his car that had failed to detonate. "I'll return this to the old bastard that sent it," Greene vowed.

Not long afterwards, the night before Easter, 1975, Birns left a go-go bar, walked to his Lincoln Mark IV, and opened the driver's door. A bomb exploded, breaking windows for blocks and cutting Birn's body in two. Greene henchman Kevin McTaggert later told the FBI that his boss had hired Hell's Angel Enos Crnic to kill Birns and had paid him $7,500 for the job.

Less than two months later, Birns's allies retaliated. On the night of May 12, 1975, Mo "the Mechanic" Kiraly detonated a dynamite bomb in a storefront under Greene's second-floor apartment, where he was sleeping with his girlfriend. The blast hurled Greene into a refrigerator, cracking a few ribs. His girlfriend was unhurt. The next day, police found a second bomb attached to Greene's back door—a block of tetrytol, a military explosive, strapped to a three-gallon can of gasoline. Kiraly had intended the small dynamite package to trigger the powerful bomb at the back door, but its fuse had been improperly placed. Otherwise, police said, the bomb would have turned the entire block into flaming rubble.

After the botched assassination attempt, Greene sat in his tiny front yard, bare-chested, the Irish tricolor flag fluttering above him on a pole, the sun turning his skin a burnt sienna as reporters asked him who he thought was trying to kill him.

As the battle between Greene and the Mafia escalated, each near miss added to his legend of invincibility. Part of his protection was the same kind of shield Jackie was using; like Presser, Danny Greene worked as an FBI informer. His handler was Pat Foran, who would take over as Jackie's exclusive handler a year later.

After Greene survived the blast at his apartment, he was contacted by John Nardi. According to Edward Kovacic, head of Cleveland police intelligence at the time, Nardi recruited Greene to his side in the battle against the Cleveland Mafia, arguing that "your enemies are my enemies. Let's fight them together."

Nardi knew that Greene had the muscle—Hell's Angels, hoodlums, and Mob-connected thugs—to help him make a move on the Cleveland family. Though Nardi probably didn't know it, Greene also had the FBI to alert him whenever it picked up intelligence about the Mafia's plans to kill him. It gave him a fantastic edge over his enemies. "If we receive information that there is a threat on their life, we will advise them," FBI supervisor Foran said of his informants. "I think it's our moral responsibility." Jackie, of course, enjoyed the same protection.

Nardi's biggest problem was Leo "Lips" Moceri, the new underboss of the Cleveland family and a cousin of boss Jack White. Moceri had the reputation in Mob circles of being a worker, or killer. Across the country, underworld old-timers knew Moceri as a prolific hit man who, like White, had been a Prohibition-era member of Detroit's notorious Purple Gang. In Toledo, Ohio, in the thirties, Moceri had been indicted for three separate murders, but was acquitted each time. Jug-eared, nicknamed Lips for his fat drooping mouth, and muscular despite his sixty-nine years, Moceri had made a small fortune as a loan shark, mostly in Akron. In 1973 alone he had loans totaling more than $100,000 on the street at one time. Moceri's partners were Tony "Dope" Delsanter, Jack White, and their youngish crew of collectors and enforcers, among them Collinwood's Pasquale "Butchie" Cisternino and Eugene "the Animal" Ciasullo, two of Greene's sworn enemies.

Moceri resented John Nardi, considering him an opportunist who took advantage of the temporary disorder in the Cleveland Mafia after the death of Scalish. Moceri and his associates theorized that Nardi, once a likely heir to the Cleveland family, was bitter because Scalish had never inducted him into the Mafia. Moceri was the first to realize that Nardi was stockpiling muscle and weapons while encroaching on his crime territory. Several weeks after Scalish died, Moceri confronted Nardi outside the Teamsters Joint Council 41 building.

"Keep your hands off the Akron rackets and get rid of Danny Greene," the underboss ordered.

"I'll do what I damn well please!" Nardi shouted back.

250

"Do you know who I am?" Moceri demanded. "I'm Leo Moceri and no one pushes me around!"

The heated argument ended with the mobsters spitting in each other's faces, the ultimate insult. It demanded revenge.

Jackie was acquainted with the antagonists on all sides of the Mob war. He was closest to Maishe Rockman, who represented the Mafia's interests in the Teamsters. What Jackie privately assured these dangerous men about his loyalties can be discerned from reading the pages available from the informant files of Presser, Hughes, and other Mob associates. The files suggest that men on each side of the Mob war, at least in the beginning, thought that Jackie Presser was in their camp. One of the FBI's top Mob sources reported, "Nardi is aligning himself with some very powerful underworld characters such as Dominick Bartone, Tony Panzerelli, Danny Greene, Frank Favaro, and Jackie Presser of the Teamsters." A master at balancing, Jackie seemed to be deliberately, dangerously playing both sides at once.

Eventually, however, he quietly threw in his lot with his friend Rockman and the Cleveland family. It was an obvious choice; he had known Rockman for years, trusted him, and figured his side was going to win.

For a while, however, it looked as if he had picked wrong. On August 22, 1976, Lips Moceri drove up from Akron to Murray Hill in his girlfriend's Lincoln Continental, his Mercedes having been stolen a few months earlier. Jack White invited him to a clambake at St. Joseph's Church, saying that everybody from the old neighborhood would be there. Moceri turned him down, saying he had work to do, and headed off. It was the last his friends ever saw of him.

On September 1, Moceri's girlfriend called the Akron police and told them that Lips had been missing for days. That night, police found her Continental, empty and untouched except for a spot of blood in the trunk. A witness reported seeing a stocky redheaded man getting out of the car. Moceri, the brutal Mob enforcer and former Purple Gang member, was never seen again.

The murder of Moceri—a made member, the underboss no less—was a national embarrassment to the Cleveland Mafia. Jack White vowed to revenge his cousin's murder. Once reluctant to go to war, he poured his considerable resources into several different schemes to kill Nardi and Greene.

Just after Moceri was murdered, Jimmy "the Weasel" Fratianno flew into Cleveland from the West Coast and met with *consigliere* Tony "Dope" Delsanter. It was not a coincidence. As an FBI informant, the Weasel wanted to or was instructed to inject himself in the middle of a tense situation. Fratianno had to know that he might learn something in Cleveland that he could trade to the FBI if he got in trouble later on—an insurance policy, the wise guys called it.

"It's a war now," Delsanter told him.

"You'll have to make new guys," the Weasel said.

"We can't even remember the ceremony, it's been so long since any new members were made in Cleveland," Tony Dope replied.

"I'll help you make new members," Fratianno offered. "I just did one on the West Coast not too long ago."

A few weeks later, Fratianno joined Moceri's replacement, new underboss Big Ange Lonardo, Tony Dope, and Jack White in the basement of the Roman Gardens, a popular restaurant in Murray Hill. In the dark room around a table sat the new recruits, John Calandra and Teamsters "public-relations consultant" Tony Liberatore, president of Laborers Union Local 860. A gun and a knife sat crossed on the table. Fratianno mumbled some words in Sicilian and then intoned the Mafia's rules in English: never talk about family business, no drug dealing, no pimping, no fooling around with the wife or family of an *amico nostra.*

And finally, "You come in alive and go out dead."

Bill Presser and his son plotted throughout these tense times. They wanted to find a way for Jackie to take over Bill's seat on the Teamsters executive board. It was a tricky maneuver. If Bill resigned as vice president before the June 1976 IBT general convention in Las Vegas, the twenty-three hundred delegates would vote on his replacement from nominations taken from the floor. That would be difficult to control. The more certain course was for Bill to resign after the convention at an executive board meeting, nominate Jackie to take his place, and hope a majority of the seventeen voting members on the board would go along.

Fitzsimmons supported Bill on this, remembering how the Plug had helped him thwart Hoffa's comeback only a couple of years earlier.

But Bill didn't want to take chances, and before the summer convention, he asked Roy Lee Williams to tell Fitz that he supported Jackie.

Williams didn't particularly like Jackie. Jackie was nearly a generation younger than most of the Teamsters vice presidents and had been active in the union for only a decade. He also created the impression that he was the spoiled, corner-cutting beneficiary of his father's hard work. Bill Presser made unethical side deals and he accommodated the Mafia, but he had also swung a bat during the bloody thirties. What had Jackie done other than keep his fat fingers clenched to his father's coattails? The old-timers sneered at Jackie's public-relations proposals, though they had to admit that projecting a cleaner image might help to keep the government off their backs. Williams decided to support Jackie.

Besides improving their public relations, Jackie also wanted the executive board to approve a plan to set up clubs for retired Teamsters. He was scheduled to give a speech about the program at the IBT convention, but a group of International officers acting behind the scenes kept him off the podium during all four days of the convention. They wanted to put Bill Presser's ambitious son in his place. But they did support the idea, and convention delegates voted overwhelmingly to create a retirees' department to be administered from Teamsters headquarters.

A few weeks after the convention, Jackie started a bold, ambitious plan to try to take over the union presidency.

In July 1976, Jackie met with FBI agent McCann and coughed up information he'd known for more than a year: Fitzsimmons had met several times with "the number-one man" of New York's Genovese Mafia family at a Scottsdale, Arizona, estate. Jackie didn't know the mafioso's name or his address, but he had seen the house, a Spanish-style mansion surrounded by walls topped with barbed wire. Men with suits, ties, and shotguns patrolled inside the high, wrought-iron front gate. Huge guard dogs roamed inside the estate, which he guessed to be four or five acres. Later, the FBI brought out maps and photos of Scottsdale mansions, but Jackie couldn't pin it down.

Before he could completely sabotage Fitz, however, Jackie first had to take over his father's position as vice president on the Teamsters executive board. Aware of the power of imagery, Jackie had already checked into Cleveland's Mt. Sinai Hospital and undergone its well-known starvation diet, living on liquids under strict supervision. "I was tired of looking like a thug," he explained. He lost so much weight—115 pounds—that he paid a plastic surgeon to remove the baggy skin flapping around his eyes.

At the same time, Jackie had the PR firm Bellamy and Halbin work up a prototype for a national publicity campaign that he would try to sell to the IBT executive board at its quarterly meeting in October. This was to be his audition for vice president, his chance to impress the old-timers in the Teamsters hierarchy and let them know that he had the ideas, the speaking ability, and the commanding presence to sit on the ruling board of the nation's biggest, most powerful labor union.

Jackie was nervous about the October 1976 presentation. He desperately wanted to make a good impression. He walked to the lectern dressed in a conservative new suit, the smallest he'd worn since his navy days three decades earlier. Jackie made his pitch and fielded a few routine questions. That was it. He turned to leave. Then, Jackie recalled, "My dad asked me to wait a minute. Then he looked up. There were tears in his eyes."

"Fitz," Bill Presser said, "there's something I want to say, and I'd like my boy to hear." The Plug said that he planned to retire, that his health was shot and he couldn't go on.

Jackie said that he and Fitz were shocked by the announcement. They had no idea Bill wanted to retire so soon. "Fitz didn't say anything for a minute or two, and my knees were knocking, I was so weak," Jackie said. "Then Fitz looked up and started talking about what a great man Dad was. But then came the real shocker. He [Fitz] turned to me and said to the other guys sitting around the table, 'I'd like to nominate Jackie to take his place. Are there any objections?'"

The vote was unanimous. "I had no idea in the world it was going to happen," Jackie insisted.

Jackie's version of the most important step so far in his union career is romanticized and misleading. Actually, his father had talked about retiring from the executive board since at least 1970, after his operation for stomach cancer. Diabetic, grossly overweight, and inactive, by 1976 the Plug was debilitated. But he did what he had to do to get his son elected: hold on past the general convention and lobby Roy Williams. Weeks before his "surprise" election, Jackie resigned his well-paying positions with the Hotel and Restaurant Employees Union. It was hardly a coincidence. It just so happened that the Teamsters constitution barred executive board members from holding positions in other unions.

As a Teamsters vice president, Jackie was courted by businessmen as well as other vice presidents seeking support for pet programs. He was exposed to a rich new field of information about loans, schemes, and business ties. For an FBI snoop, it was a great opportunity. It also posed new dangers.

As an informer at this rarified level, Jackie was privy to meetings, deals, and loans known to only a few powerful teamsters, underworld figures, and business leaders. A serious problem was presented by the FBI's coding system, which identified its informants by city. The FBI coded a snitch from Cleveland with the letters CV, followed by a number. A San Diego source was coded SD, and so on. If inadvertently disclosed, FBI informant reports about high-level Teamsters wrongdoing coded CV would point like a gun to one person—Jackie Presser.

Also in late 1976, Jackie's contact agent, Marty McCann, told him privately that he planned to retire in February 1977. Jackie felt uneasy. He didn't want to be handed off to a new agent; it would mean that another person would learn that he and Tony were moles inside the underworld. Jackie demanded special protection, and the FBI acquiesced. After a series of meetings, including one at the Palmer House hotel in Chicago, FBI director Clarence Kelley approved unique arrangements to handle Jackie. His new contact agent, Special Agent Patrick Foran, typed Presser's allegations and information on plain white paper and carried it by hand or shipped it in an unmarked envelope to FBI headquarters in Washington. There, the informant desk broke down the high-level intelligence and distributed it to the various field offices that needed to undertake follow-up investigations. Sometimes the information was simply indexed and filed. "Headquarters carefully filtered and screened the information so as not to have it in any way traceable back to Mr. Presser," said Oliver Revell, the FBI's second in command.

A registered FBI informant since July 3, 1968, Tony Hughes had burrowed deeply into the good graces of Mafia boss Jack White.

255

Hughes visited him at least once a week, chatted about what was going on, and took tidbits back to Marty McCann. White didn't discuss important family business around Hughes, but the boss did share some news he had recently picked up: "Nardi wants to hit Jackie, Maishe, and Harold Friedman," White told Hughes. "He wants to wipe out all the Jews in charge of the Teamsters and take it over himself."

If he did, anyone wanting labor peace, sweetheart contracts, or patronage jobs would have to go through Nardi. He'd quickly become a millionaire. Maybe he'd even pay off some his long-overdue gambling markers.

Hughes quickly broke the news of the murder contracts to Jackie, Harold, and the FBI. Jackie and Harold had Teamsters-supplied body-guards, usually ex-boxers packing pistols, but they were hardly Secret Service caliber. So they took extra precautions. Jackie and Harold hurried to the Cleveland Police Department, registered their own handguns, and asked if they could get permits to carry concealed weapons. "They're scared to death of something," Andy Vanyo, chief of the police intelligence unit, remarked at the time.

Carmen noticed it as well. Jackie was more nervous than she ever remembered, and he always made certain to carry one or two guns in his briefcase. Their house out in rural Russell Township was secure and well-lighted. One night, Jackie heard a noise in the basement, leaped up, and asked, "What's that?"

"Sounds like something in the basement," Carmen remembers saying.

"Carmen, take Max down there," said Jackie, frightened.

She said she padded down there with the dog and looked around. Nothing unusual. Back at the stairs, she looked up. There stood Jackie, white-knuckled, gripping a loaded shotgun.

Soon thereafter, Jackie stayed home for a couple of weeks, not leaving for work or meetings. He drew the shades throughout the house, avoiding windows and daylight like a vampire. He continually called Tony Hughes or the FBI, trolling for news about the intrafamily feud.

The warfare escalated. On the night of September 10, 1976, at about half-past eleven John Nardi stepped out of the Italian-American Brotherhood Club on Murray Hill and walked to his Oldsmobile, which was parked under the streetlights a few steps away. As he lowered himself into the front seat, one or two cars pulled up and someone with a carbine fired six shots—one shattering the windshield, four piercing the side of the car, and another ricocheting off into the dark.

Nardi fell flat on the floor, his heart racing. After a few minutes of silence, he sat up, unharmed, and drove home—without calling the police. The next day, he played dumb when detectives came to ask about the gun battle. Nardi didn't even let them examine his car. Later, Hughes informed the FBI, Nardi said he knew who had ambushed him. "Five of them guys are gonna go," Nardi predicted, "and you're going to be reading about it in the newspaper."

As if there weren't enough going on with all the bombings and botched killings, the Cleveland Mafia infiltrated the local FBI office in February 1977 and swiped its top-secret list of local informants. It took the FBI several months to uncover this security breach and frantically warn its pack of informers. By then, the underworld seethed with paranoia.

As Jackie later discovered, his old friend Tony Liberatore, the two-thousand-dollar-a-month "public-relations consultant" for Hoover-Gorin, had pulled the strings in the theft of the FBI's snitch list, which at the time was one of the most egregious breaches of security in the FBI's sixty-nine-year history. A pardoned cop killer, Liberatore presided over Laborer's Union Local 860, which supplied unskilled workers for northern-Ohio construction projects and highways. Like Jackie, Liberatore was a union boss who sought public acceptance and political connections, and in 1975, Cleveland mayor Ralph Perk appointed him to the Cleveland Regional Sewer Board. It was a plum assignment for a union official; the public sewer authority took bids from companies to build and repair sewer lines and treatment plants. Many of the construction companies employed laborers from Liberatore's local.

Even before his recent induction into the Mafia, Liberatore had tried to impress Jack White with his connections and cunning. Liberatore harbored a desire to take over the crime family some day. In the sixties, long before the Mob's civil war, he befriended Danny Greene when Greene was running errands for Frank Brancato. Greene stayed loyal to Liberatore—"I'd take a bullet for Tony," he'd say—while Liberatore secretly conspired against his former friend.

257

Liberatore's associates included Thomas Lanci, another two-thousand-dollar-a-month Hoover-Gorin beneficiary, and Kenneth Ciarcia, a salesman for a Lincoln dealership. It was through Ciarcia that Liberatore and the Cleveland Mafia obtained the FBI's informant list. One of Ciarcia's co-workers was Jeffrey Rabinowitz, who was engaged to an FBI clerk, Geraldine Linhart. Jeff and Gerri had dinner at Ciarcia's home several times, and both were impressed with his stories about his influential friends. Recently divorced, Gerri Linhart was trying to sell the house she had received in the settlement, but a land-contract dispute over the sale was dragging through court. At a Christmas party in 1976, she approached Kenny Ciarcia and wanted to know if he had friends who could resolve the court case in her favor. Ciarcia walked outside to his car, which was equipped with a telephone. He returned moments later. "It's all been taken care of," he lied.

In February 1977, Gerri and Jeff attended a dinner party at Ciarcia's house. He took her aside and set the hook: "You want something from me, and I need something from you." Look in the FBI files, he suggested, and see what they have on James "Jack White" Licavoli and Tony Liberatore. She agreed to help.

Back at work, when no one was looking, Gerri Linhart searched the FBI indexes and found a Licavoli report dated February 2, 1977. She copied it and turned it over to Ciarcia. "I want you to destroy it" she said. "Don't worry, there's nothing good in it anyway," he replied after scanning it.

Ciarcia gave the purloined report to Liberatore, who rushed it to Jack White to impress him with his cunning. It was an eye-opener for the Mafia; the eight-page single-spaced report revealed that the FBI had developed at least two high-level informants inside the Cleveland family circles. The report noted a variety of Teamsters funny business, such as the fact that John Trunzo, a business agent for Local 507, was running an illegal gambling game on the Hill and that Teamsters official "John Nardi exercises a great deal of control over Mickey Rini," the retired Teamsters Local 400 officer "who in turn influences city hall in Cleveland, Ohio. The source stated that most of the city jobs funneled from Nardi go through Rini and Rini was responsible for the employment of John Milano, Tony Milano's son, as an inspector."

The stolen report also detailed the ongoing Mob war: "Butchie Cisternino told Jack White some time ago that John Nardi was making a move for power locally but that Jack did not want to believe it or did not believe it. The source stated that White indicated that he did not want to get mixed up in any type of squabble."

White and Liberatore were intrigued by the informant codes on the FBI report. If they could figure out who the snitches were, they'd solve a few problems.

Nardi may not have realized it, but he was under Mafia surveillance in the spring of 1977. His moves in and out of the Teamsters joint council building were closely monitored. Tom Lanci was in the thick of it. Every day for a few weeks, he would take a phone call at the clothing store where he worked, and a man's voice would announce, "Sam went to lunch" and mention the time. Later, another man would call and simply ask, "When did Sam go to lunch?" and Lanci would tell him. He didn't know what was going on at first, but since Liberatore, the man he affectionately called uncle, had asked him to relay the messages, Lanci did so without question. He thought it was a silly ruse, since he recognized both voices as minor Teamsters officials who worked in the same building as Nardi.

Nardi frequently switched cars and as a precaution usually parked at a nearby gas station and walked down an alley to the Teamsters office. On May 17, 1977, he parked in the Teamsters fenced lot. That morning, two of Danny Greene's gang members warned Nardi that a murder attempt was imminent. The Irishman had just learned about it from one of his top sources.

"Don't worry, Jack White is my friend," Nardi told the two messengers. "I've known him all my life."

About three o'clock that afternoon, Nardi left the building and walked to his car. Another car was parked next to it, its passenger door packed with a remote-control bomb loaded with nuts and bolts. The bombed was mounted low and directed upwards to the spot where Nardi would stand while unlocking his car. As Nardi opened the car door, someone triggered the charge. The bomb shattered the union-hall windows and shot the vinyl roof from Nardi's Oldsmobile 98 over the two-story union hall and into a parking lot two hundred feet away. The bolts packed in the bomb shot out like shrapnel and punched Nardi full of holes.

The blast stripped off his clothes, and he was spewing blood. Nick Nardi, a Teamsters official, raced out of the building and tried to revive his older brother, who was bleeding furiously, his legs shattered. "It didn't hurt," John Nardi said. Twenty-six minutes later, he was pronounced dead at a nearby hospital.

Before the police arrived, a Teamsters leader, most likely Bill Presser, ordered the joint council doors to be locked. This infuriated detectives, who wanted to come inside and search for witnesses. As Teamsters workers filtered out of the gap-windowed building on their way home, they refused even to give their names.

Danny Greene had lost his powerful ally, but he seemed unfazed and determined to carry on. As usual, he sat bare-chested in a lawn chair in his Collinwood front yard while a bodyguard scrutinized cars passing on the quiet street. "I have a message for those yellow maggots," Greene said of Nardi's killers. "That includes the payers and the doers. The doers are the people who carried out the bombing. They have to be eliminated because the people who paid them can't afford to have them remain alive. And the payers are going to feel great heat and pressure from the FBI and local authorities."

As an FBI informer, Greene knew what he was talking about.

In a series of telephone calls over the spring and early summer, Ciarcia began to pressure Gerri Linhart to steal the FBI informant list, even though he still hadn't taken care of her contract dispute. Even so, in late June or early July, Linhart simply walked into the FBI's informant room and copied down the names and corresponding symbols of ten informants. She recognized only one of the names—Danny Greene. Liberatore met her at the Lincoln dealership. When she hesitated to turn over her handwritten list, he assured her, "No one is going to get hurt." He reminded her that he was trying to take care of her lawsuit. "I know a lot of people," he said.

Linhart was a good negotiator. She started talking about her problems getting rid of her old house and her need for a down payment on a new one. "We'll take care of that," Liberatore replied. He left the room for a moment, came back, and handed her a thousand dollars, cash, saying there'd be more.

Over the next few months, Linhart stole several reports about Jack

White, a list of license plates of FBI undercover cars, and an FBI affidavit asking permission to tap the phone of Teamsters official Carmen Parise, who was loan-sharking out of a Murray Hill gambling joint called the Card Shop. Still, Liberatore pressed for more information. Some of Jack White's FBI reports contained informant codes not found on the first list she gave them. Find out more, they urged her.

In August, Gerri Linhart walked into the FBI's unlocked, unprotected informant room. She carried a yellow legal pad. She pulled some three-by-five-inch cards from a file and copied down the symbol numbers and names of fifty-six informants. Liberatore was pleased and later loaned her $15,000 for a down payment on the home she and her fiancé were building.

When Jack White saw the purloined informant list, he couldn't believe his eyes. One of the informants was Tony Hughes. White must have felt sick. He had known Tony's family for decades and talked to Tony all the time. Another was John "Curly" Montana, a murderer and suspected fence. Because of his special security arrangements, Presser's name wasn't on the Cleveland FBI office's list of informers. But both Hughes and Montana were, and they were also close friends of Jackie.

In August, Jimmy the Weasel flew in for the funeral of his close friend Tony Delsanter, who had died of natural causes. After the service, Jack White and the Weasel chatted about their old friend. Then White unfolded a piece of paper and said, "Look at this."

It was an FBI report from the San Diego field office to the FBI director. "We've got a connection in the FBI office through some broad," White explained. "She stole a list of stoolies, and now we know two of their names, Tony Hughes and Curly Montana."

Fratianno tried to remain calm. If she kept digging, she might find his name in there, too. "Can she find shit out about Los Angeles? We've got some stoolies there, too," Fratianno said.

White replied that the woman was working on getting more information.

Fratianno felt the noose tightening around his neck. Though he had informed to the FBI in California, the field office probably sent copies to the Cleveland office, since his mother lived there and he visited home frequently. The Mafia's mole in the FBI might uncover his secret any minute.

After Delsanter's funeral, the Weasel hurriedly called a retired FBI agent he knew in San Francisco and told him that the Cleveland family had stolen the local FBI's informant list. The ex-agent said he didn't believe such a thing was possible.

Oh yeah, the Weasel replied. Here are two snitches, Tony Hughes and Curly Montana. Check it out.

Fratianno hoped that by alerting the FBI, it would plug the leak and save his hide. Meanwhile, the FBI warned Tony Hughes that he was in danger. Jackie was terrified, too, even though he was assured that his name wasn't anywhere to be found in the Cleveland office. But the bureau had recklessly allowed a clerk to steal its top-secret informant list in the first place. How could Jackie be sure that someone else hadn't goofed up and recorded his name somewhere?

As a safeguard, the FBI reportedly gave Jackie a pocket-sized radio transmitter, similar to a remote-control garage-door opener. The idea was for Jackie or his bodyguard to stand at a safe distance before starting a car, raise the transmitter antenna, aim, and spray the car with radio waves, thereby setting off any possible bombs.

Jackie was extremely jumpy at home. With their children grown and living on their own, Jackie and Carmen had moved into a huge apartment in Shaker Heights, which she decorated with expensive antiques and tasteful pieces of art. While taking the garbage down the hall to the trash chute one night, she inadvertently left the door open behind her.

"You dumb son of a bitch," Jackie screamed when she returned after a minute. "You left the door open!"

"He really thought he was going to be killed, because he never swore at me like that before," she recalls. Also, Jackie's bodyguards not only walked him to the apartment building door, but they started bringing him inside as well. Life was precarious for a top-echelon Mafia informant.

In the fall of 1977, Jack White's assassination crew adopted a new strategy. Wars were won by good intelligence. So the Cleveland Mafia, borrowing one of the FBI's most effective techniques, installed a wiretap on the phone at the apartment of Danny Greene's girlfriend. Carmen Marconi, a forty-seven-year-old electronics wizard who held patents for burglar alarms, rigged the illegal tap and attached a tape recorder. Another of White's crew retrieved the tapes and passed them on to Raymond Ferrito.

Ferrito had become a familiar sight around Cleveland. A thin, nervous, forty-eight-year-old hoodlum from Erie, Pennsylvania, Ferrito had served time in California with Jimmy the Weasel. Many months earlier, the Weasel had introduced Ferrito to Tony Delsanter, Jack White's *consigliere*. With Greene on the rampage, the Cleveland family was looking for good recruits, and Ferrito seemed likely. He had the will to kill. He proved that in 1969, when he lured Julius Petro, an ex-gangster from Cleveland, into a car at the Los Angeles airport, waited for a jet to roar overhead, then calmly put a bullet through his head. Delsanter and White probably weren't aware that Ferrito guzzled antacid for his ulcerous stomach and smoked marijuana incessantly to stay calm. Their plan was for him to help them kill the charmed Danny Greene.

Ferrito spent weeks tailing Greene around Cleveland, living in hotels, watching for patterns and an opening. It was frustrating; the Irishman was armed and cautious. In meetings with White, Big Ange Lonardo, and their underlings, Ferrito complained that he wasn't getting enough support, and he lashed out in frustration.

By fall 1977, Ferrito was listening to the tapes of Greene's phone calls, but he complained that the tapes were always two or three days old when he got them, and thus worthless for planning an ambush. After weeks of listening, picking up scraps of information about the Irishman's movements and plans, the Cleveland Mafia got lucky. Greene developed a loose filling, and his girlfriend used the bugged phone on October 4, 1977, to make an appointment for him with his dentist two days later.

The next day, Ronnie Carabbia brought Ferrito to a meeting with Jack White, Big Ange, Butchie Cisternino, and John Calandra. They played the tape of Greene's girlfriend making the dental appointment and decided this was the best opportunity yet to nail him. The hit team sprang into place, picking up two supposedly clean cars that had been obtained earlier—one a bomb car, the other a getaway car. The bomb car was a maroon Chevrolet Nova with a hollowed-out passenger door.

Welded in the door was a heavy steel-plate box with an open end aimed outward like the barrel of a cannon.

Shortly before Greene's appointment, Ray Ferrito gingerly placed the bomb in the passenger door, covered it with a blanket, and waited for Greene to arrive. The Irishman was late. He parked his car in the middle of the medical building's lot and walked inside carrying a blue Adidas gym bag. Ferrito parked the bomb car next to Greene's while the dentist worked on the loose filling. Twenty-five minutes later, Greene left. It was shortly after three o'clock. "Have a nice day," the receptionist told him.

In the back seat of the getaway car, Ronnie Carabbia held the detonator, a black transmitter with a long antenna, the kind used for flying large model airplanes. They watched as Greene unlocked the car and climbed in. Ferrito eased the blue Plymouth escape car toward the freeway, and Carabbia flipped the switch.

An ear-shattering blast rocked the medical building and sent up a fireball that for a second bathed the area in intense white light. Greene was killed instantly. The bomb ripped off his clothes and stripped the flesh from his back, leaving a bloody, amputated corpse dressed only in brown zip-up boots. His left arm was thrown a hundred feet, an emerald ring still on a finger. The explosion drove the Celtic cross he wore around his neck deep into the parking-lot asphalt. His gym bag, almost untouched, dropped next to the car. Inside, the FBI retrieved a 9-mm. pistol with two clips, a list of license plates of his enemies, a news article about how easy it was to obtain terrorist weapons, and a Catholic holy card picturing the Mother of Perpetual Help.

A few hours later, Jackie and Tony Hughes learned that Greene had been killed by a car bomb. Now they were really scared. The Irish Gang was sure to retaliate immediately against White and his allies, themselves included. At the moment, however, Tony was in Hillcrest Hospital, recuperating from hemorrhoid surgery. It wasn't a good idea to be staying where anyone could find out your room number with a phone call. He checked out, met Jackie, and they hurriedly left town. "It was a big scramble," Carmen recalls. "They all went to Florida." There they moved from hotel to hotel, waiting for weeks until they got word it was OK to return.

Before he fled Cleveland, Jackie admonished Carmen, "Now don't touch my car! Whatever you do, don't touch my car!"

Headstrong, almost perversely rebellious, Carmen of course drove Jackie's car. Nothing happened.

Two days after the killing, Ferrito met with Jack White. "We're going to make you a member of our thing," White told him.

"That'll be great," Ferrito replied.

"Now maybe things will settle down," White said, "and we can make a buck."

The war was over. Jackie's side won. Now he could relax a bit after months of walking a tightrope between conflicting camps.

"Jackie was a master at balancing," Carmen Presser recalls. "Jackie knew what he was doing at all times. I heard both sides. I used to sit and listen to the phone calls. If you listen to this over and over every day, you know what's going on. Don't ever think Jackie was caught in the middle. He knew exactly what he was doing at all times. He was balancing the two factions. Jackie was a master."

19

Informing

"Some guy takes a broad to a hotel, he shacks up with her, I'll bet you there's a dime dropped on the guy."

JACKIE PRESSER

By the late seventies, Jackie strode with increased confidence through his conflicting worlds. With his father's help, he had pulled off a bait-and-switch maneuver to land on the Teamsters executive board. He had survived a Mob war. And he was steering the FBI toward his Teamster antagonists with both hearsay and solid information.

To those who had known him—friends familiar with his bungled marriages, botched business opportunities, and embarrassing expulsion from the Hotel Employees Union—it was quite a surprise that Jackie Presser had turned his life around so dramatically. "I don't know if he woke up one day and said, 'I'm going to do something with my life,'" recalls Presser's close friend, Paul Locigno, the former Teamsters governmental-affairs director. "Everybody can argue what his motive was—political, it was his father, he wanted to clean up the union. The bottom line was he had a game plan and he had a program. In his own way, he was giving the union back to the membership and getting rid of the people who only wanted to take from the union. The biggest thing that irked Jackie was not if Teamsters officials were riding around in big cars with large salaries. He didn't want people around who didn't work."

Other than his father, Carmen says, "Jackie was never very close to anybody." Tony Hughes, his best friend throughout the seventies, said he had no idea that Jackie had had a daughter he never saw, and

266

took kickbacks from the Hoover-Gorin PR firm. Jackie had to keep his secret lives separate, and keeping his distance was how he achieved it. Whether consciously or not, Jackie also worked at telling the cover stories he needed in order to live a double life.

"Jackie practiced lies," Carmen Presser explains. "He'd make up a story in his head, and it would sound real good to him. He'd tell the story several times, in practice, to work out the kinks. After he told the story a few times, he began to believe it. He'd tell you and not even think about it." Faced with a slip of his tongue or a conflicting story, Jackie Presser could without hesitation spin a convincing cover—a potentially lifesaving skill.

"I'll never forget the time Jackie came home and started telling me a story," Carmen says. "He had been to Vegas, and this man came up to him and told him this and that. So he told me this long incredible story about what had happened to him. Later, I was putting his things away, and there was this magazine. I started reading it, and the whole story he told me was in the magazine." She laughed at the memory. "You couldn't get mad at him for it."

Another way Jackie protected himself was to make certain to warn his Teamster associates, but not too loudly or repeatedly, about the ever-present danger of snitches. At a Joint Council 41 meeting in June 1978, for instance, he predicted a wave of suffocating FBI scrutiny. He knew what he was talking about because in large part he sparked such investigations, in particular one into John J. "Skippy" Felice, president of Teamsters Beverage Drivers Local 293.

"Very fortunate for the government, the greatest thing they got going for them is informers, guys that don't like each other," Jackie lectured. "Some guy takes a broad to a hotel, he shacks up with her, I'll bet you there's a dime dropped on the guy. I'm not just talking about Ohio. I've seen some really good guys go down the tubes for no reason at all. It's getting worse and worse, and if we don't do something about it, there's a lot of guys in this room that won't be around. You can bet on that."

By late 1977, after a year as a Teamsters vice president, Jackie proved to be one of the bureau's more valuable organized-crime informants. He provided high-level intelligence about the Hoffa murder, Mob-connected Hollywood power broker Sidney Korshak, and which casinos were secretly owned by what crime families. The breadth of his

267

information was impressive, some of it undoubtedly learned from talking to his father. His handler, Patrick Foran, went by the book more than Marty McCann had in memorializing Presser's information. In 1977 alone, Foran wrote up a couple of hundred pages of reports, typed on plain white paper and hand-carried to FBI headquarters, where they were kept with thousands of other pages in the PROBEX file, a catchall investigation into various Teamsters cases, in particular Hoffa's murder. Presser was called the PROBEX source. Unlike any other source at the time, his information wasn't even indexed, in order to protect him.

Some of the most intriguing information Jackie gave had to do with Hoffa's kidnapping and murder. In an interview with two FBI agents days after Hoffa disappeared, Jackie was circumspect and dismissive. "Hoffa's going to show up," he told the two agents, in front of Rotatori. "He's pulling a publicity stunt." Two months later, before a federal grand jury in Detroit, Jackie refused to answer questions about Hoffa, citing the Fifth Amendment protection against self-incrimination.

His private views, which he never expected to surface publicly, were more detailed and revealing. They can be found in his FBI informant file.

"After Hoffa got out of jail, he demanded a piece of the pie," Presser told his FBI handler. "He had set up Central States, but now Dorfman was running the show with Nick Civella. Dorfman wouldn't give Jimmy any loans, but he kept pushing."

One of the first loans Hoffa wanted approved was for $1 million to invest in coal mines in Pennsylvania, Jackie said. Dorfman blocked it. "Hoffa kept pushing, pushing, and so Dorfman went to Civella and asked him to get Hoffa off his back."

Civella met with Hoffa and told him to back off, but Hoffa refused. Shortly after this meeting, Hoffa disappeared, Jackie explained. This revelation is the first report by an insider—both a teamster and a Mob insider—that the Kansas City Mafia boss was linked to Hoffa's killing.

Jackie also pointed with certainty to the involvement of Hoffa's foster son, Charles "Chuckie" O'Brien, in the kidnapping and murder. In the years leading up to his disappearance, Hoffa had alienated and angered O'Brien, Jackie revealed.

A Teamster organizer, O'Brien had been extremely attentive to

Hoffa while he was imprisoned, visiting him frequently and bringing messages in and out, Jackie told the FBI. "When I get out of here, I'm going to make sure you've got a good job with the union and make some money," Hoffa was said to have promised O'Brien. After Nixon commuted Hoffa's sentence, he didn't keep these promises, Jackie said, but instead continued to treat his son, Jimmy Hoffa, Jr., as "the apple of his eye." O'Brien was upset and turned from Hoffa to Detroit racketeers Anthony "Tony Jack" Giacalone and Mafia capo Tony Provenzano—all of whom were named as prime suspects in the Hoffa murder.

"By the spring of '75," Jackie told the FBI, "Chuckie hated Hoffa and his son so much that he was spreading word to the outfit people that Jimmy Hoffa was talking to the FBI."

The crowning indignity in O'Brien's eyes was when Fitz fired him and Hoffa didn't step in to help save his job, Jackie explained. So Chuckie turned to the Giacalones, who convinced Fitz to give him another chance. He was rehired and sent to organize workers in Alaska. "As a result of all this, Chuckie was very bitter to Jimmy Hoffa," Jackie explained. "Instead, he got very close to Tony Jack and Tony Pro."

O'Brien, who was in Detroit the day Hoffa was kidnapped, was one of the last people to see Hoffa alive, according to Presser. He drove the car that picked up Hoffa at the Red Fox restaurant on July 30, 1975; Hoffa, a paranoid man, wouldn't get into a car unless he trusted the driver.

"Without any doubt" in his mind, Jackie told the FBI, O'Brien "was the one who set up Jimmy Hoffa the day he disappeared."

During the early Carter years, Jackie continued to unleash a flood of underworld scuttlebutt to the FBI. His favorite targets included mobbed-up insurance magnate and Central States "consultant" Allen Dorfman, Cleveland Teamster rival John J. "Skippy" Felice, Jr., and even Roy Lee Williams, the powerful teamster who helped Jackie get elected IBT vice president the year before. In March 1977, for instance, Jackie explained to the FBI that Fitzsimmons was trying to pry Dorfman from the Central States Pension Fund, which now topped $1.6 billion in assets. Fitz was tired of Hoffa's old protégé, a greedy, egotistical braggart who was getting sloppy and bringing too much FBI attention to the fund.

"Dorfman's doing everything short of killing Fitz to get him outta office," Presser said. "He wants Williams or Harold Gibbons to replace Fitz because he and the Chicago outfit can control those guys.

"If you could get Dorfman in a jam, every big outfit guy in the country who's dealt with Central States could be prosecuted. Here's the names of two guys who used to work with Dorfman but he got 'em fired. They're really mad at him. You talk to them, they might be able to nail him for you. They both got papers showing the phony stuff he did to get loans for outfit guys."

Jackie went on. "There's a contract out on Dan Shannon because he won't do what Dorfman says. It's through Nick Civella. Fitz got wind of it and got the hit called off, telling 'em it would bring too much heat on us."

Shannon, director of the Central States Pension Fund, took the threat seriously. The ex–Notre Dame football star wore a bulletproof vest and traveled with a bodyguard for several months. "I worked like a son of a bitch to get rid of that Shannon, you know how hard I worked on that," Civella later told a Mob associate.

In April 1977, at a three-day Teamsters executive-board conference in Las Vegas, Fitzsimmons did everything he could to avoid Dorfman. It was a darkly humorous scene: the chief of the nation's most powerful union scurrying around, afraid to talk to someone who, on paper, was supposed to be an underling. The last day of the conference, Dorfman cornered Fitz and walked him into a back room.

"I want my insurance contract renewed with Central States," Dorfman insisted.

Fitz refused.

It didn't matter. Dorfman was clever and wired. He went to see Roy Williams, head of the Central States Conference, who gave him a ten-year renewal on his contract. Months later, when Fitzsimmons learned about this insubordination, he revoked Dorfman's unusually long contract.

"Dorfman got mad and got ahold of Nick Civella in prison," Jackie told the FBI. "Civella went to Roy and Tony Pro, and they put the pressure on Fitz. By Thanksgiving, Fitz was walking around afraid he was gonna get hit."

Fitzsimmons caved in. By January, he had approved a compromise. Dorfman received a three-year insurance contract with the Central States fund.

There did come a time when Jackie took credit publicly for helping the Justice Department charge a Teamster employee with a crime. He said that he had turned in his niece, Cindy Presser, an assistant bookkeeper at Joint Council 41, for embezzling from the union. The story made good copy; Jackie was so tough and dedicated that he'd turn in his own relatives if he caught them stealing from the Teamsters. Like the other dramatic stories he told about himself, this one wasn't true.

From October 1977 to February 1978, Cindy Presser, Bill Presser's twenty-two-year-old granddaughter, had forged and cashed union checks worth $47,990. The joint council lawyer, Bob Rotatori, uncovered the fraud after his law firm hadn't received its retainer checks for a few months. He called the Teamsters bookkeeper and learned that the checks had been issued, endorsed, cashed, and returned. He went over to look at the endorsement, and Cindy Presser's crude crime was uncovered. Why no one noticed that Cindy had suddenly come into a lot of money was unclear.

Rotatori didn't look forward to breaking the news to Bill Presser. "He and Faye had helped raise her," Rotatori said. "He was very close to her." A week later, Bill and Rotatori drove to Columbus for a meeting of the Ohio Conference of Teamsters. "I didn't have the heart to tell him" before the meeting, the lawyer said. They stopped afterward at the Greenleaf for dinner and Bill's customary piece of pie. There, Rotatori told him that his granddaughter had embezzled from the joint council.

"He cried," Rotatori remembered. "There were tears on his face. Big, huge tough guy. He cried."

"What do we do?" Presser asked.

"You have to authorize me to take this to the federal government."

"If you have to do that, you have to do it," Bill said.

"I'm aware of it, you're aware of it, we have to do it this way," Rotatori said.

Bill Presser repaid the money and hired a good lawyer for Cindy, who pleaded guilty, received counseling, and served three months in prison. In newspaper interviews thereafter, Jackie said that it was he who had turned in his niece. He cited this as evidence of his dedication to protecting the dues of the rank and file. "That always irked me," Rotatori recalls. "Jackie never had a damn thing to do with it."

As an undercover FBI operative in the union and in the Mob, Jackie Presser made a career out of betraying trust. Were his motives noble, like the wartime double agent who puts his life on the line for the good of his country? Or was something else at work?

"He didn't want any bosses," explains his former wife Carmen, who knew him for more than twenty years. "He wanted to be the boss. He wanted to go straight up the ladder with power. He loved power. And if he got rid of everybody around him, then he didn't have to listen to them. Don't think for one instant that Jackie cared about the people."

Rotatori agrees with Carmen. "Jackie was so consumed with wanting power that he played this double game. He used the federal government as much as the federal government used him. I think it was a calculated plan of his whereby he got rid of his enemies."

An FBI supervisor insisted that Jackie wanted to get back at the Mob for corrupting his father. The Mob had used Bill to obtain millions of dollars in Central States loans but had never rewarded him for his risks, Jackie said. Cuyahoga County Republican chairman Bob Hughes, a friend of Bill and Jackie's, doesn't endorse that theory. "I don't think Jackie would get mad about something that happened ten years before," Hughes said. "I did not ever hear Jackie say he was resentful of Auippa in Chicago, for instance."

The nature of the beast is such that an informant endangers those closest to him. "I think most people are not comfortable with informants," Bob Hughes said. "People think they're stool pigeons and finks. Whatever the rationale, people are uncomfortable with that. If you're an informant, you tend to hurt your friends. You hurt people who trust you."

Jackie especially hurt Carmen Presser. They had started to drift apart the minute they were married in 1971, but his secret life with the FBI closed him off even more. He didn't feel he could tell her about

272

it. "He used to come home and tell me everything that had happened," Carmen says. "Because there wasn't anything he had to hide. We were very, very close. Then it seemed the more covertly he had to live his life, the less I would know, and the less close we were, and the less he talked to me about things."

Jackie had pretty much moved out of their Shaker Heights apartment and was living with his girlfriend in a high rise in downtown Cleveland. It devastated her. "You don't understand what a man like that can do to a human being. If you get a person who treats you like no one else in your whole life has treated you, with such gentleness and such kindness and such compassion and love. And then suddenly, from nowhere, they turn and treat you worse than anyone you've ever known has treated you, it blows your mind. It destroys you. You don't know what to do. You don't know whose fault it is or where to turn. You don't know what happened. So you become like a violent animal. I started drinking. I didn't know what to do. I was in such pain. Let me tell you—I'm a strong person, and he almost killed me."

During this time, Jackie sent Carmen out of town to their condominium in Boca Raton, Florida, saying that he'd come down and see her. But there were always excuses why he couldn't make it. Jackie's secretary, Gail George, showed up instead and stayed at their condo for a few days, taking a brief vacation. Carmen said that George was very rude to her, referring to Jackie as "Mr. Presser" and making herself seem important and more in tune with Jackie than Carmen was. It enraged her.

Back in Cleveland, after stewing over the incident for a while, Carmen visited Local 507, went into an office where George was working, and locked the door behind her. "Hi, honey," Carmen said cheerfully, seeing a look of panic come into George's eyes.

Carmen took off a shoe, gripped it like a club, and bashed the secretary in the head. While George screamed, Carmen wrestled her to the floor and hit her repeatedly, asking calmly, "Now are you ever going to talk to me like that again?"

"No! No! No! I promise!"

She hit her some more—"only in the hairline where it wouldn't show," Carmen remembers—then stopped, satisfied that George had learned her lesson.

Later, after Jackie had moved out permanently, he called his

273

estranged wife and said that he was dispatching one of his union business agents to come to the apartment and pick up his suits. He asked her to please have them ready.

Carmen cut the back out of the expensive suit coats and snipped off a leg from each pair of pants. She folded them neatly and packed them in a box. You couldn't even tell they had been mutilated. "I wasn't going to dress him up for somebody else," she says. She called the business agent, and he came and picked them up.

20
Rebels

"No damned Communist group is ever going to infiltrate this union."

FRANK FITZSIMMONS

While he was tiptoeing around feuding Cleveland Mob factions in 1976, Jackie faced another problem at home. Some of the rank and file were sick of his heavy-handed rule and had joined the small rebel movements taking hold in Cleveland, Detroit, and other Teamsters strongholds across the country.

Hoffa's disappearance a year earlier had sparked the reform movement. In search of Hoffa's kidnappers, the FBI, the IRS, the Justice and Labor Departments, and numerous police departments all put heat on the union and the Mob. For a moment, the Teamsters hierarchy seemed unsure, about to stumble, which gave the rebels a tiny opening. Cleveland became one of the hotbeds of rebellion.

The first group of reformers on the scene was the Professional Drivers Council (PROD), a Ralph Nader–inspired group run by savvy activist lawyer Arthur L. Fox. PROD started out lobbying for improved truck safety, sounding the themes of Nader's successful campaign against General Motors. PROD used news releases, press conferences, and picket lines to cast the Interstate Commerce Commission as a villain that allowed big trucking companies to flout federal safety regulations.

Soon PROD developed into a sturdy, sophisticated challenger of corrupt Teamsters leaders. Just before the 1976 IBT convention, the reformers dropped a bombshell on the Pressers. PROD's research di-

275

rector, John Sikorski, a Harvard graduate who worked summers as a teamster on Cleveland loading docks, had spent several months in the Labor Department's records rooms, poring over the financial reports of all Teamster locals, joint councils, and conferences. Blandly titled "Teamsters Democracy and Financial Responsibility," his report exposed one of the union's dirtiest secrets, the massive salaries and benefits paid to its officers. The salaries were a sneaky setup. Most teamsters didn't realize that Jackie had been collecting six separate paychecks, one each from Local 507, Joint Council 41, the Ohio Conference of Teamsters, the International, the Hotel and Restaurant Employees Union, and Harold Friedman's Bakery Workers Local 19. His 1974 take-home pay—$177,000. Harold Friedman himself, an unknown local leader, hauled in $181,000, giving Cleveland the distinction of being home to the world's two highest-paid labor bosses.

In the face of the reformers' complaints, Jackie reacted just as Big Bill, a true believer in J. Edgar Hoover's Red menace, had taught him. Jackie smeared the rebels as Communist agents who planned to take over the union movement and enslave the country. It's hard to believe that Jackie believed his own rhetoric. He most likely used the Joe McCarthy tactics out of convenience. "Commies?" one of Jackie's closest advisors said with a chuckle. "Jackie used that to entrench himself in the union. He was a shrewd politician, and he used the issue. He was willing to take on these guys who other people were paranoid of. Jackie got a lot of mileage out of that internally at the International. He was looked upon as taking these guys on and having a program and an agenda."

Over the Memorial Day weekend of 1976, the Ohio Conference of Teamsters bought a full-page advertisement in the *Plain Dealer* that asked, "Who is attacking the Teamsters Union?" The ad gave a colorful answer: "An unholy alliance of political midgets, some lying media gossip peddlers, and a few self-appointed labor 'reformers' whose secret motives are destructive and un-American." Jackie's ad didn't mention that other folks targeting the Teamsters included employees of the Justice Department, the FBI, and the IRS.

An unforeseen by-product of Jackie's defensive strategy was that national attention was focused on tiny PROD, which had only two thousand members out of the 2.3 million Teamsters. "Presser did more for the Teamsters rank-and-file reform movement than just about any

276

other Teamsters official," Sikorski recalls. "His huge salary, the brazenness of his wealth, his connections with management—people couldn't picture him doing an honest day's work in his life."

The battle intensified by the 1976 IBT Convention held in Las Vegas in June. Jackie was co–sergeant at arms, which meant that he provided security on the convention floor, at its meeting halls, and around Fitzsimmons and other key leaders. He imported numerous big business agents from Local 507, including Tony Hughes and Skip Felice.

Outside the convention hall, PROD members made an issue of Jackie's astronomical salary by distributing leaflets and selling their exposé on Teamster finances to reporters. The criticism couldn't have come at a worse time for Jackie. He was slimmed down, PR honed, trying to convince his elders on the International executive board that he should succeed his father, and all reporters wanted to know was why he banked so much of the members' dues. "I am the representative of the new leadership in labor," he insisted to reporters. "I am an educated labor leader who is concerned about improving the economic health of my community." Besides, management lawyers got a hundred dollars an hour or more to negotiate contracts, he argued. "Why shouldn't I get as much?"

Then Fitzsimmons, who was getting poor PR advice from Jackie, gave the rebel Teamsters a tremendous boost. Normally a bland, droning speaker, Fitz in his keynote address launched an unexpected, blistering attack on PROD before the national press corps. "For those who would say it's time to reform this organization, that it's time that the officers quit selling out their membership, I say to them, go to hell!" Fitz said. The 2,254 convention delegates obediently roared their approval.

"I promise you," Fitz went on, "as long as I have a drop of breath in my body, no damned Communist group is ever going to infiltrate this union." Turning to the press gallery he said, "Why the hell don't you investigate that kind of organization to find out where they get their money or who is trying to destroy this labor organization?" The delegates stood and cheered. Fitz wrapped it up, "Teamsters are without peer as an organization dedicated to the service of mankind." More thunderous applause.

"It helped PROD, absolutely," former director Sikorski says of

Fitzsimmons's attack. "When he did that, it made us a big issue. It got us a lot of press, both there and in Washington, D.C. Herblock even did a big cartoon."

Shortly after the 1976 convention, another reform group, Teamsters for a Democratic Union (TDU) was founded. Unlike PROD, TDU ignored Capitol Hill and concentrated instead on grass-roots organizing and trying to elect its own local union officers. Kenneth Paff, a Teamster driver from Local 407 in Cleveland, became a key TDU organizer and spokesman. Once a member of the International Socialist Party, Paff quickly ran afoul of some PROD activists, who objected to such TDU tactics as selling Communist party newspapers at organizing meetings of blue-collar workers and truck drivers. Fox and Sikorski even sent out a letter to their PROD chapters, pointing out TDU's Socialist background. Jackie got his hands on the letter and happily disseminated it. "There was some silly Red-baiting on PROD's part, in retrospect," Sikorski admits. "TDU showed they could organize the troops. Our competition only lasted a year or two."

Paff and the radicals were a tiny cadre inside TDU. Most of its members were simply fed-up truck drivers and dock workers who wanted a decent contract and union leaders who would fight to enforce it. Jackie hammered on Paff's background in an attempt to tar the entire TDU outfit. In September, Jackie learned that TDU was holding its first national conference at Kent State University, forty miles south of Cleveland. He and his staff whipped up a counterdemonstration and shipped seven busloads of retired Teamsters to Kent. The Teamsters milled around, held up signs, and passed out leaflets that called TDU "radical Socialist agitators." Jackie felt that he was playing hardball, letting TDU know he was watching their moves.

"That was kind of dumb on his part and good for us," Ken Paff recalls. "Jackie was a big shot, and here he was picketing us. We were just a small band of dissidents. Here were all these paid officials picketing. We took their photos and circled their names and wrote on their salaries and gave them to the reporters."

Jackie hated the pesky Paff. "He's a big crybaby, a loudmouth, a nothing guy who's never done anything," Jackie said. The guy doesn't "represent a flea." He's a "stupid bastard, an erratic guy."

278

Jackie was pleased with the news coverage of his counterdemonstration. Bashing dissidents seemed like a good way to rally his troops and look forceful on television. Later, at a meeting of local Teamster leaders, Jackie discussed expanding his TDU-bashing into a national campaign. "It isn't only our International union that's being attacked by these subversives, radical and Socialistic-type people," he said. "We're going to have to spend some time and money and work to show that this is a national program, and it's not just aimed at the Teamsters. They started with the Teamsters, but they're getting into all facets of organized labor."

Though few believed TDU represented a Commie threat capable of toppling the republic, Jackie's Red-scare tactics did accomplish something. He sent a message to Teamster members not to join or have any contact with the dissidents. Teamsters dissatisfied with their union were afraid to join TDU or PROD; they didn't want to lose their job or their good health, as Detroit Teamster rebel Pete Camarata had. Camarata had criticized the union on the floor of the IBT convention, only to find himself smacked around by one of Presser's business agents outside the convention hall. Back in Detroit, he said he was fired from his job for no good reason.

The Hoffa case also lurked in the back of any would-be rebel's mind. Look what happened to Hoffa after he threatened to return and expose Teamsters corruption, members reminded one another. He mysteriously disappeared, and no one was charged. If he wasn't safe, what chance did a lone rebel trucker stand?

Paff admits that Presser's most effective technique against the TDU was the implied threat of violence. It was enough to keep many unhappy Teamsters away from reform meetings. If new members did show up, they would often find a squad of large business agents standing silently at the back of the meeting room with their arms folded, staring as if to say, We know who you are and will remember you were here. This hampered recruitment much more than Presser's Red-baiting.

Even so, by reacting with such vehemence and might, Jackie inflated the rebels to mythic proportions. "People were saying to us, 'You guys must have balls all the way down to the floor,'" Paff says. "The Pressers overreacted to us. It's like a guy's got a fly on his foot and he shoots it with a machine gun and now he doesn't have a foot."

279

By spring 1977, Jackie was boasting that he had won the battle against the rebel groups. "We're starting to push PROD out of Ohio," he told his fellow union leaders. "TDU is all but dead in this area. This has been a lot of hard work. It takes a lot of know-how to fight these Socialists."

Behind the scenes, Jackie was smart enough to realize that the dissidents had latched onto good issues. The union hierarchy would have to sieze the initiative, respond to complaints, and co-opt the rebel forces. "We've had dissident membership, and that membership in some instances are one hundred and fifty percent right . . . because the people that represent them are neglectful," Presser said privately. The reformers did change his thinking. His father's old-fashioned, tight-lipped autocratic rule wouldn't work anymore, and Jackie warned his local presidents that they'd have to make changes. At one joint council meeting, he told the assembled union leaders that the Teamsters would be holding workshops instead of golf outings from now on.

> If you officers and officials don't talk to your membership and start to tell the truth to them about what the hell is going on in this union, we ain't going to have a union. If we ain't got a union, you ain't got a job. And that's the way it works, and that's what these outsiders are trying to accomplish.
>
> One big problem that we found within this International is that most of the elected officers that are from the old school—and surely those young kids that are being elected today by the membership—don't know how to run a local union. We found local union officers that are buying Cadillacs when their local union treasuries are under ten thousand dollars. We found local union officers that have a payroll that is in excess of the yearly income. We found union officers that are attending conferences and local union meetings and entertaining their membership with whiskey, food, and sandwiches, and the local is running in the red. We found officers of local unions that are doing things that are absolutely unheard of.

Jackie said it was time for Teamster officials to clean up their act: "We should start telling our business agents, executive board members, and elected officials what we're all about and why we have to do the thing that we're doing, so that you don't get indicted, so that you don't turn around and say, 'Somebody's putting the heat on. Somebody's dropping dimes on me.' And then they find out that you were getting manicures and dry cleaning and haircuts, you're buying your broad gifts and taking your wife with you on trips, and all of the time you knew it was illegal." Jackie knew his topic well; he had been dropping dimes to the FBI for several years.

By the late seventies, PROD and TDU had moved closer together. TDU downplayed its early Socialist roots, and PROD moved from truck safety to corruption fighting. Both agreed that the way to chase out the corrupt Teamsters leaders, a small but powerful minority in the 1.8-million-member union, was to have union officers, from the general president on down, elected democratically by secret ballot of each union member. The current system—with local officers and delegates picking the president every five years at the IBT convention—gave too much power to the Teamster brass.

In 1979, PROD was assimilated into TDU, and TDU moved its headquarters from Cleveland to Detroit, a larger Teamsters center and the home of President Fitzsimmons, their main target. Of course, Jackie took credit for the move, saying he drove TDU out of town. "He got a lot of mileage out of it," one of Presser's advisors recalls.

Paff disagreed. Over the next few years, thanks in large part to Jackie Presser, TDU would only get stronger.

21
Bribing a Senator

"Don't worry about it. I'll have that committee."
SENATOR HOWARD CANNON

Bill, Jackie, and the Teamsters lost their key to the back door of the White House during the Jimmy Carter years. No more secret sessions with top White House advisors like the ones Fitzsimmons had enjoyed with Charles Colson, plotting to take on antiwar demonstrators and liberals, and to help Bill Presser, if possible. In 1976, members of the Teamsters executive board couldn't agree among themselves which presidential candidate was the lesser evil. They didn't make an endorsement, Carter won, and the Teamsters found a White House even more closed off than expected.

Bill and Jackie Presser were used to being pampered by politicians. Ohio DRIVE, their political action committee, was the most active in the Teamsters, and elected officials in Ohio practically begged for their endorsements and contributions. "Money talks," said Tony Hughes, who screened candidates. It was certainly upsetting to the Pressers to find their mundane requests for White House favors falling on uncaring ears. For example, Ohio state representative Rocco K. Colonna, an auto worker who had campaigned for Carter, called the White House asking for a Carter letter congratulating Bill, who was being feted at yet another testimonial dinner. Under previous administrations, such perfunctory greetings were issued almost automatically. But this time, the Carter aide who fielded Colonna's request, unfamiliar with Bill Presser, called a Labor Department official who dumped a bucket of

282

slop on the idea. The Carter aide wrote a sarcastic memo noting that Presser's "record of service" had been "the subject of numerous criminal investigations" then instructed an underling to turn it down.

The union kept trying to cultivate friends in the Carter administration, thinking perhaps of Hoffa's favorite saying, "Every man has his price." In early 1976, after Jimmy Carter broke from the primary pack, the Central States Pension Fund deposited $18 million into the National Bank of Georgia, controlled by Carter's best friend Bert Lance. At the time, the three-person trust department didn't manage an account over $2 million. Lance said that he had nothing to do with the Teamsters' deposits. Before it could be seen whether the Teamsters had been able to construct a pipeline into the White House through Lance, his shaky banking practices forced him out as Carter's budget director, only eight months into the new administration.

Jackie even went so far as to ask Jimmy the Weasel sometime in the first half of 1977 whether he had a contact within the Carter camp who might help with a favor. Fratianno replied that he had just the man in mind: William Marchiondo, a New Mexico lawyer with political connections who, along with his friend Jerry Apodaca, the New Mexico governor, had been an early Carter supporter. Fratianno said that Marchiondo bragged that the Carter administration was indebted to him. Apodaca's cousin also worked as an associate legal counsel for Carter.

The Weasel called Marchiondo and told him that Jackie Presser needed a White House favor. Marchiondo said he'd try to help. In return, the lawyer asked about getting legal work referred from the Teamsters. By late 1977, Fratianno said, he had introduced Jackie to Marchiondo. Nothing came of this contact, which suggests that Presser may have been using Fratianno to see if anyone in the White House had Mob ties. With this juicy tidbit in hand, Jackie could pad his FBI résumé.

By 1978, the biggest challenge facing Fitz, Jackie, and the union was the proposed deregulation of the trucking industry. The Interstate Commerce Commission regulated truck lines doing $31 billion of business a year. The ICC set freight rates, dictated where and what companies could haul and how much they could charge. The ICC even regulated who could enter the trucking business, making freight hauling about as financially risky as owning the local electric company.

The Teamsters and the companies loved the setup. Freight haulers weren't undercut by gypsy or nonunion outfits. The union always won impressive pay raises for its members, and the truck companies didn't care how much they had to shell out; they simply passed on their costs by getting the ICC to grant a rate increase, which it always did. For decades, regulated trucking had been a stable, highly profitable component of the U.S. economy.

The Carter administration wanted to slay the cash cow and deregulate trucking, believing this action would slow inflation by increasing competition among companies. They'd have to cut rates to survive, meaning lower shipping costs for companies ranging from food stores to automakers. "If there is any other industry with a greater potential for competition, I don't know of it," Carter anti-inflation czar Alfred E. Kahn once said of trucking.

The Teamsters, whose three hundred thousand freight drivers would be affected by deregulation, considered the idea an abomination. By late 1978, it was widely reported that Senator Edward M. Kennedy was going to introduce a trucking-deregulation bill in the Senate Judiciary Committee, which he chaired. This really riled the Teamsters brass. A deregulation bill was bad enough; worse, a member of the Kennedy family—the union's bête noire in the fifties—was sponsoring it. They would do whatever it took to stop his bill.

The Teamsters chiefs got a lucky break, or so Roy Williams and Allen Dorfman thought. Senator Howard W. Cannon of Nevada wanted to buy a choice parcel of Teamsters real estate at the precise time Kennedy's deregulation bill was supposed to start wending its way through Senate committees and out onto the floor. Cannon, the influential chairman of the Senate Commerce Committee and a ranking member of the Armed Services Committee, could kill or at least tie up the legislation.

The senator lived in the exclusive Las Vegas Country Club Estates, which, like much of Las Vegas's choice real estate, abutted a vacant 5.8-acre parcel owned by the Teamsters Central States Pension Fund. In November 1978, the fund's new government-appointed assets administrator, Victor Palmieri Company, solicited bids for the land, known as the Wonderworld parcel after its previous owner. The winning bidder wanted to build three nine-story condominium buildings on the land and linked his purchase to a favorable rezoning. The last thing Cannon's wealthy neighbors wanted was hundreds of new residents spoiling their view and property values. They banded together and rallied to stop the high rises.

Cannon attended one of the protest meetings, and he and his neighbors decided to buy the Wonderworld plot to protect themselves. The senator, who had business partners active in Teamsters-financed casinos, offered to call Allen Dorfman. He knew Dorfman was the man to see about getting a Teamsters favor.

Since the McClellan hearings in the late fifties, Dorfman had been tarred as a Mob man. Yet Cannon, a U.S. senator, a member of the gentleman's club, wasn't the least bit shy about asking the notorious labor racketeer for help. According to Dorfman, the two men had known each other since Cannon's days as the Las Vegas city attorney in the mid-fifties. Since then, Howard Cannon had compiled a less than sterling record. Originally from Utah, he was a bumpkin when he first arrived in Las Vegas. "He had on those thick, crepe-rubber-soled shoes and a bright sport coat and a bright pair of slacks—he sure as hell didn't look much like a potential United States senator!" recalled Norman H. Biltz, the Nevada real-estate developer and political kingmaker. A key insider in Nevada's bipartisan political machine, Biltz and his group put up the money for Cannon's 1958 Senate race. "An attorney here took Howard under his wing and really taught him how to make a speech, what to say and what not to say, and carried him through the thing," Biltz said.

Dr. Frederick M. Anderson, a surgeon and a University of Nevada regent, had thought about running against Cannon that year. "A prominent investigative reporter, Ed Reid, who later wrote *The Green Felt Jungle*, came to me with a story that indicated shady dealings on the part of Cannon as city attorney in an award of a garbage franchise," Anderson recalled. "That could, I think, have changed many votes. Reid said he would back it with proof in the newspaper if I would break it on television or radio. After talking with him considerably, and although I believed him to be truthful, I finally told him that I didn't want to win that way even if there had been improper conduct."

Over the next two decades, Cannon was accused of everything from stuffing ballot boxes to using his Senate seat to enhance his land

285

holdings. He has denied the charges and thrived in Nevada's rough-and-tumble political arena. Cannon's 1975–76 campaign finance reports raised eyebrows. They listed thirty-three contributors who were involved in or associated with organized crime or top officials of firms linked to organized crime. A Cannon aide said that you couldn't run for Nevada office without taking contributions from the gambling industry.

On Wednesday, January 10, 1979, in his private Las Vegas office, the senator sat down with Allen Dorfman and Roy Williams and a Teamster lawyer named Ed Wheeler. In a less private outer office were William E. Webbe, a Dorfman employee, and Cannon's son-in-law, Robert Bjornsen, who chatted about how the senator might go about buying the vacant Teamsters land.

Inside the inner sanctum, a conspiracy was put in place. As a key participant later admitted, Williams and Dorfman asked Cannon to oppose Kennedy's proposed trucking deregulation bill after it was introduced. Cannon asked about buying the 5.8 acres abutting his fancy home. Williams then promised the senator that he and his neighbors could buy the property if Cannon would tie up deregulation legislation in his Commerce Committee.

Cannon, Dorfman, and Williams ended the meeting and came to the outside room where the other two men sat.

"You take care of your end, and we'll take care of our end," Williams said to Cannon.

"Don't worry about it, I'll have that committee," Cannon said. "You tell me what you want . . . and we can work this thing out together."

They had a deal, a simple quid pro quo. The Teamsters' enticement to Cannon was the exclusive right to purchase the Wonderworld acres for $1.4 million—$200,000 less than the current high bidder.

Two days before Kennedy introduced his bill, the White House detected that the Teamsters, for some puzzling reason, didn't seem to be as vociferously opposed to Kennedy's bill as it had to past deregulation proposals. On January 20, Carter's chief domestic policy adviser Stuart E. Eizenstat wrote to the president, "We should support this bill. . . . The Teamsters will not endorse it, but they do not oppose it with nearly the force that they oppose complete deregulation of price

286

and entry." By then, many in the Teamsters hierarchy knew that Cannon was going to help out.

Kennedy unveiled his deregulation bill in the Senate Judiciary Committee on January 22, 1979. Cannon immediately insisted that the bill—which proposed to outlaw rate-setting—belonged in his Commerce Committee. Kennedy's bill was snagged and was never even introduced.

While the Teamsters and the Mob were teaming up to battle deregulation, a team of Chicago FBI agents was trying to convince their supervisors to blanket Dorfman's insurance offices with wiretaps and bugs.

Tapping Dorfman was the first step in an ambitious plan hatched by Chicago FBI agents and the Chicago Strike Force to pinch off the cash flooding the Chicago Mafia through Dorfman and Las Vegas casinos. The agents had been compiling intelligence from different sources, some of it from Jackie Presser via FBI headquarter's informant desk, that revealed Dorfman as a hidden owner of Las Vegas casinos to which he had steered Teamsters loans. In return for the loans, casino owners such as Allen Glick allowed Mob associates to skim unreported cash. Also, Jackie and other Mob sources told the FBI that Dorfman had hidden interest in the Slots-A-Fun and Bingo Palace casinos.

The Chicago Strike Force chief Doug Roller was gung ho on the proposed investigation, but the FBI agents' supervisors—assistant special agents in charge, or ASACs—were decidedly cool. "I remember it clearly, a January morning in '79, in my office, when the two ASACs of the bureau were questioning the dedication and the resources of the project," Roller recalled. "They said it was going to be too much money and manpower and resources. And they really didn't think it was appropriate. We had a pissing contest over the importance of the case."

The strike force won and Operation Pendorf (*Pen*etrate *Dorf*man) kicked off. The first crucial step was getting court permission to install wiretaps. Roller knew that the probable cause—the reasons he and the FBI agents gave a judge to convince him to approve a wiretap—had to be airtight. Later defense lawyers would try to attack the wiretap application, which was known as a Title III affidavit. If their assault was successful, Operation Pendorf could collapse like a house of cards, no matter how incriminating the intercepted conversations were.

The probable cause for the first Pendorf wiretap application consisted of detailed, current intelligence from several FBI informers. Though neither Roller nor the agents were told, one of the key Title III informants was Jackie. His intelligence on Dorfman—that he partly owned and skimmed from two Las Vegas casinos—arrived in Chicago on plain white paper. FBI agent Peter Wacks used it and several other informant reports to craft an affidavit that convinced a federal judge to allow the wiretap investigation to go forward.

On January 29, the FBI obtained court permission to tap thirteen telephone lines out of Dorfman's insurance offices in the western suburbs of Chicago. The bureau's black-bag experts—agents trained to pick locks and bypass the fanciest security systems—entered Dorfman's offices seven times to plant microphones. Then the FBI set up a cover company nearby, North American Plating Company, where agents in business suits arrived like clockwork each morning to put in grueling twelve-hour shifts monitoring the wiretaps. Agents were instructed to "bring in lunch and other necessities" and to stash their "guns, handcuffs, bullet pouches, etc." in briefcases so as not to blow their cover.

The largest court-ordered wiretap surveillance in Justice Department history had commenced.

After the first meeting with Cannon, Williams stepped out of the picture for the moment and let Dorfman and his associates take care of the senator. As director of the Central Conference, Williams was busy bargaining the National Master Freight Agreement, to be presented for a vote by long-haul drivers in April. Drivers wanted a hefty raise to keep up with the raging twelve percent inflation, but the White House had asked Fitzsimmons to keep the Master Freight Agreement raises under Carter's seven percent voluntary wage guideline. Fitz said fine, as long as he saw some "handwriting in the sky" that the Labor and Justice departments were easing up their corruption probes into Central States. A week later, the Labor Department filed a civil lawsuit against the Teamsters and the administrators of Central States Pension Fund. Fitz and the IBT executive board reacted angrily. If Carter won't back off, neither will we. The vice presidents voted to give Fitz permission to call a national strike.

Meanwhile, Dorfman was conniving to get the Las Vegas parcel into Cannon's hands. Dorfman discussed his moves with his handler in the Chicago family, Joey "the Clown" Lombardo, an ex–hit man who rose up to become a powerful caporegime who controlled Dorfman, the outfit's porn interests, and other rackets. Dorfman talked tough and strode through Las Vegas and La Costa like a conquering warrior. But wiretaps revealed an obsequious side to the Mob's front man. When Lombardo barked an order, Dorfman jumped.

Luckily for Dorfman and the Teamsters, it turned out that ex–casino owner Allen Glick had submitted the high bid for Wonderworld, $1.6 million. After some discussion, Joey the Clown and Dorfman figured that Glick would drop his offer if they asked him to. Dorfman sent word of this plan to Williams, who concurred. It was too risky for Dorfman, Lombardo, or Williams to solicit Glick. They decided that Thomas O'Malley, forty-six, and Andrew G. Massa, sixty-five, two Central States trustees, would travel at union expense to see Glick in San Diego.

Williams dispatched the Teamsters Central Conference's Falcon 20 jet to pick up the two Chicago men and speed them to California. They met with Glick, appropriately, at La Costa.

"Allen, could you please withdraw your bid?" Glick was asked. "We'd appreciate the favor. Senator Cannon has put in a lower bid, and the union wants him to get the property."

They went on to explain that Cannon chaired a congressional committee that was going to tie up the hated deregulation bill. Not only that, they added, but Mr. Dorfman wants Cannon to buy the property.

That last detail caused Glick to snap to attention. The next day, he told Victor Palmieri Company that he was withdrawing his $1.6 million bid. A few days later in Chicago, Joey the Clown reached Dorfman associate Bill Webbe on one of the bugged telephones and asked for any news.

Without using Glick's name, Webbe said that the San Diego developer had dropped his bid.

"He says he's willing to turn it down?" Lombardo asked.

"Oh, he turned it down—flat out," Webbe said.

"Beautiful," Lombardo replied. Later on, he boasted, "OK. Another good move by me. I'm like an old-time general. They'd better give me some stars."

By February, Cannon's neighbors dropped out of the venture, and the money they put into a down-payment fund was returned. But Bjornsen, with Dorfman's hidden financial backing, continued to push to buy the parcel. On February 9, 1979, Bjornsen resubmitted a bid for $1.4 million. The same day, another Las Vegas developer submitted a higher bid of $1.6 million, knocking out the Cannon offer once again.

Dorfman and Lombardo were vexed when they learned of the new bidder. Luckily, it turned out to be a friend of Glick. They told him to get the guy to drop his bid, and Glick, ever obedient, quickly did.

Driving off high bidders was a new tactic for Dorfman and the Mob. Only a few years earlier, all Dorfman or Bill Presser or Fitzsimmons would have had to do was say the word and Central States trustees immediately would have accepted Cannon's low offer. The Victor Palmieri Company, however, sold Central States Pension Fund real-estate by sealed bids, making the process difficult to manipulate.

In March, Williams telephoned Dorfman to see how the Cannon deal was progressing, but he ended up talking to Webbe. Williams ordered Webbe to complete the deal quickly. "I don't want to hear no more bullshit," Williams said.

The difficulty that Dorfman, Lombardo, and the Teamsters were having in steering the land to Cannon illustrates the much larger problem the Mob was having with Central States in the late seventies. After twenty years of freewheeling deals, defaults, kickbacks, and low-interest loans, the Mafia's bank got religion. It started when Central States administrator Dan Shannon, brought in by Fitzsimmons and Bill Presser to "reform" the fund, refused to approve any new real-estate loans. For this subversive act, Dorfman put out a contract on Shannon's life.

By 1977, Fitz had bowed to pressure from the IRS and the Justice Department and turned over the fund's asset management to two outside companies, Victor Palmieri Company and Equitable Life Assurance Society. Palmieri was assigned to run the fund's investments west of the Mississippi River. Equitable Life had the remainder.

Dorfman howled in protest. The independent asset managers cut into his action. He asked Mafia boss Civella to pressure Roy Williams to throw out the two firms. Dorfman "went every place he could to get pressure put on me by Nick Civella to change back to the way it used to be, knowing that that was impossible under the law," Williams said.

So upset was the Mafia with losing a grip on Central States that Civella, Dorfman, and other Mob guys convened on March 25, 1979, at Kansas City's Crown Center Hotel to discuss a way to get it back. They thought they were being careful by meeting at the last minute in a room at the low-profile Crown Center Hotel. No way could the FBI put a bug in there that afternoon.

The mobsters hadn't counted on diligent Kansas City FBI agent William N. Ouseley, who had been alerted to the meeting by Chicago agents monitoring wiretaps of Dorfman's offices. Ouseley corraled seven agents, who staked out the Kansas City airport. Dorfman and Lombardo were spotted, and Ouseley tailed their taxi to the hotel.

The agents wanted to get to a room on the same floor to observe the conclave. But they got even luckier. The hotel rented Ouseley the room next door, which was separated from the mobsters' hotel room, room 1539, by two separate doors with a space between. Ouseley knelt and pressed his ear to the metal door jam. To his surprise, he said he could hear the wise guys talking clearly. Twisted like a contortionist, he kept his ear on the door and took notes on a pad for nearly two and a half hours. He was spelled only briefly by a colleague.

He heard Joe Agosto, a Las Vegas casino manager, tell Civella, "We got work to do. We got to get the fund back. Get good lawyers. Got moves to make, lot of scheming to do. . . . We got to put it back together the way it was, for now and for the future."

Civella said that he had been working with Williams to regain control of Central States in a way that would "protect Roy" because "he's a friend of mine." Civella said that he had assured Williams that "I'm not asking you to do something that will open the penitentiary door."

One of the favors needed, Civella was overheard to say, was the firing of Equitable and Palmieri, the by-the-books companies now man-

291

aging the pension-fund's assets. Roy Williams was the one to perform this service, Civella explained. "Whatever [Williams] needs, I have taken care of," Civella said. "We give him money."

But who would replace the independent managers? someone at the meeting wondered. Civella responded that he didn't have a preference, as long as it wasn't Dorfman. Not that he didn't like Allen, just that Dorfman's presence would attract government scrutiny. "Allen has ego problems," Civella said after he excused Dorfman from the meeting. "The government would swoop down if they hear that it's Allen who's running things."

"Allen has to be close to Roy on the QT, just like two peas in a pod, like you and I," Joe Agosto told Civella.

On April 23, 1979, a few weeks after the Crown Center meeting, Nick Civella summoned Williams to a meeting in Kansas City to talk about how the Mob could get its claws back into the $2 billion fund. The second most influential Teamster in the country dutifully complied and was chauffered by an underworld minion to the home of Phil Simone, a Civella relative and truck-terminal manager. Williams was comfortable meeting at Simone's home. At least if the Teamsters official was caught by surveillance, he'd have a plausible excuse for seeing truck executive Simone. Even so, Williams took precautions. Afraid that federal agents might be watching the house or Nick Civella, Williams ducked down and hid on the floor of the Cadillac before the car pulled up to Simone's house and into the garage at quarter after two that afternoon. Dorfman, Civella, Sam Ancona, and others were waiting for him. Dorfman, who did much of the talking, said at one point, "We want the Shannon people out of there. We want Central States back like it used to be."

Williams listened respectfully and said he'd see what he could do.

The overhears and wiretaps and bugged conversations pouring out of Dorfman's insurance offices titillated the FBI agents, but they couldn't figure out what crimes were being plotted. Dorfman, Lombardo, and other participants discussed their schemes in veiled terms, referring to "that guy," "the local guy," "the man," and other vague figures. The FBI agents also overheard "the senator" mentioned a few times.

Early in the investigation, FBI agents picked up the telephone call between Cannon's son-in-law Bjornsen and Webbe of Central States. The agents understood the call to be about some kind of a real-estate transaction and concluded, erroneously, that it involved the sale of the Aladdin casino, not the property next to the Las Vegas Country Club that Cannon wanted to buy. Further confusing the matter, monitoring agents didn't even know who Bjornsen was and for many weeks misspelled his name "Ornsen" and "Ewing" and "Euing."

Every thirty days, the Chicago Strike Force and FBI office had to reapply to federal court for permission to extend the wiretaps on Dorfman another month. At each application, the Justice Department faced the burden of showing that the taps were productive and moving the investigation forward. It was difficult. Nothing was overheard about Dorfman secretly owning the Slots-A-Fun or the Bingo Palace, which had been a key reason for the wiretaps in the first place. The Chicago FBI supervisors, not excited about Pendorf in the first place, weren't pleased with the case.

"There was always the specter of the axe falling on it," Roller said. "It disappeared when we got Cannon."

In mid-March, the FBI asked Jackie about the confusing wiretapped conversations involving Webbe, Dorfman, "the senator," someone named Ornsen, and some sort of Teamster land deal in Las Vegas. Presser gave them the key that unlocked the mystery: Williams cut a deal with Cannon, Jackie explained. He's going to kill the deregulation bill in his Senate Commerce Committee in exchange for a bargain-basement price on a piece of Las Vegas real estate owned by the fund. Bjornsen is Cannon's son-in-law. Jackie knew this because Williams made the mistake of telling him.

All the pieces clicked into place for the FBI.

Meanwhile, the Palmieri Company still hadn't approved the sale to Cannon through his son-in-law. The management company continued to solicit bids for Wonderworld, and Williams was angry. He had made a promise and had yet to deliver on it to the senator. On April 26, Williams called Bill Webbe at the Central States offices.

WILLIAMS: Did ya ever find out anything more on that west thing?

WEBBE: Yes, uh, they turned down the last offer that was given. That was a very fair offer.

WILLIAMS: Yep.

WEBBE: And Allen was out there this week, and he's out there now.

WILLIAMS: Yeah, I know he is. I talked to him on Monday.

WEBBE: . . . I reported to him what happened, and he said, well, he's gonna meet with, uh, the son-in-law and also get to, to the other guy and find out what they wanna do next.

WILLIAMS: . . . We made a commitment.

WEBBE: Yeah, I know.

WILLIAMS: And now we've got no other bidders.

WEBBE: I know it.

WILLIAMS: And we've got a piece of property that's six acres that is appraised at $900,000 and what are we gettin', a million four?

WEBBE: A million four.

WILLIAMS: . . . And I just can't see, so I sent the lawyers . . . out there to find out what in the hell was wrong, 'cause I got whistled in by the senator to find out what was wrong. And of course I know what he done with deregulations.

WEBBE: That's right.

WILLIAMS: He put them on the back burner.

WEBBE: That's exactly right.

WILLIAMS: And then he was willin' to take on a fight with Kennedy.

WEBBE: And he did.

WILLIAMS: Yeah, and he got that bill out of Kennedy's hands.

WEBBE: That's right. He, he did everything he said.

294

On May 21, 1979, about half-past four in the afternoon, Teamsters vice president Donald Peters, who ran Local 743, the largest in the area, dropped in to see his friend Allen Dorfman and have a drink while the evening rush hour thinned out. Central States employee William Webbe was in Dorfman's office.

Their chitchat was interrupted a few minutes later. It was Senator Cannon on the phone, calling to ask Dorfman for a status report on the Wonderworld land he wanted to buy. Dorfman apologized for the delays and told Cannon to have his son-in-law resubmit their $1.4 million bid.

After he hung up, Dorfman announced, "Senator Cannon."

"How's he doing?" Peters asked.

"Huh? We fucked him around like no man has ever been fucked around. Get Bob Borgensen . . . on the phone."

"Bjornsen?" Webbe said.

"Bjornsen, what the fuck ever his son-in-law's name is," Dorfman said.

"He took care of deregulation, didn't he?" Peters asked. The entire Teamsters executive board seemed to know about the scheme.

"Huh?" Dorfman said.

"Did he take care of deregulation?" Peters repeated.

"Of course," Dorfman said. "But we ain't fulfilled our commitment to him yet. You know, I'm surprised he still even talks to me."

A few minutes later, Dorfman told Peters that he had to meet Cannon on June 1 in Las Vegas to make another request. "You know why I gotta meet the senator on June 1st? This is even funnier. Gotta go for another favor. A favor for Dusty Miller. You know, I'm gonna wear out my welcome with this guy. I keep going to him for favors, he keeps performing, we keep delivering him shit."

Then Dorfman griped about how easy it would have been in the old days to get the Central States Pension Fund to sell Cannon the vacant land. One word from someone like Williams or Fitz or Presser, and it would be done. Even now, if the trustees had just made up their minds, stuck together, and called Palmieri to say they wanted to sell the land to Cannon, Palmieri would have had to do it, Dorfman said.

"And the worst part about it," Dorfman marveled, "they [the trustees] know who it's for, and they know why it was done. 'Cause Roy went and told 'em." Dorfman couldn't understand why the Central

295

States trustees—half of them Teamsters, the rest trucking-company executives—didn't push the Wonderworld sale out of self-interest. Fitzsimmons wasn't helping Cannon get his land either, Dorfman felt. He told Webbe he was fed up with Fitz.

"I've already told him, 'I don't give a fuck what you [want],' " Dorfman said. "I told Fitzsimmons, 'Say listen, fuck you and your de[regulation]!' I told him right at the wedding last Sunday. I says, 'Fuck you and your commitments, pal.' I says, 'You think this fucking road is a one-way street, you got another fucking guess coming. You don't make commitments to United States senators and then don't fulfill them.'

"And he says, 'Well I don't know why it wasn't fulfilled.' I said, 'Well, I ain't the fuckin' boss of the International Brotherhood of Teamsters. You are. You ain't figured it out.' I says, 'Did this guy perform on everything that he was asked to?' He says, 'He sure did.' "

Cannon never got the real estate he wanted. Palmieri sold it for $1.6 million to another group of investors. By the end of 1979, the federal investigation had kicked into high gear, and the Chicago Strike Force had subpoenaed travel records, started calling witnesses to a federal grand jury, and transcribed thousands of reels of intercepted phone calls. Operation Pendorf went public.

Roy Williams was scared. So were Dorfman's Central States associates Bill Webbe, Thomas O'Malley, and Amos Massa. But egotistical Allen Dorfman, who had survived a quarter century of federal scrutiny, told them not to worry. "Gentlemen, gentlemen, tell me what you did that was wrong?" he asked at a January 7, 1980, meeting at his offices in suburban Chicago. "Nothing, not a fucking thing."

Then Dorfman suggested their alibi when questioned by the grand jury. "You went with the concerted effort to sell this piece of property. And if it were at all possible and they were the successful bidders, you wanted that property to go to Mr. Bjornsen. He happened to be Senator Cannon's son-in-law. What the fuck business is that of yours?"

A dozen or so miles away in a high-rise Loop office building, Doug Roller, Chicago Strike Force prosecutor Gary Shapiro, FBI agent Peter Wacks, and others were making it their business. Dorfman had made it easier for them.

"If Dorfman hadn't been such a cheap motherfucker, they

296

wouldn't have even had this this case," Roller later recalled. "The price Victor Palmieri [Company] wanted was $1.6 million. All Dorfman had to have done was come up with that $200,000 for the senator through other machinations." The Teamsters would have had him in their pocket and not left a steady six months of telephone calls for the FBI to intercept and interpret.

"To Allen Dorfman and the Mob, $200,000 was nothing," Roller went on. "But that would have been too easy. They'd have to front their own money. That's a total antithesis to the mentality of organized crime. They don't give, they take. So they go get themselves in a jam for $200,000."

22

Presidential Politics

"But Newt, he's never been indicted."

EDWIN MEESE III

By early 1980, word had circulated widely through the Teamsters and the underworld that Frank Fitzsimmons was afflicted with lung cancer and undergoing tests and treatment. Not wanting to be caught off guard and miss an opportunity to install his candidate as Teamsters president, Nick Civella—the single strongest Mafia voice in the union, Jackie told the FBI—launched a campaign for his hometown boy, Roy Williams, nicknamed Rancher because he raised quarter horses as a hobby.

On January 11, 1980, Nick Civella met with his brother Carl, a Kansas City Mafia capo, in the visitors room at the federal prison in Leavenworth, Kansas. Nick Civella had been imprisoned for violating parole. Though they used code names, the brothers spoke openly about promoting Williams. They didn't know the Kansas City Strike Force and the FBI had placed a hidden, court-approved microphone in the visiting area.

Nick Civella had earlier instructed his younger brother to recruit backers for Rancher by lobbying Bill "Plug" Presser. The key was to talk to the Plug's underworld handler, Maishe Rockman, and get him to convince Presser to back Williams, Nick said.

CARL CIVELLA: Me and him try to get to the Plug. Talk to 'im about the—did you want one of us to go talk to 'im?

298

NICK CIVELLA: No!

CARL: You wanted—

NICK: No!

CARL: He [wasn't] quite sure if you wanted me or—

NICK: All right. Here's what I said. Word should be gotten, should be gotten through Maishe.

CARL: Yeah.

NICK: That big fat Plug likes him [Williams] too. . . . Maishe could take care of it. Boy, we gotta sell Maishe first, then later sell them. That's the way it's got to be or should be. He's the most logical. I can't see of anybody else they would want. Fat Guy, knows, uh, R [Rancher] real well. An' that son [Jackie], even though they never got along too good, uh, knows the guy.

A week later, Carl again visited Nick in prison, after Williams had apparently learned of their plans for him. Roy was acting "like he's the king already," Carl told his brother.

Maishe was coming to town to pick up skim money, and Carl said he'd tell him to intercede with Bill Presser.

NICK: Maishe get my message?

CARL: He's comin' back from St. Louis tonight. . . . I'm gonna send 'im some money, right. I got twenty-five put away for 'im. If we get some more, I'm going to send him twenty-five more. There's another package of six-fifty. I'm going to tell him to go see the Plug and tell the Plug that that's what [we] want.

The FBI also had a strong interest in Fitzsimmons's medical condition, and Jackie kept his handlers informed. By April, Fitz had lost considerable weight and looked terrible. He fell asleep during executive board meetings in Miami. Though very ill, Fitz seemed more concerned about his son, Richard, vice president of Local 299 in Detroit, who had just been sentenced to thirty months in prison for taking bribes from trucking-company officials to assure labor peace. Fitz was

299

furious that his relatively unimportant son was getting locked up while wealthy mobsters like Al Dorfman flew about the country first class, making deals and playing golf with powerful politicians. Fitz also worried about his own neck. From what the Teamsters president was hearing, the Justice Department's Pendorf investigation in Chicago and its Straw Man probe of Las Vegas casino skimming and the Kansas City Mafia were dead certain to put the squeeze on the Detroit and Chicago mobsters he had had dealings with through Central States. A Chicago grand jury had already started subpoenaing records and witnesses.

"If the government squeezes hard enough, some of these guys might cough me up as part of a deal," Fitz confided to Jackie. "I'm getting too old for this kind of aggravation."

Keenly aware of Fitzsimmons's troubled state of mind, Jackie urged the FBI to recruit him as an informant.

"This is the time to get to Fitz," Jackie said. "But don't approach him at work. It's got to be some place neutral. Give me time and I'll come up with a good spot for you. Meantime, here's the name of one of Fitz's best friends. He's reasonable. Maybe you can get to Fitz through him."

While the vultures circled Fitzsimmons and the Mafia talked up Williams, Jackie Presser got involved in a presidential campaign of another sort. He fell for Ronald Reagan, the former head of the Screen Actors Guild and a conservative in tune with Jackie's feelings about class, dissidents, and Communism. It was an odd romance if one considered that the Teamsters had hated Reagan when he was governor of California. Under the headline "Right Winger at Work," the February 1967 *DRIVE Reporter* blasted Reagan when he broke with tradition and for the first time named a businessman to head the California Labor Commission. According to his speeches, radio commentaries, and campaign literature, Reagan opposed the union shop and instead advocated right-to-work, which was anathema to unions. A free-market advocate, Reagan didn't believe in tariffs, restrictions, and price-setting regulation. The AFL-CIO leadership blasted Reagan and backed Jimmy Carter in 1980. But Jackie blamed Carter for trucking deregulation and for the Labor Department's lawsuit against the Central States Pension Fund. Jackie alone among powerful labor figures embraced Reagan.

300

Before Jackie was deeply immersed in the presidential campaign, he suffered the first hit in a volley of accusations that linked him to the Mafia and should have cooled off Reagan's mating dance with Jackie and the Teamsters. Jimmy "the Weasel" Fratianno told a San Francisco jury in the embezzlement trial of Teamsters leader Rudy Tham that Jackie had admitted being controlled by the boss of the Cleveland Mafia. Though this was true, Jackie replied through his publicist that he had never even talked to the Weasel. "I have no knowledge of what he is talking about," Jackie said. He would later contradict this statement.

The allegations wafted in from California—Reagan country—but they evidently didn't offend Reagan, Meese, and the campaign crew. Two weeks later, Jackie all but publicly announced that he, the IBT vice president with a Midwest territory of 1.4 million teamsters, was going to do everything he could to help put the Gipper in the White House.

That summer, about the time Reagan won his party's nomination, the Chicago Strike Force sent the Justice Department a political hot potato in the form of a memo seeking permission to indict six men for supposedly taking part in a scheme to bribe Senator Cannon: Joseph Lombardo, Allen Dorfman, Roy Williams, Central States trustees Thomas G. O'Malley and Andrew G. Massa, and Cannon himself.

The Justice Department didn't seem particularly keen on indicting Cannon. It was explained privately to Chicago Strike Force chief Roller that the FBI had intercepted only one telephone call—fairly innocuous on its face—between Cannon and Dorfman. The Justice Department and the Chicago Strike Force haggled for a while over indicting Cannon, and eventually Roller was overruled. That didn't mean the others targets in the case—Dorfman, Roy Williams, and their associates—were off the hook. But Roller realized that without a Cannon indictment, the case against the others was weakened. He kept his disappointment within the department. "In my fifteen years in the Department of Justice, I have never seen any response by my superiors to political pressure," Roller said in a recent interview. "The closest thing was the decision not to indict Cannon. This is speculation. It was summer of an election year. It wouldn't have done the Democrats any

301

good to have a powerful senator linked to organized-crime figures. I don't know if there were other factors at work."

By August, Reagan and Jackie had forged a close political relationship, and Reagan accepted an invitation to speak at the annual meeting of the Ohio Conference of Teamsters later in the month. Jackie was elated, particularly because he was going to host a small, private lunch with Reagan before the speech. Jackie believed that Reagan would be the next president and that finally, after four years of Jimmy Carter and deregulation, the Ohio Teamsters would have a pipeline into the White House. Only this time, Jackie knew that he would be the president's man, not Fitz, not Roy Williams, and not Jimmy Hoffa, wherever he might be.

Jackie wanted his father to join him and Reagan for lunch. But though Bill was intensely proud of his son, he didn't think it was a good idea. He hated all the hoopla, and he worried—accurately, as it turned out—that reporters would make an issue of his criminal record and use it to embarrass Jackie and the Republican candidate. Jackie convinced him to attend anyway.

News about Reagan's lunch with Jackie made the rounds and upset organized-crime authorities, TDU dissidents, and even old friends of Reagan and Meese. Clarence Newton, a retired FBI supervisor from the Sacramento organized-crime squad, had worked in the mid-seventies as a special assistant to Governor Reagan. Newton knew Fratianno and the activities of the California Mob. When he heard about Reagan's lunch with Jackie, Newton called his old friend Edwin Meese. Newton said that he warned Meese, "Jackie Presser is nothing but an organized-crime hoodlum."

"But Newt," Meese protested, "he's never been indicted."

This didn't sound like the former Alameda County deputy district attorney who had directed Governor Reagan's hard-line crackdown on anti-war demonstrators in Berkeley's People's Park.

"Ed, you sound more like a defense lawyer than a prosecutor," Newton said, disappointed.

In his speech to the Ohio Conference of Teamsters, Reagan espoused views that greatly diverged from his conservative, anti-labor philosophy. Since the sixties, Reagan had railed against big government and its tangled nest of regulations. He sang a new song in Columbus. Reagan, the free marketeer, called the Carter administration's deregulation program "ill-conceived and not in the best interest of transportation requirements of the country." He had bartered his consistent ideology for Teamsters clout, and Jackie couldn't have been happier.

The Ohio Teamsters wielded more clout than other unions and special-interest groups because it had millions of dollars and a grass-roots network of leaflet distributors, envelope stuffers, and telephone callers. The Ohio Teamsters' political action committee, Ohio DRIVE, was loaded with money, due in large part to Jackie. A year later, he took the program to the national level, making it a top priority. Jackie practically forced local Teamsters officials to get their members to give one dollar a week from their salaries to DRIVE. "People would come and say they have a problem, and Jackie would look in the book and see if they were in the DRIVE program," said a Presser insider. "If they weren't, his enthusiasm would fall off." He wouldn't go out of his way to help them, and they quickly got the message.

The Ohio Teamsters gave the Reagan campaign little money but lots of services, such as the use of phone banks and a state-of-the-art rolling stage, complete with electrical outlets and a broadcast system, that could be hauled from city to city by a rig. According to Teamster records, Reagan spoke from this platform seven times during his campaign and his eight years in office, and it was used at his inauguration ceremonies in 1980 and 1984.

In October, the IBT executive board met at La Costa to decide, among other matters, whom to endorse for president. Jackie gave a charged-up speech, blaming Carter for deregulation, inflation, and a host of ills. Jackie's stirring speech swayed a large number of undecided votes and the IBT board threw their support behind Reagan. Tony Hughes, Jackie's confidant, said that Presser had linked the Teamsters' endorsement to a promise from the Reagan camp to move slowly on deregulation. Jackie admitted as much. "We lost our major battle, which was deregulation," Jackie told a meeting of Ohio Teamsters officials. "President Reagan and his people, through our union, are now considering reviewing the deregulation issue, which will be a benefit to the Teamsters."

Two weeks after Reagan's landslide victory, Reagan visited Teamsters headquarters, which stood in the shadow of the Capitol. Fitz, despite his poor health, met Reagan and Vice President–elect George Bush on the marble front steps, then ushered them through a throng of clapping and cheering employees and up to a noon meeting of the IBT executive board. During the twenty-minute visit, Reagan waxed on about his days as Screen Actors Guild president, fighting what he said were Communist attempts to take over the union. None of the vice presidents asked Reagan about his support of state right-to-work laws, which prohibit making union membership a condition of employment. (Reagan opposed a national right-to-work law, saying it was up to the states to decide.) None of the Teamsters officials asked Reagan about his controversial plans to relax occupational-safety regulations, which had sparked outcries from other labor unions. Fitz and Jackie wanted a love-in, and for twenty minutes, that's what they got.

Jackie's efforts paid off. On December 15, Meese and Reagan politicos selected Jackie as a senior adviser to the White House transition team. It was one of the proudest moments of his life. The young man who had stolen cars and hustled card games on Murray Hill was now part of the Establishment, a senior adviser to the President. At least for that moment, Jackie had escaped his shadowy past and become respectable.

Later that day, Jackie's father attended a meeting of Cleveland-area Teamsters officials. Bill was still shaking his head in amazement. "You're in the only state in the union and with the only man in the entire American labor movement now sitting on the Cabinet of the president of the United States," he said. "We're very fortunate. How he did it with bubble gum and mirrors, I still can't figure out, but he did it."

Jackie let it be known that he would be picking the new Secretary of Labor, as well as helping to decide who would fill key spots at the Transportation Department and the Interstate Commerce Commission. Within a day, Teamsters for a Democratic Union, newspaper editorialists, and congressional critics of the Teamsters reacted in outrage. "He doesn't represent the Teamsters, but if you want a spokesman for millionaires and organized crime, get Jackie," said TDU's Ken Paff. Representative J. J. Pickle, Democrat from Texas, couldn't believe it either. "I am convinced that we are not truly in the Christmas season, but rather around the time of April Fools'."

As he would prove time and again during the Reagan years, Reagan counselor Ed Meese seemed blind to even the most staggering conflicts of interest. Jackie's case was no exception. At the time, the

304

Labor Department was suing Jackie and other teamsters, charging them with squandering millions from the Central States Pension Fund. Yet the Reagan transition team was letting Jackie help select a Secretary of Labor, the person who would be settling or pushing that lawsuit to trial.

The next day, Jackie took two more blows. Testimony from a New Jersey crime commission linked Jackie to Camillo "Bill" Molinaro, a Cleveland Mafia member on loan to New Jersey's DeCavalcante crime family. After being arrested in 1975 for illegally performing an abortion, Molinaro gave police a three-hour confession. Among his revelations, Molinaro told police that when the Mob needed money from the Teamsters, they contacted Jackie Presser. He said Jackie had helped him get four loans—ranging from $500,000 to $2 million—from the Central States Pension Fund. Jackie had to defend himself again. He admitted talking to Molinaro on the telephone several times but said he never helped him. The guy is just trying to promote himself, said Jackie. "I'm positive the president-elect would not make an appointment like this unless my record was impeccable." The same day, the *New York Times* published an editorial attacking Reagan for rewarding Jackie. "The appointment is a sad one for an administration—not yet in office—from which much better is expected."

Jackie worried that the barrage of bad publicity would cause the Reagan camp to drop him. But Meese stood firmly behind him, and kept him on the team.

In January, a telegram was sent out under Fitz's name to all the IBT vice presidents. "You are urged to attend these inaugural activities in order to utilize these activities for the purpose of shaping the policies of the incoming administration to the betterment of our members." Jackie wanted the union to have its presence felt at the ceremonies. John Climaco, Presser's lobbyist Paul Locigno, and nearly all of his crew, except Harold Friedman, made the trip. Jackie was the gadfly of the inauguration ceremonies, flitting from party to party. "We were invited to the inaugural ball for the president of the United States," Harold later told a meeting of Teamsters leaders. "Jackie Presser attended, your secretary-treasurer. I couldn't go. I was too busy here. He went to eight of the balls, and we were invited, and it's kind of nice, I guess."

After the hoopla died down, Bill Presser marveled at how successful and respectable his prodigal son had turned out—having lunch with Reagan, battling Congress over deregulation, pushing DRIVE to new heights. "I had a lot of conversations with Bill about how overwhelmed he was with how Jackie turned the corner," says a high-ranking Teamster who had been close to both men. "Lots of times he said he'd wake up and think about it and couldn't believe Jackie had accomplished all this."

A decade earlier, Bill had kicked Jackie out of meetings when he had something important to discuss with Fitzsimmons. Now, in his old age, he went on and on to the local presidents about how his progressive son was bringing the union into a new age.

"Beyond me stands a young man who can put me in the shadows, and I don't take a back seat to any man," Bill said. "He can't put me in the shadows about yesterday's type of operation and many things that fit into today's operation. But when it comes to the progressive type of operation, he loses me so fast that I can't even start when he's already down the road.

"I'm very, very proud of him, our vice president. He's one of the very few with any guts or brains that knows what he's doing up there. The problem is jealousy. That's all it is. Men have been sitting there twenty, thirty years, their cans are so frozen to the chairs they're sitting on that they can't get off the chairs. It isn't their fault. It was the evolution of time."

In late December 1980, nearly six months after its informal notice to the Chicago Strike Force, the Justice Department publicly announced that it had closed its investigation into Howard Cannon. The senator wouldn't be indicted. Williams was relieved. It didn't mean that he or Dorfman or the others were off the hook. But his lawyers told him that the Justice Department would have a hard time bringing charges against him, the supposed bribe giver, once it had admitted it didn't have a case against the person who was supposed to take the bribe.

By now, Frank Fitzsimmons was being treated for lung cancer in a California hospital near his La Costa home. He was going to have to step down and wanted vice president Joe Morgan, from Hallandale, Florida, not Roy Williams, to succeed him. But Fitz, confined to bed, couldn't do much about it.

306

Civella continued to promote his boy Williams and again made his wishes known to Maishe Rockman. Maishe and Civella decided the next step was to get the Chicago and New York bosses to go along. Sometime that spring, Maishe, Big Ange Lonardo, and Jack White traveled to Chicago to discuss the issue with Mob leaders. According to Lonardo, the three Cleveland mobsters met in a restaurant at the city's outskirts with Chicago boss Joey Auippa and underboss Jackie Cerone. Following Mafia protocol, Auippa asked Rockman, who wasn't a made Mafia member, to leave the table while they discussed family business.

"Joe, whatever we're doing here, Maishe could explain it better to you than we could," Lonardo told the boss.

"Well, I didn't know, I'm sorry," Auippa replied. "See if he's still outside." Someone looked, but Maishe had already left.

After some discussion, Auippa said that the Chicago outfit would join the Kansas City and Cleveland families in backing Williams. Part of the deal presented by Lonardo was Civella and Rockman's agreement that Jackie would be named director of the Central Conference, taking over the position Williams would be vacating. Auippa said he'd go along with that, too, though he didn't trust Presser. Soon, Rockman returned to the meeting, and Auippa apologized for asking him to leave. Rockman said he wasn't offended.

Back in Cleveland, Lonardo made plans for Maishe and him to see Fat Tony Salerno and tell him about their conspiracy. He called Peanuts Tronolone at his travel agency in Miami and said "make a meet with that fellow."

Big Ange and Maishe convened at Salerno's clubhouse in East Harlem a few days later and told him about the plan to back Williams.

"Was Chicago satisfied with Roy?" Salerno asked.

"Yes."

"Well, OK, we'll go along. . . . I'll call Sammy Pro and get him to line up delegates."

Williams wanted to know what Fitz was going to do. Though Civella assured him that he had the support of the crime families, Williams said he'd never run against a sitting president. "I'll vote for Fitz even if they have to bring him in on a stretcher," he told Civella.

On May 5, 1981, Frank Fitzsimmons died in California while the IBT executive board was meeting there. Williams told the assembled

307

vice presidents that he was running for president and added that he didn't care if any of them ran against him. He also said he thought he was going to be indicted in the Cannon bribery case but that he would "weather the storm."

"If any of you do run against me and I beat you, your careers on the executive board are over," Williams threatened. He promised to kick them off the ruling board and replace them with his loyalists.

No one challenged him. The board named George Mock as an interim president and scheduled an executive board vote on Fitz's successor in ten days.

Several days later, Williams was home in Kansas City, sick in bed, when Nick Civella's messenger, Teamsters official Sam Ancona, paid a visit. Civella is making calls to help you, Ancona said. A few days later, Civella himself met Williams at a hotel near the Kansas City Royals ballpark and said he had "made some telephone calls and would make some more, and I wasn't going to have any trouble being elected," Williams recalled. Civella was right. Ten days after Fitz's death, the seventeen voting members of the executive board elected Roy Williams as the new Teamsters president to fill the term that would expire in three weeks.

Though Williams was sitting president, Jackie Presser made some contingency plans to run against him at the election scheduled to be held at the IBT convention in June, Tony Hughes recalls. Presser was banking on the chance that Williams would be indicted before the convention, thereby giving Jackie a chance to position himself as a reform candidate. "He bought a lotta Jackie Presser stuff, banners," Hughes says. "We went out to the convention [and] they talked him out of running. Roy Williams told Jackie he was gonna be head of the Central Conference. That's what Jackie told me. Roy Williams said he only wanted to be president for a term and then it would be Jackie."

On May 22, 1981, only a few days before the IBT convention, union president Roy Williams, Allen Dorfman, Joey Lombardo, and two of their associates were indicted in Chicago for conspiring to bribe Senator Cannon to tie up a deregulation bill.

Williams thought the timing was deliberate. In his June 1 opening address to the 2,200 handpicked delegates at the Las Vegas IBT convention, Williams unleashed a furious defense.

"These charges are a damn lie. If you heard Senator Cannon, he

308

only met me one time and he had never talked to me, and he had certainly never discussed any sort of bribe or anything compared to it. I have and will continue to fight deregulation with every ounce of energy in my body in an open and honest manner, as every Teamster in America has." Applause.

"No indictment will stop me. Neither will politicians, people that want to be recognized at somebody else's expense. And no indictment will stop me from fighting for the economic survival of all our Teamster brothers and sisters." More applause.

"I will tell you that neither a federal bureaucracy or headline-grabbing politicians are going to run the largest labor union in the world." Loud, sustained applause.

On the morning of June 4, 1981, the fourth day of the Las Vegas convention, Jackie Presser took the podium and, with a straight face and convincing emotion, told the delegates,

> I have the distinguished privilege of placing in nomination the man who will be our next general president, and who will lead this, the greatest labor-union organization in the world, to new heights and greater expectations. . . .
>
> And like every courageous leader who has stood at the helm of this union, he has withstood in a calm, honest, and irreproachable manner attacks from ill-informed, dishonest, headline-seeking elements who are trying to undermine the greatness of this union. . . . And for that, we owe him a great debt of thanks for standing in the forefront—in the line of fire—to take the heat for all of us. That is what the stuff of courage is made of. . . .
>
> "I am proud to call him a friend. I am proud to walk at his side. And I will be proud to serve him."

As Jackie nominated Williams for IBT general president, the Rancher received a standing ovation. Minutes later, Williams, a Mafia puppet, won a predictably lopsided election.

At a time when tens of thousands of drivers lost their jobs because of deregulation and companies asking for give-backs on the Master Freight Agreement, the delegates voted to give Williams a forty-four-percent pay raise, bringing his salary as president to $225,000.

Back in Kansas City a few days later, Williams met with Civella, who was very sick, at their usual hotel near the Kansas City Royals ballpark. He told the don to discontinue paying him the monthly $1,500 skimmed from Las Vegas casinos.

"I'm taking over as president, and I don't want the money anymore," Williams said he told Civella. "I don't need it. I would rather not have it." Civella agreed.

As part of the deal to get elected, Williams knew he was expected to name Jackie as director of the Central Conference, the second most powerful position in the union. But Allen Dorfman, one of Williams's strong backers, scared him off.

"Jackie is despised in Chicago," Williams remembers Dorfman saying. "If you want to get us all killed, you appoint him." The Chicago Mafia considered Jackie an untrustworthy fink who wouldn't give Dorfman the run of the Central States Pension Fund.

Williams relayed the warning to Jackie. "You've got a problem in Chicago. Before I appoint you, get your problem straightened out with Dorfman."

Dorfman also told Jackie he'd be killed if he showed up in Chicago after being appointed head of the Central Conference of Teamsters, Williams said.

"To hell with him," Jackie told Williams. "I don't like him anyway." Jackie never settled with Dorfman, and Williams didn't appoint him Central Conference director.

On the afternoon of July 18, 1981, Bill Presser died of a heart attack at his condominium in suburban Lyndhurst, Ohio. He was seventy-four, wealthy, and had seen his firstborn surpass him in the labor movement. Reagan sent a telegram to Jackie that said, "Those of us who care share some measure of your loss and pray that you will be comforted at this difficult time."

Roy Williams flew to Cleveland for the funeral three days later. In a brief speech he called Bill "the consummate trade unionist, a guiding light for the rest of us younger officers. . . . He was a mentor and my friend for thirty-three years."

Judges and politicians who had bowed before Big Bill, currying favor and soliciting contributions, showed up in force at Miller-Deutsch Memorial Chapel in suburban Woodmere. Ohio governor

James Rhodes, Cleveland mayor George Voinovich, and seven or eight IBT vice presidents were on hand.

It was a day of mixed feelings for Jackie Presser; he loved his father, but he wouldn't have to stand in his shadow anymore. He was finally going to be judged on his own. He was in charge. "I was privileged to spend fifty-five years with my father," Jackie said. "He was an outstanding parent. He devoted his life to the betterment of mankind. He was a person of great wisdom, integrity, and compassion."

After the service, a procession of Cadillacs and shiny cars wove through the suburbs for a dozen miles, tying up traffic and the manpower of several community police forces. Strangely, many Cleveland Mafia members—Bill's allies—were absent. Maishe had warned Big Ange and the others to stay away; the Presser family said it didn't want them there, he explained. But the reasons were much more complicated than that. The Cleveland FBI office had told Jackie it was setting up surveillance. Helping a few friends, Jackie sent out the warning.

The Bureau wanted to update its intelligence files. It wanted to keep tabs on new alliances by writing down license-plate numbers and snapping surveillance photos. Bill's funeral was an intelligence opportunity too fruitful to pass up. The FBI set up its stakeout two hours before the service.

Parked nearby was a van with smoked-glass windows. Inside, two Labor Department agents, George "Red" Simmons and Jim Thomas, were snapping photos from a camera mounted on a tripod and equipped with a telephoto lens. They had the same idea as the FBI. "Everybody who was everybody from Cleveland came," Thomas recalled. "Mayors, congressmen, all the union leaders, every petty thief in the world. Many attorneys, many accountants. The whole Jewish community." There were some mobsters, but mostly from out of town.

The FBI agents and the Labor investigators clicked away with their cameras, each unaware of the other. In theory, the two Cleveland offices were supposed to work labor-racketeering cases together under supervision of the Strike Force Against Organized Crime. But that was just a theory. It was a good thing they weren't working together at the crowded funeral. The FBI wanted to protect Jackie Presser. Simmons and Thomas wanted to prosecute him.

Their collision was inevitable.

23

The Chase

"Jackie Presser gets a piece of everything."
ANTHONY LIBERATORE

The Labor Department's organized-crime squad and the FBI field office in Cleveland hadn't been coordinating their efforts for at least two years before Bill Presser's funeral. Sometime in mid-1979, Jim Thomas recalls, he and his boss climbed into an elevator and rocketed up an ugly, black modern box in downtown Cleveland known as the Federal Building. They were paying a courtesy call on their rich, entrenched, famous investigative colleague, the FBI.

They strode past roomy wood-paneled offices, decorated with giant official FBI seals and a portrait of the director, and into a meeting room with two FBI agents. One was Patrick Foran, the aggressive, blatantly ambitious head of the Cleveland FBI's organized-crime squad. One of the elite in the 180-agent Cleveland field office, Foran kept the bureau's top-secret informant list and led the Mob squad, the office's sexiest, most mysterious outfit. When it suited him, he would take calls from reporters trolling for off-the-record tidbits to feed readers craving news about the Mafia. He was also the handler of the FBI office's top snitch, Jackie Presser. Thomas, a former IRS agent, knew Foran well and was one of the few guys able to get past his prickly shell. Both were Irish cops at heart. Foran grew up in the Bronx, Thomas in Cleveland's Old Angle, a working-class Irish neighborhood known for Friday-night fish frys and boxing gyms.

Foran and his fellow FBI agents didn't like Labor agents investigating Mob guys. Up until a year ago, organized crime had been the bureau's exclusive turf. Then in April 1978, the feisty, headline-grabbing Senate Permanent Subcommittee on Investigations heard testimony from strike force chiefs of major cities who accused Labor Department bureaucrats of letting the Mob continue to infiltrate the Teamsters and other unions. Then a few senators unloaded. "Participation by the Labor Department in the organized-crime program has been little more than a numbers game," Senator Charles Percy of Illinois fumed. "Some even consider it a charade. On paper, sixty-four Labor Department compliance officers are listed as working full time on organized-crime matters. But in fact, the actual number of man-years committed to the program is less than half that figure."

In April 1978, Senator Sam Nunn of Georgia and others on the subcommittee introduced legislation that would create an investigative office, the Inspector General, for each major Cabinet department and agency. In addition, the proposed law created a special Office of Labor Racketeering in the Labor Department; its mission was to battle organized crime's takeover of unions and their health-care and retirement funds. The FBI fought hard to scuttle the legislation, testifying against it at hearings, but it was enacted in November.

In theory, the Labor agents in the new organized-crime squad were supposed to work in concert with IRS and FBI agents, all under the orchestration of local Strike Force prosecutors. In practice, problems quickly cropped up. It didn't take long for the FBI, especially in Cleveland, to begin picking on the new kid.

At the meeting with the FBI, Thomas and his supervisor pulled out a list of ten or so labor-racketeering cases they were working on and shared it with Foran. At the top of their list of targets were Bill and Jackie Presser, followed by a batch of less powerful figures, including John J. "Skippy" Felice, Jr., of Teamsters Local 293 and Salvatore "Sam" Busacca of Teamsters Local 436. Foran and the other FBI agent scanned the list, Thomas says, checking off the cases the bureau was on top of. We know about this, this, this, this, and this, Foran noted, indicating that the bureau possessed intelligence or was looking into each local and each union official the Labor agents had listed.

Except one. Jim Thomas was struck by the fact that Foran didn't have a word to say about the FBI investigating Jackie Presser. That didn't tell Thomas that Jackie was an FBI snitch, but it did suggest that

Presser-affiliated unions might be rich virgin territory for Labor agents to plow.

Jim Thomas had become a Labor Department organized-crime investigator in March 1979 and was assigned a nook in cramped offices one floor beneath the Cleveland Strike Force. Sitting at the desk facing him was a sturdy, hard-nosed, redhaired, sometimes florid-faced ex-DEA agent named George Simmons. Everybody called him Red. Simmons and Thomas had gotten to know each other a little over the years, chatting and trading war stories as they waited to testify to federal grand juries. They hit it off and were assigned to cases as partners.

They had complementary styles and skills as investigators. Thomas, an Irish Catholic born in 1941, caught attention with his mop of white hair and gift of blarney. Trained as an accountant by the Jesuits at John Carroll University, Thomas could talk to anyone. He lulled them with his gab, listening, empathizing, relaxing them, eventually getting them to reveal what he wanted to know. Simmons, four years younger than his partner, grew up in Cleveland's Waspy east exurbia. He graduated from Kent State University, worked first as a suburban policeman, then as a U.S. Drug Enforcement Administration agent for nine years. He was smart, extremely skilled at using evidence to craft search-warrant affidavits. "We hit it off excellent on one case," Thomas says. "We both tried not to get caught up in the bureaucracy. We may not wear a suit and tie every day, but we'll get the job done. Our attitude was our job is to put people in jail. And we were both willing to work long hours."

After surveying the labor-racketeering landscape and learning of the FBI's lack of interest in the Pressers, Simmons and Thomas decided to target Jackie. "Here was the only Teamsters local that the FBI wasn't working on, so we thought we wouldn't step on anyone's toes when we did it," Simmons said years later. "That's how naive we were."

Another reason the agents targeted Jackie was that they inherited a couple of small, unexplored leads about him. One lead, for example, was that Teamsters funds may have been funneled to Jackie through inflated payments to his brother's cleaning company, which was paid more than two thousand dollars a month to clean Joint Council 41's small suite of offices. "We came up with the idea," Thomas says. "First, we sat down and decided why screw around with [the small fry] when we can take Jackie down? Jackie was supposed to be invincible.

314

It was a challenge. Second, it would put Labor's organized-crime office on the map."

Over the years, other Cleveland law enforcers had wanted to investigate Jackie. Doug Roller, chief of the Cleveland Strike Force from the mid- to late seventies, thought it was extremely odd that the bureau hadn't worked up a case on Presser. Roller knew plenty of shenanigans were going on; before taking over the Chicago Strike Force, he co-authored a 1977 Justice Department report on labor racketeering that said that Jackie and his father's Teamsters Joint Council 41 employed union officials who were Mob figures. In fact, at a meeting around 1978 with FBI agent Foran, Roller asked, "Why don't you try to come up with something on Jackie Presser?"

"Just because his father was a crook doesn't mean he's one, too," he remembers Foran saying.

Roller, of course, had no idea that Jackie was working as an FBI informant. Simmons and Thomas didn't suspect it at first. By August 1980, they had convinced their supervisor to let them pursue the Presser leads. But before they dove into the task, mindful of Presser's clout, they called on Steve Olah, the new Cleveland Strike Force chief. "We have carte blanche to go after Jackie," Red and Jim told him. "Any reason we shouldn't, tell us up front." Olah gave them the green light.

Months later, the two agents tailed Jackie for two weeks to get an idea of his habits and the people with whom he associated. While staking him out, Jim Thomas recognized one of the men Presser met with. It was FBI organized-crime-squad supervisor Robert S. Friedrick.

The agents met again with Olah and told them they suspected that Jackie was an FBI informer. "We don't want to waste our time making a case and then have to drop it because of the FBI," Thomas recalls saying. "Tell us right now if we should move on to somebody else."

"If you make a case, I will prosecute him," Olah said.

In some cities, FBI and Labor agents worked well together. When it came to investigating Jackie Presser, this cooperation was lacking from the start.

It was no secret in Cleveland and elsewhere that the FBI wanted

Labor agents to confine their probing to audits, the necessary but unglamorous legwork needed to prove certain labor-union crimes. By statute, Labor agents could audit a union's financial records at any time, whereas the FBI was required to get a subpoena. That suggested, at least to the FBI, that Labor investigators were supposed to stick to their balance sheets and calculators. To actually go into the field, interview wise guys, squeeze them, scare them, shake something loose, well, the bureau felt this was its territory. Furthermore, FBI agents were allowed to carry guns, unlike Labor agents. What could Labor agents do in a jam, pull out their pencils?

One Friday a month for several years, the Cleveland Strike Force held a meeting with representatives from the IRS, FBI, DEA, Labor, Customs, Secret Service, and Alcohol, Tobacco and Firearms. Investigators talked about cases they were working on, trading ideas and information. "That was the real concept of the strike force," says Thomas, who attended several of the sessions. "That went on for two years. The FBI would come in—Pat Foran, George Grotz—and not say a word, and everybody else would spill their guts. Then everybody else finally said, 'I'm not going to spill my guts if the FBI doesn't. Forget it.'" The meetings stopped.

About the time they targeted Presser, the Labor agents moved into larger offices on the eighteenth floor of a building that, coincidentally, overlooked the squat brick building that housed Presser's Local 507. Red and Jim set up a telescope pointed at the union hall and its parking lot. Without leaving their office, they knew who came and went into Jackie and Harold Friedman's sanctum.

During this time, a pair of reporters began snooping into Jackie's union affairs. One was Mairy Jayn Woge, a silver-haired crime reporter who appeared disorganized, even scatterbrained, but actually was cunning, at times brilliant, at convincing sources in law enforcement and the underworld to open up to her. Perhaps because she seemed harmless, federal agents as well as sources close to the Pressers fed her tips, raw intelligence, and allegations. Often the information never found its way into print, because Woge would be unable to document, organize, and singlehandedly write a sophisticated investigative piece that could pass muster with the editors and the newspaper's lawyers.

She had received the tip that Harry Haler, a one-third partner in the tiny Hoover-Gorin firm, had filed a 1977 lawsuit in state court in Los Angeles in which he claimed that the Pressers and the Teamsters had cheated him out of money. The outlines of Presser's kickback scheme were laid out in Haler's pleadings. He had dropped the lawsuit in 1978, allowing Presser to breathe a little easier. Los Angeles reporters had overlooked the lawsuit, but now Woge was rummaging around in the case.

Word of interest soon filtered back to Jackie. Considering himself a public-relations pro, he called the *Plain Dealer* editors to ask them to call off their reporter. He had no trouble reaching David L. Hopcraft, the paper's executive editor. Hopcraft was under orders from the paper's editor and publisher, Thomas Vail, to attend to Jackie's concerns. After all, Teamsters drove the trucks that delivered the more than four hundred thousand copies of the morning paper calling itself "Ohio's largest." Furthermore, the Teamsters was the only one of the newspaper's five unions that could call a strike and single-handedly shut down the paper.

At the time, the *Plain Dealer* and the *Cleveland Press* were locked in a bitter, winner-takes-all circulation battle in an economically depressed town. Their newsstand copy price was fifteen cents when most other metropolitan dailies were selling for a quarter. The *Press*, the afternoon paper, was losing the battle, but a one- or two-month strike at the *Plain Dealer* was all it would take to rejuvenate the *Press*. A *Plain Dealer* strike would shift all the supermarket and department-store advertising to the ailing *Press*, giving it a tremendous surge of cash and another year or two of life. Jackie held each paper hostage; if he wished, he could strike either with a phone call.

Vail, swayed perhaps by repeated complaints from Presser and his publicists, told Hopcraft that he thought some reporters went out of their way to embarrass Presser because of supposed hostility between the Newspaper Guild and the Teamsters. Actually, the newspaper scrutinized Presser and the Teamsters far less than it did the local electric utility, the school board, or other powerful institutions. "I met with Jackie on several occasions," says Hopcraft, who enjoyed schmoozing with politicians and business leaders. Broad-shouldered, perennially tanned, Hopcraft was quick to laugh, displaying a crooked tooth that had earned him the newsroom nickname Snag, from the cartoon character Snaggletooth the Lion. "Jackie was always very sensitive and unhappy with *Plain Dealer* coverage. Because of his unhappiness with the paper, I was sort of picked as the guy to smooth the troubled waters."

Presser had learned—either from family members, a Mob associate, or (Hopcraft's theory) a mole in the *Plain Dealer* newsroom—that Woge was looking into the Haler kickbacks. In a meeting with Hopcraft, Jackie blistered Haler, calling him a con, a fraud, and the possessor of an impressive forty-year string of criminal convictions. Clearly, Jackie had ordered someone to investigate Haler's background. Jackie also expressed doubts as to Woge's fairness, claiming that she was out to get him. Hopcraft said he agreed with his concerns—a tactical error that later gave Presser and his lawyers the opportunity to threaten a lawsuit. Hopcraft told Jackie he was assigning another reporter, Walt Bogdanich, to the story.

"Jackie had said all these things to me over the years, how there was some connection between [Mairy Jayn] and some of the people who used to hang out on the Hill," Hopcraft remembers. "They clearly saw her as someone being used by the government and the gangster element of the Teamsters to weaken Jackie and solidify whatever control they did or didn't have on the union. I think she is the kind of person who could be used. I believed it. That's why I got Walt involved in it. Because nobody's going to use Walt."

Bogdanich, who went on to win a Pulitzer Prize in 1988 for his work at the *Wall Street Journal,* was the paper's top investigator, an intense and competitive reporter who had put together several important exposés of the Teamsters' misdeeds in Ohio. Bogdanich and Woge quickly hit the paper trail, tracing Haler, Presser, and the Teamsters' money through court records, incorporation papers, and FBI records. Within two months, and after dozens of interviews, the two reporters had pinned down most of the Hoover-Gorin kickback scheme. Lawyers and editors reviewed the stories and prepared them for publication. In the week before the series was to run, Bogdanich and Woge called Presser at the Local 507 union hall and left several messages. They also requested an interview with Presser in calls to Jackie's Cleveland PR firm. Bogdanich and Woge never suspected that Presser, the target of their probe, had been talking all along to their executive editor.

318

† † †

On Friday October 8, 1981, two days before the *Plain Dealer* exposé was to be published, one of Presser's publicists explained to Bogdanich and Woge that Jackie wouldn't talk to them unless he first read a draft of their stories. This was a maneuver to buy time. The *Plain Dealer*, like almost all newspapers, had a policy against letting the target of an investigation enjoy a prepublication review of its news stories.

The same day, a Labor Department agent in Las Vegas visited Duke Hoover and slapped him with a Cleveland grand-jury subpoena for his firm's financial records. Red and Jim had known for days that Bogdanich and Woge had come up with a dynamite series on Hoover-Gorin, and the two agents convinced the reporters to give them two days' notice before the series was published. That way Red and Jim could get a subpoena in place to preserve the Hoover-Gorin records. For the next several days, the Labor agent in Las Vegas staked out Hoover's office, watching to see if boxes were moved out or thrown in the trash. Duke Hoover was nervous, but he had been through this in 1973 when a federal grand jury in New York had asked for the company's records. Nothing had happened back then.

On Saturday afternoon, just hours before the exposé rolled off the presses, Jackie said that he talked to Hopcraft, who assured him the story wouldn't be published, saying, "Won't they be surprised when it doesn't run." Hopcraft denies saying this.

On Saturday night, Jim Thomas, excited and a little nervous, drove downtown to the *Plain Dealer*. At precisely 10:20 each night in the *Plain Dealer* lobby, a stack of the next day's first edition was trundled out and available for sale. Thomas grabbed one and whipped through the first part of the series. He couldn't believe the story. It was fantastic! Wait until Red saw this!

Jackie picked up the Sunday *Plain Dealer* and felt sick. Splashed across page one was the headline "Presser is accused of taking kickbacks."

The story—the first installment of a two-part series, published on August 23 and 24, 1981—began with a punch. "International Teamsters Union Vice President Jackie Presser, heir apparent to the union presidency, received about $300,000 in cash kickbacks from a public-relations firm that did business with the Teamsters, according to a

319

sworn deposition and other information obtained by the *Plain Dealer.*"

It was his old partner in crime, Harry Haler, who did him in. Jackie had realized years earlier that he should never have gotten involved with a con like Harry. After they had their falling-out in 1977, Haler had filed a lawsuit in state court in Los Angeles claiming that the Teamsters owed him $590,000. Now, four years later, *Plain Dealer* reporters had obtained Haler's court pleadings. His sworn statements made fascinating reading. Haler admitted that for a year starting in mid-1972, he had kicked back $25,000 a month to Jackie—a total of $300,000.

The Monday installment of the series sported the headline "Presser . . . U.S. informer" and provoked another cry of anguish from Presser and his entourage. This was one of the lowest moments of his career. Combined with the previous day's exposé, this story seemed to finish off Jackie in one-two fashion. "Teamster Union leader Jackie Presser was a secret government informant before and after he allegedly accepted cash kickbacks in connection with a Teamster public-relations agency."

The story explained that while he collected the $300,000, Jackie and his dad served as government informants. The story suggested government misconduct by pointing out that IRS agents had filed reports with the FBI about the kickbacks from the Hoover-Gorin public-relations firm, but that follow-up investigations never took place. The implication was obvious: the FBI had ignored the kickback charges to protect its prize informant.

The *Plain Dealer* devoted more than one hundred inches of copy, complete with text, photos, index, and sidebars, to expose Jackie as a thief and a snitch. The wire services picked up the stories and gave them wide play around the country. It was a disaster for Jackie. The kickback story wasn't what was so devastating; it had happened years ago, and people had come to expect such behavior from Teamsters leaders. What really hurt was the newspaper's pulling the cover off his relationship with the feds. If his friends in the union believed he was a secret agent of the government, he would never corral the executive board votes he needed to succeed Roy Williams as top boss. Who would trust him?

Of course, the way his union associates felt wouldn't matter if he got assassinated. If the wise guys on Murray Hill or in the Chicago

320

family believed he was a snitch—as some had suspected for years—they'd dispatch one of their hit men to give him a brief, final lesson.

The *Plain Dealer's* revelations were a particularly hard blow because they came just when Jackie was riding highest. His enemy in the union, Roy Williams, was under indictment in Chicago for conspiring to bribe Senator Howard Cannon and might have to step down, clearing the top job for Jackie. At the moment, Jackie was enjoying a terrific relationship with President Reagan and the White House, something his father, a felon, never could have achieved. Jackie had spent two days in Washington in June, polishing his image with influential reporters and newscasters at breakfast meetings set up by the top-drawer Republican public-relations firm of Gray and Company. He was pleased with the subsequent coverage. The *Washington Post,* for instance, had reported, "The Cleveland union leader is clearly becoming a national power within the union. The emergence of Presser already has given rise to speculation that he is the heir apparent to the sixty-six-year-old Williams."

Everything was clicking along according to his game plan until the newspaper reporters forced him to go back to his playbooks.

The Presser exposé buoyed the spirits of many of the paper's veteran reporters. It was a tough, well-documented investigative series, some of it based on confidential sources, that exposed wrongdoing by a mighty community leader and an institution—the Teamsters—that had escaped scrutiny for years. It was heartening to see that this kind of reporting was supported by the managers of the *Plain Dealer,* a paper not renowned for its muckraking. A couple of days after the series appeared, editor and publisher Tom Vail, an old-money Princeton man whose great-grandfather had founded the paper, made one of his infrequent trips through the newsroom and spotted Bogdanich.

"Good job, Walt, right on," Vail said, pumping his fist.

"Well, we're going after some pretty powerful people," Bogdanich replied.

"Don't worry about it. Good job."

Bogdanich couldn't have imagined that a year later his editors would cave in and take a completely different attitude toward the Presser series.

† † †

The day after the series ran, Red and Jim met Harry Haler at the Culver City Ramada Inn and took pages of notes while he outlined the kickback scheme detailed in the *Plain Dealer* and in the IRS investigative reports. It was clear that he hated Jackie. "He screwed me out of $300,000," Haler said. He was enjoying the opportunity to stick it to Presser once again.

"Who do you work for?" Haler asked Red and Jim at one point.

"We're Labor agents under the Cleveland Strike Force."

"Do you work for Dave Margolis?" asked Haler, a Justice Department buff.

Margolis was the head of the Justice Department's organized-crime unit. In fact Red and Jim did ultimately work for Dave Margolis.

"If you guys continue to work this investigation, two things will happen to you," Haler predicted. "You'll ruin your careers, and you'll probably be fired. That's what happened to the two IRS guys I worked with, John Daley and Gabriel Dennis."

Dave Margolis, like many other Justice Department supervisors, knew all about the notorious informant Harry Haler and didn't trust him enough to give the go-ahead on indictments based on his testimony. They knew all too well the stories about the legendary Haler, who had once conned a Senate investigating committee into digging up acres of Michigan farmland looking for Jimmy Hoffa's body.

While it was true that IRS-intelligence agents Daley and Dennis had made several important IRS cases based on accurate, raw intelligence provided by Harry Haler, he also brought them trouble. By practical definition, a good informant, someone like Jackie, is a coconspirator or a criminal—still active, if he's worth anything. He rarely talks to government agents out of patriotism. He either wants to eliminate his enemies, improve his plea-bargaining position if he's in trouble, or create an indebted agent-friend—an insurance policy—should he ever face indictment or a grand-jury appearance. Good investigators realize that they step into a danger zone each time they rely on an informant's facts. If a handler goes too far in protecting an informant, the agent could get reprimanded, fired, or indicted. A top snitch can send an investigator's career skyrocketing or bring it crashing down.

"Let us worry about Dave Margolis," Red and Jim told Haler at the Culver City Ramada Inn. "Now tell us exactly what happened."

322

Haler explained the kickback scheme, volunteering names and telephone numbers. He even called some of his couriers to tell them to cooperate with the Labor agents. For a week, Red and Jim rolled through southern California on a fascinating quest, talking to money changers, bagmen, and former Hoover-Gorin employees. "One of the high points," Red says, "was when Vince Martinico turned green."

Vince Martinico, a.k.a Vince Martin, was one of the couriers Haler said he used to carry payoffs to Jackie. Martinico worked at a liquor distributorship. When Red and Jim dropped in to see him unannounced, Martinico told his secretary to brush them off.

"Please, just show him my card," Thomas said.

She took it back and Martinico ran out to see them.

"Let's step outside on the sidewalk," Jim Thomas said.

"What's this all about?" Martinico asked.

"Have you read the newspapers in Cleveland? Harry Haler said he used you to carry kickbacks to Jackie Presser from Hoover-Gorin."

Martinico started. His face changed color. He didn't know what to say. "He was in a position to deny it, he had every opportunity to deny it, and he turned green," Red says. Now all they had to do was get him before a grand jury, quickly.

The two agents called the Cleveland Strike Force and convinced prosecutor Steve Jigger to wire a grand jury subpoena for the terrified Martinico to them immediately. By the time they served him with the subpoena the next day, he had retained a lawyer who advised him to shut up.

Before they left Los Angeles, Red and Jim made a low-key visit to the intelligence unit of the IRS. A friendly source went to a file drawer and pulled out a stack of Daley and Dennis's reports of their meetings across the country with informants Harry Haler, Frank Fitzsimmons, and Bill and Jackie Presser. Later, they drove out to Daley's Los Angeles home to talk to him about Haler. It was a depressing scene. Here was an investigator, like themselves, Thomas recalls, who had been a top organized-crime fighter, a dedicated agent who broke in during the heady days in the early sixties when Attorney General Robert Kennedy poured resources into the fight against the Mob. Now Daley was recovering from a heart attack, living in a small home that "was almost a shack," Thomas says.

"He was telling us a tale of woe, all these great investigations he did, and then the IRS relegated him to the file room. . . . He was a broken man."

Before Red and Jim left his house, Daley warned them about getting involved with Harry Haler. "You don't know the horse you're getting on. The Justice Department will go after you."

Back in Cleveland, Red and Jim took a phone call from Rick Lind, the FBI agent in charge of investigating labor racketeering. Lind volunteered that he had information about Jackie Presser that might help them. Red and Jim stopped by the FBI office to hear the intelligence, but Lind instead ushered them into the office of Joe Griffin, special agent in charge of the Cleveland FBI office. Griffin greeted them warmly and asked in a friendly way how the Presser probe was going. "We want to help you guys," Thomas recalls him as saying. "Any equipment you need, whatever."

Instead of volunteering information about Presser, Griffin asked Red and Jim questions about Haler. They were noncommittal. The meeting ended without the FBI offering one speck of information about the activities of Jackie Presser.

On their next trip to Los Angeles, several weeks later, Red and Jim sat down with Duke Hoover and his lawyer. This was their first look at the smooth-voiced ex–disc jockey. He had graduated to pin-striped suits—still polyester—and a diamond pinkie ring. Hoover easily fielded an hour of chatty, small-talk questions—where're you from? How'd you get into the business? Then Red abruptly announced that Haler had admitted that Hoover had funneled kickbacks to Jackie though the PR firm. What about it?

Something darkly humorous unfolded. Duke Hoover, former broadcaster, began to stammer and stutter each time the agents brought up the kickbacks. He couldn't get out an answer. Red and Jim smiled. They had really hit a nerve. They took his reaction to be yet another confirmation of the *Plain Dealer* exposé.

By this time, Jackie was extremely upset. The two agents were probing into his affairs in a very obvious and public fashion. Jackie's associates, family, and friends were all aware that the Labor Department was turning up the heat. A highly publicized investigation could hurt him more now than at any other time of his career. It would spook his friends in the Reagan administration, causing them to pull back after all the work he had done to insinuate himself into the White House. It looked to Jackie like the two agents were working hand in glove with the news media. He remembered that the strike force had issued a subpoena for the Hoover-Gorin records several days before the damaging *Plain Dealer* series.

Jackie consulted his lawyer, John Climaco, whose attack-dog style of law brought him results as well as trouble. They brainstormed, trying to find ways to thwart the mounting pressure from the Labor agents, and decided to launch an attack on Haler's credibility. Climaco and his staff quickly compiled an impressive dossier on the con man. In a memo sent to Presser a few months after the series was published, Climaco wrote, "Haler, who uses ten other aliases, is a felon with numerous convictions and an arrest record dating back to 1942. Mr. Haler has been described as a 'treacherous rogue,' 'double-dealer,' 'informant,' and 'the plague,' with one common thread running through all descriptions—that he is a pathological liar who cannot and should not be believed."

Meanwhile, Steve Jigger, the strike force prosecutor, asked the FBI for its reports on Haler. For reasons unexplained, the bureau didn't provide the records. By January, Simmons and Thomas had completed the legwork on the Hoover-Gorin probe and waited for the strike force to call Duke Hoover, Vince Martinico, and other key witnesses before the grand jury. Hoover and Martinico, who had refused to reveal anything other than their terror to the Labor agents, could have broken the case wide open in the grand-jury room. But Jigger never called them. "I begged him to give Martinico immunity and call him to the grand jury," Thomas says. "I have no idea why he didn't."

Jigger was certainly wise enough to heed the warnings of his superiors. He knew his boss, Dave Margolis, wouldn't approve an indictment based on Haler's testimony. Only Jigger didn't tell this to Red and Jim, and they kept pushing the case.

On the morning of March 10, 1982, Anthony "Tony Lib" Liberatore, the Cleveland Mafia capo, waited in his car in the parking lot at Cleveland's Edgewater Park, a strip of land overlooking a nine-hundred-foot bathing beach and the downtown skyline. He was facing trial for conspiring with other Cleveland Mafia figures to murder labor leader Danny Greene; he was also appealing his conviction for bribing the FBI clerk who had stolen the bureau's informant list. Liberatore desperately needed a friend in the federal government—that's why he agreed to meet with Red and Jim. Liberatore figured that if he gave the two agents worthwhile information, maybe they would help him cut a deal with the strike force and solve some of his legal difficulties. Liberatore hated Jackie Presser, blamed him for his legal problems, and suspected him of being an FBI snitch. Now Liberatore was going to roll over on Jackie. Serve that fat bastard right.

Red and Jim wanted to ask Liberatore how he and Tom Lanci, two Mob guys, ended up getting paid handsomely by Hoover-Gorin. Also, did they kick back their salaries to Jackie?

Simmons and Thomas pulled up at half-past nine, climbed into Liberatore's car, and flopped out their IDs. "We want to talk to you about Hoover-Gorin," Thomas said. "We can't and won't talk about your trial or your appeal."

Liberatore agreed.

"So tell us what you got out of Hoover-Gorin," Thomas said.

"Two thousand dollars a month," Liberatore replied. "It lasted about a year. I used the money to buy CDs."

"Did you do any work for it?"

"Some consulting," he said.

"What did Lanci do?"

"He told me he was getting two thousand dollars a month and kicking back fourteen hundred to Jackie," Liberatore explained. "Tommy kept six hundred dollars for his taxes and his trouble."

"We're interested in Tony Hughes," Thomas said.

"He hasn't worked for the union since he and Jackie opened their restaurant," Liberatore said. "He's just Jackie's bodyguard and gofer. Plus he and Jackie and Curly Montana are loan-sharking and fencing stolen jewelry. Jackie and Curly also got some dental clinics with the union. About three years ago, they tried to set one up in Detroit."

Liberatore went on for forty-five minutes, coughing up solid allegations, hearsay, and speculation. "You have to understand," he said at one point, "Jackie Presser gets a piece of everything."

326

† † †

About the time the two Labor agents talked to Tony Lib, they began shifting their investigation to a new front. Red and Jim uncovered witnesses and hard evidence of a much better, more recent scheme involving Jackie—that he may have placed relatives and mobsters in no-show jobs on the Local 507 payroll. The no-shows included Mafia associates John Nardi, Jr., gambler George Argie, Sr., and Tony Hughes.

Nardi's father, organized-crime figure John Nardi, Sr., was a gun runner and dope dealer who had been blown up in the Teamsters Joint Council 41 parking lot in 1977. As an eleven-year-old boy, Jack Nardi was taught by his father how to handicap race horses. Ever since, Jack Nardi, Jr., had gambled, hustled, and scammed. But unlike his father, he couldn't put together a big score or a lasting criminal enterprise. Without steady income, Jack neglected his family, which deeply concerned his father. In 1972, John Nardi, Sr., the chief officer of Teamsters Local 410, called on Bill Presser, his old business partner in the jukebox business, and got him to agree to give his son a job at Local 507. A day or so later, Jack Nardi and his father visited Jackie Presser at the Local 507 office. Nardi later recounted their conversation.

"You will be a business agent, and we'll pay you three hundred dollars a week," Presser told him.

"What do I do?" young Nardi asked.

"We'll call you and let you know."

Nardi said that Jackie never called him, but each week, a three-hundred-dollar check was mailed to his house. Once he asked his father if he should be working. "Don't worry about it, just take the checks," John Nardi, Sr., told his son.

From 1972 to 1978, Jack Nardi didn't work one single day for the Teamsters, but he was paid $109,800. Even after his father was killed, Jack Nardi retained his status as a ghost employee. At his father's funeral, Jackie worked his way through the receiving line. Gripping young Nardi's hand, Presser told him, "Your job is safe."

While Jack Nardi was supposed to be working for Local 507, he held down various jobs throughout Ohio as an electrician and a leasing agent. In November 1978, his free ride came to an end. Jackie Presser called him to a meeting at the Forge and told him he was fired. "The heat's on," Nardi remembers Jackie saying. "You've got to get off the payroll."

Bob Friedrick, Jackie's last FBI handler, gave a different reason for Nardi's firing. Jackie had told him that Jack White, the Cleveland Mafia boss, ordered Jackie to remove Nardi from the payroll because the Mafia didn't want the Teamsters supporting a rival in the now-decimated Danny Greene–John Nardi faction of the Cleveland crime family.

On March 1, 1982, the Cleveland Strike Force issued a subpoena for the financial records of Teamsters Local 507 and Jackie and Tony Hughes's restaurant, the Forge. This move alerted Jackie, Harold Friedman, and their lawyers to the Labor investigators' new front in their war against Jackie Presser. Thomas and Simmons were examining tips that Jackie gave no-show jobs to friends in the Mob and that he and Tony Hughes may have funneled money to themselves by having the union pay bills at the Forge.

The next day, Simmons and Thomas dropped in on the Forge after lunch and asked for Tony Hughes. They decided not to embarrass him in the restaurant. "We're here to serve a subpoena, and we don't want any fanfare," Thomas told him. "Do you want to go in the kitchen?"

Hughes invited them to sit down for a cup of coffee. "Do you want the books now?" Hughes asked.

"No. You have to do it this way."

"We didn't do anything," said Hughes, who claims that the following conversation took place:

"You know, we're after your boss," the agents said. "We're going to get your boss and his family. We think you're skimming from the Forge. We've had numerous reports you're skimming."

"You guys are so full of it," Hughes retorted. "Sure, we're making a lot of money skimming. That's why we're taking money out of our own pockets to pay the bills and we're trying to sell the place. Who's telling you all this?"

"Harry Haler."

"Are you sure it isn't Mairy Jayn or something?" Hughes asked.

"No, it's Harry Haler. We sat with him in a restaurant in another city not too long ago and he told us that Jackie Presser is doing these things."

Red and Jim deny that they mentioned Haler or getting Jackie Presser. But Thomas said he did ask Hughes, "What are you going to do after you sell the restaurant?"

To which Hughes replied, "I guess I'll go back and work for the union."

By April 1982, Hughes had found someone to buy the restaurant, lawyer Jerry Milano. He paid $160,000 for the equipment, inventory, and fixtures. Jackie and Tony's restaurant was $600,000 in debt. But only $17,500 was owed on secured bank loans. The rest was tens of thousands in unpaid taxes and bills: $60,000 to the IRS, $56,000 to the Ohio Bureau of Workmen's Compensation for unemployment insurance, $35,000 to the Ohio Department of Taxation, $26,000 in county taxes, and so on. Businesses that supplied meat, eggs, and produce were severely punished by the Forge's closing. Zide Egg Company of Cleveland was owed $27,813, Michael's Finer Meats in Columbus lost $34,586, Produce Service was stiffed $6,405, and on and on and on— bakeries, linen suppliers, plumbers. "They just drained all the money out of it," said someone familiar with the Forge's books.

After talking to Hughes, the two agents turned their attention back to Jack Nardi. They culled six years of Nardi paychecks from the financial records they had subpoenaed and totaled them. It was an impressive sum—$109,800, one of the largest suspected ghost-employee cases the Labor Department's racketeering office had ever run across. Red and Jim reached Jack Nardi by telephone and set up a meeting with him in a restaurant in a Cleveland hotel.

Tall, about 6'2" and 180 pounds, Nardi wore a brown toupee and flashed nervous, darting eyes. He spoke smoothly, only revealing his lack of education by occasionally misusing a word. The agents fanned out the copies of the paychecks. "Yeah, those are mine," Nardi admitted.

"What did you do for them?"

"Nothing," Nardi said. "I wanted to work, but Presser never called me."

Without hesitation, he told them he hadn't been to Local 507 once in six years. Red and Jim were elated. They had just obtained a

329

seemingly airtight confession, from a Mob-connected guy, no less. Finally, after months of hard work and harassment, they had found their smoking gun.

In May 1982, Jackie's uncle Allen Friedman was out of work, taking medicine for his inoperable heart condition, smoking a couple of packs of cigarettes and gulping up to ten Valiums a day. His life was falling apart. Shortly after Bill Presser died in July 1981, Allen had a final blowup with Jackie and retired from Local 507. Jackie had wanted to dump him for years but couldn't because Bill had promised his wife he'd look out for Allen. Meanwhile, Jackie complained to everybody about his uncle, even to his FBI control agent Bob Friedrick.

Allen "was threatening everybody," Friedrick once said under oath. "He was going to kill this person, he was going to kill that person, he wanted to kill Jackie. When he saw Tony he was going to kill him, because he had a gun. Supposedly he came into the office one time, 'Where is Tony Hughes? I'm going to kill him.'"

To make a living in retirement, Allen Friedman switched sides and marketed himself as a consultant to companies facing organizing drives. He printed up a sales brochure with his message, "Unions have gone too far." But business was so pitiful that he turned to an old standby, loan-sharking. Allen borrowed $30,000 from loan-shark Martin "Mutt" DeFabio, who operated out of the Card Shop on Murray Hill with the blessing of Jack White. Allen told Mutt he was going to put the $30,000 on the street, go into the loan-sharking business, and make some easy money.

But once he got the bankroll, Allen got greedy. In typical Friedman fashion, he flew to Las Vegas and began gambling, tossing big bills on casino tables, trying to make a big score. Mutt DeFabio quickly heard about it and dispatched someone out to Vegas to protect his investment by yanking Allen out of the casinos. By the time DeFabio's man got there, Allen had squandered about $20,000 of his $30,000 stake.

Later, DeFabio visited Allen at his home to collect late payments on the loan. He found him sitting in the family room with his wife, Nancy. "You motherfucker," Mutt told him. "Come outside."

Once outside, Allen doubled over, crying out as he eased himself

330

to the ground. His wife called an ambulance, then screamed at Mutt, "You killed my husband! You killed my husband!"

"Let that motherfucker die," Mutt replied.

Friedman went to the hospital and word circulated to the Presser and Friedman families what had happened. Tony Hughes, an old hand at loan-sharking, visited Mutt. "Give the guy a break," Hughes said.

"Break? He ruined me, took every fuckin' dime I got," Mutt said.

"I'll see that you get your money back," Hughes said. He made arrangements for Allen to repay on an easier schedule.

Several times after that, Mutt DeFabio had to visit Friedman to collect, and the same scene would unfold. "The few times I hadda go, he pulled that fake heart attack and he would, you know, his wife kept sayin', 'If anything happens to my husband, I'll kill you,' " he said, laughing.

Before Allen attempted loan-sharking, he tried to open a restaurant in Euclid, a blue-collar city along Lake Erie just east of Cleveland. After borrowing some seed money from the Transamerica Financial Services bank, he decided he needed another loan. So he invited the loan officer, Patrick J. Mann, out to the proposed restaurant site. Once there, Allen pulled out a gun, pointed it at Mann's head, and suggested that he'd kill him if he didn't approve the additional loan. Mann approved the loan as well as several others Allen applied for, some under false names, including that of Terence Freeman, a Local 507 business agent and Allen's close friend.

The restaurant never got off the ground, and Allen, squeezed by a Mob loan shark as well as by his other creditors, became increasingly desperate for cash. He called on Robert Duvin, a management labor lawyer who was a good friend of Harold Friedman and Jackie Presser. At this time, Allen wasn't on speaking terms with Jackie, so he employed Duvin to relay a message.

"Tell Jackie I need $100,000 for my debts," Allen said. "Not just $10,000 or $15,000 like before. If he doesn't give me the money, tell him I will kill him."

Duvin promptly drove to Local 507 and told Jackie about Allen's strange visit and bizarre threats. "Don't worry about it," Jackie said. "I'll take care of it. My uncle Allen is crazy."

Such was the tangled state of Allen Friedman's life on May 12, 1982, a beautiful spring day, when Jim Thomas drove out to Beachwood, Ohio, and knocked on the front door of Friedman's white frame ranch home. Allen's young wife Nancy answered the door, wrapped in a bathrobe. Thomas identified himself, and she began to cry. "Things have been so hard lately," she wept.

"I'm not going to hurt him," Thomas said. "I just want to talk to him about his nephew."

Thomas stood on the porch for a half hour, talking to her about her life, Allen, and the Presser family. Then Allen pulled up in his car and got out. He carried dry cleaning in one hand and the morning newspaper in the other. "C'mon in," he told Thomas.

Allen sat on the couch, pointed Thomas to a chair and asked, "Coffee?"

Without much prodding, Allen began to talk about how he, not Jackie, was the father of Local 507. He was the man who could talk to the rank and file, organize a shop, and run a picket line. He told him how he broke off from the Pressers and started his own independent warehouse workers union, Local 752. Then he showed Thomas the videotape he used to pitch himself as a labor consultant. It had a tinny soundtrack and showed Allen speaking before an empty hall. It was as captivating as watching grass grow.

Thomas had signed up to take the afternoon off to play golf, but if Allen was going to talk, then Thomas was willing to stay all day, which he did, asking for drink after drink—pop, diet pop, Coke, coffee, and water—anything to stay in the apartment and keep the conversation moving forward. And in true Friedman fashion, Allen bloomed in front of his audience of one seemingly empathetic listener. Allen spun stories of picket lines and organizing drives, showing the persuasive skills that made him a good union organizer, while off to the side, frequently interrupting, was his slim, henna-haired wife with the high-fashion cheekbones. "Shut up, Allen," she kept saying. "Shut up. You'd better shut up."

Allen even took Thomas into a small room in the house where the walls were covered with framed family photos. In the middle of a grid of photos was an empty space. "Bill Presser's picture used to hang there," Allen said. "I took it down. He didn't back me in a fight with Jackie."

Then, without realizing the danger of his words, Allen told a story he had told many times before and since. In fall 1976, Jackie and

The Chase

Harold Friedman had come to the hospital to visit him after he had had his latest heart attack while organizing for his Local 752.

"Uncle Allen," he recalls Jackie saying, "The doctor and my mom told me that you only have a year or a year and a half to live."

"Well, what about it?" Allen replied.

"We would like for you to transfer your members into our local," Jackie said.

"Jackie, I owe a lot of money. I went into great debt to finance this local."

"We'll pay off all your debts," Presser said.

"If you take my black business agent with you," Allen said, referring to his buddy Terence Freeman. "And you have to promise me never to fire him and pay off all my debts."

Jackie agreed, but Allen was wary and said he needed to hear Harold Friedman, who ran Local 507's day to day affairs, agree to the conditions. Several weeks later, when he felt better, Allen met Harold and Jackie at the Local 507 offices and they reached an agreement. Considering them inventory in his own private company, Allen said he "sold" his members to Jackie. Local 507 received the 1,300 members in Allen's independent Local 752 and his salary was raised to one thousand dollars a week from $750 and was to be paid until he died. It was as if a conglomerate had bought out a smaller competitor, a common practice in the business world but improper and illegal in the labor movement.

Allen didn't die. After several months, he felt better and began coming to Local 507 in the mornings, looking for something to do. Jackie and Tony Hughes and Harold didn't want him around the office and wouldn't even give him a key, Allen said. Occasionally, he'd try to enter the offices and a new secretary, not knowing him, would refuse to buzz him in. Allen would blow his stack, sending his blood pressure rocketing, then pound and kick the door until a business agent ran up, saying, "It's OK, let him in, let him in!"

Once inside "they wouldn't let me do nothing," Allen said. "I would show up and nobody would talk to me. I would sit in a waiting room like a big goof reading magazines, and I just decided the heck with it."

When Friedman was done with the story of how he sold his little union local and didn't work, Thomas was very glad he had missed his

333

afternoon golf date. "Do you realize what you've just done?" Thomas said. "You've just confessed to a crime."

"What crime?" Allen said. His wife, who had repeatedly told him not to say anything, started crying.

"In fact, I'm going to serve you with a grand jury subpoena right now," Thomas said, pulling it from a pocket.

Allen didn't like this turn of events, but at the moment he disliked his nephew even more. After some discussion, Allen told the Labor agent that he would appear before the grand jury and would answer questions about Jackie. Thomas hurried back to his office and dictated a long memo that recounted the interview. When strike force prosecutors heard about Allen's admissions, they got excited. That made two confessions, Nardi's and Friedman's. They just might indict Jackie Presser after all.

It's called baby-sitting a witness. Nearly every day, Thomas called Allen, checking his condition, keeping him in line. Thomas and his boss, Dave Williams, took him to lunch at a fancy restaurant, where Allen repeated his account of turning over his union local to Jackie and Harold Friedman for a thousand dollars a week for life. Thomas talked to Nancy Friedman on the phone as well, and she gave him some advice. "You better get Allen down there before the grave-setting," she warned.

In early June, roughly a year after Bill Presser's death, the family was going to have a ceremony at the cemetery in which an engraved headstone would be placed on his grave. Faye Presser was coming from Florida, and nearly the entire Presser and Friedman families planned to attend. It looked to be a rare, emotional reunion and at least a temporary rapprochement between Jackie and his uncle Allen. After the placing of the stone, when he'd be awash in family feelings, Allen wouldn't hold enough anger in his heart to hurt Jackie at the grand jury, Nancy Friedman believed.

Thomas said that he begged the strike force to call a special grand jury to hear Allen. "I told them, 'Get him in! Get him in!'"

But the strike force didn't get Allen in before the ceremony. He came in less than a week later, carrying a letter from his doctor stating that he was too sick to testify. Strike force prosecutor Steve Jigger, his feet up on a desk, was unwinding after presenting a string of witnesses to the grand jury on another case. "What's this," Jigger asked, reading the letter. "Well, are you afraid to testify or what?"

Friedman took offense. "Get me out of here," he told the two agents.

Red and Jim were crestfallen. They knew Allen would have coughed up Jackie if the strike force had presented him to the grand jury just after he had confessed.

"I'm sorry I let you down," Allen told them later. "But you've got to understand. Jackie's my nephew, and I still love him."

Red and Jim continued their quest to build a no-show embezzlement case against Jackie Presser and Harold Friedman, focusing on the four ghost employees. The two Labor agents worked on finding Local 507 records that would back up Nardi and Friedman's confessions to show that the two men had never worked. It was a difficult task, but they had some luck. Harold Friedman compulsively insisted on documenting his employees' actions. Business agents signed in and out on one form and listed every factory and shop they visited on another. There were expense reports and telephone logs and up-to-date rosters. Furthermore, all union meetings were recorded by stenographers, who noted who attended and what exactly was said.

The strike force had obtained some of this with a subpoena, but Teamsters lawyers said much of these records didn't exist. In late September, however, Red and Jim located the company that printed all the forms Harold Friedman used. It was a gold mine. Now Red and Jim now knew exactly what records they needed to obtain, and Red began crafting a search warrant affidavit.

Many Labor Department racketeering cases fizzled after an informant told them about a mobster or a relative with a no-show job. Without the benefit of a confession or lengthy around-the-clock surveillance, it was extremely difficult to prove in court that someone took a union paycheck without working. With luck, an agent might find a no-show living in another state while collecting a union paycheck, but that was unusual.

Nardi's word that he had never worked wasn't enough by itself to indict Jackie, but Red and Jim built a strong case using Harold Friedman's compulsive records. They found the shop where Friedman had pads of sign-in sheets printed. All the business agents were listed except Nardi, Hughes, Allen Friedman, and George Argie, all of the suspected no-shows. Also, every Local 507 business agent was reimbursed for out-of-pocket expenses, such as buying hot dogs or coffee for picketers or buying meals on the road. A business agent always incurred expenses. Between 1972 and 1978, Local 507 expense reports filed with the government revealed that Jack Nardi was never reimbursed a penny for expenses. This was extremely suspicious. The agents knew they could use this in a trial to buttress Nardi's confession.

Jim and Red appreciated the irony. Harold Friedman had always said that the way to beat snoopy government investigators was to document everything on paper and keep it forever. Now his yards and yards of beloved paperwork had twisted into the rope they would use to hang him.

24

The Fix

"You know anybody connected with the Plain Dealer?"

MAISHE ROCKMAN TO FAT TONY SALERNO

It was a familiar routine for Jackie. He'd put aside phone calls and family on Sunday mornings and talk confidentially to FBI special agent Bob Friedrick. Friedrick was a graduate of the U.S. Naval Academy, a quiet, intense man with only a dozen or so years of FBI experience. Even so, he was already the head of its prestigious organized-crime squad in Cleveland. He had also commanded the FBI's SWAT team, drawing upon his combat experience in Vietnam to perform the dangerous, precise work with skill.

Though he had been Pat Foran's understudy in the organized-crime squad, Friedrick had less down-and-dirty street experience than many other agents. While Foran was decribed as making decisions unilaterally and arrogantly, Bob Friedrick liked to discuss tactics with other agents, brainstorm a bit, and make sure major moves were well thought out and thorough.

Jackie cultivated Friedrick carefully, flooding him with charm, and the agent found himself swept away on a wave of good feeling. It didn't take long before he broke one of the FBI's most important rules in handling informants. He got too close.

At this stage of their weekly debriefings, Jackie seemed to make a point of dumping on Teamsters president Roy Lee Williams, who had been accused of bribing Nevada Senator Howard Cannon and was awaiting trial. If Williams dodged conviction, Jackie wanted to be certain he gave the FBI every possible weapon to knock his rival out of the picture. At a February 1982 meeting with Friedrick, for instance, Jackie revealed that Williams kept a $250-a-day suite at the Hyatt Regency on Capitol Hill, just across from IBT headquarters.

"Roy has probably only used it ten times," Jackie said. "But his real close pal uses it all time. The guy is Roy's bagman, and he keeps the suite stocked with food, whiskey, and women. He uses the phones for business."

Jackie continued, "He and his buddies come to the International in a van sometimes in the morning and cart off machines, calculators, fireproof safes, you name it. These guys are looting the International!"

Friedrick, unfamiliar with all the Teamster characters and their significance, took notes in a spiral-bound notebook. Then he reported the allegations on plain white paper to the FBI informant desk in Washington. He made sure to disguise Jackie as his source, listing Presser by his code name, ALPRO.

Friedrick considered Presser an extremely helpful source. In June 1982, for instance, Jackie told him how the FBI could develop another high-level Teamster snitch, one who had a possible pipeline into Mob activity in Philadelphia—IBT vice president Maurice Shurr.

"Maury Shurr is a very weak guy," Presser told Friedrick. "He's done some wrong things. Some sweetheart contracts, other stuff. I'll check around and get some details for you. If you approach him right, he might be willing to cooperate completely with you guys."

Jackie and Tony Hughes met frequently with Friedrick in the summer and fall of 1982. One reason was that they were tired of Simmons and Thomas's relentless pursuit and wanted the FBI to stop them somehow. The two Labor agents had tromped into his union hall to serve subpoenas on Jackie's business agents. Then they came back with more subpoenas for samples of his handwriting and asked him to write out the name Harry Haler twenty-five times. The agents dragged his secretary down to the grand jury. Then they subpoenaed his girl-friend Cindy, who worked part time at Local 507. They even slapped a subpoena on his son, Gary, while he was carrying his laundry into a dry cleaner two blocks from the union hall. Simmons served him in the store, placing the subpoena on top of a basket of clothes Gary was carrying. Startled, unsure of what was happening, Gary threw up his

338

hands as if in a stickup, dropping his laundry. Jackie was furious when he learned of this, feeling that his son had been deliberately humiliated in public.

Furthermore, Jackie's relatives and friends kept telling him that two guys named Simmons and Thomas had dropped by unannounced and asked a bunch of nosy questions about him and the Teamsters. Jackie had had more than enough.

"What's going on?" Jackie would ask Friedrick. "Why can't you do something about those guys? I thought the FBI was going to take care of the Labor Department for me."

At first, Friedrick didn't know how to answer these questions and shared Presser's concern about the Labor Department's investigation. He passed along Jackie's complaints to Jim Moody, chief of the organized-crime unit at FBI headquarters in Washington, D.C. Moody told him that Presser had nothing to worry about, that the bureau would take care of the Labor Department investigation. He told him to continue to gather intelligence from Jackie and reassure him that the FBI was going to help.

Friedrick truly believed that the FBI brass would get the Justice Department to call off Red and Jim or at least would refuse to indict Jackie and Tony. Presser was too valuable a source. He was the FBI's mole inside the highest levels of organized crime. "Don't worry," he reassured Jackie time and again. "It will all be taken care of."

In the months after the damaging *Plain Dealer* exposé, Jackie complained repeatedly about the newspaper to Friedrick and even threatened to punish it by forcing its Teamsters Union drivers out on a wildcat strike. That would fix them.

Indeed it would. Then Cleveland-area food chains and department stores and real-estate companies would sink all of their advertising dollars into the *Cleveland Press,* giving new life to the dying afternoon newspaper owned by Presser family friend Joseph Cole.

"Don't do it," Friedrick warned Jackie. "It's going to wash itself out." Not long afterward, Jackie informed his handler that the Mafia and Roy Cohn were going to help him with his *Plain Dealer* problem. Friedrick didn't believe it.

For years, the Teamsters had enjoyed a corrupt relationship with the *Plain Dealer*'s management, Presser informed the FBI. The paper's powerful labor-relations director had paid Carmen Parise, head of the newspaper drivers Teamster local, a thousand dollars a month for negotiating a softer contract, Jackie said. Parise, a Mafia associate, was also a loan shark.

Furthermore, Presser told the FBI, the *Plain Dealer*'s assistant to the publisher, Alex Machaskee, asked him in 1980 to help put the rival *Cleveland Press* out of its misery by creating "problems" with its Teamsters local. Jackie said that he told Machaskee he wouldn't help, that he strongly believed Cleveland should be a two-paper town. Machaskee has denied the charges.

The relationship between the Mob and the newspaper was cinched tighter after Jackie began griping about Bogdanich and Woge's exposé to Maishe Rockman, his advisor and Mob handler. Jackie vehemently insisted that the stories were vicious lies supplied by a con man whom he once thought he could trust. Jackie knew that if he could convince Maishe, the most powerful Mob figure in town, of his innocence, then Maishe could sway Jack White and the other leaders of the Cleveland Mafia.

For reasons he has yet to reveal, Maishe believed Jackie and decided to see what he could do to help restore the good name of the son of his dear friend Bill Presser. Jackie would then be deeply indebted, and Maishe knew such a debt could be profitably collected when Jackie became general president of the Teamsters.

Despite years of street talk by Cleveland and Chicago Mafia figures about the coincidences that pointed to Jackie's being a government informant, Maishe refused to believe it. Many times Maishe and White's lawyer argued about Jackie Presser's loyalty. But shrewd, streetwise Maishe Rockman always stood up for him—even now, just a few months after the *Plain Dealer* published seemingly indisputable stories about Jackie being a snitch. "No one I ever knew got in trouble by him," Maishe would rationalize.

Unbeknownst to Rockman at the time, Jackie had already supplied the FBI with the incriminating information used in the Justice Department's Strawman probe, a case that a few years later put Maishe and the heads of the Kansas City Mafia in prison for skimming cash from Mob-controlled Las Vegas casinos. "Maishe Rockman is in jail because of Jackie Presser," an FBI agent confided. Standing up for

Jackie was his father's Achilles' heel, Maishe's son said shortly after Jackie died.

In the spring of 1982, as Roy Williams went to trial on charges of bribing Senator Cannon, Rockman decided the time was right to lobby other Mafia families to support Jackie as Williams's successor. Rockman, who had better Mafia-commission contacts than anyone else in the Cleveland family, promoted his plan with underboss Angelo "Big Ange" Lonardo and Cleveland Mafia boss James "Jack White" Licavoli.

If Roy Lee loses his case, he'll have to step down, Maishe told them. We should be ready with a new man. We should start pushing Jackie. It'll bring prestige to the Cleveland family.

Lonardo would later testify that he and Jack White didn't trust Jackie to do what they wanted but that Maishe convinced them he held sway over Presser. The Cleveland Mafia leaders finally agreed to throw their support behind Jackie and to lobby for him with the Mafia families in Chicago and New York.

Rockman and Lonardo worked together on the project. They were a natural team, each married to a sister of the late John Scalish, the Cleveland Mafia don from the forties to 1976. Jack White stayed out of lobbying for Jackie. He wasn't interested in setting up out-of-town meetings, talking in code through intermediaries, and traveling to Chicago or New York to meet and pay respects to ranking mafiosi. "I hate all that greaseball stuff," he would say. Also, White was under indictment for racketeering and had to ask the government for permission to travel out of state. All in all, he'd rather play golf.

Maishe and Big Ange drove to Chicago in Rockman's car, a black Cadillac fitted with an oversized gasoline tank and a secret compartment to hide skim money. They met Jackie Cerone, underboss, and Joey Auippa, boss of the Chicago family, in a downtown Chicago hotel room. They got right down to business.

"Williams is facing hard time, and we should be ready with our guy for president," Lonardo told the two Chicago Mafia leaders.

Then Maishe Rockman presented his case for Jackie Presser, promising, "I can control him."

"I don't like Jackie Presser," Cerone said bluntly.

"Why not?"

"He's an informant."

"Don't worry about him being an informant, he's not," Maishe insisted. "I can control him."

"We got other fellows we would like to put in," Cerone said. He mentioned Teamsters vice presidents Andy Anderson, Joe Morgan, and Don Peters. "The Chicago family is very close to these guys," Cerone went on. "We can control them."

But Rockman was persuasive, vouching for Jackie. He said he'd known Jackie Presser for years, had known his father since childhood. "Jackie is not a government snitch, and I know I can handle him," Rockman insisted.

The meeting broke up before the four powerful mobsters reached an agreement as to which Teamsters vice president to back for the top slot.

"We'll think about Presser and let you know," Lonardo recalled the Chicago mobsters saying. "Now, why don't we all go to dinner?" Lonardo and Rockman begged off, saying they had to get back to Cleveland.

A few weeks later, a Chicago family higher-up called Maishe on the telephone and broke the news: the Chicago family would go with Presser. That pleased Big Ange, and he went to work. First he called John "Peanuts" Tronolone in Miami, *consigliere* of the Cleveland Mafia and owner of Peter Pan World of Travel. He told Peanuts to purchase airline tickets and set up a meeting with Fat Tony Salerno in New York City. A day or two later, Big Ange and Maishe flew United Airlines to New York and journeyed to Fat Tony's social club on East 116th Street in East Harlem. There they filled in Salerno about their meeting with Auippa and Cerone.

"They think Jackie's an informant," Lonardo said.

"If you need any help, I'll call them," Salerno offered.

"No, Chicago agreed to go along with him," Lonardo said. "Now, can you line up delegates?"

Fat Tony said he'd call Sammy Provenzano, a Teamsters international vice president and the brother of Genovese family capo Tony Pro, chief suspect in the Hoffa murder. Fat Tony said he'd get Sammy to put the arm on delegates who'd be voting at the next Teamsters convention.

342

Later in Cleveland, according to Lonardo, Maishe had a private talk with Jackie Presser and told him about the support he and Big Ange had lined up for him during their trips around the country. "If you get elected, don't think it came only from me," Maishe told Jackie. "You can thank Chicago and New York and Angelo for it."

While this was unfolding, Jackie's lawyer, John Climaco, the legal equivalent of a street fighter, began collecting information about Harry Haler. He wanted to know all about the man who claimed that Climaco's biggest client took kickbacks and was a government informant. Finding dirt on Haler was easy enough. But Climaco also learned that when Haler's testimony could be corroborated independently, the Justice Department had used him as a witness and had obtained convictions.

Rockman knew that Jackie had to counteract the *Plain Dealer* story accusing him of being a federal informant. He'd never become Teamsters president wearing a snitch jacket, and Maishe wanted him in. With Jackie in the top Teamsters job, Maishe stood to gain enormous clout in the underworld.

After he learned of Haler's criminal track record and heard Jackie's denials, Maishe believed that Jackie had been slandered, and he went to work. In mid-1982, Maishe and Big Ange again traveled to New York to see Fat Tony. At the social club, Rockman told Salerno about Haler and the *Plain Dealer* story that had devastated Presser. Then Rockman asked, "You know anyone connected with the *Plain Dealer*?"

"No, I don't," Salerno replied. "But wait a minute, I'll try to find out."

He told his aide-de-camp, Vincent "Fish" Cafaro, to call their lawyer, the notorious power broker Roy Cohn, former chief counsel to Senator Joseph McCarthy in the days of the Red menace. Lonardo and Cafaro both later described what happened.

Fish came back to the room a moment later and announced that Cohn was on the line. Salerno went out and talked to him for a while, came back, and told Rockman and Lonardo that Cohn said he represented the owner of the *Plain Dealer*. Salerno told them he hadn't wanted to discuss Jackie and the newspaper over the telephone and had agreed to meet Cohn in a few days to see what could be accomplished.

Salerno employed Cohn only for certain legal problems. When the powerful Mafia boss needed someone to fight for his freedom at a criminal trial, he hired a high-priced litigator, someone who would prepare the case meticulously by filing motions, conducting independent investigations of witnesses—basically accomplishing a task for which Cohn didn't have the skill or patience.

But Cohn was worth his hefty fees in other, more intangible, ways. As federal wiretaps show, Cohn allowed Salerno and other Mafia powers to use his law office to conduct their criminal operations. Sitting in Cohn's office at the law firm, Saxe and Bacon, his driver waiting outside, Fat Tony could relax, knowing that for the moment he was free from electronic surveillance, the bane of his life. Except in rare instances, judges wouldn't authorize a wiretap of a lawyer's office, since discussions with clients are privileged by law.

For his part, Cohn didn't suffer moral qualms about letting his office be used to further his client's criminal enterprises. Indeed, Cohn did far more than let Fat Tony dial a telephone with impunity. During the early eighties, he served as an occasional bagman. Joe Culek, a New York construction-company official, told federal agents that he once stuffed $20,000 into an envelope, then "ran on foot" to Roy Cohn's office, handed the loot to Cohn, and instructed him to give the bribe to Salerno. Culek was buying labor peace to complete a big Manhattan construction project.

After Maishe and Big Ange returned to Cleveland, Salerno met with Cohn and told him he would like the *Plain Dealer* to run a retraction about Presser taking kickbacks and being a federal informant. It was easy for Cohn to call on Si Newhouse, the paper's owner, and ask him to dish out an editorial favor for a friend, client, or prospective client. Cohn and Newhouse were close friends, and Cohn had brokered editorial favors in the past.

The intimacy between Cohn and the Newhouses had begun in the thirties, when Roy and Si met at New York's Horace Mann School for Boys. Cohn called Si "my best friend" and Si once described Cohn to reporters as "one of the most extraordinary men I've ever met." For most of their lives, they talked to each other nearly every day. Si and his family took vacations with Cohn, cruising the coastal waters of Mexico in Cohn's leased yacht.

Despite Cohn's unsavory reputation and scrapes with the law, the Newhouses, one of the richest families in America, always stood by him. When Cohn went on trial in 1963 in New York City on charges of giving false testimony and intimidating grand-jury witnesses, Si Newhouse frequently visited him in the courtroom, lending moral support. Around this time, Cohn, facing legal bills and IRS hassles, borrowed $500,000 interest-free from old man Sam Newhouse, founder of the country's largest private media empire. Cohn never paid it back.

Robert Blecker, a law professor at New York University Law School and a friend of Cohn, told Cohn biographer Nicholas Von Hoffman about the lawyer's clout with the Newhouses. "Roy once told me that . . . in those towns where there was a Newhouse newspaper, it was the only newspaper in town, which means the editor of that newspaper is quite an influential person. So if anyone ever got into trouble in any city in which there was a Newhouse newspaper, Roy could go to Si and Si could go to the editor and there you have a leading member in town who could do a favor. Roy was a favor broker."

So it was not at all unusual for Cohn to ask Si Newhouse to pull strings for Teamsters vice president Jackie Presser.

In late summer 1982, *Plain Dealer* executive editor Dave Hopcraft was informed by Norman Newhouse, Si's brother and the man who was directly responsible for the family's newspapers, that the company had agreed to extend the statute of limitations for Jackie Presser to file a libel lawsuit. Norman said that he wanted to appease Presser, and the extension would give everyone time to come up with a way to make Jackie happy.

Hopcraft was amazed by the call. This was the first time Norman Newhouse had become involved in what was basically a local legal problem for the *Plain Dealer*. When Newhouse told him to satisfy Presser, Hopcraft realized that Norman's idea of a solution wouldn't pass muster as a model of journalistic integrity.

Later, Newhouse lawyer Charles Sabin flew into town and met Hopcraft and publisher Vail for supper at the Union Club, a Waspy private club. Sabin told them that the Newhouses wanted to soothe the unhappy Jackie Presser. Sabin said he had heard that Presser didn't take $300,000 in a series of kickbacks, wasn't a federal informant, and that the government was closing its investigation.

On the hot spot, Hopcraft devised what he thought was a solution with integrity. "If what you're saying and Climaco's saying is true— that the government has investigated and Jackie is not in jeopardy— then I'll follow our policy," Hopcraft told Sabin. "Get the government to say that, and I'll write a front-page story that says Jackie was investigated and the government is not pursuing it." At the time, the *Plain Dealer* had a policy of giving a story about a person's acquittal the same prominence as the original story about his indictment.

Hopcraft's proposal seemed fine with everybody at the table. For the moment, he didn't think he was selling out. Over the next couple of weeks, Hopcraft began making phone calls to the strike force, to the local U.S. Attorney, J. William Petro, and eventually to David Margolis, head of the Justice Department's organized-crime section. "Look, the strike force was quoted in our paper as saying it was investigating Jackie Presser for kickbacks," Hopcraft argued. "If the case is closed, it's only fair you should announce that as well."

On July 28, 1982, keeping up the pressure and aware of Maishe's work behind the scenes with Cohn, Presser demanded a retraction in a letter to Tom Vail. He threatened to file a libel suit. The threat made an impression, but it was essentially empty. Presser knew he could never sit still for the exhaustive discovery of a real libel suit. Any decent lawyer would unearth secrets Jackie would rather keep buried, especially the fact that he was indeed an FBI informant.

Pressed by Hopcraft, Margolis sent a letter dated October 4 to Climaco saying that the Hoover-Gorin kickback probe was closed. Though the Justice Department almost never admits that an investigation is closed, Margolis had an easy excuse to explain why he sent the letter. The kickbacks to Presser had occurred more than seven years ago. By law, bribery charges had to be brought on such crimes within seven years. The deadline had expired a few months earlier.

A week before the Margolis letter, Jackie had bragged to friends that he "had the government on the run"; that the *Plain Dealer* was going to run a retraction of its story that he took kickbacks; and that the newspaper was going to pay him $2 million in damages.

On Thursday, October 6, Hopcraft told reporter Walt Bogandich that the Presser kickback case had been closed and that a story would be run. Fine, Bogdanich said, as long as you also mention that the seven-year statute of limitations had expired on bringing charges based on those allegations. To his dismay, Bogdanich gradually learned that the story Hopcraft envisioned would contain much more information than a few paragraphs about an investigation being closed. Essentially, it was going to be a retraction.

"What are they saying is wrong with the story?" Bogdanich asked Hopcraft. "Please, listen to the tapes. Read the documents." There was documentation for every fact, phrase, nuance, and allegation, he insisted.

Hopcraft replied, "It doesn't matter. I'm sure it's documented, Walt. The orders are coming out of New York."

As Hopcraft later explained it, "Here's how the play went—from [Jackie's lawyer] Climaco to Roy Cohn to Si Newhouse to Charley Sabin and Norman Newhouse." According to a close Presser adviser, Climaco called Cohn because Jackie told him that Roy Cohn had already been brought into the scheme. "Si Newhouse wasn't very amenable right away," said a Teamster insider at one of the meetings. "There was a lot dialogue."

Demands for corrections or retractions occur all too often in the newspaper business, and the routine at the *Plain Dealer* was simple: a lawyer or subject of a story would lodge a complaint, provide his evidence of a mistake (if he had any), and then an editor would ask whomever wrote the news story for his documentation. If a mistake was made, a correction would be printed immediately on page two. Sometimes, the paper's lawyers at Baker and Hostetler, nationally known for its libel practice, took part in the process.

What was happening to Bogdanich and Woge was unprecedented; they knew it and Hopcraft later admitted it. The Cleveland lawyers who reviewed their story before publication were never consulted about the retraction. Nor were the editors concerned about the veracity of the story, though Bogdanich pleaded with them to listen to the evidence.

After talking to Bogdanich, Hopcraft relented for a moment and said he would try to resolve the dispute behind the scenes. He asked the reporter not to tell anyone about it in the meantime. Bogdanich agreed.

While Salerno, Cohn, and the Mafia conspired to help him, Jackie had confidently been telling friends that his powerful allies in the government would soon stop Red Simmons and Jim Thomas's heavy-handed probe and smack them back into their place. The two Labor investigators were lightweights, Jackie said. Climaco sarcastically referred to them as Freebie and the Bean.

Instead, Red and Jim had convinced the strike-force prosecutors that a search of Presser's Local 507 was needed to get evidence about the no-show employees. About eight o'clock on Friday morning, October 8, a team of ten agents from the Office of Labor Racketeering, several of them imported from Chicago, sealed off Local 507, trapping Jackie's secretary and a few other employees inside. No one could go in or out at first. The agents moved slowly from room to room, sifting through drawers and files.

Climaco was called and he rushed to the building, but he wasn't allowed inside. He was furious. He stalked around the building. Spotting *Plain Dealer* reporter Stephanie Saul, he asked her how she knew about the search. She was noncommittal. He joined some of the teamsters milling around and said, "That bitch, how did she know about this before I did?"

The search had caught Jackie and his lawyers unawares; they had barely had time to celebrate the Justice Department's letter closing the Hoover-Gorin case. They didn't know what sort of incriminating evidence the Labor agents, after picking through Jackie and Harold's desks, might drag out of the union hall. Who knew what Harold the Archivist had squirreled away?

Climaco thought that the search was a retaliation by the Labor agents after learning of the Margolis letter. Actually, Red Simmons's search affidavit had been written two weeks earlier. The search had been planned a week before Margolis wrote his controversial letter.

Inside Jackie's office, the investigators found X-rated videotapes, slingshots, crossbows, antique firearms, and a small waste basket half-filled with valuable gold coins. On Harold Friedman's desk, the agents grabbed a file folder containing the pay stubs of Harry Friedman, George Argie, Sr., John J. Felice, and Jack Nardi and a copy of the court decision in *United States v. Bane,* the landmark no-show employee case.

Jackie was in the middle of a meeting with FBI agent Bob Friedrick when he was called at home and told about the search. The FBI hadn't been notified or invited to help with the search—a significant departure from normal procedure. Usually when the strike force needed extra bodies to secure a building during a search, the 180-agent FBI office provided the personnel. It was clear that the Labor Department's racketeering office was deliberately keeping the FBI away from the Presser probe. Friedrick's boss, Joe Griffin, was furious when he learned about the search. He called Olah, the strike-force chief, and demanded to know why he wasn't told about it.

"It was on a need-to-know basis," Olah fired back. "Besides, I've been here over ten years, and the bureau has never shown any interest in investigating the Pressers." Olah took another shot. "By the way, is Jackie an FBI informant?"

No, Griffin replied. Absolutely not.

Olah was playing a game, Thomas said years later. Olah knew Jackie was the FBI's snitch. To irritate Griffin and the FBI agents, Olah let the two Labor agents chase Jackie Presser, never believing they'd be able to build an indictable case.

It was a game of chicken. The strike force was pitted against the FBI, with two bull-headed supervisors, Steve Olah and Joe Griffin, butting heads. Olah pursued Presser; Griffin protected Presser. Both knew he was an informant, but neither would acknowledge it or discuss how to handle the dilemma. Olah wanted Griffin to tell him that Jackie was his snitch and then ask him to back off. Griffin couldn't stomach Olah and wouldn't give him the satisfaction of being asked for a favor. So both headed straight at each other, unswerving and unthinking, egos clashing.

Later in the day of the search of Local 507, Bogdanich learned conclusively that his editors didn't care how well he and Woge had documented the series and that Roy Cohn was somehow involved. A conspiracy, he thought. In the newsroom late Friday afternoon, he told

Newspaper Guild leader Robert Daniels about the proposed story and how he was being denied input or a chance to read it. Within minutes, the word buzzed across the sprawling newsroom, and reporters and editors gathered in clumps, trying to find out what was going on. Steve Hatch, the Guild's executive secretary, held an emergency meeting in the newspaper's executive dining room. Guild members were outraged when they learned about the proposed retraction, Cohn's involvement, and the strange behavior of Hopcraft, blindly following orders from New York.

The reporters were riled and confused. Many believed that *Plain Dealer* management was capitulating to Presser and the Teamsters out of economic blackmail. One theory making the rounds was that Presser had promised the paper's owners that the Teamsters would go easy during the next contract negotiations, thereby saving hundreds of thousands of dollars in wages. Teamsters Local 473 represented the newspaper's drivers. Its contract was the yardstick by which the other unions at the *Plain Dealer* measured their gains. If the Teamsters agreed to a five-percent raise, the other unions fell right in line.

In an interview for this book, Hopcraft discounted the economic-blackmail theory. "John Climaco never said, 'Screw you, we're going to close you down!' Jackie Presser never said, 'Screw you, we're going to close you down!' " But, Hopcraft pointed out, he didn't know what Jackie may have said to the paper's publisher and business managers.

"You have to remember the timing here," Hopcraft explained. "There is no way in God's green earth the *Cleveland Press* could survive as a newspaper unless you can get the Guild or the Teamsters to close down the *Plain Dealer* for six months. Even then, it would have just extended the *Press*'s life for a couple of years."

It clearly wasn't a good time for the owners of the *Plain Dealer* to refuse a request from Jackie Presser.

On Sunday, October 10, 1982, the *Plain Dealer* ran an awkwardly written story, without a byline, on page one under the headline, "Justice closes kickback investigation of Presser."

The story read in part, "David Margolis, chief of the Justice Department's Organized Crime Division, issued the following statement: 'In regard to . . . an article which appeared in the *Plain Dealer*

350

on August 25, 1981, alleging that Jackie Presser took a kickback from Hoover-Gorin and Associates, Inc., please be advised that the Justice Department considers this matter closed.' "

The rest of the article consisted of quotes from John Climaco attacking Haler and the *Plain Dealer* and defending Presser. "The closing of this investigation vindicates Jackie Presser, who from the beginning denied that there was any truth in these allegations," the lawyer said.

The story didn't mention that the seven-year time limit had expired for bringing kickback charges against Presser. Bogdanich and Woge had demanded that this be included. Hopcraft said that he had tried to get it in but had yielded to Presser and Climaco's pressure when they refused.

In his unusual letter to Climaco, Margolis didn't deny the meat of the second part of the *Plain Dealer*'s Presser series: that Jackie and his dad were informants. In fact, Margolis's letter never even mentioned it. But the phony news story, written by Hopcraft, did quote Climaco on the topic. "The IRS as well as the Justice Department have advised me that Jackie and William Presser have never acted as informants." A few paragraphs later, Hopcraft was quoted as saying that "Climaco's characterization of . . . the statements of federal authorities is correct." In other words, the newspaper was saying that Jackie wasn't a snitch.

"That story," reporter Bogdanich would later say with disgust, "was a total fraud."

The morning the retraction appeared in the paper, Presser met as usual with FBI agent Bob Friedrick. It was early, and Jackie hadn't put in his front uppers. He walked up to the agent displaying the front page and a huge gap-toothed grin. "Everybody was elated at the retraction," said one of Jackie's closest friends in the union. "That was needed. If he didn't get that, he would have had trouble getting the presidency. That was the milestone. That was mandatory. Everyone knew that." FBI agents and supervisors who knew Jackie was working as a top-level snitch were elated, too. Now he could use that article to deny it and perhaps live a lot longer.

Later that Sunday morning, about sixty reporters came downtown on their day off for a Guild meeting to figure out the next move. Reporter Dick Peery, an old hand and a union activist, took the floor and told the assembly, "I remember Roy Cohn from the days of the Communist witch hunts. If he is involved in this, I can assure you something very unethical is going on."

The reporters threw up what's known as an informational picket line on the sidewalk in front of the *Plain Dealer* building and near a bus stop that sported the paper's promotional slogan, "When the News Breaks, We Put It Together."

Before the picketing started, the Guild's buttoned-down labor lawyer, wearing a tie and glasses, warned the rag-tag picketers to walk in an orderly line, behave, and not impede anyone entering the building. Citing case law, he warned the protesting reporters that informational picket lines have more legal restrictions than strike picket lines. And above all, he lectured, do not use obscenities.

As soon as the lawyer was out of earshot, reporter Jack Hagan, a newsroom cutup, smiled and quietly began a singsong chant, "Hopcraft is a cocksucker, Hopcraft is a cocksucker." The picket line broke up laughing.

The Associated Press, United Press International, and the three local TV stations were alerted to the protest and scurried to the scene to hear Guild leader Hatch blast the newspaper's actions. The story was "a capitulation to powerful interests . . . intentionally misleading and a serious abuse of the press," Steve Hatch charged. Noting that Hopcraft had written the so-called news story, Hatch remarked, "If that's the kind of reporter he is, Hopcraft should find another line of work." Reporters carried picket signs saying, "Jackie Presser, *Plain Dealer* Editor and Publisher" and "When the News Breaks, We Apologize."

Sunday afternoon, Jackie and Climaco held a press conference, claiming that they were upset with Hopcraft. They had demanded that their retraction be displayed across the top of the front page, above the fold, just as the original series had been. But the retraction appeared below the fold, they complained.

Several days later, Jackie's publicists distributed 150,000 copies of a new issue of the union newspaper, *Ohio Teamster.* Splashed across the front page of the tabloid was the headline "Retraction Vindicates Pressers and Spells Victory for All Teamsters." Underneath was printed the *Plain Dealer*'s story. Jackie was featured in a front-page column, saying that the newspaper had admitted that it "printed lies about my father and myself being federal informers."

352

This retraction is a bombshell for the news media and a reason for all Teamsters to celebrate. Year after year our International Union, our officers and members, even our pension funds, have been taking it on the chin from a sizable number of jackals in the news media and from certain entities and individuals in the government structure who play ball with the jackals. . . .

A month after the death of my father, the former international Vice-President Bill Presser, who had often been vilified by the *Plain Dealer*—the newspaper began a series alleging that I had taken kickbacks from a Las Vegas public relations firm and also alleging that my Dad and I, along with our late General President Frank E. Fitzsimmons, had cooked up a corrupt deal with government officials in which we would act as informers. . . . At that point I decided I had to try to end the continued stream of baseless accusations against the Teamsters and the Pressers, no matter what it cost.

This issue of the *Ohio Teamster* was Jackie's victory flag. He had it distributed to members of Congress, newspapers, and community leaders. A few weeks later, at an annual convention in Columbus, Jackie waved the article before a crowd of teamsters. They applauded as he proclaimed his innocence and vowed to carry on his struggle to protect their rights.

Meanwhile, a copy of the retraction was mailed to Fat Tony Salerno, and the boss, pleased with his handiwork, forwarded it to the heads of the Chicago Mafia. Fat Tony wanted to show them that his candidate for Teamsters president wasn't a stool pigeon after all.

With a little help from the Mob, Jackie Presser was back on track.

25

Obstructing Justice

"In a last ditch effort to stop the Presser indictment, the FBI joined in an operation with mob attorneys and [an] organized crime affiliate . . . to neutralize key government witness John Nardi."

LABOR DEPARTMENT INTERNAL MEMO

Walt Bogdanich and Mairy Jayn Woge were bitter about their treatment, but the controversy soon died down. It would be several years before bits and pieces of the retraction story were revealed in wiretaps and informant testimony used in criminal cases in New York. But even then, none of the city's dailies gave it any attention. By then, Walt was reporting for the *Wall Street Journal*, Mairy Jayn had been relegated to the police beat. They were shocked to learn that their series had been sabotaged by Fat Tony Salerno.

By the end of 1982, Simmons and Thomas were disappointed with the way the strike force was pursuing the Presser embezzlement case. After they searched Local 507 and seized key records, they felt everything was in shape for an indictment. But first, prosecutor Steve Jigger had to write the prosecution memorandum—pros memo, everyone called it—and send it to the Justice Department and get David Margolis to approve it.

"It was a constant struggle with Steve Jigger," Thomas recalled several years later. "He was always trying to have one-upmanship. You cannot understand, unless you were there, the frustration. Why? He's a coward."

Red and Jim were obsessed with the Presser case and took their frustration out on Jigger. He, on the other hand, was splitting his time between the Presser probe and a bribery case involving Mahoning

354

County sheriff James Trafficante, Jr. The sheriff was charged with taking kickbacks from the Youngstown Mob to ignore their illegal gambling games. He was acquitted.

Feeling that the probe was moving too slowly, Simmons and Thomas tried different ploys to goad the strike force into action. Thomas called this "stirring the pot." It meant going into the field, tailing Tony Hughes, dogging Allen and Harry Friedman with questions about the Pressers, and asking companies that did business with Local 507 if they paid kickbacks to Jackie. Essentially, it was guerrilla warfare on as many fronts as the Labor agents could open up.

"We'd go see Harry Friedman and crank him," Thomas said. "He'd go back and tell Harold Friedman what we talked about."

Red and Jim often used the office telescope to see when Tony Hughes left the union hall. Then they would tail him until he spotted them and pulled over in his car.

"What do youse guys want?" he'd ask.

"Get in the car, Tony."

He'd climb in the backseat and they'd talk. Simmons and Thomas floated misinformation, veiled threats, rumors, anything to shake him up. "Tony talked to us," Thomas said. "He was sharp but not that sharp. He played the dumb-pug role, dressed up in a suit and tie. 'What do youse guys want?' That was his way of finding out what was happening, and he'd go back and tell Jackie. Jackie couldn't very well talk to us."

The Labor agents also dug for leads by calling on the ex-wives of Teamsters business agents, who had never had much of a marriage or home life to start with. Business agents under Harold "Genghis Khan" Friedman worked twelve-hours days, six on Saturdays, then had to go out to dinner at nice restaurants a few nights a week with Harold.

"The business agents ran with a fast crowd," Thomas said. "We'd wait until they got a twenty-five-year-old, and when they got divorced, we'd go knock on the door of their ex-wives. They were pissed off and wanted to cut the balls off these guys. We'd sit there, listen to their problems."

The agents used a calculated strategy: rile up Jackie, Climaco, their business associates and relatives, and wait to see if anyone said anything incriminating. It worked. When the investigation was in a slump, stirring the pot became great sport. "It was fun, because it made something happen when nothing was being done," Simmons said. "It was fun to see the investigation go forward."

"One time, I had to hold Red back from hitting Jigger," Thomas said. "It was an act. It was very calculated. As we'd pull into the garage before the meeting, we figured it out. I'll do this, this, this, and this. You do that, that, and that."

It didn't endear them to their bosses, which may have hurt their case in the long run. They alienated Jigger, who was assigned to work with them. "Those two couldn't even tie their own shoelaces," he once complained.

In the fall of 1982, shortly after the search of Local 507, the Labor Department's nearly completed ghost-employee investigation had reached a critical point. "We began to detect a major counterattack on the part of the Teamsters—and, unfortunately, on the part of some FBI agents—to stop the investigation and to gather derogatory information on the [Labor] agents," Dave Williams, Red and Jim's supervisor, noted in a memo to his superiors. "I began reporting that to my superiors. We spoke daily during the early winter months of 1982 and 1983."

Into this highly charged atmosphere, John Climaco launched one of his patented heat-seeking letters, a carefully crafted partisan accusation, chock full of selective incidents and details, that he hoped would damage the credibility of Simmons and Thomas as Labor investigators. As a labor lawyer in Cleveland, Climaco knew of the long-standing personality conflict between the Cleveland FBI head, Joe Griffin, and the Cleveland Strike Force chief, Steve Olah. Climaco's letter drove the wedge between the two agencies even deeper and shifted attention from Jackie's suspected crimes to the personalities of the Labor investigators. Usually lawyers saved such argument and opprobrium for the courtroom. But if Climaco could create doubts about Simmons and Thomas in the minds of their strike-force superiors, some of whom were already annoyed at them, then the combative Climaco was a giant step closer to snatching Jackie from danger.

On December 8, 1982, in a twenty-four-page letter to Margolis, Climaco wrote, "To recount for you all the persons to whom Special Agents Simmons and Thomas have made wild accusations concerning our clients would be an overwhelming task. We will outline for you, therefore, only a few of the more serious accusations."

Climaco's first example was a Cleveland-area businessman interviewed by the two agents.

The first statement the Special Agents made was: "We've got you. . . ." "You are going to jail for paying kickbacks to Jackie Presser." Naturally the man was startled by this untrue accusation. Specials Agents Simmons and Thomas, in an apparent attempt to frighten him, told him he should immediately turn over his books and records or they'd obtain a subpoena requiring him to testify before a Grand Jury. . . . To date (obviously because the record and this man's testimony would be exculpatory in nature) . . . Simmons and Thomas have not requested your local office to subpoena the man.

Climaco described another incident in which the agents visited the president of the Cleveland Five Hundred, which held an annual Indy car race in downtown Cleveland over the July 4 weekend that attracted crowds of 250,000. On July 1, 1982, the businessman had labor problems with the workers who were erecting the massive temporary grandstands.

According to Climaco,

The interview took approximately fifty-five minutes with the first forty to fifty minutes consisting of small talk. During the last five minutes of the interview, [the man] was asked if he knew Jackie Presser, to which he responded that he did. He had met Jackie Presser once. . . . The Special Agents stated: "We know you have been having labor trouble. You have been having trouble with the Carpenters Union and a few other unions." Then they asked: "How much money did you pay Jackie Presser to make your union problems go away?" . . .

[His] response was: "What the hell are you talking about?" The Special Agents replied: "Isn't it a fact that you paid money to Presser to make your labor problems go away?" Again [he] stated that "That's a lie!" The Special Agents then said: "You had lunch with Jackie Presser." [He] replied: "Yes, I did, and there were four or five other people present from the Cleveland Foundation Five Hundred Board." [He] then related how the lunch was

357

prearranged and, only by coincidence was it on the same day as they had labor problems.

Explaining this exchange years later, Simmons and Thomas say they got a tip from a reliable informant and, upon their supervisor's instruction, checked it out. They say their questioning was more subtle than Climaco recounted. Thomas adds, however, "We were stirring the pot."

In November 1982, Jack Nardi, son of slain Teamsters Mob figure John Nardi, popped up as a target, triggering the tracking radar of Jackie and John Climaco. The affidavit Red and Jim used to obtain the Local 507 search warrant had been filed in the office of the federal clerk of court, according to normal routine. At this point, their theory of the Presser ghost-employee case became public. Their affidavit noted that Nardi and Allen Friedman were grand-jury witnesses and self-avowed ghost employees.

As a result, Jack Nardi and Allen Friedman were put in the middle of the strike force's battle with Local 507 and the FBI. Jackie and his lawyers now knew which witnesses they had to subvert or destroy in order to preempt Jackie's looming indictment.

Allen hurt the government case just by being himself. He was moody, up and down on Valium, changing his tune frequently. He hated his nephew and would bury him in court, he told Red and Jim. Then he backtracked, saying he couldn't hurt his family by testifying against his own blood. What worried Simmons and Thomas even more was a report from one of their snitches inside Local 507 who had overheard Harold Friedman explain that Allen had agreed to fake a heart attack to avoid testifying. If successful, Allen was supposed to be rewarded with a new car from Jackie.

"Make no bones about it," Thomas said. "We used the media many, many times. When we did the search warrant . . . we let it all hang out in there. We used Allen and Nardi's names. Once it was [filed in the court], the media would grab it, and no one could quash it. We put the names in there, absolutely. We wanted people to know about them. Hopefully someone would try to bribe them or dirty them up, and that's exactly what happened. That's when they went after Nardi."

On December 9, 1982, Jack Nardi was snared in a sting operation put together by Presser, Climaco, and the Cleveland FBI.

At the time, Jack Nardi was in desperate financial straits. He owed seven thousand dollars to cover bad checks to two Cleveland racetracks. He had a mortgage on a four-bedroom house with a pool in Boca Raton. And he had recently been indicted in Florida for grand theft, charged with conning businessmen into buying ads in a magazine that didn't exist. If he had had money, maybe he could have settled up and convinced the racetracks to drop the charges. But Nardi, a reckless gambler, was tapped out. And hanging over his head was his admission, made months earlier to Red and Jim, that he had never worked a day for the $109,800 that Teamsters Local 507 paid him from 1972 to 1978.

Nardi's mother and his uncle Nick knew that Jack had been interviewed by the Labor agents. In fact, Thomas had called Nardi's mother the spring before and asked how to reach her son. She put him off, telling him to call Nick Nardi.

Nick Nardi, head of Teamsters Local 416, the jukebox-workers outfit, admitted to the two agents that he didn't know what his nephew ever did for Presser's local. "I'm not close to my nephew," Nick Nardi said. "The only time I hear from him is when he calls and asks for money. I've never seen him around the joint council or Local 507."

Jack Nardi's wife, Terry, told the agents essentially the same thing. She and her husband had gotten married in 1976, and she said she noticed soon after that Local 507 payroll checks arrived in the mail each week. If Jack was out of town, she endorsed and deposited the checks, even though she knew he didn't work for the union. She knew better than to ask her husband questions about that arrangement or any of his other mysterious business deals.

Coming from a Teamsters family as well as a Mob-connected family, Jack Nardi should have known to zip his lip around federal agents. His relatives begged him not to testify against Presser, arguing that Jackie was too powerful and vindictive and would make it rough for Uncle Nick, who still had to deal with him on Joint Council 41.

In the fall, Jack Nardi later recalled under oath, his uncle gave him the idea that Presser might pay him if he changed his testimony or disappeared. This wasn't the first time someone tried to tamper with Nardi's testimony. By the end of November, desperate for money, Jack Nardi decided to see if he could entice Presser to bribe him for changing his grand-jury testimony. Nardi's gambling buddy in Cleveland, Sam Rapisarda, put the plan in motion. Rapisarda ran into John Joyce at Elsner's Health Club in Shaker Heights, a popular *schvitz*. He knew that Joyce, an ex–suburban police chief who liked to rub shoulders with wise guys, was now working for the Teamsters. Jackie had put Joyce in charge of the Teamster-sponsored public housing for the elderly.

"Jack Nardi wants to meet with your guy," Rapisarda told Joyce.

"What's it about?" Joyce asked.

"Jack told the grand jury about never working after Jackie hired him," Rapisarda said. "He'll deny it or get lost. But Jackie's gotta help him with some markers he's got at the track. Or maybe loan him some money."

Joyce listened carefully, then said he'd be in touch.

The next day, Joyce, Presser, and his lawyer, John Climaco, met at Jackie's Local 507 office. Joyce told them about Nardi's overture. Eager to please his boss, Joyce said he'd visit his boyhood friend Nardi and wear a concealed tape recorder to see if he could record Nardi asking for a bribe. If Nardi took the bait, Climaco would be able to destroy Nardi's credibility as a witness against Jackie in the payroll-padding investigation.

Jackie reacted angrily. "No way!" he screamed. "You could be endangering yourself. We don't know what the hell is going on. He's a liar. He's a punk."

Climaco was wary. "Jesus, I can't advise you," he told Joyce. "You might be going into something and who the hell knows." Climaco said he thought it might be a sting set up by Simmons and Thomas to trap Jackie.

Climaco and Joyce ended up telling Cleveland FBI chief Griffin that Nardi asked for a "loan" of $20,000 to change his testimony. Griffin agreed to set up the sting on Nardi. He didn't have to be told that destroying the credibility of Nardi—the Strike Force's main witness against Jackie—would help protect the FBI's top informant.

The FBI quickly dug up a body tape recorder and bought a plane ticket for agent Nelson Gordon to accompany Joyce to Florida. Less than twenty-four hours before the sting, Griffin finally told strike-force chief Steve Olah about the operation, presenting it as a *fait accompli*

360

with all the details ironed out. Olah reluctantly approved the sting.

Curiously, the day before the sting, Climaco's twenty-four-page attack on Red and Jim had landed on Margolis's desk at the Justice Department in Washington. That served as a distraction while Presser and the FBI teamed up to snare Nardi.

Down in Fort Lauderdale, FBI agent Gordon helped Joyce conceal the recorder in the small of his back. He listened in on a remote receiver as Joyce and Nardi sat in a singles' bar and talked over a couple of drinks.

Joyce, once an ambitious police officer, knew many Cleveland mobsters personally, including Jack Nardi's late father. While police chief, Joyce spent hours drinking with them at a hotel bar in Beachwood, the upper-income suburb where he ran the police department. "They'd all meet at the Sheraton," said Robert H. Abrams, deputy police chief at the time. "When we were surveilling the area, you had to reserve a parking place, with all the feds and Cleveland police intelligence guys out there watching."

To the dismay of the Beachwood police, their chief was out carousing with Big Ange Lonardo, Joe "the Hat" Lanese, and other organized-crime figures. Other law-enforcement outfits picked this up on surveillance, and soon cooperation dissolved between the Beachwood detectives and the Cleveland police intelligence unit. "John was playing both sides of the fence," says Abrams, now Beachwood's chief of police. "Monday, Wednesday, Friday we'd see him with the wise guys. On Tuesday, Thursday, Saturday, he was with the Feds. He was out hobnobbing with Marty McCann."

The Beachwood police force became so demoralized because of Joyce's behavior that nearly two dozen policemen, almost the entire force, met with the mayor and said that Joyce had to go. The mayor agreed, and Joyce left quietly, taking a job offered by Jackie. "We had enough information to make a criminal case, but we didn't want to embarrass the department," Abrams says.

In the singles' bar, Nardi felt comfortable with Joyce and didn't suspect a thing. After small talk about the weather and their families, they got down to business.

NARDI: I'll be honest with ya . . . I need $20,000 like right away. Otherwise, I'm going to blow whatever I got up, you follow me.

361

I just want a loan. I don't want it to be given to me. . . . I'll go to bat for him.

JOYCE: What do you mean go to bat?

NARDI: I'll say whatever he wants me to say. There's one thing though. If they come back and indict me, you got to pay my lawyer's fees. They may turn around and indict me.

JOYCE: On what?

NARDI: The same thing they're gonna indict Hughes, and they're going to indict G. G. [Argie] and all the rest, taking money with knowingly not working.

JOYCE: They told you that?

NARDI: . . . . That's what they told me. I don't know how true it is.

JOYCE: I'm just saying, I do know those two guys are crazy.

NARDI: I want a lawyer's fee and bail bond, that's all. I'll, I'll, I'm stand up.

JOYCE: You're willing to recant your testimony?

NARDI: Oh, absolutely.

JOYCE: Well, what are you going to say?

NARDI: Very simple, I'll say, "I told them what I had to say or they were going to send me to jail. What would you do? I'd say anything they wanted me to say, wouldn't you?" . . . . I'll say, "I was scared they were gonna turn me over to the sheriff."

Even though he had Nardi's offer, Joyce continued to probe, asking repeatedly about the actions of Simmons and Thomas while FBI agent Gordon listened nearby.

JOYCE: But did those two guys knowingly, I mean, did they come out and say that?

NARDI: Oh, they knew that I was under the impression they could turn me over . . . in five seconds.

362

Presser, Climaco, and Harold Friedman were thrilled when they learned that Jack Nardi had solicited a bribe while the FBI was listening in. Climaco shared the damaging tape with the strike-force prosecutors, confident that he had destroyed their best witness against Jackie. Climaco thought that the case should be dropped.

Red and Jim were furious. Their boss, Dave Williams, later sent a scathing memo to the Labor Department's inspector general, Robert Magee. "In a last ditch effort to stop the Presser indictment, the FBI joined in an operation with mob attorneys and organized-crime affiliate John Joyce to gather derogatory information on [Simmons and Thomas] and to neutralize key government witness John Nardi."

On December 13, Red, Jim, Steve Olah, and FBI agent Rick Lind met to discuss the Nardi sting. Olah decided that Nardi and Rapisarda should be arrested for bribery. He told the FBI to contact Joyce again, to tell him to have Nardi fly up to Cleveland to collect the $20,000. We'll arrest and try Nardi right here in Cleveland, Olah said.

If Nardi came to Ohio and was indicted for bribery, he'd be under the Justice Department's control, and they'd have more leverage to compel Nardi's testimony against Jackie. Climaco didn't like this turn of events. He felt that the strike force should drop the Presser investigation, since its main witness was now banged up.

A week later, FBI agent Lind and Olah met again to discuss Nardi's attempt to solicit a bribe. Lind said that Climaco and Joyce wouldn't continue the sting by bringing Nardi to Cleveland to pick up the $20,000.

Olah said fine. He would request a warrant charging Nardi, and the FBI would arrest him in Florida. Olah added that he wanted Simmons and Thomas to interview Nardi once he was in custody in Florida.

The FBI didn't want to cooperate in anything that might hurt Presser. Lind said that the FBI wouldn't let Red and Jim fly in the FBI plane; since it was near Christmas, the two agents probably couldn't get a commercial reservation.

Thomas walked out of the meeting. He came back a few minutes later, saying he had just made reservations.

Then Lind told them the Nardi case was not a high priority and FBI action on it might be slow.

If the Cleveland FBI was so swamped with important work, Dave

Williams asked, how did it ever find the time to put together its cross-country sting of Jack Nardi so quickly?

Well, Lind finally allowed, maybe the arrest could be made the next day. But a day later, he told the strike force that the FBI was having tremendous difficulty finding an agent in Palm Beach to arrest Nardi. Clearly, the Labor agents felt, the FBI was doing everything it could to impede their investigation into Jackie's payroll-padding scheme.

"It seemed to us at the time that they, Climaco and Presser, were controlling the case against Nardi," says Steve Canfil, a Cleveland Strike Force prosecutor who worked on the Presser investigation. "The bureau sort of had to get permission from Climaco to go ahead with it. It was a highly unusual situation."

The Nardi sting ended up backfiring on Presser. Nardi's bribe solicitation could certainly be used to impeach his testimony, but it didn't really destroy his story. He wanted money and had agreed to change his testimony for it, but in the taped conversation with Joyce, Nardi had never said that he had lied when he first admitted to taking Local 507 paychecks without working.

"We discussed it [a few days after the sting] and it didn't really seem to hurt our case," Canfil says. "On the tape, Nardi never said he was lying to us about it. He had been telling the truth and would lie for money. It didn't hurt what he told us originally."

Simmons and Thomas ended up getting hurt, however. Climaco's attacks on their integrity tarnished them with Margolis. Despite a show of support by the Cleveland Strike Force, Margolis said he didn't fully trust the agents. "Those two guys scare me," he said. He didn't insist that the Presser embezzlement case be dropped, as he had done two months earlier in officially closing the Hoover-Gorin kickback case. But Simmons and Thomas's careers were ruined in the Labor racketeering unit. How could they ever get Margolis to sign off on one of their investigations? The FBI even investigated them for unprofessional conduct, but the case went nowhere.

"As far as I know, Margolis based his opinion on the stuff Climaco had written," Canfil says. "I know that Olah trusted them. I trusted them."

† † †

Red and Jim continued to pound the pavement, driving around northern Ohio in search of friendly witnesses, Thomas at the wheel much of the time, Simmons slouched in the passenger seat, making up for the sleep he lost going to law school at night. They were becoming demoralized. They hadn't fully realized that their careers as Labor investigators were over.

They spent some days inside the office, picking page by page through bushels of subpoenaed financial records, collecting data and paper cuts. For a break, Thomas would wander over to the eighteenth-floor window and peer down through the telescope aimed at the Teamsters Local 507 hall just to see who was around and what was going on. His favorite thing to see was Harold Friedman's big blond bodyguard, a business agent named Gerry Yontek, standing guard as Friedman's girlfriend and secretary, Barbara Walden, strolled her tiny dog around the fenced Teamsters parking lot. It made Thomas laugh.

During this slow period of the investigation, Red and Jim found sustenance in the vision of actually, physically, arresting Jackie Presser.

Over the years, Jackie had defended himself to reporters and congressional committees by proclaiming that he had never been arrested, indicted, or even so much as served with a subpoena. It was a bold lie—he was convicted in Cleveland in 1947—but it was an effective rebuttal to critics who questioned why the Reagan White House climbed into bed with a racketeer. His claim about never being arrested always irritated Red and Jim, and they hoped they'd be the first ones to publicly shatter that claim.

Criminal investigators get an emotional payoff when they arrest their targets. After weeks or months or maybe years of work, an agent or detective confronts his suspect, tells him he's under arrest, and for at least the time it takes to obtain bail, the suspect's freedom is denied.

But in labor-racketeering cases, this sort of emotional payoff was rarely satisfied. The target was typically a businessman or labor official, often a community leader of some stature. Out of courtesy, prosecutors would call the target's lawyer, tell him about the indictment, and give him the option of having his client turn himself in. An arrest would be unnecessary. So for labor investigators, the end of a successful investigation was often anticlimactic, the urge for a final "Gotcha!" unsatisfied.

So in their investigative reports, Red and Jim noted that one of their informants, someone close to Jackie and his family, revealed that Jackie had told friends he owned a home in Israel that could serve as a safe haven in case he ever had to flee the government or the Mafia. It was probably another of Jackie's fish stories, but the two agents loved to hear about it. They made certain to weave this intelligence into their reports as a way of building a case that Jackie might bolt when indicted. Armed with these reports, a strike-force prosecutor could make a sales pitch to a federal magistrate to try to convince him that Presser would flee the country if indicted, and that the Labor agents would therefore need a bench warrant for his arrest.

With an arrest warrant in hand, Red and Jim would speed out to wherever Jackie happened to be at the moment, preferably some place public, after they had tipped off the newspapers. It would be a delicious moment for them to tell Jackie Presser, one of the more powerful men in the country, to put his hands behind his back, cuff him, and read him his rights.

"We really wanted to put the handcuffs on him," Thomas said. "Big ones."

26

The Marble Palace

"You got the support of all the families on the East Coast. You're gonna be the next president."

ACTING CLEVELAND BOSS PEANUTS TRONOLONE

On December 15, 1982, Jackie Presser received what he considered great news. Allen Dorfman, Roy Williams, and three of their associates were found guilty by a federal jury in Chicago of conspiring to bribe Senator Howard Cannon. Two of the biggest obstacles in Presser's path to power were now gone. Dorfman, his bane, would be out of the picture for years, unable to collar IBT vice presidents like Don Peters and persuade them to oppose Presser's programs. And Williams in all likelihood would have to step down as Teamsters president.

Dorfman was stunned by the verdict. He had expected to beat the felony charges, as he had done three times in the past. Cannon had even gotten up on the witness stand and testified on his and Williams' behalf. Williams, suffering from emphysema, was devastated. He had told Jackie he was certain he'd be acquitted.

Jackie repeatedly told his FBI handlers that if Dorfman ever talked about casino skimming and Central States kickbacks, he could put away the top Mafia leaders in Chicago and several other cities. If there was ever an opportune time for Dorfman to roll over on his Mob friends, this was it. He was sixty years old and facing fifty-five years in prison. His fortunes couldn't be much worse. Not only that, but within the next few months, Dorfman faced an extortion trial in Chicago and a kickback trial in San Francisco, and Labor Department lawyers had just seized control of his insurance firm, Amalgamated Insurance

Agency Service. The seizure cut off the $11 million a year that the Central States Pension Fund paid Dorfman to process 1.8 million health and disability claims. The Labor Department claimed that Dorfman, through his firm, had robbed the pension fund of at least $5 million.

His immediate problem was a February 10 sentencing hearing before federal district judge Prentice Marshall. If the judge gave him prison time—a virtual certainty given Dorfman's record and reputation—his usefulness as a financier to the Chicago Mafia was all but at an end.

Soon, scuttlebutt floated through the underworld that Dorfman was negotiating a deal with the Justice Department, incriminating mobsters in exchange for a reduced sentence. In fact, as Jackie told the FBI, Dorfman had been dropping hints that the Chicago outfit had better use its influence to keep him out of prison or else he might become an informer.

On January 20, 1983, a blustery cold Chicago day, Dorfman dressed for work. He pulled gray wool slacks on over black bikini underpants, donned a fashionable gray shirt, a soft white V-neck sweater, and a black herringbone sports coat. The sharp outfit complemented his silver hair and bushy black eyebrows. His legal troubles had him somewhat depressed, though his lawyers had scored a victory a few days earlier in getting the government seizure of his insurance company invalidated.

Around lunch time, Dorfman pulled on a warm camel-hair topcoat, climbed into his Cadillac, and picked up a good friend, Mob associate and bail bondsman Irving Weiner. They stopped first at a video store, where Dorfman rented a Paul Newman movie, *The Verdict*. Then they parked in the lot behind the Hyatt Hotel in Lincolnwood, a northwest Chicago suburb, within clear sight of a busy intersection. As Dorfman crossed the lot on his way to the hotel's restaurant, two men slipped up behind him. "Hey, this is a stickup!" one said.

Irv Weiner later said that he heard a slight pop, "what sounded like a beer can being opened." He turned, saw the gunmen, then ran behind a car as several more pops sounded. Eight rounds from a silencer-equipped .22-caliber semiautomatic handgun struck Dorfman in the head at close range. Allen Dorfman had just kept thirty years of Mob secrets the hard way.

According to FBI informants, wiretaps, and surveillance, Joey Auippa, the Chicago boss, had personally approved the murder. FBI director William Webster suggested that Dorfman had been assassinated to prevent him from becoming an informant. But Dorfman's longtime lawyer, Harvey Silets, said, "The idea that he would capitulate or throw in the towel is anathema, impossible." The U.S. Attorney for northern Illinois, Dan K. Webb, admitted, "Dorfman was not cooperating with us at all."

When Jackie learned of the Dorfman hit later that day, he blanched in fear. "He was very concerned that Chicago was so crazy that they'd whack a guy in broad daylight," an FBI agent said. If the outfit was willing to stage a public hit behind a busy hotel during lunch hour, what would stop it from carrying out its threats to kill Jackie for being a stool pigeon?

Shortly after Williams was sentenced on February 10, he was blasted by Senator Orrin Hatch, Republican from Utah and chairman of the Senate Labor Committee. Williams brought "disgrace and shame" on the labor movement and should resign immediately, thundered Hatch, one of organized labor's strongest foes. Williams should step down voluntarily or be forced out by the Teamsters executive board at its next meeting on April 19, he continued. As it so happened, Williams did resign on April 20, but it had nothing to do with Hatch. He stepped down as part of an agreement to stay out of prison while he appealed his conviction.

Though Jackie had talked for years about running for Teamsters president and had even brought a stash of campaign supplies to the 1981 IBT convention, it was Williams's conviction that kicked Jackie's campaign into high gear. His secret campaign network, placed inside the union bureaucracy after Williams became president in June 1981, now proved invaluable. Wallace Clements, the Southern coordinator for Teamsters DRIVE, provided intelligence from across the country about which state and local officers supported him. Duke Zeller, the union spokesman, kept tabs on who inside the International's headquarters sided with Jackie. Paul Locigno and others built bridges of support from Presser to Capitol Hill. By the time Williams was convicted, Jackie had five solid supporters among the seventeen voters on the board: Weldon Mathis from Atlanta, Edward Lawson from Vancouver, Canada; Arnie Weinmeister of Seattle; Bobby Holmes out of Detroit; and Jesse Carr of Alaska. Even with his own vote, Jackie still fell three votes short of a majority. The leading candidate was Ray Schoessling, a longtime power in the Chicago-area Teamsters who had worked since 1981 as IBT secretary-treasurer, the number-two position in the union. The swing bloc—five votes—was controlled by Joe Trerotola of New York, head of the Eastern Conference. Jackie had to sway Joe T.

Like Jackie's father, Joe T had been baptized in the labor movement in the bloody thirties. For decades thereafter, he coexisted in particular with New York's Genovese family, run lately by Fat Tony Salerno. To stay alive and stay in office, Joe T let mobsters operating as Teamsters officials, hoodlums such as Harry Davidoff and Patsy Crapanzano, have the run of the New York City joint council.

"It's like the three monkeys: hear, speak, and see no evil," said a high-ranking Teamsters official. "Joe T's the old school, just like Jackie's father. If you didn't know he was a teamster in New York, you'd think he was one of the warmest guys. He's at peace with himself. Very smart. Never pushed his authority around. You'd never think he has political power, and he's been sitting there for years. The guy is a class act. He is a warm, compassionate guy. He's a family man. He goes to church every day, him and his wife. He is not inherently an evil person."

Jackie knew he had to satisfy two special-interest groups—the Mafia and the federal government—to be elected and survive as general president of the Teamsters. "I'm not going to take the job unless I get the blessing from the government and the boys," he confided to a close friend. Once again, he stepped out on a high wire stretched between the two forces that could destroy him.

On February 4, Jackie met with Joe T and asked for his support. At the time, Trerotola had a firm grip on Teamsters locals in New England, New York, New Jersey, Delaware, and Pennsylvania, having just squelched a takeover attempt by vice president Sammy Provenzano of New Jersey.

Jackie beams after being picked as a senior adviser to the Reagan transition team, December 1980. *(UPI/Bettmann Newsphotos)*

Presidential candidate Ronald Reagan with Jackie in September 1980. Reagan agrees to reverse himself and oppose trucking deregulation in return for Teamsters support. *(Teamsters)*

Jackie's son Gary, early 1980s.

At his coming-out party as the Teamsters president, Jackie talks with Senator Robert Dole and greets Senator Orrin Hatch, April 1983.

George Bush thanks Jackie for the Teamsters' endorsement of Reagan, 1984.

(UPI/Bettmann Newsphotos)

Jackie and his fifth
wife, the former
Cynthia Jarabek.

Teamster General Counsel John Climaco, the legal equivalent of a street fighter.
(CSU Press Archives)

Fat Tony Salerno, with cigar, with his associates outside his card shop. Vincent "Fish" Cafaro, far right, is now a government witness against the Mob. *(Courtesy of FBI)*

Milton "Maishe" Rockman and Fat Tony Salerno run into Roy Cohn outside his law office, 1984. Maishe and Fat Tony used Cohn's office to discuss Mob business since Rockman, under bail restrictions in the Kansas City skim case, couldn't leave Ohio except to see a lawyer. *(Courtesy of FBI)*

Nick Civella, the Kansas City Mob boss who controlled Teamsters president Roy Williams. *(Wide World Photos)*

Big Ange Lonardo the day he is sentenced to life in prison for conspiracy to traffic in drugs. He decides to become an FBI informer. *(AP/Mark Duncan)*

Harold Friedman (32218) and Tony Hughes (32217), arraigned on embezzlement charges, 1986.

Jackie's uncle Allen Friedman, after testifying against
boyhood friend and Teamsters Vice President Harold
Friedman, 1988. *(UPI/Bettmann Newsphotos)*

The current Teamsters president, William J. McCarthy,
a throwback to the old days.

George "Red" Simmons and James Thomas, Labor investigators who pursued Jackie, hurting their careers in the process.

Jackie, the pontifex maximus in a cream-colored sport coat, is carried into the 1986 Teamsters convention in Las Vegas. *(James Hamilton)*

"You've got my backing," Joe T promised Jackie. Then the old-timer mentioned two of the new vice presidents in his area, Walter Shea and John Cleveland. "Don't worry," he reassured Jackie, "they do what they're told."

The FBI—at least at the field-office level—had encouraged him to run for high office many times, Jackie said. This wasn't surprising, since it would make Jackie, already a great mole inside organized crime, the top labor-racketeering source in the country. With the blessing of the FBI, Jackie knew that he could risk making enemies as he climbed the ranks, reassured that the bureau's vast intelligence network of sources, wiretaps, and agents would alert him to and protect him from assassination attempts. Just as important, the FBI wouldn't be trying to nail him every time he jaywalked. "Jackie thought he'd be the first president to go through and not get indicted," a friend said. "The job wouldn't be the electric chair."

By the spring, John "Peanuts" Tronolone, a hard-of-hearing old man who ran a Miami travel agency, took over as acting boss of the Cleveland family. Boss Jack White and his crew were in prison for their roles in the bombing murder of rival gangster Danny Greene. Big Ange Lonardo had recently been convicted of conspiring to traffic in cocaine and had been sentenced to 105 years in prison. Peanuts, the only ranking member left, became the de facto Cleveland boss. Since he lived in Miami, the new boss spent more time on airplanes between the two cities than tending to the crime family's dwindling business.

Even though Maishe Rockman and his brother-in-law Big Ange Lonardo had journeyed to New York and Chicago months earlier to line up support for Jackie, some last-minute lobbying was needed after Williams's conviction. In the first week of April, Jackie had an unsettling meeting with his old friend, Maishe Rockman. Maishe walked in accompanied by Tronolone, which upset Jackie. He never wanted to be seen with made members; that was why he, like his father before him, used Maishe as his intermediary.

"Roy Williams is finished," Tronolone told Jackie. "You got the support of all the families on the East Coast. You're gonna be the next president."

Jackie showed gratitude and respect but didn't like this turn of events.

"There's gonna be some requests from the families, and you're gonna have to do some favors," Tronolone said. "All requests will come through me. I know Maishe used to screen 'em for you. Now that you're gonna be president, you have to deal with a family guy about family business." He said that Fat Tony Salerno would have final approval on all deals.

Tronolone said that if he was faced with an emergency, Jackie could reach him by telephoning Peter Pan Travel in Miami and leaving a message under the code name Pasquale.

Jackie did his own lobbying, too, promising favors to Teamsters delegates to line up their votes. "I seen him promise the same job to four or five guys," said Tony Hughes, who was at his side much of the time. "Once he's president, what are they gonna do, complain? Who's gonna go against him when he's the man?"

By April 19, with Joe T on his side, Jackie had ten solid supporters. Before the election in Scottsdale, Jackie came out of a meeting and told reporters, "I have the votes. Yes, I think I'm going to win. The Teamsters executive board will support me, and we are going to change the image of our union. The change is long overdue." His rival, Schoessling, knew that he had lost and withdrew. To present a unanimous front to the rank and file, everybody agreed that night to vote for Jackie—except one vice president. Joe Morgan was the holdout. The night before the executive board meeting at the La Posada Resort Hotel in Scottsdale, Joe T asked Morgan to take a walk with him. The next morning in the hotel coffee shop, Morgan spotted Jackie, shook his hand, and said, "I'm going to vote for you."

On April 21, 1983, Jackie Presser was unanimously elected general president of the International Brotherhood of Teamsters, the largest labor union in the United States. "I will be accessible and will run an open, honest administration," he intoned. "I ask that you judge me accordingly, by my performance and my actions. I intend to lead in a new way, a new direction, for a new day for the International Brotherhood of Teamsters."

Jackie didn't make a gesture of support or say thanks to outgoing president Williams. In fact, Jackie didn't once mention his name. The board did entertain a motion to spend members' dues to pay Williams's legal fees in the Cannon bribery case—$534,467. The motion passed unanimously.

Otherwise, everybody was happy. The Mafia believed that they

372

had their agent in place, ready to dish out lucrative favors. The FBI believed it had its top organized-crime source in place, a fat, 5'9" walking, talking human microphone. Jackie made sure not to let either side think otherwise.

Back in Washington a few days later, President Reagan called and pledged to work closely with Jackie and the Teamsters. Presser's new governmental-affairs director, Paul Locigno, and the staff put together a big party for Jackie. As befitted Jackie's powerful new post, the party attracted the Washington elite, including Reagan chief of staff James Baker, Vice President George Bush, Senate Republican leader Robert Dole, and a cast of lesser lights. "You ever think you'd be standing here?" asked Timothy F. Hagan, an elected official from Cleveland. "Hell, no," Jackie replied. Unsolicited, he said, "I'm going to clean up this damn union."

FBI director William Webster, cautious and politically sensitive, closed out Jackie as a high-level FBI snitch the day after he was elected Teamsters president. Webster didn't want the bureau to be put in a position where anyone could misconstrue the FBI as secretly running the Teamsters union. A former federal judge who aspired to the U.S. Supreme Court, Webster insisted on being addressed as "Judge" instead of "Director," which irked many of the agents.

Webster was also aware of an even stickier problem—Jackie's tight White House ties. He was meeting and dealing with Meese, Bush, Rollins, Donovan, and others. If they continued to use Jackie as a source, the FBI would, in effect, be bugging the White House. Not that he would, but Jackie could put the FBI in a very uncomfortable position by bringing back dirt from the White House.

In closing out Jackie as a registered informant, his contact agent, Robert Friedrick, was told to accept any new information ALPRO offered on his own initiative and to question him about it, but Presser was not to be "tasked"—directed by Friedrick to seek information needed for other active investigations. At least that is what the orders were on paper. But in fact, as Presser's FBI files show, the FBI continued to task him, relaying requests for information from Los Angeles and other regional offices to Friedrick, who then went out to question Presser.

This supposed hands-off arrangement was intended to be temporary. The FBI's number-two man, Oliver "Buck" Revell, and many
others in the bureau were pleased with Jackie's new position. What a
tremendous spot for a top-echelon informant—inside the nation's most
corrupt union, with its ties to major crime families, elected officials, big
banks, Fortune 500 companies, and a host of other powers. On May
10, Revell wrote a five-page memo to Webster, asking that ALPRO be
reopened as an informant but under new stricter instructions that
would enable the FBI to skirt possible political quagmires. "ALPRO's
relationship with the bureau and his trusted position with the LCN and
its associates presents the FBI an unparalleled opportunity to have a
meaningful impact upon organized crime's significant control of the
IBT," Revell insisted. He proposed that Jackie be given twelve rules,
including:

- His assistance was voluntary and wouldn't keep him from being
  arrested for crimes except those authorized in advance;
- He couldn't take part in any violence; if he learned of plans to
  commit violent acts, he had to discourage them and notify
  contact agent Friedrick;
- The bureau wouldn't accept information about legitimate political activities (meaning he'd have to keep his Communist-con-
  spiracy plots involving TDU dissidents to himself);
- And the FBI wouldn't direct his legitimate union activities.

Within days of Revell's May 10 memo, the bureau learned that
Jackie had been subpoenaed to testify before the Senate Labor Committee. It was a dangerous predicament for a top Mafia mole. Though
it was unlikely that a senator would ask him flat-out if he were an
informant, the FBI couldn't be certain. Senator Hatch, though a
Presser sympathizer, was unpredictable. Senator Sam Nunn, the
Georgia Democrat, had been a vociferous, effective Teamster critic for
years. And Senator Howard Metzenbaum, Jackie believed, was his
sworn enemy. Jackie told the FBI he knew how he'd handle the question. Simply say, "No, I'm not." Deny it, as he had done many times
before.

Everyone in the FBI chain of command seemed to think that was
the right way to solve Jackie's dilemma. Everyone except the director.

Webster alerted Revell, James Moody, all the way down to Friedrick that if Jackie perjured himself at the committee hearing, Webster would tell the congressmen. He would do it privately, in executive session to protect Presser. But Webster said he couldn't have him lying to a branch of the government. Lower-level supervisors and agents thought Webster's position would endanger ALPRO. Then, instead of a handful of FBI agents aware that Jackie was a bureau informant, an entire Senate committee would know. FBI agents had griped for years about leaks of sensitive information from Capitol Hill. This new development was certain to put Presser at risk.

Webster didn't sign Revell's five-page memo, which kept Jackie off the informant list. Though Jackie had a code name and a contact agent, he could split hairs honestly and tell the Senate Labor Committee he wasn't an FBI informant.

Other Washington honchos also proceeded cautiously in their relationships with Jackie. For example, White House counsel Fred F. Fielding, worried about damaging Reagan's reputation, advised against sending Jackie an invitation to a White House state dinner while Jackie was still under investigation in Cleveland. But Fielding's advice to keep Jackie at arm's length was ignored. "Teamsters are always under investigation," a top Reagan aide told him. Even so, Presser backed out of a June 7 state dinner at the last minute, claiming that he had to be in Chicago that day to testify at a Senate Labor Committee hearing. He knew there'd be other White House invitations.

After several weeks, Presser had his team in place. It was a mixed bag of appointments. Tony Hughes was named an organizer for the International, which meant a $50,000-a-year pay raise. John Climaco took over as Teamsters general counsel, boosting his law firm's fortunes. Jackie appointed ex–loan shark Carmen Parise as national head of the newspaper drivers' division. Parise was the same man Jackie had described to his FBI handlers three years earlier as a Mob associate who took kickbacks from Cleveland *Plain Dealer* managers. Jackie's bodyguard and frequent companion was Local 507 business agent Bobby Kavalec, ex-president of an outlaw biker club. And Jackie made John Joyce the director of the Teamsters HUD-financed housing projects. Joyce, the ex–police chief who associated with wise guys, later caused a ruckus when he said that he was going to put out a contract on a HUD official who had turned down twelve of Joyce's requests for HUD financing. Joyce said he was joking, but the official, Robert Wilden, HUD director of elderly housing, felt threatened, and an internal investigation was launched.

As a symbol of his new open leadership, Jackie agreed to testify before the Senate Labor Committee on June 7, making him the first Teamsters president in a quarter of a century to answer questions from a congressional committee. The committee was holding hearings on the proposed Labor Management Racketeering Act of 1983, supported strongly by Senator Sam Nunn, Labor Committee chairman Hatch, and Senator Edward M. Kennedy. The act required a union official to leave office for ten years the minute he was convicted of racketeering or a crime involving a labor union, rather than being able to collect a salary while his appeal dragged on. The Teamsters, alone among big unions, publicly attacked the bill, even though Reagan supported it. Jackie argued that the act would create a double standard unfair to union officials. Why should a union official lose his job when the corporate type who conspired or kicked back wasn't forced to leave his company?

Lane Kirkland, AFL-CIO president, strongly supported the act, disagreeing sharply with Jackie's philosophy of the union as a business. Without referring to Presser, Kirkland remarked, "Union office is a calling, not a business. We feel that union officers have to be held to the highest standards of conduct, not just the standards of the market-place."

One reason Jackie may have agreed to testify was that he was acquainted with committee chairman Hatch. Through Ohio DRIVE, Presser gave $1,500 to Hatch in September 1981, making the Utah senator one of only two candidates outside the state to receive Ohio DRIVE money that year.

Just before the hearing, a labor-committee lawyer came in and asked Presser, sitting in a waiting room, "Do you mind if we swear you in? We'd like to swear you in."

Climaco objected, but Jackie said OK. Climaco was upset and suspected that a trap was being laid. They don't have to have sworn testimony, Climaco insisted. Cancel your appearance. Jackie told Climaco to calm down and forget about it. As it turned out, Climaco's instincts were right.

376

Jackie skillfully handled the senators' questions, deflecting the tough ones and scoring points with the easy ones. Then Senator Nunn executed a slick carom shot that preempted one of Jackie's potential defenses in the embezzlement case unfolding in Cleveland.

NUNN: Mr. Presser, a review of the annual reports for the years 1971 through 1981 indicated that you occupied a position of either secretary-treasurer or treasurer of Local 507 during that time, is that correct?

PRESSER: Yes.

NUNN: Was it accurate to say that your salary varied from between $70,000 to $220,000 a year in that ten-year period?

PRESSER: Yes.

NUNN: Your average salary was about $140,000?

PRESSER: Yes sir.

NUNN: According to the annual report of Local 507, the local collected approximately $1.5 million in dues during 1982. Is that approximately correct?

PRESSER: I really cannot pull the figure out of the air, but I would presume you must be right.

NUNN: According to my calculations, that would mean that approximately fifteen cents of every dollar paid by union members constituted your annual salary, is that correct?

PRESSER: According to that figure, yes sir.

NUNN: Do you feel you deserve that large a salary as an officer in the 507 local?

PRESSER: Yes.

NUNN: What did you do for that salary?

PRESSER: I founded the union, I built the union, I implemented its programs, instituted health and welfare pension programs. I negotiated contracts for holidays, vacations, sick pay. I did all the things that were required to establish retirement clubs, Christmas parties, stewards' affairs, blood banks, newspaper editions, housing, food.

NUNN: So you were very much involved in the management of all the facets and details of that local, is that right?

PRESSER: I ran that local, yes.

NUNN: During that time frame?

PRESSER: Most of the time.

NUNN: How many hours a week did you spend, approximately?

PRESSER: I really could not tell you, Senator. Sometimes I worked seven days a week, sometimes I work five. Sometimes I get to work at six o'clock in the morning, and I do not go home until nine or ten o'clock at night. It is not strange to find me there on a Saturday or a Sunday. As a matter of fact, there is a standing order that my office opens at seven or seven-fifteen and closes at eight or eight-thirty every night.

NUNN: So Jackie Presser was very much involved in that union, in that local's activity, and you did spend an enormous amount of time and were involved in its activities and earned your salary, is that what you are saying?

PRESSER: Yes sir.

NUNN: . . . Did you sign the checks?

PRESSER: Yes. I used a facsimile because I am on the road a lot. So I do not sign all the checks. We do have a facsimile in the office.

NUNN: Did you review them when you got back?

PRESSER: Yes.

NUNN: You kept up with the finances?

PRESSER: Yes.

After the hearing, Climaco was upset. Nunn had smoothly and firmly locked Jackie into saying, under oath, that he had signed checks and knew all about Local 507 finances. Jackie, if indicted, couldn't claim he knew nothing about the paychecks of Jack Nardi and Allen Friedman, thus giving up a possible defense strategy. The questions, crafted by Nunn aide John Sopko, a former Cleveland Strike Force attorney, had been carefully choreographed. "We knew what the hell was going on and what Jackie Presser was saying," Sopko said. "We read the newspapers and put it together."

Meanwhile, Jackie was riding high. He got good press reviews simply for testifying and answering all the questions. But later, Steve Jigger, the Cleveland Strike Force attorney, used Presser's answers to Nunn's questions as ammunition in a memo asking his bosses to prosecute Presser.

To put a high gloss on his image as a progressive new labor leader, Jackie hired Robert Gray of Gray and Company, the polished $350-an-hour lobbyist who was friends with Senator Paul Laxalt, CIA director William Casey, and many of the Reagan cabinet. Gray quickly collared a brace of Washington power brokers for a June 20th coming-out party for Jackie at the plush Georgetown Club. Two Clevelanders, Paul Locigno, the newly promoted Teamsters governmental-affairs director, and Paul Russo, undersecretary of labor, hosted the event. A steady procession of black limousines dropped off the Republican elite at the private club—Secretary of Labor Raymond Donovan, Ed Meese, former Reagan adviser Lyn Nofziger, Representative Jack Kemp, Senators Hatch, Robert Dole, and Ted Stevens, former senator Robert Taft, and thirty or so lesser lawmakers and lobbyists. The Teamsters under Presser was firmly back in the Reagan camp. "We didn't have to convince Jackie," said one participant. "He's a Reagan lover."

The Reagan administration, champion of less government and the free market, paid Presser back. It sidetracked a bill that would have eliminated the ICC and the last traces of federal regulation in trucking. A deal had been cut between the White House and the union: the bill stalled on Reagan's desk, and the Teamsters supported him for reelection.

On July 14, Uncle Allen popped up and stung Jackie again. Allen Friedman didn't demand money to pay off his gambling markers or to buy a restaurant. On that day, Friedman was indicted for taking Local

507 paychecks without working, and a trial was set for September. Several weeks later, he gave a candid on-camera interview to reporter Brian Ross of NBC in which he said, "Jackie Presser should have been in jail dozens of times, going back thirty years. He thinks I won't testify against him. . . . But I don't like the things he's done, double-crossing me, doing what he's doing to the working people."

White House counsel Fielding picked up the news of the indictment and Friedman's indiscreet remarks on network television. He warned Meese, Chief of Staff James Baker, and Deputy Chief of Staff Michael K. Deaver to quit inviting Jackie to state dinners. Keep him at arm's length, Fielding advised.

This time, the White House staff seemed to heed the warning. They pulled back an invitation, already in the works, for Jackie to attend a White House dinner. Jackie was extremely annoyed. Reagan political aides such as Edward J. Rollins made sure to smooth Jackie's ruffled feathers; Reagan needed the endorsement of the Teamsters for the 1984 campaign. "Presser is key for us," one official remarked at the time. "Do you just walk away from a union president who has such a tremendous political network, or do you stand by your friends?"

On September 28, 1983, Allen Friedman was convicted by a jury of embezzling $165,000 from Local 507 by taking paychecks without working. Now the Cleveland Strike Force's scenario was plain for all to see: federal prosecutors would use Friedman and Jack Nardi to make a case against Jackie.

With his uncle convicted and threatening to testify against him, Jackie was afraid the strike force was going to nail him. On September 30, after talking to Friedrick, Jackie decided to take a huge, irrevocable, risky step, one he had feared he might have to take one day. He decided to call in his markers with the bureau, to use the catastrophic insurance policy he had funded with eleven years of providing intelligence about the underworld.

Tell the Justice Department honchos about all the outfit guys I put away, Jackie said, and ask them to please give me a break.

Buck Revell wanted to help Jackie, considering him too valuable a source to abandon. Furthermore, nothing in the Allen Friedman embezzlement case suggested that Jackie had personally enriched himself from the no-show union employees. Revell wrote a lengthy memo to the director, giving him background on Jackie and listing his impressive accomplishments as the FBI's premier labor-rackets informant and key provider of probable cause for crucial court-approved wiretaps.

The Justice Department, Revell wrote, has a strong embezzlement case against Presser based on an investigation by Labor Department agents. The FBI didn't handle this investigation because the Cleveland FBI field office, when asked, repeatedly told the Cleveland Strike Force they had no valid allegations against Presser. However "it was common knowledge in the Cleveland area that numerous individuals were employed by Presser as no-shows. Consequently, the strike force initiated its own investigation."

Revell went on. Three men had been identified as no-show employees of Presser's Local 507—Jack Nardi, Allen Friedman, and Tony Hughes. "It should be noted that Hughes is CV 3963-TE. And it was through this individual that ALPRO was developed."

Then the bureau's number-two man made his pitch. "ALPRO has been a quality informant for the FBI for a number of years. Initially ALPRO provided information to the bureau through CV 3963-TE, the individual mentioned above." Revell then listed the instances in which Jackie had helped the FBI in important cases: conviction of Vito Mango, president of Truck Drivers Local 413; conviction of Mob associate Skippy Felice, secretary-treasurer of Beverage Drivers Local 293 and Teamsters Industrial Workers Local 73; probable-cause informant for a wiretap that "ultimately led to the indictments and convictions of five LCN figures and eleven associates in Cleveland, Ohio"; wiretap informant several times in the Pendorf case that had convicted Allen Dorfman, Joey "the Clown" Lombardo, and Teamsters ex-president Roy Williams; wiretap informant in the ongoing Strawman investigation of Las Vegas casino skimming; and providing information that "led to the conviction of a major IBT labor racketeer in San Francisco."

Those were the highlights, Revell wrote. "ALPRO has provided information concerning LCN figures, associates, and labor racketeers primarily in Chicago, Kansas City, Las Vegas, Los Angeles, Detroit, Cleveland, and the New York City metropolitan area." Revell would later say, "Without [Presser's] information, I doubt that we would have had a number of the cases that I have cited."

In the memo, Revell recommended that the FBI ask Stephen S. Trott, head of the Justice Department's criminal division, to halt

Presser's indictment since Jackie had helped the bureau tremendously and would continue to do so.

Revell was thorough in his memo to Webster, and he added a caveat. If the indictment against Presser was dropped, "congressional hearings might be held" to make sure politics didn't enter into the decision. FBI and Justice Department supervisors would have to tell the truth if subpoenaed, he added. To head off such a breach of Presser's security, the FBI could advise the committee members of Presser's cooperation in a secret executive session. The danger, of course, was that many more people would know of Presser's hush-hush activities, increasing the possibility of leaks. Revell didn't have to mention that congressional hearings probing whether the FBI had pressured the Justice Department for a big favor for a top informant would be controversial and would possibly create unflattering headlines during Webster's watch.

Before he sent the memo to Director Webster, Revell discussed the top-secret matter with Steve Trott, the number-four man at Justice. According to an internal FBI memo, Trott told Revell that the Justice Department would give Jackie a break—whatever the FBI wanted. Trott added that he thought the bureau would have to explain the maneuver to the Labor Department's inspector general, J. Brian Hyland, as well as the supervisor and agents on the Presser case.

Revell attached the news from Trott to his long memo to the director. He also sent a cover note: "Judge, please review and let's discuss in private. Buck."

Webster certainly recognized the value and necessity of in-place informants like Jackie Presser and was never shy about employing them. "The informant is the, with a capital T, the most effective tool in law enforcement today—state, local, or federal," Webster said in a 1978 speech. "We must accept that fact and deal with it in a straightforward way."

Webster decided to let Presser's investigation proceed without FBI intervention. Perhaps he was thinking of Revell's warning about the political fallout that could result from what would certainly be a high-profile decision not to indict Presser. "He wanted to be a Supreme Court justice," complained an FBI supervisor familiar with the decision. "He wouldn't make a decision, afraid it would blow up in his face." Perhaps he felt that just because Presser was a valuable source didn't give him the right to break the law.

As a result, the Presser embezzlement case continued, and Bob Friedrick got even more frustrated. His superiors kept telling him to assure Jackie that the ghost-employee case was going to go away.

In October, less than six months after Jackie promised to take the Teamsters in a "progressive new direction," he gave the blessing of his high office to a gang of Teamster officials who trampled over police to attack a meeting of union dissidents in Detroit.

The 1983 assault was the work of BLAST (Brotherhood of Loyal Americans and Strong Teamsters), a group of a couple of dozen Ohio Teamsters funded by Presser to travel to the 1981 IBT convention in Las Vegas. Jackie said the Ohio Conference of Teamsters sent the BLAST crew to Las Vegas as part of an "educational" program.

Outside the convention hall, the BLAST members harassed and intimidated TDU leafleteers, snatching flyers and tearing them up. One key BLAST member was Jim Reese, of Warren, Ohio, a former TDU member. Reese became national leader of BLAST, capitalizing on his experience inside TDU by echoing Jackie's favorite theme. "I was one of the misguided Teamsters that TDU uses to further their own goal in socialism," Reese said in the August 1983 *Rank-and-File Defender*, a BLAST tabloid. "They believe in a communist form of government and want to use the finances and resources of our union for their own goal of socialism."

On October 15, 1983, TDU held its eighth annual rank and file convention in a Hilton Hotel in Romulus, Michigan, just outside Detroit. Security was tight. A few weeks earlier, BLAST members had bragged at their shops and loading docks that they were going to break up the TDU convention. Learning of this, Ken Paff and the TDU staff hired extra police to insure peace for the two-day program.

Early that morning in Cleveland, Dayton, Youngstown, and Toledo, Ohio, and Flint, Michigan, BLAST members met at their union halls, then climbed aboard rented buses to travel to Romulus. The group included at least two presidents of Teamsters locals, a vice president, two secretary-treasurers, three union trustees, an organizer, and about a dozen business agents. Some brought six-packs of beer to guzzle during the four-hour bus ride. After arriving at the Romulus Ramada Inn just before ten o'clock that morning, about 150 pent-up Ohio BLAST members poured out of the buses, formed columns, and marched to the nearby Hilton Hotel. They were joined by some Detroit BLAST members who had arrived earlier in their own cars. They carried signs saying "TDU doesn't speak for Teamsters" and "TDU funded by employers."

The picketing, which lasted ten minutes, was a cover for a well-executed attack on the Hilton Hotel where the dissidents were staying. First, a scouting party of four BLAST leaders tried to get past hotel security to find the TDU meeting room. But a private security guard, a Romulus police sergeant, and two hotel managers refused to let them in, saying the hotel was reserved for registered guests only. About seventy BLAST demonstrators broke ranks and pushed up to the glass double doors, screaming and shouting, demanding to be let in. Inside, Ken Paff and the TDU leaders, not wanting to confront the mob and start a riot, told their followers to go to their hotel rooms until police defused the situation.

Moments later, BLAST demonstrators rushed the doors, smashed through, and knocked aside the four men, including the police officer Sergeant Ray Van Poelvoorde. They tore at his holstered service revolver, pulled off his keys, and snatched his hat and threw it like a Frisbee. BLAST leader Reese rushed in, spotted Paff in a tangle on the floor, and got in a few good kicks. The BLAST crews ran into the ballroom and gleefully tore down TDU's banners. Reese took the stage, grabbed the microphone, and told the 160 or so BLAST demonstrators milling about, "The motion is to abolish TDU! All in favor . . ." The room erupted. "Aye!"

It was only 10:15 A.M., and the BLAST guys were eager for a fight. But with no dissidents to confront and the police certain to arrive any minute, their leaders herded them back outside. Cheering, laughing, disappointed at their easy victory, the Teamster wrecking crews got on the buses for the return trip. One carried a captured TDU banner, a trophy of war, and later hung it on a wall back at BLAST headquarters in Ohio.

Presser immediately got a full report on the assault. Though he usually informed the FBI of the slightest, sometimes dubious, indiscretions of Teamster officials and mobsters, he didn't mention this well-planned attack, which was not only a state crime, but a violation of federal labor laws that say that union members have the right to assemble and discuss their views without intimidation.

One of Jackie's minions provided him with photographs of the fracas. At a Joint Council 41 executive board meeting on October 31, Jackie—who had promised Congress an enlightened New Day for the Teamsters—gave the BLAST goon squads his blessing.

> I know all about that BLAST program taking place in Michigan. I must have gotten a hundred calls. I know exactly what happened there. I was pleased to see that there are Teamsters that want to stop all that crap, but I want to say something to all of you that I think is very dramatic, OK?
>
> The thing that affected me the most about last Sunday in Detroit was that there were a lot of guys there—I got the pictures of who was there—I could have imagined a lot of stronger, tougher guys going there, tough truck drivers—but I was looking through the pictures, and you know who was in the front line of a real wild fight with state highway patrolmen and police there? The secretary-treasurer of our joint council, Bill Evans, who had two heart attacks. I wouldn't have let him go there in a hundred years.
>
> Bill, I've got to tell you, you're a hell of a guy to take it on yourself. I would have been there, but I'm not you. He was screaming and fighting and shoving and pushing and swinging like the rest of them, so you know, when the chips are down, that's where it's all at. . . . I'm going to tell you something. We should be doing more of that. I'm going to tell you. I'm not going to let up on these people.

It's hard to believe that Jackie's law-and-order friends at the White House would have approved of this response.

Copies of Jackie's endorsement of the BLAST raid were sent to every local in Ohio, the idea being to let the rank and file know it was useless to criticize their union. The BLAST raid intimidated unhappy teamsters, keeping them from speaking out or joining TDU. "It hurts you," said TDU's Paff. "People don't come out. They're scared." And Teamsters honchos got what they wanted—members too afraid to try to take back their locals from corrupt officers. With the violence endorsed by the Teamsters' all-powerful president, it seemed hopeless to even try.

Several weeks after Jackie gave the BLAST crews his imprimatur, they disrupted another TDU meeting and beat up several dissidents.

Jackie had a tough November. On the eighth, he underwent a triple-coronary-bypass operation at Cleveland Clinic. As usual, he was told to quit smoking and lose weight if he wanted to stay alive. The next day, there was a commotion in the hallway outside his room. Carmen Presser had come to visit her estranged husband, but the hospital staff wouldn't let her in. She began to yell that she had a right to see her own husband.

"I had been really angry with Jackie and was wishing he would die," Carmen recalls. "I went in and saw him and felt such pity for him. I got down on my knees, and I thanked God that he didn't die. I never wished him dead again. I went to sleep that night. I had a dream. During the dream, the Lord came and touched my hands, and when he touched my hands there was a feeling of intense love for God. After that I was saved. I woke up and said, 'Jesus lives.' " She prayed for Jackie after that.

The FBI was also worried about his welfare. On November 17, criminal-division supervisor Sean McWeeney wrote to Buck Revell, telling him that Jackie gave them permission to tell the Labor Department's inspector general that he was an informant whose intelligence had helped crack several important labor-racketeering cases. McWeeney wanted to know how to proceed. On November 20, Webster said to go ahead and tell Labor Department inspector general Hyland about Presser and the strike force but to make it clear that the FBI wasn't recommending or requesting that Presser be given a break in his embezzlement case.

Friedrick's supervisors didn't mention this decision to him. So when Presser kept asking him when the FBI was going to stop the two Cleveland Labor agents from hounding him, Friedrick told Jackie not to worry. The investigation was going to go away. Jackie, good at detecting a con, could hear the sincerity in the agent's voice. Friedrick was telling the truth as he knew it, believing what his supervisors were telling him.

Meanwhile, Friedrick continued to gather valuable intelligence from Jackie, who was for the first time dealing with the messengers and intermediaries of Fat Tony Salerno, Nick Civella, and other crime bosses. As president, Jackie had become privy to deals and schemes at the highest levels of the underworld.

On one occasion, Jackie heaped dirt on Los Angeles–based IBT vice president M. E. "Andy" Anderson and Mob-connected entertainment lawyer Sidney Korshak:

"About two years ago the International gave Andy $60,000 a month to organize dock workers out there," Presser informed. "He's gotten a million two so far. Out of this, Korshak got $800,000 for legal fees. Only Korshak hasn't handled any cases. Plus, they've only brought in about two hundred guys to the union. That's nothing for all that money. Andy was supposed to spend it on organizers, on literature and stuff. There was none of that."

At another of his regular meetings with his FBI handler, Jackie dumped on powerful IBT vice president Joe Morgan. "He holds a bunch of his big conferences and meetings at a Ramada Inn in Biloxi," Jackie said. "The word is Morgan's got a hidden ownership in the place." If convicted of using his union position to line his own pockets, Morgan could be stripped of his union offices and $231,821-a-year salary.

Jackie's New York Mafia handlers were concerned about his health, too. They wanted him to be fit so they could squeeze him for favors. But so far, the new Teamsters president hadn't been dishing any out; instead, he was taking news of the Mob's proposals back to the FBI. Fat Tony was heard on a wiretap complaining, "We ain't making enough money with this guy."

On March 6, 1984, union official Carmine D'Angelo met Fat Tony Salerno and his aide, Vincent "Fish" Cafaro, at the Social Club, 2244 First Avenue in New York. D'Angelo was the longtime president of Bakery Workers Local 102 in Ozone Park, Queens. Formerly a Teamster, D'Angelo had known the Pressers for years and had frequent contact with Jackie after he was elected president. In fact, Jackie sent a letter to a powerful Teamster leader in Kentucky, asking him to help "his dear friends" Carmine D'Angelo and his son Charles become honorary Kentucky Colonels.*

SALERNO: How is that guy, Jackie?

D'ANGELO: Jackie Presser? Ya know, he had open-heart surgery. He's good now.

SALERNO: He's good now?

D'ANGELO: Yeah, in fact, my president . . . [said], "Maybe you can talk to Jackie. He's raiding the AFL-CIO."

SALERNO: Yeah.

D'ANGELO: He's not raiding. The typographical union came to him, but they want to merge with him. So I called Jackie. I said, "Now Jackie, I got a disturbing phone call. I understand you're raiding." He said, "I don't raid anybody. Never did, never will."

SALERNO: Jackie's not like that.

D'ANGELO: No, he's not.

Only later did Fat Tony begin to learn what Jackie was truly like.

---

*It was treacherous having Jackie as a friend. The same day he wrote this letter, Jackie also informed the FBI that Carmine D'Angelo was the new intermediary between Joe T and the New York Mafia, replacing Joe "Stretch" Strachi, who had died.

388

27
Cover-up

"You get close to people in combat."
FBI SUPERVISOR BOB FRIEDRICK

It was a quarter to noon, June 6, 1984, at the Palma Boys Social Club, and Fat Tony Salerno was disgusted. "Did you read in the papers that Jack Presser is a stool pigeon for the government?" he asked two of his soldiers at the family's hangout in East Harlem, New York. "I think these fuckin' Chicago guys are going to knock my brains in."

Acting on the assurances of Maishe Rockman, Salerno had gone to great trouble to persuade the Chicago family that it could trust Presser to be their agent inside the Teamsters. But Robert L. Jackson and Ronald J. Ostrow, two highly skilled, seasoned reporters in the *Los Angeles Times*'s Washington bureau, changed all that on June 6. Longtime partners, they had been breaking stories on the Presser investigation as it mysteriously bounced its way around the highest levels of the FBI, the strike force, and the Labor Department. Jackson and Ostrow had developed tremendous Justice Department sources over the years. Now these sources confirmed that Jackie Presser was an FBI informant, despite a newspaper retraction of the same story two years earlier. This fact was significant; it suggested why the Cleveland Strike Force was having such a hard time bringing its case against Jackie. Their exclusive read in part:

> Teamsters union president Jackie Presser, the target of a federal
> corruption investigation in Cleveland, has been an informer for

389

the FBI since the 1970s, according to current and former federal law enforcement officials.

Presser's cooperation with the FBI, considered rare for a high-ranking official of the scandal-plagued union, is believed to have complicated a Justice Department decision on whether to seek his indictment by a grand jury.

That decision was considered sensitive because Presser has been virtually alone among major labor leaders in his political support for President Reagan.

The news electrified the Mob and the Teamsters Union. Newspapers all over the country picked up the story from the *Times*'s wire service and ran it prominently.

Sitting at a card table in the clean, bare storefront, Salerno, clenching his ever-present cigar, continued his tirade, which was picked up on a court-approved wiretap.

"The Teamsters said that [Presser was a snitch] in 1970, for God's sake," he said. "Now, again." How could Presser do this to him? Fat Tony asked his respectful audience—soldiers Dougie Rago, sixty-two, and Louis J. Rotondo, seventy-two. Fat Tony was worried because he had convinced the Chicago outfit that Presser wasn't the informer everyone said he was.

" 'What stool pigeon?' I told them. I said I knew his old man . . . like I know you. I know the kid, the old man. I used to meet him down in Miami."

Fat Tony went on to explain how he had even cleared up Jackie's problem with the Cleveland newspaper that had reported he was a fink. "I grabbed ahold of Roy Cohn," he explained. "Roy Cohn's friend who's an editor in Cleveland. And he picked up that paper, and the first thing you know they made a front line, a front headline page. An apology, what they said about him. So I sent the fuckin' paper to Chicago. Now it comes out that he's a stool pigeon again. (Pause) Ah, screw the guy. I can't understand it. Why would he want to squeal on the Teamster guys?"

This wasn't news to the FBI. Jackie had told Bob Friedrick about his plans to fix the *Plain Dealer* front page before the fact. The FBI agent didn't believe it possible, but he wrote a memo for the file about it anyway.

390

The whole underworld was in an uproar—anyone who dealt with the Teamsters had something to worry about—but Fat Tony, as Presser's ultimate handler, had the most to lose, his prestige and more. He had just sent a couple of mobbed-up businessmen to Jackie to ask him to toss them some of the union's insurance business. What if Jackie informed on them and they got convicted? According to Mafia code, Fat Tony would be responsible for making sure Jackie was killed. The Chicago outfit might even try to "knock his brains in."

At four in the afternoon on that dark day, Salerno was still complaining to Vincent "Fish" Cafaro, his right-hand man, driver, and numbers overseer, about Presser the stool pigeon. "When I heard this this morning, Jesus Christ almighty," Salerno said to Fish. "Here I am, sticking up for the fucking guy. I just got through sending a couple guys over there, that Mel and what's his name, ah, Miltie. That thing there, insurance. (Pause) But who the hell knows what he's doing. Right?"

"Maybe he's not our politician," Cafaro said.

"All I ever did [for] this guy [was] favors," Fat Tony griped. "Chicago wanted to kill [him]."

Elsewhere, reaction was swift. Jackie cancelled his appearance at a conference in Washington, D.C. The FBI, fearing a Mob hit, threw up surveillance on Presser and Hughes and opened an investigation into who had blown his cover.

Not everyone was as sympathetic to Presser as the FBI. "He'll have to go to work in a bulletproof limousine," said William Winpisinger, president of the International Association of Machinists. "I don't know anyone who respects a stool pigeon, either in or out of the trade-union movement."

The Chicago outfit sent its underboss, Jackie Cerone, to New York to talk with Salerno and figure out what to do. "We know he's a stool pigeon for the FBI," Cerone said.

Salerno, his prestige on the line, said, "I want proof, not talk." Salerno's pal in the Bakery Workers Union, Carmine D'Angelo, also a friend of Jackie, recounted the meeting to him to assure him he had nothing to worry about with Fat Tony. Jackie promptly told the FBI.

Jackie's high-pressure life was beginning to take its toll. On June 15, he checked his 335 pounds into the respected Cleveland Clinic for five days of tests. Meanwhile, Labor investigators Red Simmons and Jim Thomas saw their three-year-long case finally reach fruition. Strike-

391

force prosecutors Steve Olah and Steve Jigger had carefully crafted a hundred-page prosecution memorandum outlining the embezzlement case against Jackie, Local 507 president Harold Friedman, and ghost employee Tony Hughes. They sent the memo to strike-force chief Dave Margolis and his deputy, Paul Coffey. As a courtesy usually afforded white-collar defendants in sensitive or complicated cases, Olah and Jigger told lawyers for the three Teamster officials about the impending indictments and gave them a chance to present reasons why the case shouldn't go forward.

Simultaneously, Olah and Jigger were told that Presser and Hughes were FBI informants. They had strongly suspected as much. They then reviewed the two men's informant files to see if the FBI had authorized Jackie to keep ghost employees on the payroll. In 1976 and again in 1980, the attorney general had tightened up guidelines that allowed an FBI handler to give his source permission to commit crimes as part of his cover. Everything had to be documented. The closest thing the strike-force lawyers could find was a 1983 memo saying that the FBI gave Presser permission to put George Argie, a gambler and close associate of Cleveland boss Jack White, on the Local 507 payroll. With Argie on the Local 507 payroll, Tony Hughes could pick up intelligence through him about White's activities and relay it to the FBI, as most days Argie knocked off before noon and went to lunch with Tony.

News of Jackie's impending indictment infuriated Friedrick, Jackie and Tony's FBI contact agent. He felt that Jackie and Tony were being persecuted by the Labor investigators and the strike force. "I began to think the bad guys were the Justice Department and the Labor guys and good guys were Jackie Presser and Tony Hughes," he would say a few years later. "I began to think like them. That these [other] guys were abusing their investigative responsibilities."

By now, Friedrick had become close to Presser. "You get close to people in combat," Friedrick once explained. "Socially, we weren't close. We never had a drink together or met in a bar. I never met Presser where I didn't pull out a notebook and take notes. We were close professionally—because of the mission."

Hughes and Presser did small favors for the agent. Hughes got summer jobs for some teenage boys in Friedrick's neighborhood. He gave Friedrick tickets to the circus and some sporting events. A friend

392

of Friedrick's applied to the Teamsters Service Bureau for money to buy athletic equipment for the inner-city kids he counseled. Hughes made sure the Teamsters granted the program $1,500. In turn, the agent even made a fishing rod for Tony's son, who liked to go boating on Lake Erie. "I met with those guys on Mother's Day and Father's Day," Friedrick would explain several years later when questioned by the Justice Department about their relationship. "This was serious stuff. I was identifying with these people now. In my mind, maybe I'm looking at this thing from their point of view. I'm not looking at it from the FBI's point of view, but rather as one of them."

At nearly each of their meetings in 1984 and 1985, Jackie asked Friedrick about the Labor Department and strike force's case. "When is it going to go away?" Jackie inquired. Friedrick reassured him that everything was fine, echoing the words of his superior, James Moody, unit chief of the organized-crime division.

On July 3, the FBI got a chance to save Jackie and Tony. Paul Coffey, fresh from his review of Presser's voluminous informant files, came to Cleveland to interview the three FBI supervisors who had dealt with Jackie and Tony. The Justice Department wasn't about to indict the administration's key supporter without having the FBI on board.

They met at the home of Patrick Foran's in-laws. Jackie's second handler was now a supervisor. Also attending the meeting were Friedrick; Roy McKinnon and Fred Fehl, both former heads of the Cleveland FBI office; Marty McCann; and FBI supervisor Jim Moody. Friedrick hoped that Coffey would see how helpful Jackie and Tony had been to the bureau and then give them a break. The FBI supervisors told Coffey how they handled Presser and Hughes, about the investigations they had assisted, and other general points.

Though the theory of the strike force and Labor Department's case against Presser had been discussed in the newspapers—Allen Friedman and Nardi were no-shows—it is significant that none of the FBI agents came forward to say that he had authorized the no-shows. If the crimes had been authorized, this would have been the right time for the FBI agents to make the point. They did not.

On July 13, 1984, Jackie's lawyer Climaco met with strike-force section chief Margolis, Jigger, and Olah in Washington and tried to stave off Jackie's indictment by bluntly attacking the two Labor investigators, the grand jury, the Cleveland Strike Force prosecutors, and the government's two key witnesses, Allen Friedman and Jack Nardi. The meeting was recounted in a lengthy Justice Department memo.

"Thomas and Simmons said they were out to get Presser," Climaco said. "Not only that, they've deliberately leaked information to the news media as a way to tarnish venue here. How can we get a fair trial?"

Raising his voice, Climaco went on. "Allen Friedman is unreliable. I truly believe he's insane. He tried to extort Jackie for $100,000, even threatened to kill him. The man is out for revenge and has been going around telling people Harold and Jackie screwed him. Well, he just wants to be a white knight for a book he's writing."

Climaco said that Jack Nardi worked for Bill Presser at the joint council, and that Local 507 "subsidized" his salary. As soon as Jackie found out he wasn't working, he fired him. "Nardi is a convicted felon, an attempted extortionist," Climaco said. "He's written bad checks, you name it. His credibility is seriously damaged."

Despite the frightening *Los Angeles Times* report about his being an informer, Jackie didn't hide out. He was determined not to let it bother him, even though the FBI was warning him to be careful. He and his girlfriend, Cindy Jarabek, a former secretary for Local 507, kept up their social life. In July, he and Cindy dined at the home of August A. Busch III, the chairman of the board and president of Anheuser-Busch, the giant St. Louis brewer and Teamster employer. A few weeks later, on Jackie's birthday, Washington lobbyist Bob Gray threw a party for Jackie at one of his favorite Washington restaurants, The Palm, known for its huge steaks. Gray had commissioned a portrait of Jackie and gave it to him at the party. Jackie was touched. "Your personal gift will be a lasting reminder of our friendship for all the world to see," he wrote to Gray a few days later. "I really like the portrait, even if you failed to render all the kinks in my armor."

Was Jackie happy at the top? Or was sitting on the Teamsters throne an empty experience? His father was dead and his two children distant. As an informer, true friendship was impossible. He could not enjoy the self-satisfaction of being loyal to anyone. He even spurned

394

Tony Hughes, and turned instead to the Reagan crowd, with its sugary style and brilliant manipulation of public opinion. "He wanted to turn his collar, blue to white," Hughes said, disappointedly.

Jackie's impending indictment didn't cool advances from the White House. It was a presidential election year, and Reagan needed the Teamsters' endorsement again. On August 20, Reagan campaign manager Ed Rollins and Secretary of Labor Raymond Donovan ventured to a Teamsters meeting in Dallas to have breakfast with Jackie. "We want your endorsement again," Rollins told him. "We remember who our friends were, and we hope that you remember what we've done for you when it comes time for your endorsement."

Behind the scenes, Jackie reached an agreement with the Reagan camp. The Teamsters would endorse Reagan for president if the White House got rid of Donald Dotson, the conservative antilabor chairman of the National Labor Relations Board, the supposedly neutral arbiter of labor-management disputes. A corporate lawyer from Pittsburgh, Dotson had pushed the board from its traditional centrist position to a decidedly probusiness stance. Both the Teamsters and the AFL-CIO were up in arms. During his tenure, Dotson allowed the NLRB's backlog to soar to over thirteen hundred cases, about three times the normal amount. The White House had tried to rein him in. White House personnel director John Herrington had called Dotson in for a meeting and explained that the White House was angling for the Teamsters' endorsement and didn't want the NLRB to queer the opportunity with unfavorable rulings in the near future. Dotson, a former Reagan Labor Department official, said he was stunned. Herrington denied the conversation took place.

Eager to please the Teamsters, White House chief of staff James A. Baker quietly approved Dotson's replacement. But Jackie, anxious to take credit for slaying one of labor's bêtes noires, revealed to a *Plain Dealer* reporter that the Teamsters' endorsement of Reagan was linked to Dotson's demotion. The story exploded in Jackie's face; the White House, wanting to avoid outcry about a pungent political deal, pulled back. "We tried to make it happen," a Reagan source said, "but because Presser is out there stating the price of endorsement, hell, we can't do it."

Once again, Reagan had to retreat from Jackie's eager embrace. Presidential aides vetoed his scheduled appearance at an August 30 meeting of the Ohio Conference of Teamsters. Vice President Bush took Reagan's place. Arm and arm with Jackie, smiling broadly, Bush walked to the microphone and addressed the Teamsters that afternoon. After his speech, Bush told reporters he was unconcerned about Jackie's embezzlement investigation. "We have a system of justice in this country that people are innocent until proven guilty," Bush said. "There have been a lot of allegations. The endorsement has nothing to do with that."

With the Republicans on his side again, Jackie was satisfied. The next thing he needed to do was to clear up his problems with the crime families. Maishe Rockman helped him here. "Who did he hurt?" Rockman asked when confronted by Mob members who didn't trust Jackie. In September, Joe Iacobacci, a Cleveland mafioso, met with representatives of the Buffalo outfit and New York's Columbo crime family concerning a non-Teamster matter. Later Iacobacci told Tony Hughes, "They agreed that Jackie was all right."

If he stayed alive long enough and gave the FBI enough dirt to get indictments on some of the corrupt vice presidents on the International's executive board, Presser planned to replace them with younger Teamster leaders who didn't have as many Mob ties. Throughout the fall, he filled in Friedrick about the vice presidents he wanted to bump from the board.

"Ted Cozza from Pittsburgh is a made member," Jackie said. "Joe Morgan from Miami owns part of a cold-storage company that was financed by a Central States loan. The company employs about two hundred Haitians that aren't in the union. . . . Joey Auippa and his underboss meet every Saturday at 6:30 A.M. in the steam room at the Oakwood Hyatt Hotel. Tony Appa, he's a big Teamster guy there, meets with them sometimes, too."

Most importantly, Jackie told the FBI that William McCarthy, the man he thought about making secretary-treasurer, wasn't liked by the New York bosses or their New England counterpart, Raymond Patriarca. "When Patriarca heard we were thinking about appointing McCarthy, he got upset," Presser told the FBI. "Somebody once put a tap on McCarthy's phone and heard him running off about 'the fucking dagos.' Patriarca got really ticked."

In mid-October, Jackie appointed Weldon Mathis of Atlanta as his secretary-treasurer.

† † †

Jackie and John Climaco were happy to learn that Simmons and Thomas had left the Labor Department. Climaco's letters attacking their integrity had had an impact. The accusation, combined with Red and Jim's aggressive stirring-the-pot techniques, made the strike-force honchos in Washington nervous. Some of their colleagues were disappointed but couldn't blame them for leaving. Red and Jim battled FBI obstruction, intra-agency rivalry, the combined clout of Jackie Presser and his union, periods of strike-force lethargy, and still made a case against Jackie. "I'll tell you one thing," said an FBI agent intimately familiar with the investigation and the surrounding controversy. "Those guys did a hell of a job. I've got to give them that. Those guys are good investigators. They really made that case."

Red and Jim were angry. They filed a libel suit against Climaco, saying that he had defamed them in his letters to their superiors in Washington and that their superiors fell for it. "There was no way we could function any more at the Labor Department," Simmons said recently. "We had drawn the line so many times with the strike force, with Coffey and Margolis. They made it very clear through comments that came back: 'They're crazy. Those guys scare me.' What hurt was Climaco's charges that we were lying to the strike force, hiding evidence, fabricating evidence. Olah knew Climaco and knew how Climaco operated and took it with a grain of salt." An FBI probe turned up nothing to substantiate Climaco's allegations. He says he was doing his job, being an aggressive advocate for his client.

Without Justice Department backing, they moved to the investigative arm of the Defense Department. By November 1984, they were learning their way around contract and procurement fraud.

On January 31, 1985, Jigger and Olah polished their draft into the final Presser prosecution memorandum and submitted it to their superiors. They asked that Jackie be indicted for embezzling $700,000 by giving no-show jobs to Mob associates Nardi, Friedman, and Hughes.

But first, Jackie had to sidestep the President's Commission on Organized Crime, which was looking into drug dealing and labor racketeering. One of its targets was Jackie, much to the chagrin of the FBI, the White House, Presser, and John Climaco. Investigators focused on Presser's role in encouraging elected Teamster officials to attack a 1983 TDU meeting in Michigan and on his fantastic investment in the Front Row Theatre, a suburban Cleveland concert hall that featured a revolving stage. His eleven-month investment of $134,000 in the Front Row had made him a millionaire.

Climaco sparred with the commission's deputy counsel, Stephen M. Ryan, demanding legal discovery of commission files and challenging Jackie's subpoena. Jackie took the fight to federal court, lost, and was forced to appear. He now found himself in a tricky spot. Though Ryan assured him otherwise, Presser could be asked questions that might hurt him in his payroll-padding case in Cleveland.

On April 23, 1985, he appeared before the commission deep in the heart of Chicago, where the outfit hated him and where Dorfman, two years earlier, had gotten nailed at noon in a public parking lot. Jackie was jittery. He was sworn in, exercised his Fifth Amendment protection fifteen times, and then quickly left the hearing room, surrounded by his retinue. They marched to the elevators and rode one down to a secure parking lot deep in the Dirksen Federal Office Building.

For security during these days, Jackie, a gun collector, packed a tiny antique derringer in his sock. That spring, he and one of his top aides had a meeting in the West Wing of the White House. Before one of the staffers came to escort them inside, Jackie remembered the gun. He pulled it from his sock, looked around, and stashed it in a flower pot on the main steps to the Executive Office Building. After the meeting, Jackie checked to see if White House security had found his gun. It was still in the flower pot. He palmed it, then slipped it back in his sock. "We laughed and laughed about it for days," the aide said. "It was in broad daylight right on the White House grounds. Anybody else and they would have been arrested. But that was Jackie. He always landed on his feet."

Jackie's fate rested in the hands of high-level Justice Department officials who had to make the tough decision—whether Jackie's value to the FBI outweighed his allowing his uncle and Mob associates to siphon off $700,000 in salaries without working. By early June, Margolis agreed that Presser should be indicted, and Deputy Attorney General Lowell Jensen concurred. Meese wasn't consulted; he had stepped aside because of his ties to Jackie during Reagan's two presidential campaigns.

On June 5, 1985, the top brass of the Justice Department met with their FBI counterparts to give them the news about Presser. Stephen Trott, head of the Justice Department's criminal division, said Presser was going to be indicted, probably at a June 24 session of the grand jury in Cleveland.

Later that day, Friedrick learned from FBI headquarters that Jackie was going to be indicted. The agent couldn't believe it. For at least three years, his bosses had reassured him that the Labor Department's case had no merit and would go nowhere. He had told Presser this dozens of times. "I felt like I had been betrayed and was out there all by myself," he said later.

He met with Jackie and broke the bad news. Jackie was furious. "How can they do this to me after all I've done for you!" he erupted.

Friedrick didn't have an answer. A true believer in the FBI, he was crushed. He couldn't believe that FBI headquarters wanted to lose Presser. Convinced he was acting for the greater good of the FBI, Friedrick took the first step in what would unfold into a tremendous scandal.

"Look, do you trust your lawyer?" Friedrick asked.

Jackie said he could trust John Climaco.

"You've got to tell him about our relationship," the agent said. "It's the only thing left. Tell him about Nardi and Friedman and say they were kept on the payroll by FBI authorization. We have to get this information out."

Jackie was surprised at the suggestion.

"I'll meet with your lawyer, explain it to him," Friedrick said.

"You'd do that for me?" Presser asked, disbelieving.

"That's all we've got left," Friedrick said.

The conspiracy began. Presser would weave a convincing new cover story, as he had so many times in the past. They arranged a meeting with Climaco on June 9. Before he arrived, Friedrick was nervous, quizzing Jackie and Tony repeatedly. "Are you sure we're doing the right thing? Does Climaco understand the seriousness of this thing? He could be in jeopardy for his own life from the Mob"

Presser insisted on going ahead. "I could be in a lot of trouble for this," Friedrick said. The fourteen-year veteran FBI supervisor realized he was putting his career on the line.

As he would later recount, John Climaco was flabbergasted to learn that Jackie had been a prize government informer operating under a unique top-secret security agreement approved by FBI director Clarence Kelley. FBI authorization was good news. It would knock out any criminal intent by his client.

"Why didn't you come forward with this stuff sooner?" Climaco asked the agent. Friedrick brushed him off, saying "I don't know."

Two days later, Climaco met in Washington with Margolis, Jigger, Olah, and Coffey. Climaco made a forceful, eloquent presentation as to why Jackie shouldn't be indicted. "Jackie and Tony have been cooperating with the FBI for the past ten years," Climaco said, listing some of Jackie's targets: Roy Williams, Joe Morgan, Andy Anderson. "Not one decision made regarding the Teamsters and Jackie Presser in the last ten years wasn't made without the full knowledge, discussion, and approval of the FBI. For example, Jackie wanted to be president before Roy Williams but lost interest. After Williams got convicted, he wasn't running because of the investigation and because all the past presidents went to jail. But several weeks before the election, he changed his mind at the specific request, direction, and authorization of the FBI.

"My client asks me, 'Why am I being indicted? Why can't I take the stand and say the FBI made me do it?' If Jackie's indicted, he would be executed, based on what the union's executive board tells him—the people in Chicago hate him. You will be putting a target on his back after he has been cooperating with you. He made no moves of consequence as general president without FBI authorization. The FBI ran Local 507 and the International and did a hell of a good job."

It was a bizarre last-minute twist to an already Byzantine investigation. Presser was putting himself out front in claiming that the FBI had authorized him to embezzle.

Margolis complimented Climaco on his impressive presentation. But when asked specifically which FBI agent approved keeping no-shows Allen Friedman and Nardi on the Local 507 payroll, Climaco came up empty. "We need the specifics from Jackie Presser on each one," Margolis said. Climaco agreed to get them, and a meeting was set for June 17.

Two days later, Friedrick invited Climaco to a downtown Cleveland hotel. First, the FBI supervisor had to cover his tracks. He filled out an FBI requisition slip, saying he needed the hotel room as a secure place to meet a source. He later told Tony Hughes, "Remember we met at the Bond Court [Hotel]," and Hughes quickly agreed. After Climaco arrived, Friedrick asked the lawyer what he had told Margolis in Washington, and Climaco ran down his presentation while Friedrick took notes. He needed to know what was said, so that if questioned, his account wouldn't conflict with Climaco's. "We didn't have this meeting," Friedrick said when Climaco finished. "Right," he replied.

Back at his FBI office, Friedrick wrote out a Form 209 report—an insert to an informant file—to justify the blue slip he filled out to get the hotel room. The insert described a meeting with source CV-3963-TE, otherwise known as Tony Hughes. Friedrick was covering his tracks well.

On June 16, Friedrick, Jackie, and Tony got together with John Climaco again, this time at Tony's apartment. Climaco needed the details Margolis requested about when and how the agents gave Jackie permission to pad the payroll with Nardi, Allen Friedman, and others.

Climaco met at the Justice Department the next day with Margolis as well as with Jigger and Olah, who came in from Cleveland. Climaco recounted what Tony, Jackie, and Friedrick had told him.

"Tony started with Local 507 in 1968. Before that, he had been talking to [FBI agent] Marty McCann, who encouraged him to work at the union. By late 1970, Tony had gained Jackie's confidence and told him he had a government source who could advise them on legality of what they wanted to do. I'm not sure if Marty agreed to this.

"In the early seventies, Jackie was worried about Socialists coming into the labor movement, and he ran messages through Tony to McCann. About the same time, he agreed to meet with McCann and was assured of full confidentiality and protection. After the first or second meeting, they discussed various industries that organized crime was infiltrating. Jackie felt it was destructive to the union and that the eventual control and infiltration by the Mob would produce legislation that would hurt the labor movement."

Jigger and Olah were surprised at the news, and took pages of notes.

"McCann became close to the sources, meeting with Tony weekly and Jackie less often," Climaco went on. "Later, McCann handed off Jackie and Tony to Pat Foran, after first reassuring Jackie that he had complete confidentiality. This took place at a meeting in Chicago at the Palmer House. It involved officials at the highest levels of the FBI. . . .

"They set up a procedure for Jackie to move up in the union, and he was supposed to determine where the true organized crime–Teamster connections were and where they were in other unions also, especially in the food industry and hotels. He and Foran had long discussions about abuses like casual hires, labor leasing, and sweetheart contracts. The FBI wanted Jackie to pay attention to what was going on in Chicago, Detroit, New York, and Cleveland, and Jackie agreed to try to develop West Coast contacts. At the time, Rudy Tham was the only source out there for Jackie."

Climaco made sure to present every shred of information helpful to his client. He even told the story of Jackie and Tony attending a private FBI steak roast in Washington D.C. with Foran, McCann, and Roy McKinnon, the retired head of the Cleveland FBI office. "McKinnon thanked them for all they had done for the United States and all the things they had done at great sacrifice," Climaco recounted. "He told Jackie six or eight times he was the most important source in FBI history."

Turning to the question of whether the FBI authorized any no-show employees, Climaco said that it had given Jackie permission to keep four ghosts on the payroll—Nardi, Friedman, Tony Hughes, and Argie. Climaco gave the reasons as he understood them. Nardi was hired because the Mob had asked Jackie to hire him, do it, and McCann, worried about retribution, wanted to protect Jackie as his source. Friedman was trying to extort money from his nephew and was threatening to kill him. Even though Jackie wanted to fire his uncle, Friedrick told Jackie not to do so. Tony Hughes frequented the Forge restaurant during the day because wise guys hung out there, and McCann thought Tony could pick up some good intelligence. Argie was hired to provide Tony and Jackie with a pipeline into Mafia boss James "Jack White" Licavoli, a friend of Argie's.

402

The strike-force lawyers realized their embezzlement case against Jackie and Tony Hughes was crumbling. If Presser thought he had FBI approval, how could the prosecutors prove he intended to commit a crime? Without that, the government would have to drop its prosecution. First, however, Margolis said he wanted the strike force to conduct interviews with McCann, Foran, and Friedrick.

Three days later, back in Cleveland, Friedrick packed Jackie's FBI file into a case, rented a room at the Bond Court Hotel, and asked Climaco to meet him. Once again, he asked Climaco to recount his presentation, and as the lawyer explained what transpired, Friedrick scrawled notes. "We didn't have this meeting," Friedrick said. "Right," Climaco said.

After Climaco left, Friedrick called Marty McCann and asked him to come to the hotel room. McCann, who worked only a few blocks away as security chief for LTV Steel Corporation, had already been alerted that a strike-force supervisor was coming to town to interview him

"Marty, Climaco went to see Margolis about the authorization of Nardi and Friedman on the payroll," Friedrick said.

"OK, is that what the strike force wants to talk about?" McCann asked.

"Something like that," Friedrick said. He filled in McCann on the battle between the strike force and the FBI in Cleveland, painting a bleak picture of Jackie's chances to survive if word got out of his ten-year marriage to the FBI.

"Jackie is going to get indicted on racketeering charges, and during the trial his informant file will be revealed to the judge and maybe even made public," Friedrick complained. "If Jackie takes the stand to defend himself and says anything contrary to what's in his file, the strike force will use the file to impeach him." Friedrick got upset every time he told the story; McCann also reacted angrily. Without explicitly saying so, Friedrick was very clearly sending McCann the message, We've got to help Jackie and Tony because of what they have done for us.

The agent pulled out a chronology he had drawn up and the notes he had taken during Climaco's two briefings. He read them to McCann. When he finished reading he asked, "You want to see these notes?"

"No, that won't be necessary," McCann said.

"I brought the files over," Friedrick told McCann. "You want to look at them, see if there's anything about the ghosts being put on the payroll?"

"No, I wouldn't put down anything like that," McCann answered.

Though he had started the cover-up, Friedrick hoped that his story about authorizing ghost employees was true. But he couldn't come out and flatly ask McCann or Foran. What if they said no? He didn't want to scare them off.

Pat Foran arrived in Cleveland about midnight for the next day's interview with strike-force deputy chief Paul Coffey. Friedrick picked up his former supervisor at the airport and shuttled him to his in-laws' home in suburban Bay Village. Friedrick described Presser's predicament, never mentioning that he himself had met twice with Climaco.

The next day, Friedrick invited Foran to lunch and took him on a twenty-five minute drive to Herb's Tavern, west of the city. Friedrick explained how unjustly Presser was being treated, threatened with an indictment after all the information he had given to the FBI. His life was in danger. "What I was trying to do with Pat was lay the ground-work, hoping he would come forward without coming right out and saying, You have got to do this," Friedrick later admitted.

Foran agreed that it was a shameless way to treat a top-notch bureau source. After lunch, Friedrick said, "You drive, I want to read you some notes." While Foran drove, Bob Friedrick read to him the Climaco-presentation notes, the same notes he had recited to McCann the day before. Foran didn't say much as he drove. Now Jackie's three FBI handlers all had the same story to tell when interviewed by the strike force.

Back downtown in the FBI office, Friedrick went over the notes once again with Foran, pointing out why Nardi and Allen Friedman and George Argie were hired and kept on the payroll without working. Then Foran asked to read Presser and Hughes's files, looking for anything that contradicted or agreed with Friedrick's notes.

"The message that I tried to convey was that it's show time now," Friedrick said later. "It's the end of the line. It depends on whether we do something for this guy or we don't do something whether he's going to get off."

That afternoon, they were called one by one over to the Bond

Court Hotel to be interviewed by Paul Coffey. Jigger and Olah took notes, and Jim Moody sat in. Without much difficulty, Jackie's three handlers told the same story about giving Presser authorization to keep ghost employees on the payroll.

McCann went first, following the story line that Friedrick had outlined to him. McCann claimed, among other things, that "keeping Nardi on the payroll gave Presser and Hughes entrée into the Italian faction of the union. Presser and Hughes did complain frequently that they did not think Nardi was doing what he should be doing, and I advised them to keep him on and that should Nardi be let go, I felt the Italian faction might attempt to kill Presser and Hughes in a power play, based on other information I was receiving."

Foran was next. In keeping with his nature, he was hostile and aggressive, even though Coffey's questioning wasn't confrontational. Foran told them, "Subsequent to the merger of Teamsters Locals 507 and 752, I advised Presser to keep Allen Friedman on the rolls because he was a source of information concerning a case the FBI was investigating involving Friedman and John Trunzo's illegal loan-sharking, gambling, and shakedown of union companies, which activities were being reported by Hughes and Presser."

Friedrick, low-key and seemingly straightforward, backed up the other two. By now, Jigger had practically quit taking notes. He felt terrible. It looked like four years of investigating Jackie had been wasted, all because two agencies that were supposed to work in tandem couldn't get along. At the end of the interviews he wrote a note on his pad: "game, set, match." The FBI had won. Or so it seemed.

A week later, Revell, the number-two man at the FBI, alerted Director Webster by memo about the bizarre turn of events. Two FBI supervisors and a former supervisor were saying that ALPRO was authorized to keep Jack Nardi and Allen Friedman on the payroll as no-show employees. None of the agents considered this to be a violation of embezzlement statutes. It looks like the Department of Justice would have to drop its case against Jackie. Since the investigation had generated so many headlines, strike-force chief Margolis and his deputy, Coffey, thought that dropping the case would spark an obstruction of justice investigation by Congress.

In a final note, Revell told the FBI director that Coffey was "irate." Coffey had asked McCann, Foran, and Friedrick about autho-

405

rization in a July 1984 meeting in Cleveland; now Coffey wanted to know why the hell the agents hadn't mentioned then that Presser had the FBI's permission to commit crimes.

For the moment, no one from the FBI could give Coffey a good answer.

The more Olah and Jigger reflected on the explanations McCann, Foran, and Friedrick gave about giving Jackie permission to pad the Local 507 with no-show employees, the more incredible the stories seemed. Olah had known all three as either supervisors or agents for at least a decade, and he got along with them to varying degrees. Something wasn't right.

Jigger became suspicious when he noticed that each of the agents made identical mistakes about dates and facts—such as the year Allen Friedman suffered a heart attack or when Jackie hired gambler George Argie as his executive assistant. This oddity suggested to him that their stories had been rehearsed. Also, the three agents, in describing the events, used phrases almost identical to those used by Climaco. By then, Olah had become convinced that his archenemy, FBI Cleveland-office chief Joe Griffin, and the three agents had concocted the phony story to derail Jackie's indictment.

On July 23, 1985, the Justice Department dropped its case against Jackie, Tony, and Harold Friedman, to the relief of many in the FBI. At the same time, however, the Justice Department opened an inquiry into McCann, Foran, and Friedrick.

A day later, Senators Sam Nunn and William V. Roth, Jr., two ranking members of the Senate Permanent Subcommittee on Investigations, asked the FBI, Justice, and Labor to turn over their files on the aborted four-year investigation. The committee wanted to make sure that Presser ties to the White House had played no part in having the case dropped, which was the talk of Capitol Hill. Other reports suggested that the case had been dropped because Jackie was an FBI source, but Climaco denied it. "Insanity and lies," he said. "My client is not an informant. Never was an informant. Never had a relationship" with the FBI.

Controversy over the Presser case continued to mount, with editorial writers at national newspapers demanding an explanation. "We are

406

led to believe that Mr. Presser was some kind of an informant for the FBI and that indicting him would jeopardize some other—more important?—cases," the *Washington Post* said. "But who authorized this arrangement, and why didn't the strike force know about it? What is the relationship between the FBI and federal prosecutors in dealing with informers? And what are the ground rules, not only for this case, but generally, that govern decisions to drop some prosecutions in order to preserve others—especially when public figures are involved?"

With the investigation closed, the Reagan administration rekindled its love affair with Jackie and the Teamsters. Presser wasn't as smitten this time. "He was a little bit disappointed in the Republicans because they had talked in big dollar signs and money values and it didn't seem like they were really concerned about the country as much as they should have been," Friedrick later explained.

On August 1, White House political director Ed Rollins and an aide, Linda Chavez, appeared at a Teamsters rally in Dearborn, Michigan. In a speech to the assembled, Rollins congratulated Presser "on having the tremendous burden on your head, unjustifiably for five years, put to rest for good. . . . Jackie Presser shares Ronald Reagan's faith in the men and women who made America great. . . . With leaders like Jackie Presser, we can make America stronger, better." The cheerleading paid off for Rollins. Less than two months later, he left the White House to become a partner in a lobbying firm, bringing in a huge client, the Teamsters. "I spent a lot of years doing things for love," said the balding, bearded Rollins. Now he wanted to make money. "I think I can make between three-quarters and a million dollars" a year.

About this time, an FBI supervisor alerted Bob Friedrick that the inquiry had been upgraded to a criminal investigation. Though Friedrick believed he had done the right thing—protecting Presser, being loyal to what he perceived to be the greater good of the bureau—he was afraid his obstruction and cover-up would be discovered. On August 12, the FBI called him and Presser's two other contact agents to Washington for another round of interviews. The straight-laced, religious Friedrick was considered the least likely conspirator since he hadn't handled Jackie when Nardi and Friedman supposedly worked out their unusual union fringe benefits.

Friedrick was granted immunity, sworn in, compelled to testify, and interviewed by FBI agent Ralph Regalbuto, assigned to its internal

407

watchdog unit, the Office of Professional Responsibility. Except for a few embellishments, Friedrick stuck to his original story and lied under oath.

Once back in Cleveland, Friedrick called Foran and said he hadn't told Regalbuto about his notes. "The thing you are going to have trouble overcoming was the original meeting we had in July 1984," Friedrick said, starting to go into details.

Foran, upset, cut him off. "Look, I don't want to hear any more!"

Next Friedrick called McCann, who pumped him up, saying "Hang in there. Don't worry about it."

Friedrick was tiptoeing into dangerous territory. "I was walking on eggshells, and I wanted to be very careful that I didn't say something or indicate something that would cause this thing to fail," he explained later.

Two days after his sworn interview with Regalbuto, he telephoned the agent and quietly said that he had lied to him about something and wanted to correct the record. He admitted that he, McCann, and Foran had talked about what they were going to say when questioned on June 20 by the strike force. Regalbuto noted the information.

Confused, wanting to get away from it all, Friedrick took his family on a vacation to Maine, his home state. Away from the office and his duties as supervisor of the organized-crime squad, he had time to reflect on the investigation targeting him and his colleagues. He decided to call Foran. Worried about leaving a paper trail, Friedrick left the rented cottage, located a public telephone, and pumped in enough change to reach Foran in the FBI's Las Vegas field office, where Foran was second in command.

Friedrick said that he had told the FBI's in-house investigators that he had rehearsed McCann and Foran before the first June 20 inquiry in Cleveland by reading them notes of Climaco's presentation. Foran reacted angrily. "Just tell the truth, don't be changing things," he said.

Jackie Presser still brimmed with information on the underworld. FBI supervisors had removed Friedrick as Jackie's contact agent ever since he, McCann, and Foran had become the targets of the obstruction-of-justice investigation. Two supervisors at FBI headquarters, Larry A. Potts and Donald V. North, took over.

Some of the information was ominous. "Tony Appa, an outfit guy in Chicago, is sitting down with Dominic Senese about Chuckie O'Brien," Jackie said. "Senese thinks O'Brien is talking and wants to do something about it." O'Brien, Hoffa's foster son, worked for Teamsters vice president Joe Morgan.

Three weeks later, Jackie offered a morsel about a Detroit mafioso suspected of taking part in the Hoffa murder. "Tony Giacalone gets out of jail in the next few days, and a party is going to be held for him all week. A bunch of outfit guys will be there. They'll be staying at the Diplomat Hotel in Fort Lauderdale. Tony LaPiana will definitely be there." Potts and North noted the information and put it in Jackie's file.

Meanwhile, the Justice Department closed in on McCann, Foran, and Friedrick. The lawyers in the Justice Department's internal watchdog unit decided that Friedrick was the weak link. He was the straight arrow who hadn't been around when Nardi and Friedman enjoyed no-show employment at Local 507. Earlier, Friedrick had felt a compunction to correct himself and tell the truth. If they could break him first, then they could work this conpiracy right up the ladder, possibly to his boss, Joe Griffin, and maybe even up to FBI headquarters or to Attorney General Ed Meese.

On January 6, 1986, Friedrick was summoned once again to Washington. He had given statements in June, August, and September. Now the prosecutors wanted to grant him immunity, call him before a grand jury, and compel him to testify against McCann and Foran. The prosecutors didn't realize that Friedrick had started the obstruction and had carefully recruited McCann and Foran into the plot.

The next day, Friedrick consented to a polygraph exam. Paul Minor, an FBI employee, strapped and wired Friedrick to the apparatus, asked some control questions, then moved into the danger zone.

"Are you withholding anything important about the quashing of the Presser indictment?" Minor asked.

"No," Friedrick answered.

"Do you know for sure that Presser placed Nardi and Friedman on the payroll without FBI authority or knowledge?"

"No."

"Did you ever discuss with Foran or McCann the falsification of information to quash that indictment of Presser?"

"No."

"Are you lying to me about your knowledge of what happened with Nardi and Friedman?"

"No."

Minor unhooked Friedrick, then accused him of lying. The agent broke down. He admitted for the first time that he had made up the story about authorizing ghost employees. Neither he nor anyone else in the FBI had, to his knowledge, authorized Jackie to put Nardi or Friedman on the payroll. Friedrick, who had put his career and freedom on the line for Jackie Presser and Tony Hughes, was going to get kicked out of the bureau.

"Would they do that for you?" Minor asked.

"If you'd asked me that in June, I would have said, yeah, they'll do that for me," he replied. "I know better now. They wouldn't do it for me."

Over the next two days, Friedrick gave a detailed confession to Justice Department lawyers Robert Chapman and Richard M. Rogers. Friedrick took them through his cover-up step by step, giving them a statement that, when transcribed, was over three hundred double-spaced pages long. Friedrick told the truth, he said, because "after lengthy and constant discussions with my wife, she says no matter how bad you look, you've got to tell the truth."

Friedrick's breakdown explained what had happened, but the Justice Department lawyers were still frustrated. Months earlier, one of them had casually remarked to Friedrick that his obstruction-of-justice case might turn out to be a government scandal bigger than Watergate. At the time, Attorney General Meese was being charged by critics with violating professional ethics; some career Justice Department lawyers felt him utterly capable of killing the Presser case for political reasons.

Instead, the obstruction had started with Bob Friedrick and had gone down the ranks. Despite what Steve Olah thought, and what

Chapman and Rogers may have suspected, Friedrick's bosses didn't seem to be involved. Even more aggravating to the Justice Department lawyers, Friedrick had given his contradictory statements under a grant of immunity. He couldn't be charged.

After a lunch break on January 9, Dick Rogers told the emotionally drained agent, "We'd like to see what your potential liability is." The transcript of their interview shows a discussion that was held off the record, then:

> FRIEDRICK: What do you mean? You're advising me of my rights now? Is that what you're saying?
>
> ROGERS: In a sense. What we want to do, we're still trying to figure out whether the statements that were made earlier actually constitute lies, and it appears that some of them may and others may not have.
>
> FRIEDRICK: I'll say that. You don't have to go through point by point. Yes, some of those things were lies.
>
> ROGERS: You don't have to if you don't want to. If you're tired of this, it's been a couple of days.

They went off the record again.

> FRIEDRICK: I don't understand. All of a sudden I don't have to [continue talking], but, you know, up to this point I did?

His interrogators didn't give him a straight answer but said they wanted to go over contradictions in his statements now that they had advised him of his right to remain silent.

Why go over it again? Friedrick asked them. I've already told you everything. I'm not holding back. "I'm very sensitive to right and wrong, and I guess maybe it's a poor self-image. But you know, black is black and white is white. And I've tried to play in the gray area here, and I can't do it."

The two Justice Department lawyers again suggested going over his contradictory statements.

FRIEDRICK: Well, let me ask you, is this a formal advisory of my rights? I think you've got to be honest with me too.

ROGERS: I know, that's why I hesitate to answer.

FRIEDRICK: . . . Well, my question still stands.

Chapman and Rogers equivocated. They didn't want to scare him off.

FRIEDRICK: It was my thought that I had one more chance to tell the story and not be subject to any prosecution.

Later, the Office of Professional Responsibility (OPR) used the four days of damaging admissions to get Friedrick indicted for lying and obstructing justice. But his lawyer, William Beyer, convinced a federal judge to throw out the statements since Friedrick had thought he had immunity. The Justice Department lawyers saw an important integrity case slip away. Yet again, another party involved in the Jackie Presser case had gotten burned.

On January 16, at a brief White House ceremony, Irving R. Kaufman, chairman of the President's Commission on Organized Crime, tweaked his boss. He handed President Reagan the commission's report, which soundly criticized the White House for its contacts with Jackie and the Teamsters Union. Such contacts erode the public's confidence in the government's fight against labor racketeering, the report said. "The long delays in reaching a resolution of a Department of Justice investigation concerning . . . Presser have led to a similar concern—whether Presser's support of the administration in the 1980 and 1984 election campaigns influenced the conduct of the investigation." The commission noted that a quarter of a century after the McClellan committee reports, organized crime still controlled the hierarchy of the country's largest labor union. One commission member, Eugene Methvin, later described Teamsters corruption as a "screaming national scandal. . . . The time and testimonial record would seem ripe for the Justice Department to initiate a civil RICO action to place the entire International Brotherhood of Teamsters under a court-appointed trustee."

412

That night, before a White House dinner for Ecuador's president, Reagan was asked by a reporter what Kaufman had said to him while handing him the critical report. Reagan, a little flustered, said, "Something that we really understand is that we have a problem, trying to deal with it."

"Had Jackie Presser's role been mentioned?"

"No, and well as I say, I haven't read the report, but also the commission has mandated silence on the interim report until the final report comes in."

"Don't you think the Teamsters have been in a lot of trouble through the years?" the reporter pressed on.

"As I say," Reagan said, "I haven't read it." An aide broke in, saying, "He's got some guests." Reagan quickly walked away.

Friedrick's confession resurrected the Cleveland Strike Force's embezzlement case. A new grand jury was impaneled in early 1986, and witnesses and statements were presented. Meanwhile, the Senate Permanent Subcommittee on Investigations, chaired by Senator Sam Nunn, looked into the bungled Presser probe and the tensions between the Labor investigators and the FBI. On May 9, the subcommittee issued its draft report, which accused the FBI of hampering the investigation. "The Department of Justice may have a flawed supervisory relationship with the FBI," it read in part. "Unless the department exercises its authority and responsibilities to direct the FBI and demand a full accounting of the FBI's activities as they impact on other work of the department, the same types of problems that occurred during the Presser case may well recur."

Later that day, Jackie and Tony Hughes were thrown into a panic. They learned that they were going to be indicted. Tony telephoned Larry Potts at FBI headquarters. "I hear we're going to be indicted—me, Jackie, Harold, and Bob Friedrick," he said.

Potts said he knew nothing about it.

"For what we've done, it doesn't seem like anybody is trying to protect us," Hughes complained. "We're being thrown to the wind. What are youse doing to keep us a secret?"

"We tried to keep it confidential," Potts said, "but because of what's been happening lately, your informant status has been confirmed by other sources."

"When it comes out we're informants, we're gonna say our government sold us down the river," Hughes said. "We were promised this would never happen. We have been above board on everything we done, and it has been approved. Let me tell you something. Our lives are on the line, and nobody seems to care."

"We care," Potts said, trying to reassure him. "You let us know the minute you hear anything about a threat."

Their information was right on target. Three days later, Margolis called a meeting of FBI and Justice Department brass and announced that Presser, Hughes, Friedman, and Friedrick would be indicted on May 16. Since Friedrick would be indicted for lying and covering up to protect Presser and Hughes, the two Teamsters officials would be exposed as FBI informers, Margolis said. They should be protected.

"That's our number-one concern," FBI deputy assistant director Anthony Daniels said.

"Do you think Friedrick will be in danger from Presser, since he'll be the witness that could damage his authorization defense?" Margolis asked the FBI.

"We'll watch the situation and see how it develops," Daniels replied.

The timing of the indictment couldn't have been worse for Presser. The IBT convention, held every five years, started Monday, May 19, in Las Vegas, and he was expected to be elected general president again. Also, the sixty-year-old Presser had just eloped in Las Vegas with Cindy Jarabek, the former part-time secretary from Local 507 with whom he had been having an affair for several years, starting long before his divorce that past fall from Carmen. A trim, attractive thirty-eight-year-old, Cindy Presser often wore her blond-streaked hair tucked in a bun at the nape of her neck and fancied tasteful, black designer pants suits and luxurious jewelry. Her engagement ring diamond alone checked in at three carats. Jackie and Cindy had known each other for a decade. Jackie's lawyer, John Climaco, had handled Cindy's divorce from her first husband in 1977.

Jackie felt the Justice Department had deliberately timed its indictment to embarrass him. Tony Hughes called FBI headquarters on May 14 and talked to Potts again. Hughes wanted to know what the Justice Department was going to say about the indictment. "Is it going to say in the press release we were helping youse guys?" Tony asked.

Potts said yes.

"You might as well just kill us yourself," Hughes said. "The government is trying to destroy us. I hope they do kill us. Then it will be on your conscience. You'll never get any more informants."

Potts offered to relocate him and Jackie through the federal Witness Protection Program. Hughes said forget it, then hung up.

Jackie left his Nevada honeymoon to be arraigned in Cleveland on payroll padding charges. The front steps to the federal court house were jammed with television cameramen, reporters, and photographers. A van from Local 507 pulled up and Jackie, Tony, and Harold Friedman and their lawyers climbed out. Tony and Harold moved through the throng, their mouths set. Jackie smiled and shot one-liners at a newsman. Inside the three were fingerprinted, photographed, and released on bond. Jackie knew how his father must have felt. Plug had been through the same process in the same building twice before. Now his son became part of a disgraceful Teamsters tradition, the fourth of the past five Teamsters presidents to be charged with union-related crimes while in office.

On the opening day of the four-day Teamsters convention, new Labor secretary William E. Brock, in a display of backbone that was lacking in Meese, Rollins, and President Reagan, told the Teamsters to "clean house." It was a surprise call for reform, catching Jackie, sitting only a few steps away, off guard.

"As secretary of labor, it isn't easy to hear about mobbed-up locals or pension-fund abuse—misuse of members' blood, sweat, and tears," Brock said. "It's impossible for me to ignore that. It is necessary for you to address it." Brock didn't mention Jackie by name but did toss him a bone, saying that he believed a person should be considered innocent until proven guilty. The convention hall of six thousand delegates, retirees, and visitors erupted in applause. "These are difficult things to say, but these are difficult times for the Teamsters," Brock went on, the hall falling silent. "The perception is not just that you are a union in trouble . . . but that you are bound to stay that way."

"Well, that says it all," Jackie said after Brock sat down. Other vice presidents weren't so magnanimous. Weldon Mathis later took the microphone and said he was sick of politicians coming to their conventions and criticizing the Teamsters. "Mathis's remark hurt the efforts to convince the government we were trying to reform internally,"

Teamsters lobbying director Paul Locigno said. "Weldon took it the wrong way because of his bias against Republicans. As far as he's concerned, there's never been a good Republican."

Brock's words contrasted sharply with those in an upbeat four-minute videotape greeting from Vice President George Bush. Bush's videotape was a sloppy effort; he congratulated the Teamsters on growing while other unions had slipped. In fact, the Teamsters had lost three hundred thousand members since the 1981 convention, mostly because deregulation had put hundreds of union trucking firms out of business. Bush was supposed to appear in person but backed out at the last minute, which angered Jackie.

The Teamsters convention held parties each night at the different casino hotels. The second night, the Eastern Conference of Teamsters hosted a gaudy, lavish celebration at Caesar's Palace, the gambling hall and hotel financed by Central States loans. Several thousand delegates, friends, labor officials, and reporters packed into the ballroom, enjoying an open bar with tumbler-sized drinks and grazing among tables loaded with crab claws, caviar, roast beef, petits fours, and fifteen different desserts.

Once the party got going, Jackie made his grand entrance. Trumpets sounded Aaron Copland's "Fanfare for the Common Man" as four burly weight lifters, dressed as Roman centurions with red-plumed helmets, paraded in carrying a golden litter, muscles bulging from the strain. Reclining on this padded throne, laughing, shaking hands, waving a beefy paw to the assembled multitude, was Jackie Presser, a three-hundred-pound-plus pontifex maximus in a cream-colored sports coat. "Hail, Caesar!" an amplified voice boomed. Jackie, grinning widely, said, "I never knew I'd be carried by four gorillas."

The opening night party cost $647,960, paid for by the dues of Eastern Conference members. To put this expenditure in perspective and show the conference's priorities, it had spent all of seven thousand dollars that year trying to organize new Teamster members.

On Wednesday May 21, Jackie was elected president during a four-hour roll call. The vote was 1,729 to 24. His opponent, Sam Theodus of Truck Drivers Local 407 in Cleveland, conceded a half hour into the vote, but Jackie insisted that the tally go on. "You've just seen democracy in action," Presser told the press.

Security was tight that week. After all, Jackie, through his lawyers, was now admitting in pretrial maneuvering in a Cleveland federal courtroom that the FBI had authorized him to keep no-show workers on the Local 507 payroll. Therefore, it was indisputable to anyone who read the newspapers that Jackie was an informer. But Jackie still denied it. He spread several cover stories to keep his opponents in the union and the underworld off balance. Teamsters lawyer Robert Rotatori mentioned two of Jackie's more effective covers. For the first, he would say, "It's a lie. The government is trying to get me killed." For the second, "It's not true. It's all just a defense strategy." He convinced some and at least created doubt among others. "Jackie," Rotatori said, "was a very cunning individual."

In mid-July, in the midst of the pretrial skirmishing, Cleveland Strike Force chief Steve Olah, only forty-one, died of a heart attack. Maybe the Presser case was jinxed. Reporters had their news stories retracted. Labor investigators had their careers ruined. Jackie's contact agent was indicted. Then a chief antagonist, Steve Olah, dropped dead at forty-one. A few days later, Cleveland FBI chief Joe Griffin was spotted at the funeral of his nemesis. They had feuded over turf since before the Presser case. "Joe, what are you doing here?" he was asked. According to FBI legend, Griffin replied, "I want to make sure the son of a bitch is dead."

Obesity, poor diet, three packs of cigarettes a day for nearly forty years, and the stress of living a double life all had taken their toll on Jackie. In January 1987, he checked into the Cleveland Clinic for a lung-cancer operation. Surgeons removed the upper lobe of his left lung; four days later, Jackie underwent the first of eight weekly radiation treatments. He took a long vacation in Scottsdale, Arizona, near his wife's family, and his staff pretty much ran things while he recuperated in the dry desert air.

On August 6, 1987, a warm sunny morning in Cleveland, Jackie and his wife slowly walked down the carpeted corridor of Local 507, where his climb to power had begun twenty years earlier. In two weeks, his labor racketeering trial was supposed to commence. Cindy Presser pulled her husband through a door and into the meeting hall. It was a setup. There was a roar of voices, "Happy birthday, Jackie! Surprise!" His face split into a broad smile.

417

It was a coming-out party as well as a private birthday celebration. Jackie was recovering from the cancer and radiation treatments and had even been able to play a round of golf at the Rancho Mirage resort. At the party, he saw some retired teamsters loyal to his family. He also saw Michael Benz, a representative of the Greater Cleveland Growth Association, the local chamber of commerce. Nearby stood Carmen Parise, head of the Teamsters newspaper drivers division. "I feel great, I feel fine," Jackie said, moving from guest to guest.

Sam Miller, the multimillionaire developer and major shareholder of Forest City Enterprises, a big Teamster employer, asked, "Are you really well?"

"Sam, do I look like I'm dying?" Jackie said, smiling, nimbly dodging the question.

Miller and the others hadn't seen much of Jackie since his January 13 operation. Despite rumors that he had shriveled up from cancer, Jackie was still his roly-poly self, packing at least three hundred pounds into a navy-blue suit draped over his 5'9" frame. He wore a canary-yellow golf shirt that said "Rancho Mirage" in tiny letters and a matching cap that hid his skull, which had been denuded by the radiation treatments.

"The doctors can't believe his progress," Cindy told a visitor. "My husband has a very strong constitution."

The one hundred people in the room sang "Happy Birthday," and then Jackie stood at a lectern and said, "I do not have cancer." He doffed his hat. "My hair is growing back."

Then the fun began. His friends had brought gag gifts. Jackie was an easy target since they knew he was supposed to be an aficionado of chocolate, golf, and sex. Among the gifts were huge boxes of chocolates, a box of white-chocolate golf balls, a box of exploding golf balls, a black leather whip, a candle resembling a penis, and a copy of *Sex and Aerobics* magazine.

"You people must think I'm perverted, all these gifts," he said, embarrassed. "My son is sitting here." Near the front, looking uncomfortable and colorless, was Gary Presser, twenty-nine, Jackie's only son by his third wife and a newly elected vice president of Local 507.

Jackie unwrapped a blackjack, an organizing tool more popular in his father's days. "Don't let Cindy get ahold of this," he said, waving the small leather club. "She'll give me a few whaps."

418

Jackie unwrapped a book, *Presumed Innocent,* the summer's best-selling mystery thriller. He liked the title. "Hey, Harold," Jackie called out to Harold Friedman, displaying the book. "Presumed . . . inno-cent." He drew out the words, making an inside joke. "It's a good book." That's how he hoped his jury would start out—presuming his innocence.

Jackie's embezzlement trial was delayed time and again as the govern-ment and his lawyers wrangled over discovery. Climaco insisted on getting Jackie's informant file, saying it contained proof that his client was authorized to hire ghost employees. The government refused, and the wrangling went on, focusing on Jackie's secret life as an FBI source, creating headlines in its wake.

Jackie had other pressing matters to attend to. For months, there had been whispers that the Justice Department was preparing an un-precedented civil lawsuit to place the Teamsters Union under federal control, arguing that it was the only way to rid the union of organized crime. Using the Racketeer Influenced and Corrupt Organizations Act (RICO), the lawsuit was aimed at forcing the twenty-one member executive board to resign, including not-so-secret FBI operative Jackie Presser. The suit hadn't been filed, but it was impossible to keep the massive action a secret, as teams of government lawyers, clerks, and FBI agents in Washington, New York, and elsewhere gathered records, held meetings, and wrote legal briefs. Through third parties, allies in the Labor Department's legal office sent word to Presser what was up.

Sick as he was, Jackie and his staff mounted an impressive preemp-tive strike on the lawsuit that summer. On Labor Day, the Teamsters Union fought back in full-page ads in fifteen influential newspapers across the country. "Takeovers of unions are nothing new—Commu-nists and Fascists have been doing so for decades," the ads read. "It's a sad day in the history of the United States and the American labor movement when such tactics are even considered. America . . . it can't happen here. Or can it?"

They hired the world's largest public-relations firm, Hill and Knowlton, to handle publicity for the battle. A week later, more than three thousand Teamster business agents journeyed to the Cincinnati

Convention Center to rally against the proposed takeover lawsuit. The union's chief lobbyist, Paul Locigno, and his staff drummed up personal appearances by three presidential aspirants: Jesse Jackson, Representative Jack Kemp, and Alexander Haig, who all told the unionists that they opposed the Justice Department's civil RICO lawsuit. Senator Paul Simon of Illinois, a Democratic presidential candidate, union leaders from Europe and Asia, and United Nations trade secretaries also sent videotaped speeches supporting the Teamsters.

Running a 102-degree fever from the flu, Jackie told the Cincinnati rally, "We are fed up with the government's big-bully tactics. We are not going to take it any more. We're going to fight back." The Mafia doesn't control this union, he said with a straight face, adding that there wasn't even proof that the Mafia existed.

Privately, Jackie didn't hold Reagan personally responsible for the contemplated takeover suit by the Justice Department. "I know that Meese signed off, and it wound up in the hands of a person under Ed Meese who anticipated but has not gone forward with any action," Jackie said that month to a reporter in Columbus. But at the Cincinnati rally, Jackie bitterly attacked the Reagan administration, saying it wanted to destroy the labor movement. "You know why we're first on the list? Because we're the strongest," he said. The crowd roared in approval.

The ad campaign and the rally were only part of the Teamsters' aggressive counterattack. Presser thought that the union needed more allies. On October 13, at Mel Krupin's restaurant in Washington, Edward Hanley, president of the Hotel and Restaurant Employees Union as well as an AFL-CIO board member, asked Jackie, as he invariably did whenever he saw him, when the Teamsters were going to rejoin the AFL-CIO. Chairman Lane Kirkland had promoted the idea since the late seventies. This time, Jackie accepted Hanley's invitation.

The next day, Hanley, William H. Wynn, president of the United Food and Commercial Workers Union, and Robert A. Georgine, head of the AFL-CIO's building-trades division, met with Jackie and then later with Kirkland. Everything looked fine for reaffiliation. Moving quickly, the Teamsters' executive board voted five days later to rejoin the AFL-CIO. Five days after that, the AFL-CIO's executive council accepted the plan over the weekend before its biennial convention in

Miami Beach. Presser was pleased. Throwing in with the AFL-CIO's 12.7 million members would help them immensely in fighting off the government's civil RICO lawsuit. Jackie would be able to frame the Justice Department's reform attempt as an attack on all labor unions. Today the Teamsters, tomorrow the Textile Workers.

On October 29, Jackie journeyed to Miami to address the AFL-CIO convention. With only one good lung, he bogged down in the humidity and became weak and disoriented. But this was a historic moment he didn't want to pass up. Twenty-five years ago, the Teamsters had been expelled from the AFL-CIO because of corruption and Mob ties. His father had to accept part of the blame. Now the Teamsters were being welcomed back, even though mobbed-up locals and corrupt vice presidents still existed.

Wearing a cap as usual to hide his bald head, Jackie began his speech, ignoring a prepared text. "We want to come home," he told the nine hundred cheering labor leaders at the final session of the convention. Together we can "create the greatest political giant this country has ever seen."

He spoke off the cuff for twenty minutes, at times halting and appearing disoriented. He received his biggest applause talking about DRIVE, the union's political campaign fund, explaining how it would top $10 million that year. "Our DRIVE organization on a voluntary basis goes out and gets a dollar a week from our membership on a check-off basis," Presser said. "Now that may not seem like much, but when you have five hundred thousand people paying a dollar a week, you have an awful lot of money to spend. And without money, you're going nowhere in this country. It just will never happen."

After his speech "he almost collapsed," Paul Locigno recalls. "It was heroic. He was dehydrated. He hadn't eaten in days. I don't know where he got the personal energy to walk. For him even to be lucid enough to talk was a small miracle, he had been so out of it. After that, he collapsed back in Phoenix. He did not remember giving that speech. The only thing he remembers is he and Lane Kirkland raising their arms up together."

Jackie was on target about the incredible power of DRIVE's war chest. It actually raised $8 million in 1987, making it the largest lobbying committee of any labor or business group, larger than the reigning giants, the American Medical Association and the National

Association of Realtors, neither of which topped $6 million. DRIVE contributions opened doors. Locigno and the headquarters staff eventually convinced 246 members of the House of Representatives to sign a letter to Attorney General Meese protesting the proposed civil RICO suit. "You can't get 246 members of Congress to sign a proclamation for National Pickle Week," Locigno said. Members of congress who had accepted DRIVE money were two and a half times as likely to sign the letter as those who did not, a *Wall Street Journal* survey showed. Locigno said that the letter was significant. "It was credited with making the government tone down its tactics," he said.

By the time the letter got to Meese in December, Jackie had suffered a relapse. He spent the rest of the winter in Arizona, coming home briefly at Christmas. His embezzlement trial was delayed to February 1988, then to May. The drugs and painkillers he took to treat his lung cancer and other complications made Jackie's moods swing wildly. Near the end, he cried over his betrayal of Maishe Rockman, his father's dear underworld friend from Glenville. Maishe had put his reputation on the line for Jackie with the Genovese Crime Family in New York, insisting he could control him and that Jackie was not an FBI stool pigeon. In return, Jackie had helped put the old man in prison, and now he regretted it.

In April 1988, he returned to Cleveland, still struggling to stay alive. "He called me one Saturday," said Bob Hughes, the Cuyahoga County Republican party chairman. "He came down to the office, and we sat and chatted for two hours. I concluded Jackie was dying. Absolutely dying. I looked in Jackie's eyes—there was no spark there. Pasty looking skin, his hair gone. I thought, You're looking at death. The angel of death was beating its wings in my office. . . . Jackie was just venting out his frustrations on people we knew. I think Jackie knew he was dying and felt he was ill-used. Guys he felt were bum rapping him, taking advantage of him."

By then, it was clear that Jackie wouldn't survive, and Teamsters vice presidents began jockeying for power. Weldon Mathis, the second in command, wanted to be president. So did vice presidents Walter Shea and William McCarthy of Boston. Harold Friedman threw in with McCarthy; Climaco backed Weldon Mathis; and Tony Hughes joined McCarthy and Friedman, which created problems with his lawyer, John Climaco's brother Michael, Hughes said. On May 4, the

422

other vice presidents learned that Jackie had signed a letter, presented to him by John Climaco, in which he relinquished his duties to Mathis for 120 days. Some vice presidents were upset, feeling manipulated by a Climaco-engineered power play that gave Mathis a better shot at succeeding Jackie.

Mathis told reporters that he expected Jackie to recover, but less than two weeks later, surgeons at a Phoenix hospital removed a tumor from Jackie's brain, where the lung cancer had metastasized. Jackie would never recover. He knew he was sick and in a hospital but was otherwise disoriented. He couldn't shave, read, or recall what month it was. "Jackie didn't even know what town he was in," Hughes said.

"When Jackie had moments of sanity," a close friend said, "he wouldn't have picked Weldon Mathis. The only person he respected and cared about on that whole board was Joe T [Trerotola of New York]. Because Joe T stuck by him in the end. Jackie was half in and half out. He told the board that if he had his way, he'd remove half of them before the next convention. He didn't care what he said. He didn't mask or use finesse or diplomacy."

The Justice Department had other ideas about who should run the Teamsters. On June 28, the U.S. Attorney in Manhattan, Rudolph W. Giuliani, filed a lawsuit asking a judge to oust the executive board members and to order free elections because Mafia infiltration had "deprived union members of their rights" through a "campaign of fear" that included "twenty murders, a number of shootings, bombings, beatings . . . bribes, extortion, and theft, and misuse of union funds."

That very day, a blood clot lodged in Jackie's remaining lung, and he was rushed to Lakewood Hospital in suburban Cleveland. He never learned that the government had filed the lawsuit he had fought so hard to subvert. Jackie Presser died eleven days later, on July 9, 1988.

Three days later, about six hundred people came to Jackie's funeral service—judges, elected officials, heads of local and international unions, mayors, a U.S. senator or two, and half a dozen congressmen. Some who knew him the longest and most intimately—his mother Faye, living in Miami, and his uncle Allen Friedman—stayed home. His mother was old; his uncle was angry. Teamster vice president

Harold Friedman, who had taught Jackie the nuts and bolts of the union business, made an appearance, but it was an empty gesture. He had refused to fly the flag at half-mast outside Local 507, as the rest of the Cleveland-area locals were doing. Jackie had hurt those closest to him.

It was warm, sunny morning, and the seats in the windowless funeral parlor quickly filled up to capacity, with another hundred mourners lining the aisles. The Teamsters vice presidents and other ranking officials were ferried to the Berkowitz-Kumin Memorial Chapel by buses from the downtown hotels. At 11:06 A.M., Cleveland Mayor George Voinovich began a brief eulogy, pointing out Jackie's accomplishments as a labor leader. "He was a man who loved his fellow man. He made a difference in my life. I will miss him and pray for him."

Senator Orrin Hatch of Utah followed him. "Like the rest of us, Jackie Presser made some mistakes," Hatch intoned. "I am sure that given an opportunity to relive his life, he would make some different decisions. Wouldn't we all. But the Jackie Presser who I knew and who I will always remember was a man of courage. He was the first Teamster president to come voluntarily before a Senate committee [in 1983] and respond to every single question the members of the committee decided to ask. He did so in front of all the committee, in front of the public, and under oath."

Hatch mentioned all those Jackie helped—his wife Cindy, his son Gary, and daughter Bari; Teamster members and retirees; the state of Israel. Hatch didn't note Jackie's aid to the FBI, but the thought wasn't far from the mind of one man in the crowd, ex-agent Bob Friedrick, who came on his own and blended in unobtrusively.

"May Jackie Presser stay gently with God," Hatch went on. "May he rest from the days of adversity, and may he never be forgotten by the thousands he helped through his affection, his leadership, and his friendship. We will miss you, Jackie. You were one who made a difference."

After the service, a parade of cars, limos, and buses traced the same route to Mount Olive Cemetery they had when Bill Presser had been laid to rest seven years before. Jackie had commanded center stage that day, greeting the visiting Teamsters leaders, taking telegrams from congressmen and the president, leading mourners to the burial site,

424

sharing his grief with several hundred. At Jackie's funeral, his son Gary Presser, quiet and emotionally wounded, stayed in the background except for serving as a pallbearer.

Bill Presser had handed his power down to Jackie, starting him off young, sticking with him through failure, watching him finally succeed in middle age. But Jackie didn't do that with his son. When they buried Jackie Presser, they ended the Presser dynasty in the labor movement, a reign of power that spanned more than half a century, from the birth of Teamsters' labor racketeering to a climactic showdown with the federal government.

28

Epilogue

"McCarthy used the Winter Hill syndicate gang to help enforce his union policies."

JUSTICE DEPARTMENT REPORT

After Jackie Presser's burial service, two buses of Teamster officials and their spouses arrived at Cleveland PM, a fancy Italian restaurant appropriate for the occasion. Run by a family with Murray Hill roots, the restaurant overlooked the city's industrial valley, full of truck depots and smoking forges and mills.

It wasn't a sorrowful group. Jackie had been sick for so long, his death was a deliverance. Now it remained to be seen who would replace him and what would happen to his "new day for the Teamsters" administration.

Two men stood out that early afternoon at the restaurant, turning heads as they moved among their colleagues. One was going to replace Jackie as president—Weldon Mathis, sixty-two, the acting Teamsters president from Atlanta, or William J. McCarthy, sixty-nine, a vice president from Boston. They were a study in contrasts. Mathis, tanned, speaking in slow Southern tones, moved through the crowded restaurant, smiling graciously and shaking hands. Billy McCarthy, with ruffled white hair and an off-the-rack suit, didn't mingle, instead moving quickly to and from the restaurant's pay telephones, brushing off greetings, his mind on his mission—to get nine of seventeen IBT executive board votes.

Mathis, an insider at Teamster headquarters for nearly two decades, was the early favorite. For much of the past year, he and

426

Climaco had run the union while Jackie recuperated. Some Teamster vice presidents felt that Climaco—not Jackie, as reported—was the prime mover behind the Mathis campaign. Their detractors cynically noted that Climaco's law firm would retain its multimillion-dollar account with the International and other Teamster entities if Mathis was president.

Jackie wouldn't have wanted Billy McCarthy to succeed him. McCarthy was everything Jackie had been and wanted to escape— uneducated, unpolished, a hooligan, car thief, and brawler in his younger days. McCarthy had campaigned hard for two months to line up supporters, among them Harold Friedman, who had split from Jackie after he was indicted for payroll padding along with Presser and Hughes.

Mathis counted his votes again and again; he had nine, just enough. Consequently, he didn't feel the need to reach out to vice president Joe Trerotola, who controlled five votes and who didn't like Mathis one bit. Mathis didn't know it, but a few weeks before the election, one of the votes he had counted on—Daniel C. Ligurotis, the newest vice president on the executive board—had switched camps. Mathis and McCarthy both gave Ligurotis the same sales pitch: a promise to make him head of the powerful Central Conference of Teamsters. But Chicago-based Ligurotis wanted a Teamsters jet to go along with the job. Mathis would have to take the jet from Edward Lawson, head of the Canadian Conference of Teamsters and his close friend on the executive board. He couldn't do that. McCarthy promised Ligurotis the executive jet, nailing down the vote. On July 15, 1988, after a rancorous meeting, McCarthy, with Trerotola's backing, squeezed past Mathis on a nine-to-eight vote. Still seething and badly split, the IBT executive board couldn't even agree on a motion to present its usual phony unanimous vote to the public. The old guard was back in power.

A few days later, at a news conference, McCarthy bluntly remarked that if Jackie knew he had won, Presser probably would be "rolling over in his grave."

Nothing worked out the way Jackie had planned. Throughout the five years of his presidency, he had proclaimed his term in office a "new day for the Teamsters." With millions spent on public relations, lobbying, and campaign contributions, the notion took hold. There was some substance behind it as well. Local officers actually received assistance when they called headquarters for organizing funds and model contracts.

Jackie felt himself to be a modern labor leader, an innovator of Teamsters retiree clubs, political action committees, and union-sponsored housing. But actually, the late Teamsters vice-president Harold Gibbons introduced these programs in St. Louis back when Jackie was dipping into the till at bowling alleys, still searching for love and a style to call his own. Jackie didn't act out of an egalitarian belief in the dignity of the worker—he always said the common man had no business running a Teamsters local—but out of an urge to remake his union into a middle-class, professional Fortune 500 company with pension benefits, health plans, and office Christmas parties. It was all part of his unintended quest to "turn his collar." Acting president Weldon Mathis would have walked the path Presser had marked, holding himself out as a clean, modern labor leader. Compared to other IBT vice presidents, Mathis's transgressions were minor; he had been accused of voting irregularities at his home local in Atlanta, and he had been involved in some minor dirty campaign tricks for White House aide Charles Colson during Nixon's 1972 campaign. Over the years, Presser had had nothing damaging to say to his FBI handlers about Mathis.

McCarthy, however, sounded none of Jackie's "new day" themes. McCarthy was a throwback, a union boss in the mold of Hoffa and the Plug, men who concentrated on bread-and-butter issues and shunned the press and Madison Avenue techniques. First, McCarthy fired Teamsters general counsel Climaco at an executive board meeting, then he removed Presser loyalists Dan Darrow, head of the United Parcel Service drivers locals, and Carmen Parise, head of the newspaper drivers locals. Later, he turned his wrath on Jackie, calling him a "crooked stool pigeon" who lied to the FBI. "There was a lot of phoney-baloney stuff in there," McCarthy said in his Boston brogue. "Anything he did was for his benefit."

The day after McCarthy was elected IBT president, his hometown paper, the *Boston Globe,* gave him a clean bill of health. A news story quoted union sources as saying that McCarthy was a back-to-the-basics leader. "He is also regarded as having run one of the cleanest Teamsters locals in the country and has never been connected with any

Teamster-related corruption," the newspaper reported. Jeremiah T. O'Sullivan, chief of the Justice Department's Boston Strike Force, told the *Globe* he knew of no ties between McCarthy and the Mob. McCarthy had never been charged with a crime, either, O'Sullivan added.

But interviews and documents uncovered for this book reveal a much different picture of the president of the nation's largest labor union. Born and reared in Boston, McCarthy grew up in the city's slums, the son of an epileptic mother whom he had to escort as a boy. "I would have to go with her everyplace," he said. "And she would take a spell, and they'd want to arrest her for drunk, for drinking."

At fifteen he stole a car, was spotted by Boston police in his Charleston neighborhood, and led them on a chase. He abandoned the car near Teamsters Local 25, jumped into the cab of a ten-wheeler, and hid on the floor. When its driver returned from a tavern, McCarthy said he talked the man into taking him on his run to New York City. Young McCarthy became friends with his savior and spent Sundays helping the man wash and repair his rig, falling in love with trucks. Around this time, he was caught in some mischief and a parish priest pulled him into the church sacristy for a lecture. The future Teamsters president spotted a pad of blank baptism certificates and hatched a plan. He returned with a friend, who distracted the priest while the resourceful McCarthy stole some of the blank records. He forged one to make himself old enough to get the chauffeur's license he needed to get a truck-driving job. At seventeen, he joined the Teamsters.

He drove for Benjamin Motor Express, making the Boston to New York runs, with an overnight layover, three times a week. For each run, he made sixteen dollars plus four dollars in expenses, sixty dollars a week. "Every Saturday you would get paid, and you got paid cash," McCarthy said. "Then I would have to go behind the trucks in the platform, way down back, and had to slip the boss a ten-buck kickback. . . . What the hell, I didn't want to do it. But I said, hell, I want the job, too." Ten dollars—one-sixth of his weekly wages—was a hefty sum in those days.

In 1946, he was business agent of Truck Drivers Local 25; by 1955, he took over as president. Hot-tempered, impatient, appearing slightly crazy to his enemies, McCarthy ran the local with an iron fist, working ten- and twelve-hour days. He took over the joint council, then was named a vice-president in 1969. Among his friends was Howard "Howie" Winter, the one-time leader of the Winter Hill gang, an organized-crime faction from Somerville, Massachusetts. Winter joined McCarthy's local as a young man and spent a dozen or so years there helping McCarthy get reelected with heavy-handed campaigning. Winter didn't threaten McCarthy's opponents, the Teamster official said. "I wouldn't allow it."

However, according to a 1977 Justice Department report strictly intended for internal use, McCarthy had considerable Mob help maintaining control over Local 25 during the fifties and sixties:

> International vice president and organizer William J. McCarthy is closely linked to Gennaro Angiulo of the Boston LCN. McCarthy is said to utilize the syndicate's muscle to maintain his power. This power solidifies not only his position in the two international offices he holds but also as president of Joint Council 10 and Local 25. . . .
>
> President William McCarthy is a close associate of Boston LCN figure Gennaro Angiulo. McCarthy used the Winter Hill syndicate gang to help enforce his union policies. Local 25 is under investigation by the FBI and the Department of Labor for misuse of union funds. There is a suspected alliance between Sal Provenzano of New Jersey and McCarthy. There is also a connection between Local 122 IBT and Local 25. Most recently officers of Local 122 have been successful in putting members of the Winter Hill gang on the payroll of a local Budweiser plant, although all these men are members of Local 25.

McCarthy had other influential friends. Raymond L. S. Patriarca, Mafia boss of New England, was overheard on an FBI wiretap on June 7, 1965, saying that he knew McCarthy very well and that James J. "Buddy" McLean, a Winter Hill gang leader, probably controlled him. Patriarca said he was extremely close with McLean.

Thereafter, McCarthy had fleeting contact with the FBI. In February 1974, the FBI questioned him about the firebombing of trucks and the slashing of truck tires during a long-running dispute between a Schlitz beer distributor and a trucking company with Local 25 drivers. Schlitz had given a distributorship to a new company in Springfield,

Massachusetts, and the new competitor was moving into Boston and taking over accounts that had employed Local 25 drivers. McCarthy said he knew nothing about it and that he had not made threats.

In 1976, FBI agents asked him about Hoffa's mysterious disappearance. Specifically, the agents wanted to know what Central States consultant Allen Dorfman and casino owner and former Hoffa lawyer Morris Shenker might have said about Hoffa's comeback. McCarthy said he knew the two men, but little else.

Had he ever heard that Hoffa considered cooperating with the Justice Department as a basis for having his parole restrictions removed? the agents asked. McCarthy said no.

Did he know anything about payments or bribes that may have been made to insure that Hoffa was restricted from taking part in union activities until 1980? the FBI wanted to know. Again, McCarthy said he knew nothing.

And what of Charles Colson and his relationship with Fitzsimmons and getting those restrictions placed on Hoffa? McCarthy told the FBI he knew Colson as a lawyer for the Teamsters but that was about it. In 1982, he was questioned by FBI agents about Teamsters contributions channeled to the Reagan campaign through Secretary of Labor Raymond Donovan. He said he knew nothing about it.

Fighting the Justice Department's cleanup lawsuit fell to McCarthy's longtime Boston lawyer, James Grady, and the New York law firm of Mudge, Rose, Guthrie, Alexander and Ferdon, Richard M. Nixon's former employer. They began negotiations with the U.S. Attorney's office in late 1988. Before long, the deep divisions on the executive board, unhealed since McCarthy's election, ripped open and began hurting the Teamsters. The government lawyers had planned to pit one group against the others and achieved a tremendous breakthrough in January 1989. Three vice presidents—Weldon Mathis, Edward Lawson from Vancouver, and Don L. West from Birmingham—tried to settle the case separately from the rest of the IBT executive board. It was the McCarthy-Mathis split surfacing again. These three Teamster leaders knew that if the union lost the civil RICO case, they and the other board members faced possible economic devastation. By law, the Justice Department could not only strip them of all union positions but could also make them forfeit their pensions. Since they were all making from $200,000 to $300,000 a year, they each stood to lose more than a million dollars in future earnings and pension money. But the three men also agreed that the union needed some reforming. They eventually signed an agreement in early March endorsing election reforms as well as the appointment of an independent officer to throw out corrupt Teamsters Union officials. Significantly, the three acknowledged in their carefully worded agreement that there was some Mob control of the union. It was a devastating blow to the IBT board.

Lawyers Randy Mastro, Marla Alhadeff, Peter Sprung, and Richard Marks from the U.S. Attorney's office in New York made another offer to the McCarthy forces. They wanted the union to adopt secret ballot elections by the rank and file for top officers, appointment of a Teamsters czar to oversee operations and discipline union officials, and the resignations of five Teamsters vice presidents the Justice Department felt were Mob-influenced, including Joe Trerotola from New York; Harold Friedman of Cleveland; Don Peters from Chicago: Joe Morgan from Miami; and Ted Cozza from Pittsburgh. McCarthy and Grady rejected the offer. They were old-time negotiators, not used to moving from their positions until the eleventh hour.

Meanwhile, lawyers for the union had been demanding to see Jackie and Tony Hughes's informant files as part of pre-trial discovery in the lawsuit. They probably thought they'd never get the top-secret materials—the FBI had never allowed such informant information to be released—and could create delay or confusion by wrangling over the ALPRO files. But on March 8, only five days before trial, the government entered more than three thousand redacted pages of Presser and Hughes's secret files into the court record. The ALPRO files incriminated several executive board members, especially Peters and Morgan.

Marathon negotiations kicked off over the weekend before the trial. At about half-past one in the morning on the day of the trial, an agreement was reached. None of the current executive board members would have to resign. They had preserved their jobs for the short term, but they had agreed to give extraordinary powers to a court-appointed administrator and two other key officers.

The administrator could veto any expenditure or purchase he felt was improper. He also could file corruption charges against officers, suspending or firing them. His burden of proof was the lowest possible; he had only to show just cause to dismiss someone for corruption. That meant that newspaper articles, hearsay testimony, and other evidence could be used at a hearing. The administrator's actions were final and binding, subject only to appeal in federal court.

The agreement also called for the appointment of a powerful elections officer, who was to oversee direct, secret rank-and-file elections of the general president and other top jobs when the current officers' terms expired in 1991.

The third court-appointed watchdog was an investigations officer, who had subpoena power, the right to examine ledger books and financial records, take sworn statements, and look into any situation that hinted of Mob involvement or any other form of corruption. Armed with this information, the administrator could then remove tainted union officers.

The Teamster brass probably didn't realize what it had given up. The executive board gave the new administrator the tools with which to remove them. "It was an incredible slam dunk at the last minute," said Randy Mastro, the lead Justice Department lawyer on the case.

Billy McCarthy was either fearless or crazy. About two weeks after the civil RICO lawsuit was settled, but before the administrator took over, McCarthy awarded a $3-million-a-year Teamsters printing contract to a tiny Sudbury, Massachusetts, company owned by his son-in-law, Joseph Treacy. The company, Windsor Graphics, gave its address as Treacy's home, where an answering machine handled inquiries. In a matter of weeks, the administrator would begin looking into union spending and contracts. The printing contract seemed a blatant conflict of interest, though McCarthy defended his actions. The bids had been sealed and were awarded to whomever had the lowest.

Next, McCarthy deliberately thumbed his nose at the Justice Department and its settlement. After promising to rid the Teamsters of corruption, McCarthy, in his first executive board appointment, named as vice president Local 283 president George Vitale of Wyandotte, Michigan. Vitale had twice been convicted of labor racketeering—once for taking payoffs, the other for illegally using union funds to buy his wife a car. He was hardly the most inspiring choice. Furthermore, Vitale was a close associate of Anthony LaPiana, whom Jackie Presser once described as "the new Allen Dorfman" because of his Mob ties and his lucrative insurance business built with Teamsters health and welfare funds. "We have mixed signals on the Detroit family 'owning' LaPiana," said a Labor Department official. "He may get orders out of Chicago." LaPiana is the son-in-law of Vincent Meli, a Detroit rackets figure from the Hoffa days. Vitale had even removed his Local 283's health and welfare plan out of the huge, efficient Michigan Conference of Teamsters plan and placed the business in LaPiana's hands. LaPiana's National Labor Union Health and Welfare Fund operated at a loss in the early eighties, mostly because of bad business practices and seventeen-percent administrative fees, about double the industry standard, Jackie informed the FBI. By 1983, the fund owed $2.5 million in unpaid claims, and LaPiana and Vitale put the arm on vice president Bobby Holmes to bail them out. He refused.

In June 1983, LaPiana collared Jackie at a Teamsters meeting in Chicago. According to Jackie's remarks to the FBI, LaPiana said he represented the Chicago and Detroit crime families, both of whom wanted Jackie to "handle" the $2.5 million debt by giving LaPiana funds from the International or vice president Bobby Holmes's Central Conference. Later, LaPiana sued the Michigan Conference of Teamsters for the money and received a hefty sum as a settlement.

McCarthy's next pick for vice president was also controversial: Gairald Kiser, mid-sixties, a former officer with Cincinnati Truck Drivers Local 100. Kiser was a hulking, eccentric man who would show up in a tuxedo or other inappropriate garb at union meetings. He also fancied homburg hats and canes. Even McCarthy's supporters shook their heads over this appointment. Jackie's "new day" term had been almost completely dismantled. The union was up for grabs; not since the waning days of president Dan Tobin in the early 1950s had such high-level rebellion broken out.

The legacy Jackie did end up leaving wasn't one he had intended. The biggest, longest, most effective project he had constructed turned out to be his FBI file—2,000-plus pages of hard facts, hearsay, investigative leads, and scuttlebutt coughed up over a fifteen-year period under the FBI code names Tailor, PROBEX, and ALPRO. The Teamsters union lawyers fought hard to get his and Tony Hughes's files in the IBT Civil RICO case, and now those files have been publicly disclosed. The new administrator of the union can now use the 2,000-page file, along with other documentation, to remove mobbed-up officials in the union.

The compilers of Jackie's FBI files—Marty McCann, Pat Foran, and Bob Friedrick—were not as lucky as Jackie. They are under criminal investigation for perjury and obstruction of justice, stemming from trying to protect Jackie from Labor agents Simmons and Thomas. Once again the people who developed ties to Jackie Presser found their careers in jeopardy. Jackie, nimble for a fat man, always kept his footing while walking a high wire between the Mob and the FBI. Though a Mafia snitch, he ended up cheating his supposed executioners by dying of natural causes. That didn't matter much to him. His friends said that in the last year or two of his life, Jackie seemed to want to go out in a blaze of glory like Hoffa.

In the end, who got the better part of the deal between Presser and the FBI? Tony Hughes, who ought to know, said at first Jackie benefited more. McCann would warn him when the FBI had picked up information about John Nardi, Danny Greene, or their murderous Cleveland crew wanting to hurt him. Moreover, the FBI quit scrutinizing the Presser family and turned its attention to his rivals, some of whom deserved to be exposed. By 1980, Jackie had implicated labor racketeers Allen Dorfman and Teamsters chief Roy Williams in a bribe scheme, and that tipped the balance in favor of the FBI. Three years later, June 1983, the FBI compiled a hyperbolic list of Presser's accomplishments so Oliver B. Revell, the FBI's second-in-command, could try to convince his boss to ask the Labor investigators to back down. Despite the puffery, Jackie did help the Justice Department convict ranking mobsters in Kansas City, Chicago, Cleveland, and New York.

He probably could have become Teamsters president as Rob Williams had done—throwing in wholeheartedly with the Mob. But Jackie didn't have to make such an iron-clad devil's pact once he became the FBI's prize mole inside the underworld. Instead he employed a conservative tactic for a man from a family of gamblers: He hedged his bets by becoming an informer, buying an insurance policy from the FBI.

In the end, the FBI's most secretive informant became its most celebrated.

435

Notes

1. EARLY DAYS

In addition to interviews with Presser relatives and family members, some of whom requested anonymity, this chapter drew upon the Jewish Community Center records at the Western Reserve Historical Society, the former *Cleveland Press*'s newspaper morgue now at Cleveland State University library, and *The Encyclopedia of Cleveland History* (Indiana University Press, 1987), an invaluable 1,127-page work of scholarship. No similar reference book currently exists for an American city. Also helpful were county birth, death, and marriage records, and census cards of the Cleveland City School District, and the huge labor history collection—oral histories, union records and newspapers—at the Ohio Historical Society.

Page
9
"We were growing up"
Interview with the author.

10
"Jackie was in charge"
Interview with the author.

11
"I remember the streets"
Jackie Presser oral history, Ohio Historical Society.

12
Allen's fondest memories
Interview with the author.

14
"I beat up on kids"
Interview with the author.

15
"I was one of the very"
William Presser oral history, Ohio Historical Society.

2. THE RACKETS

In addition to interviews, this chapter was based on articles in the *Cleveland Press* and *Plain Dealer*, grand jury reports, police records and *Marstan Hat Cleaners, Inc., v. William B. Beckerman, William Presser, et al,* Cuyahoga Common Pleas Court, case no. 431341.

Page
17
Carley's troubles had started
Carley's Dry Cleaning Corp. v. International Association of Cleaning and Dye Houseworkers, William Presser, et al, Cuyahoga County Common Pleas Court, case no. 483322. The court records included affidavits of William G. Jones and other employees that recounted the conversations described.

19
"The labor movement when I started"
Plain Dealer, July 19, 1981.

"The smell was terrible"
Interview with the author.

21
In a scathing report
Though grand jury proceedings were shrouded in secrecy, in Cuyahoga County, at least, grand jury foremen were expected to issue a report at the end of their terms. These reports—ranging from one perfunctory paragraph to dozens of pages—were then typed into docket books. The practice continued to the fifties and these fascinating reports detail the changing face of crime in Cleveland.

Eliot Ness didn't look
Cleveland, the Best-Kept Secret, by George Condon (Doubleday, 1967). Also, articles in the *Cleveland Plain Dealer, Press* and *Cleveland News.*

23
"Realizing the possibilities, the gang"
Silent Syndicate, Hank Messick. The book is unfortunately out of print and difficult to locate. It is said that the former Cleveland syndicate members, respected citizens of Las Vegas, Miami, and Los Angeles by the book's 1967 publication date, bought thousands of copies of the book and destroyed them.

24
But Ness should have recognized
Silent Syndicate, Hank Messick.

25
"Few people realize the nature"
Cuyahoga County grand-jury report, 1937, Cyril O'Neil, foreman.

3. YOUNG JACKIE

This chapter drew upon interviews with Allen Friedman, Abba Schwartz, Jack Kleinman, Pauline Walls, and others. Official investigative files on the Mob's jukebox rackets
are voluminous. Until Senator Bender aborted the hearings, groundbreaking work was
performed by "Investigation of Racketeering in the Cleveland, Ohio, Area" (known
informally as the Cleveland rackets hearings), Special Anti-Racketeering Subcommittee of the Committee on Government Operations of the House of Representatives,
83rd Congress, second session, in September 1954. Also essential is the record of the
McClellan rackets committee, known officially as the Senate Select Committee on
Improper Activities in the Labor or Management Field, January 30, 1957, through
March 1960; the Chicago Crime Commission files 60–78, four volumes on jukebox
rackets; and the John F. Kennedy pre-administration papers at the John F. Kennedy
Library, Box 803, folder "Coin-op Music, Amusements and Cigarette Vending Ma-
chine Industry: Findings."

Page
32
School administrators
Census Card, Jack Presser, Cleveland City School District.

"I was hard to contain"
Jackie Presser oral history, Ohio Historical Society.

"He was a hoodlum"
Interview with the author.

"He was what you call the neighborhood bully"
Interview with the author.

32–33
"He was a wonderful combination"
Interview with the author.

34
"Almost every level of the jukebox"
The Jukebox Racket, Virgil W. Peterson, Chicago Crime Commission, September
1954.

36
One restaurant owner
Gilles testimony, Cleveland rackets hearings, 1954.

37
Once in place, Presser's system
Cleveland rackets hearings, 1954.

38
"I was quite successful,"
William Presser oral history, Ohio Historical Society.

Five years later
Report of the Cleveland Rackets, 84th Congress, first session, 1955.

His father's vending
Jackie Presser oral history, Ohio Historical Society.

39
During the drives
Author interview with Rotatori.

"Our contract calls for"
Investigation of Racketeering in the Detroit Area, Joint Subcommittees of the Committee on Education and Labor and the Committee on Government Operations of the House of Representatives, 83rd Congress, first session. Known informally as the Detroit jukebox hearings.

40
DeSchryver, who was either brave
Ibid.

41
"They have been instrumental"
Cleveland rackets hearings, 1954.

42
"He always wore a suit"
Interview with the author.

44
"He seemed torn"
Pauline Walls letter to the author.

arrested on August 16, 1947
Throughout his career, Jackie said he had never been arrested or convicted. Not true. Records of his arrest and conviction are not found in Cleveland police files or routine court records. However, a daily appearance docket book for Cleveland Municipal Court for 1947, moldering in the dark and dust of the attic in the old Cleveland City Jail, held this secret.

46
In December 1944
Presser's cigarette and candy cartel is described in the records of the criminal anti-trust

action, *U.S. v. Tobacco and Candy Jobbers Association, Inc., William Presser, et al*, Northern District of Ohio, case no. 20338.

47
Presser's union men
Ibid.

48
Rockman had known Bill
Based on Angelo Lonardo's testimony in *U.S. v. Anthony Salerno, et al*, Southern District of New York, case no. 86 CR 245, and the Senate Permanent Subcommittee on Investigations, Hearings: Twenty-five Years after Valachi, April 1988.

"I want you to sell"
Cleveland rackets hearings, 1954.

4. STEALING CARS

The FBI investigated Allen Friedman's car-theft ring extensively, and Jackie obtained portions of those files in 1977 when he filed a Freedom of Information/Privacy Act request. I obtained those records as well as several dozen additional pages on the car ring through a FOIA request. The records were located under Cleveland FBI file numbers HQ 26-128423 and CV F.O. 26-6171. Also helpful were records in *U.S. v. Allen Friedman, et al* case numbers 19888–91, Northern District of Ohio, filed December 27, 1949.

Page
49
"I stole it"
Allen Friedman interview with the author.

52
"Jackie Presser expects us"
Jackie Presser FBI file, HQ 26-128423.

On June 2, 1949
Based on FBI records of the theft ring, File no. CV F.O. 26-6171

54
"So my brother Harry"
Friedman interview with the author.

"I took a ride with three"
Harold Friedman, February 9, 1989, deposition, *U.S. v. International Brotherhood of Teamsters, et al*, Southern District of New York, case no. 88 Civ 4486, referred to hereafter as IBT Civil RICO.

55
a curious extra detail
U.S. v. Allen Friedman, et al.

56
The man who forty years later
Allen Friedman interview with the author.

called into the warden's office
Power and Greed, Allen Friedman and Ted Schwarz (Franklin Watts, 1989).

58
Once in Toledo
Ibid.

60
At first, witnesses
Testimony of Sergeant Russell R. Jones, head of the Cincinnati vice squad, Cleveland rackets hearings, 1954.

"We did a little check
James Luken oral history, Ohio Historical Society.

5. BUYING OFF BENDER

Page
61
He kept busy.
Cleveland rackets hearings, 1954.

62
During their first year with Presser
U.S. v. Tobacco and Candy Jobbers. Also Cleveland rackets hearings, 1954.

The Justice Department had the case
Ibid.

64
"There was a lot of rumors"
Rotatori interview with the author.

"My wife is a very good"
Cleveland rackets hearings, 1954. The hearings were highlighted by the confessions of Moose Maxwell.

65
It wasn't surprising
Allen Friedman interview with the author and confidential sources.

66
Foley enjoyed tremendous
Delaney interview with the author.

68
Republican county chairman
Stillman interview with the author.

75
"Suddenly in the last"
James Luken oral history, Ohio Historical Society.

"Certain Teamsters"
The transcript of the meeting was obtained by the McClellan committee.

76
"George Starling, who is now"
James Luken oral history, Ohio Historical Society.

6. JACKIE'S FIRST SHOT

In addition to interviews, this chapter drew upon the court records in *Hotel Workers v. Jackie Presser, et al,* the extensive news coverage of the Dorsel's and Hotel Workers Union disputes in the local newspapers, and the personal scrapbooks and memorabilia of Oscar Zimmerman.

Page
77
He bought her meals
Goeble interview with the author.

78
"Ed Miller, the president"
Jackie Presser oral history, Ohio Historical Society.

79
"Jackie came in with the charter"
Vinegard interview with the author.

82
So strong was the Mob's control
Hotel Employees and Restaurant Employees International Union, Permanent Subcommittee on Investigations, Senate Governmental Affairs Committee, August 27, 1984.

83
It worked just as profitably
Chicago Crime Commission files.

83
The organizing drive at Dorsel's
Zimmerman interview with author.

84
"Sit down, Billy"
Weinberger interview with the author.

88
Jackie was out of town
Holohan's testimony in *Hotel Workers v. Jackie Presser, et al.*

89
Bill Presser, concerned
Power and Greed, Allen Friedman and Ted Schwarz (Franklin Watts, 1989).

90
"There isn't many things that I haven't done"
Jackie Presser oral history, Ohio Historical Society.

7. ROY WILLIAMS, THE MOB, AND KENNEDY

In addition to interviews, this chapter relied upon the McClellan hearings transcripts, the Robert Kennedy pre-Administration papers at the John F. Kennedy Library, and news stories in the *Kansas City Star,* the *Washington Post,* the *New York Times,* the *Wall Street Journal,* the *Cleveland Press,* and the *Plain Dealer.* Indispensable were the three long depositions of Roy Williams found in the records of the President's Commission on Organized Crime (1985), the IBT Civil RICO case (1988), and *U.S. v. Anthony Salerno, et al* (1986), both in the Southern District of New York.

Page
92
The interruption of this high-level
The Enemy Within, Robert F. Kennedy (Harper & Row Publishers, 1960).

At his next meeting
Williams deposition, *U.S. v. International Brotherhood of Teamsters, et al,* Southern District of New York, 88 Civ. 4486. Of the three detailed depositions—essentially confessions—William gave federal authorities since deciding to testify against the Mob, this one, taken December 1, 1988, by assistant U.S. Attorney Randy Mastro, was the most revealing.

93
The same scene unfolded
Ibid.

94
"Roy, it's a bad situation,"
Ibid.

95
"I made no bones about it,"
Williams deposition in *U.S. v. Anthony Salerno, et al,* Southern District of New York, 86 CR 245, otherwise known as the Genovese family case or simply the Salerno II trial.

Before that time
Williams deposition, IBT Civil RICO.

Some four hundred agents
The Valachi Papers, Peter Maas (Bantam Books, 1972).

In hounding left-wing idealists
After the Apalachin arrests in November 1957, Kennedy asked Hoover for dossiers on the mobsters who had been temporarily swept up in the raid. The FBI replied that it didn't have any. Disappointed, Kennedy asked the Bureau of Narcotics, which had extensive files on many of the mobsters.

97
Kennedy said
The Enemy Within, Kennedy.

98
After Sheridan left
Testimony in *U.S. v. William Presser,* CR No. 23276, Northern District of Ohio, 1960.

Four days later
The Fall and Rise of Jimmy Hoffa, Walter Sheridan (Saturday Review Press, 1972).

"there was no subversive information"
May 1958 FBI memo to Robert Kennedy.

99
Kennedy had been briefed
Memo to Kennedy from Senate investigator Arthur Kaplan, September 17, 1958. Though still under the Senate's fifty-year seal on criminal investigative records, several confidential McClellan committee memos were obtained for this book.

Kennedy: You have given jobs
These exchanges between Kennedy and Presser and Kennedy and Triscaro are taken from the McClellan hearings, September 17, 1958.

101
Hoffa was sitting nearby
Plain Dealer, September 18, 1958.

101
"took so many fifths"
Ibid.

102
a $300,000 loan
Allen Friedman says that Bill Presser discussed the plane sale with him briefly at the dinner table. Ed Partin, a teamster, FBI informant, and former close associate of Hoffa's, told Dan Moldea, author of the groundbreaking *The Hoffa Wars,* that Hoffa, Bill Presser, and others had sold munitions to Cuban forces. "I was right there on several occasions when they were loading the guns and ammunition up on the barges," Partin told Moldea. "Hoffa was directing the whole thing."

But Bartone's arrest
The Fall and Rise of Jimmy Hoffa, Sheridan.

8. EASTGATE

In addition to interviews, this chapter was based on extensive court records in *Teamsters Central States Pension Fund v. Eastgate Coliseum, et al,* Cuyahoga County Common Pleas Court, 1964, case no. 792985.

Details of the FBI's bowling alley investigation on Bill Presser and Jimmy Hoffa are among the six inches of William Presser's FBI files, HQ 92-6028 and CV 92-178, parts 1 and 2, obtained by a Freedom of Information Act request.

Page
105
Four months later,
Testimony in *U.S. v. William Presser,* CR No. 23276, Northern District of Ohio.

109
"I would have steak"
Bari Presser interview with the author.

112
On the drive back to Detroit
Hoffa's Man, Joe Franco with Richard Hammer (Prentice Hall Press, 1987).

114
"His old man was very unhappy"
Klein interview with Nevada Gaming Commission agents, March 15, 1974.

9. CARMEN

This chapter drew on a series of interviews with Carmen Presser, as well as interviews with Tony Hughes, Richie Giachetti, Bari Presser, and others.

Page
119
Jacobs arranged lines of credit [footnote]
Sports Illustrated, May 29, 1972.

10. THE LOCAL 507 STORY

In addition to interviews with Allen Friedman, Steve Kapelka, Carmen Presser, Tony Hughes, and many others, this chapter relied heavily on the more than fifteen thousand pages of verbatim transcripts of Local 507 and the Teamsters Joint Council 41. Teamster entities at the local and area level rarely kept such records, and the transcripts give a valuable peek inside the operations of the Pressers and Friedmans.

Page
126
"Las Vegas was a gold"
Time, November 28, 1969.

130
Teamsters Local 197
Memo from the Cleveland office of the Labor-Management Services Administration, Department of Labor, to David Margolis, chief of the Cleveland Strike Force, December 21, 1973. Hereafter referred to as Local 507 audit, 1973.

131
By 1971, Local 507
Ibid.

132
A few years later, Bill [footnote]
Silent Syndicate, Messick.

134
"We built up a fine"
Cleveland Press, June 18, 1968.

139
"There's a lot of poor"
Jackie Presser oral history, Ohio Historical Society.

139
As for his predecessor
The International Brotherhood of Teamsters, Sam Romer (John Wiley and Sons, Inc., 1962).

Not only did Jackie
Hoffa was the master at making seemingly innocuous changes in union bylaws. After becoming Teamsters president in 1957, he executed some canny moves at the next IBT general convention that made it extremely difficult for boatrockers or reform candidates to become union officials. For example, after the 1961 Teamsters convention, you had to have worked in a local for two years and attended half of its regular meetings before you could run for office. This slammed the door on newcomers. If by chance a local was taken over by reformers or didn't follow Hoffa's fiat, his general executive board "in its sound discretion" could merge the local or transfer members at will. If a local still resisted, Hoffa could place it in trusteeship or revoke its charter according to another 1961 rule change. With such discriminatory admission policies, the Teamsters leadership resembled the restricted private clubs patronized by captains of industry they were supposed to oppose at the bargaining table.

There was one sweeping power Hoffa didn't want. As the Teamsters president, according to the International constitution, Hoffa could expel a union member who had been convicted of a crime or who "has engaged in what is commonly termed racketeering." But in 1961, Hoffa actually gave up this discretion. He had never used it, not wanting to give in to his critics nor send the wrong message to his Mob supporters. Hoffa said he didn't want this power because the 1959 Landrum-Griffin Act already barred felons from holding union office. "Why should this convention go on record and make a more stringent rule?" Hoffa asked.

Well aware of the battles he faced with the Kennedy Justice Department, Hoffa took a giant self-serving step at the 1961 Teamsters convention, one that saved him at least a million dollars and spared Bill and Jackie Presser hundreds of thousands of dollars of expense. Urged by Hoffa and his crew, convention delegates adopted a change in the International constitution that authorized spending union dues to pay all legal bills for Teamsters officers accused of crimes. This was a fantastic fringe benefit for racketeers in the union. Now their pockets were almost as deep as those of the Justice Department.

140
For example, article 13
Local 507 audit, 1973.

141
In fact, though minutes
Ibid.

"Jackie Presser got all"
Allen Friedman 1983 grand-jury testimony.

141
Sometimes, the targeted company
Ibid.

142
"Sometimes Jackie would say"
Ibid.

Over the next seven
Convoy, October 1983.

143
"We got them a good"
Friedman 1983 grand-jury testimony.

"On picket lines"
Ibid.

144
Local 507 member Renato Cremona
Cremona v. Teamsters, et al, Cuyahoga County Common Pleas Court, 1977, case no. 966783.

"The assault was completely"
Letter, January 18, 1977, to Harold Friedman from Richard Zaletel.

Freeman didn't like this
Letter, January 17, 1977, from Custom Trim to Harold Friedman.

146
"It was a constant fight"
Friedman 1983 grand-jury testimony.

"In fact, it takes a long"
Local 507 executive board meeting, March 30, 1979.

"[Harold] would make a big"
Friedman 1983 grand-jury testimony.

147
"Every single case"
Local 507 executive board meeting, March 30, 1979.

"Over thirty thousand of our members"
Ibid.

148
"We've got the greatest"
Ibid.

11. PARDON ME

In addition to interviews, this chapter relied on articles in the *Press* and *Plain Dealer*, as well as more than one hundred pages of William Presser's pardon file, obtained under the Freedom of Information Act. Among those writing character references were former Congresswoman Frances Bolton (D-Ohio), Cuyahoga County Republican chairman Robert Hughes, lawyer Henry S. Gottfried, Rabbi Rudolph Rosenthal, and Helen J. Lyons, clerk of Cleveland Municipal Court.

Page
150
Born in 1906
A groundbreaking *Cleveland Press* nine-part series, "Money and the Mob," starting January 28, 1978, by Walt Bogdanich and Walter Johns showed for the first time how Zeve funneled money from the charity bingo games he ran into Seaway Acceptance, a loan company authorities said was controlled by the Mob. Seaway in turn loaned money to bars, vending companies, Mafia underboss Angelo Lonardo, up-and-coming pornographer Larry Flynt, and politicians.

151
"I respectfully pray"
William Presser, Application for Pardon, Department of Justice, September 28, 1966.

152
"I spent fifty-eight months"
Hoffa: The Real Story, James R. Hoffa, as told to Oscar Fraley (Stein and Day, 1975).

153
Hoffa fumed in prison
Ibid.

he "would be very happy"
Memo to President Johnson and Attorney General Ramsey Clark from Ohio DRIVE director James O. Simpkins and Mrs. William Presser, May 6, 1968.

The Cleveland police chief
William Presser's 1966 pardon application and attachments.

154
"Unless you have that"
Ohio DRIVE meeting, August 29, 1978.

"always connected with judges"
Licavoli investigation, Cleveland FBI file CV-397.

155
"Yes, Jackie will be around"
Ohio DRIVE meeting, August 29, 1978.

"Bill would be the one"
Stokes interview with the author

156
"We have to go to some"
Ohio DRIVE meeting, August 30, 1978.

A memo in Presser's pardon
Memo to President Johnson and Attorney General Ramsey Clark from James O.
Simpkins and Mrs. William Presser, May 6, 1968.

157
A final stroke
Congressional Record, June 27, 1969, p. 17639.

Feighan's son, Edward, a Cleveland-area U.S. representative, inherited his father's
Teamsters ties. The pro-labor liberal congressman has been one of the top beneficiaries
of Teamster PAC money, according to federal election reports.

158
Their venture began
This account is based on the records of *U.S. v. William Presser and James Franks,*
Northern District of Ohio, 1970, CR 70-393, and interviews with federal investiga-
tors.

161
"When I step down
Plain Dealer, October 27, 1970.

As Jackie admitted
Plain Dealer, June 17, 1973.

12. COURTING NIXON

The Nixon Project of the National Archives provided materials from the White
House's central files and special files, in particular the handwritten day-to-day notes of
Colson, Ehrlichman, and Haldeman. Also, a lengthy oral history of Colson, made
public in May 1989, clarified some important points. Unfortunately, much of the
Nixon White House material is still not available for scholars and reporters, as the
former president fights its release. The early Haler material was located at the Kennedy
Assassination Archives in Washington, D.C. Also helpful were the *New York Times,*
Washington Post, Detroit News, Wall Street Journal, and Sandy Smith's exceptional
work in *Time.*

Page
162
"There was no special"
Gary interview with the author.

163
Fitzsimmons sat down
The accounts of Fitzsimmons and Colson's meetings come from White House memos and Colson's handwritten notes at the National Archives' Nixon Project in Alexandria, Virginia. The April 29 meeting was described in a memo for Colson from aide George T. Bell.

165
Colson warned Dean
Colson memo to Dean, December 13, 1971.

166
"I get people to loan me"
Haler interview with the author. FBI report, November 30, 1963, case number LA 44-895, Special Agent John Nolan to Special-Agent-in-Charge, Los Angeles office.

170
A few weeks later
Interviews with Labor Department investigators James Thomas and George Simmons, who read the confidential reports; other federal sources.

172
By 1971, Berger
Hoffa's Man, Joe Franco with Richard Hammer (Prentice Hall Press, 1987).

"When anybody was going to run"
Allen testimony, June 22, 1982, before the Senate Permanent Subcommittee on Investigations, hearings on Mob infiltration into the Hotel Workers Union.

174
In April 1971, Colson's aide
Memo, April 13, 1971, George T. Bell to Colson, Colson files, Nixon Project.

As a gesture
Hoffa: The Real Story, James R. Hoffa, as told to Oscar Fraley (Stein and Day, 1975).

175
"Fitz wants Columbia"
Memo, Colson to Bell, March 30, 1972, Colson files, Nixon Project, National Archives.

Moore also admitted
Hoffa: The Real Story, Hoffa, p. 214.

175
Colson denies it
Charles Colson, oral history, September 21, 1988; Nixon Presidential Materials Staff Oral Histories; National Archives.

176
He accumulated only
Hoover-Gorin federal income tax return, 1971.

178
One courier recalled
Plain Dealer, August 23, 1981.

179
Colson said he fired
Colson oral history, September 21, 1988.

180
Fitzsimmons complained
Time, August 31, 1981.

Within a month or two
Ibid.

181
The wiretaps, as well as
New York Times, April 29, 1973.

"The deal with the Teamsters"
Ibid.

Peterson later said
Time, August 31, 1981.

182
A secret Watergate memo
Memo, July 3, 1974, Watergate Special Prosecution Force, National Archives

183
Colson had Presser's name
Colson oral history, Nixon Project, National Archives.

Presser's Joint Council 41
Attachments to March 19, 1973, Joint Council 41 executive board transcripts.

184
"and his muscleman"
Time, August 8, 1977.

But he still wanted
Allen testimony, "Hotel Employees and Restaurant Employees International Union," hearings before the Permanent Subcommittee on Investigations, June 22, 1982.

185
"I was supposed"
Ibid.

13. THE FORGE

Interviews for this chapter included Anthony Hughes, Martin P. McCann, Jr., Neil Morrow, Carmen Presser, Carl Milstein, John Vinegard, and others. A valuable resource for this and nearly every other chapter in the middle of the book were the verbatim transcripts I obtained of executive board meetings of Local 507 and Teamsters Joint Council 41 from 1972 to 1981, more than fifteen thousand pages complete with correspondence and union financial records.

Page
188
"They are misleading"
Cleveland Press, May 9, 1969.

"Tony Hughes is the kind"
Harold Friedman deposition, February 9, 1989, IBT Civil RICO.

191
At the March meeting
Teamsters Joint Council 41 executive board meeting, March 19, 1973.

193
"He used to come"
Neil Morrow interview with the author.

Hanley grabbed the presidency
This internal report, not intended for public disclosure, was based on research and analysis by Hope Breiding, intelligence analyst and research coordinator, Department of Justice, and written by Douglas P. Roller, Cleveland Strike Force chief, and Peter F. Vaira, Chicago Strike Force chief.

One of Hanley's first
Senate Permanent Subcommitee on Investigations report, *Hotel Employees and Restaurant Employees International Union,* August 27, 1984.

14. SKIMMING VEGAS

Periodicals, books, and oral histories about Las Vegas and gambling can be found in the Special Collections Department of the University of Nevada, in both Reno and Las Vegas. The numerous congressional reports and hearings are listed in the bibliography. Also consulted were the *Wall Street Journal,* the *New York Times,* the *Washington Post,* and the *Las Vegas Sun.* I was fortunate to have access not only to the entire trial record of the Argent case (also called the Kansas City skim case) but all discovery material obtained by the defendants, including wiretaps and surveillance reports not introduced at trial.

Page
196
In return, Hoffa routinely
Forbes, November 10, 1980.

197
The fund was losing
Ibid.

Dalitz met Hoffa
The Hoffa Wars, Dan E. Moldea (Paddington Press Ltd., 1978).

"They said I knew"
Hoffa: The Real Story, James R. Hoffa, as told to Oscar Fraley (Stein and Day, 1975).

198
"At the top of Cleveland's"
Gamblers' Money, Wallace Turner (Houghton Mifflin Co., 1965).

199
Gambler George Gordon carried
ALPRO, Section 2, October 1978.

In the summer of 1969
Time, November 28, 1969.

The two Cleveland men
Ibid.

200
"All of a sudden"
Carmen Presser interview with the author.

201
One of Glick's Hacienda
The Teamsters, Steven Brill (Simon and Schuster, 1978).

202
Along with everybody else
Glick testimony in *U.S. v. Carl Angelo DeLuna, et al,* Western District of Missouri, No. 83-124. Commonly referred to as the Kansas City skim case.

"That was something he wanted"
U.S. v. DeLuna.

"He told me to follow Bill"
Williams deposition in the Genovese family trial.

202
"Well, how much money"
U.S. v. DeLuna.

"Johnny, let's do this"
Angelo Lonardo testimony in the Kansas City skim case.

204
"I can't get there"
Glick testimony in the Kansas City skim case. All of Glick's remarks in this chapter were drawn from testimony in that trial.

206
"At the Fremont, we had"
November 26, 1978, wiretap of Josephine Marlo's residence, introduced as evidence in the Kansas City skim case.

208
Jackie told the FBI that Maishe
Lonardo testimony, Kansas City skim case.

"Let me keep you company"
Ibid.

210
"He informed me"
U.S. v. DeLuna.

15. POLISHING AN IMAGE

In addition to interviews, I consulted the *Ohio Teamster* from 1975 to 1980, the *International Teamster* for the same period, and the relevant articles from the *Cleveland Press* and *Plain Dealer*.

Page
212
"When dialysis came along"
Joint Council 41 executive board meeting, September 11, 1972.

214
"Obviously, it is some"
Cleveland rackets hearings, 1954.

A Gallup poll showed
Unions and the Mass Media, Sara U. Douglas (Ablex Publishing Corp., 1986).

215–16
"What the hell do they"
The Teamsters, Steven Brill (Simon and Schuster, 1978).

217
"I guess I'll throw"
Cleveland Press, March 7, 1975.

218
"When you're with him"
Krenzler interview with the author.

219
A wildly successful
Details of Presser's Front Row Theatre and Bally stock deals are found in a Governmental Affairs Committee report, *Criminal Investigations of Mr. Jackie Presser and Other Teamsters Officials,* December 1986.

16. SWEETHEARTS

Page
223
Williams asked Sammy Pro
Williams deposition, President's Commission on Organized Crime, September 13, 1985.

224
But Boffa got around
In spring 1985, Rispo detailed the labor-leasing scheme in depositions and testimony to the President's Commission on Organized Crime (PCOC).

225
Sheeran in turn
Rispo testimony, *U.S. v. Frank Sheeran, et al,* District of Delaware, 80 Cr. 36. Also introduced at trial were recordings made by informant Charlie Allen with a hidden FBI microphone that captured Sheeran discussing the scheme and his payments to Bufalino.

"Sometimes you had to go"
Rispo testimony before the PCOC, April 23, 1985.

226
Sometimes, if the complaining
Ibid.

227
In some cases, drivers
Rispo deposition for the PCOC, February 14, 1985.

228
Boffa called the head
Rispo testimony, PCOC.

228
In return, Rispo swore
Rispo testimony, PCOC.

"I want you to give this"
Ibid.

229
"Gene said to give this"
Rispo deposition, PCOC.

230
"Many, many times Jackie"
Carmen Presser interview with the author.

231
Authorities learned that Boffa
Vicious Circles, Jonathan Kwitny (Norton, 1979).

Throughout this time
Rispo deposition, PCOC.

232
"What the hell"
Rispo testimony, PCOC.

Though Presser's FBI informant files are extensive
The author's review of two thousand pages of Presser's FBI informant file.

Many companies were
PCOC report and hearings.

17. THE WEASEL

This chapter was based on the author's interview with Jimmy Fratianno, as well as Fratianno's testimony at various trials and congressional committees and Ovid Demaris's biography of Fratianno, *The Last Mafioso*.

Page
237
"If he [Tham] starts going wild"
The Last Mafioso, Ovid Demaris (Bantam Books, 1981).

The Labor Department was supposed
Senate Permanent Subcommittee on Investigations report, *Oversight Inquiry of the Department of Labor's Investigation of the Teamsters Central States Pension Fund*, July 1981, report no. 97-177.

458

238
"There are billions"
"Fraud and Abuse in Pensions and Related Employee Benefit Plans," hearings before the House Select Committee on Aging, November 4, 1981, report no. 97-324.

"Dorfman's company, Amalgamated"
The Last Mafioso, Demaris.

239
"I don't like Jackie"
Fratianno testimony, *U.S. v. Allen Dorfman, et al,* Northern District of Illinois, No. 81 CR 269. Also known as the Pendorf case.

18. THE MOB AT WAR

The war between the Cleveland Mafia and the Nardi-Greene gang captured the imagination of the city and received exhaustive coverage by the *Press* and *Plain Dealer.* I fleshed out these accounts with nearly one hundred pages of FBI files pertaining to Licavoli, Rabinowitz, Ferrito, and Lanci. Also useful was the thirty-three-page affidavit of FBI agent George Grotz, written to obtain a court-approved wiretap on Licavoli's Little Italy apartment.

Page
242
There's nothing to suggest
June 6, 1984, wiretap of Palma Boys Social Club, Genovese family case.

"What's with all"
Williams deposition, PCOC.

Williams knew only too well
Williams testimony, June 2, 1987, Genovese family case.

243
Other than slot machines
Interview with Fred Jurek.

244
The news hummed
FBI report of an October 28, 1983, interview with Angelo Lonardo.

"Angelo is more qualified"
Lonardo FBI debriefing, October 28, 1983.

245
A couple of years
FBI report of an October 28, 1983, interview with Lonardo.

245
Another powerful gangster
FBI affidavit by Cleveland special agent George Grotz in October 1977 for a wiretap of James Licavoli's telephone.

A few years later, John
Cleveland FBI report, *James Licavoli, a.k.a Jack White,* February 2, 1977, by special agent Thomas K. Kimmel, Jr.

246
Two weeks before trial
FBI report, CV 92-397, October 22, 1976.

247
Later, Hoffa warned
Cleveland Magazine, "The Life and Hard Times of the Cleveland Mafia," by Edward P. Whelan, August 1978.

248
Greene brought them in
Cleveland Magazine, "The Bombing Business," by Edward P. Whelan, April 1977.

249
Greene henchman Kevin McTaggert
Cleveland FBI informant report, May 15, 1978.

250
"If we receive information"
Foran's testimony on August 1, 1978, in *Ohio v. Thomas Lanci, et al,* Cuyahoga County Common Pleas Court, case no. 38130.

251
The heated argument
Cleveland Magazine, August 1978.

"Nardi is aligning"
FBI report, November 8, 1976, in file CV 92-397.

Jack White invited him
FBI interview with Licavoli, September 3, 1976.

252
"We can't even remember"
Author interview with Fratianno. Also, *The Last Mafioso,* Ovid Demaris.

254
"Fitz," Bill Presser said
The Teamsters, Steven Brill (Simon and Schuster, 1978).

255
"Headquarters carefully filtered"
Oliver B. Revell deposition, January 11, 1989, IBT Civil RICO case.

256
"Nardi wants to hit"
Hughes informant file, CV 137-3046.

"They're scared to death"
Author interview with Edward Kovacic, Vanyo's supervisor at the time.

257
"Five of them guys"
Hughes FBI informant file.

Even before his recent
Hughes FBI file.

"I'd take a bullet"
Thomas Lanci interview with the Cleveland FBI, February 23, 1982.

258
"You want something"
FBI report, Rabinowitz interviews, March 21, 1978.

"John Nardi exercises"
FBI report, February 2, 1977, *James Licavoli, a.k.a. Jack White,* CV 92-397.

260
"No one is going"
Rabinowitz, March 9, 1978, affidavit given to the Cleveland FBI.

261
"We've got a connection"
The Last Mafioso, Demaris.

263
Ferrito spent weeks
Ferrito admits to the murder of Petro and his role in the Greene killing in a series of statements to the Cleveland FBI found in file CV 92-2805.

264
"Have a nice"
Cleveland Magazine, August 1978.

265
"We're going to make"
Ferrito statements to the FBI in CV 92-2805.

19. INFORMING

Page
267
"Jackie practiced lies"
Carmen Presser interview with the author.

"Very fortunate for"
Joint Council 41 executive board meeting, June 18, 1978.

268
Presser was called
FBI internal memo from executive assistant director Sean McWeeney to John E. Otto, June 30, 1982.

In an interview with two
Three-page FBI report, August 7, 1975.

"After Hoffa got"
ALPRO, Section 1, March 1977.

269
After Nixon commuted
ALPRO, Section 1, May 1977.

"As a result of all"
Ibid.

"Without any doubt"
Ibid.

270
"If you could get Dorfman"
ALPRO, Section 1, March 1977.

"I worked like"
Crown Center Hotel overhear, March 25, 1979, introduced in Kansas City skim case.

"I want my"
ALPRO, Section 1, undated.

271
"He cried"
Rotatori interview with the author.

20. REBELS

In addition to interviews, I consulted the following written materials: TDU's magazine *Convoy* from 1978 to 1989, various PROD reports, newsletters, clips, and memorabilia generously supplied by John C. Sikorski, transcripts of Joint Council 41 meetings, the *Plain Dealer*, the *Cleveland Press*, the *Wall Street Journal*, Moldea's *The Hoffa Wars*, and a transcript of the IBT's 1976 convention.

Page
278
"There was some silly"
Sikorski interview with the author.

"He's a big crybaby"
Plain Dealer, September 24, 1978.

279
"People were saying"
Paff interview with the author.

280
"We're starting to push"
Joint Council 41 executive board meeting, March 28, 1977.

"We've had dissident"
Joint Council 41 executive board meeting, December 20, 1976.

"If you officers"
Joint Council 41 executive board meeting, June 19, 1978.

21. BRIBING A SENATOR

The White House central files and special files at the Jimmy Carter Presidential Library revealed how the Carter White House chose principle over political expediency and rebuffed the Pressers and the union. The oral histories at the University of Nevada in Las Vegas and Reno helped me trace Cannon's roots and early political career. The record of the Pendorf case, including wiretaps, surveillance reports, and discovery material provided to defense lawyers, is the spine of this chapter. Presser and Hughes's FBI files were also essential. Various internal FBI memos were consulted. In addition to interviews, I also relied on news accounts in the *Chicago Tribune*, *Washington Post*, *Wall Street Journal*, *New York Times* and *Forbes*.

Page
282
For example, Ohio state
Carter Library, White House Central Files, Presser name file, July 27, 1978, memo.

285
"An attorney here"
Biltz oral history, University of Nevada.

"A prominent investigative"
Anderson oral history, University of Nevada.

286
They listed thirty-three
Miami Herald, August 24, 1981.

Williams then promised
ALPRO, Section 2, March 23, 1979.

"You take care"
William Webbe, Chicago grand jury testimony, Pendorf case.

"We should support"
Memo, January 20, 1979, from Eizenstat to Jimmy Carter, Box 297, White House Central Files, Carter Library.

287
The agents had been compiling
Chicago FBI agent Peter J. Wacks's seventy-page wiretap affidavit, January 29, 1979, outlines the FBI's source information at that point. An August 11, 1983, airtel memo from the Chicago FBI's special agent in charge to FBI Director Webster says Jackie was Confidential Informant No. 3 in the Wacks affidavit. Presser was used in twelve subsequent affidavits in the Pendorf probe.

"I remember it"
Roller interview with the author.

288
The probable cause
Until approached for this book, Roller and other Chicago Strike Force prosecutors were unaware of Jackie's role in Pendorf, though they had suspicions. At the time, only FBI agent Patrick Foran and a few other key agents and supervisors knew Jackie had helped kicked off Operation Pendorf.

The bureau's black-bag
Chicago Sun-Times, March 31, 1982.

Fitz said fine
ALPRO file, Section 2, October 1978.

290
But Bjornsen, with
New York Times, November 4, 1982.

291
Dorfman "went every place"
Williams deposition, IBT Civil RICO.

"We got work to do"
Crown Center overhear, March 25, 1979.

292
"We want the Shannon"
Williams deposition, IBT Civil RICO.

295
"Did he take care"
May 21, 1979, hidden-microphone recording used as evidence in the Pendorf trial.

296
"You went with the concerted"
January 7, 1980, wiretap used in the Pendorf trial.

296–97
"If Dorfman hadn't been"
Roller interview with the author.

22. PRESIDENTIAL POLITICS

In addition to interviews, the following sources were consulted: the *Washington Post,*
New York Times, Wall Street Journal, Cleveland Press, Cleveland Plain Dealer,
ALPRO files, and Tony Hughes's FBI files.

Page
298
"Me and him try"
Wiretap exhibit in the Kansas City skim case.

299
"Maishe get my"
Ibid.

By April, Fitz had lost
Fitzsimmons's state of mind is described in detail in various inserts in ALPRO,
Sections 1 and 2.

300
"If the government"
Ibid.

302
When he heard about
Newton interview with the author.

303
"We lost our major"
Joint Council 41 executive board meeting, December 15, 1980.

304
During the twenty-minute
Washington Star, November 19, 1980.

"You're in the only"
Joint Council 41 executive board meeting, December 15, 1980.

305
"I'm positive the"
Washington Star, December 16, 1980.

"The appointment is a sad"
New York Times, December 19, 1980.

"We were invited"
Joint Council 41 executive board meeting, February 20, 1981.

306
"I'm very, very proud"
Joint Council 41 executive board meeting, March 16, 1981.

He was going
ALPRO file, Section 2, various inserts.

307
Civella continued to promote
Lonardo's trial testimony in the Genovese family case.

308
"If any of you do run"
Hughes FBI informant file, May 8, 1981.

A few days later, Civella
Williams deposition, IBT Civil RICO.

"He bought a lotta"
Hughes interview with the author.

310
"I'm taking over"
Williams deposition, IBT Civil RICO.

Dorfman also told Jackie
FBI report of a November 26, 1985, interview with Williams in federal prison at Springfield, Missouri.

Reagan sent
Plain Dealer, July 22, 1981.

23. THE CHASE

This chapter relied upon the complete Labor Department investigative file into the ghost employee case, the Hoover-Gorin case, and its offshoots—a three-inch stack of Labor Department ROIs (reports of investigation), File 53-M860-0004. Also helpful were two Senate Permanent Subcommittee documents, *Labor Management Racketeering*, hearings on April 24 and 25, 1978, and *Department of Justice's Handling of the Jackie Presser Ghostworkers Case*, hearings on May 9, 1986. Generous with their time and insights were former Labor investigators Jim Thomas and Red Simmons. Other interviews included Carmen Presser, Mairy Jayn Woge, Walt Bogdanich, David Hopcraft, Peter Halbin, John Climaco, Harry Haler, Steve Canfil, Tony Hughes, Jerry Milano, Allen Friedman, and Nancy Friedman.

Page
313
"Participation by the Labor"
Permanent Subcommittee on Investigations hearings, April 24, 1978.

314
"Here was the only"
Simmons interview with the author.

315
"Why don't you try"
Roller interview with the author.

317
The outlines of
ROI, George Simmons to file, re: Jackie Presser, et al, December 30, 1981.

320
After they had their falling-out
Harry Haler v. Hoover-Gorin & Associates, No. C191549, Superior Court of California, Los Angeles County.

322
"Who do you work"
Based on interviews with Thomas, Simmons, and Haler and Labor Department ROIs.

326
Simmons and Thomas pulled up
ROI, March 10, 1982.

327
In 1972, John Nardi, Sr.,
Nardi account of his no-show job is based on his testimony in *U.S. v. Harold Friedman, et al,* CR 86-114, Northern District of Ohio.

328
The next day, Simmons
ROI, March 2, 1982.

330
Later, DeFabio visited Allen
FBI wiretap of the Card Shop, a Mob gambling club, attached to a strike force sentencing memorandum in *U.S. v. Allen Friedman,* CR 83-188, Northern District of Ohio.

331
So he invited
Friedman's strongarming of Mann was recounted in his 1983 ghost employee trial.

Such was the tangled
Based on interviews with Thomas, Simmons, and Friedman and ROIs.

24. THE FIX

In addition to interviews, I relied on my own observations and experiences in the *Plain Dealer* newsroom during the uproar before and after the retraction. Materials consulted include the Labor Department reports on the investigation of Jackie Presser, various Justice Department memos, Presser and Hughes's informant files, and Nicholas Von Hoffman's *Citizen Cohn.*

Page
338
Friedrick, unfamiliar
Friedrick statements to the Justice Department lawyers, Office of Professional Responsibility, January 8, 9, and 13, 1986.

"Maury Shurr is a"
ALPRO file, undated.

338
Simmons served him
ROI, March 8, 1982.

339
"Don't worry"
Friedrick statement, January 8, 1986.

340
Parise, a Mafia associate
ALPRO file, Section 2, November 21, 1980.

Jackie said that he told
Ibid.

Jackie would then be
Author interview with lawyer Thomas Rockman, Maishe's son.

341
"It'll bring"
Based on Lonardo's testimony in the Genovese family case; before the Permanent
Subcommittee on Investigations; and in the IBT Civil RICO case.

342
"If you need any"
Ibid.

343
He told his aide-de-camp
Cafaro affidavit to the Permanent Subcommittee on Investigations, April 8, 1988.

345
Around this time, Cohn
Citizen Cohn, Nicholas Von Hoffman (Doubleday, 1988).

When Newhouse told him
Hopcraft interview with the author.

346
A week before the Margolis
Hughes informant file, September 1982.

347
There was documentation
Bogdanich interview with the author.

348–49
On Harold Friedman's desk
Based on the search warrant return filed in federal court in Cleveland, November 9,
1982.

349
No, Griffin replied
January 24, 1983, memo from David Williams, head of the Labor Department's
organized crime and racketeering office in Cleveland, to Robert Magee, Inspector
General, Labor Department.

353
"This retraction"
Ohio Teamster, October 1982.

25. OBSTRUCTING JUSTICE

Page
356
"We began to detect"
Williams memo to McGee, January 24, 1983.

358
What worried Simmons
ROI, June 14, 1982.

359
"I'm not close"
ROI, June 15, 1982.

Jack Nardi's wife
ROI, November 18, 1982.

Coming from a Teamsters
Transcript of Joyce and Nardi's recorded conversation.

360
"No way!"
Joyce deposition, May 6, 1986, to the Permanent Subcommittee on Investigations.

361
"They'd all meet"
Abrams interview with the author.

"I'll be honest"
The conversation is taken verbatim from the recording of the December 10, 1982,
meeting in Ft. Lauderdale.

363
"In a last-ditch effort"
Williams memo to Magee, January 24, 1983.

364
But Simmons and Thomas's careers

470

James Thomas and George Simmons v. John Climaco, Cuyahoga County Common Pleas Court, case no. CV 67891.

364
"As far as I know"
Canfil interview with the author.

26. THE MARBLE PALACE

Page
367
Jackie repeatedly told
ALPRO file, various inserts.

368
Soon, scuttlebutt floated
ALPRO file, Section 3, March 31, 1982.

371
"You've got my"
ALPRO file, Section 4, February 11, 1983.

Big Ange Lonardo had
Cleveland Magazine, "The Lonardo Papers," December 1985.

"Roy Williams is finished"
ALPRO file, April 18, 1983.

372
"I have the votes"
Plain Dealer, April 20, 1983.

376
Through Ohio DRIVE
UPI, May 9, 1983.

379
"We didn't have to convince"
Houston Post, Evans and Novak column, July 2, 1983.

The Reagan administration, champion
Washington Post, July 25, 1983.

380
"Presser is key for us"
Washington Post, August 17, 1983.

Tell the Justice
Revell memo to Webster, September 30, 1983.

380
"ALPRO has provided"
Revell deposition, IBT Civil RICO.

382
Before he sent the memo
Undated FBI "Routing/action slip," handwritten by Revell, attached to the September 30 memo.

"The informant is"
New York Times, July 2, 1978.

385
Copies of Jackie's
Based on a report of Brian D. Hitt, staff investigator of the President's Commission on Organized Crime, April 23, 1985.

387
Formerly a Teamster
Letter, June 26, 1984, from Presser to Marion Winstead, president of Teamsters Local 89, Louisville, Kentucky.

388
It was treacherous [footnote]
ALPRO, Section 8, June 26, 1984.

27. COVER-UP

Written material consulted included the *Los Angeles Times,* the *Washington Post,* the *Plain Dealer,* and a cache of internal FBI memos obtained by the author.

Page
389
"I think these fuckin' "
Wiretap transcript, June 6, 1984, in Genovese family case.

391
"When I heard this"
Ibid.

"We know he's a
ALPRO file, updated.

392
"I began to think the bad"
Friedrick statement, January 8, 1986.

"You get close"
Friedrick interview with the author.

472

393
"This was serious"
Friedrick statement, January 8, 1986.

Friedrick hoped that
Friedrick statement, January 8, 1986.

394
"Thomas and Simmons"
Jigger memo recounting the meeting.

"Your personal gift"
Presser letter to Gray, August 10, 1984.

395
"We remember who"
UPI, August 20, 1984.

A corporate lawyer
See the *New York Times,* October 30, 1988, for a good analysis of Dotson's tenure on the NLRB.

The White House had tried
Newsweek, August 20, 1984.

Eager to please
Plain Dealer, August 21, 1984.

"We tried to make"
Washington Post, August 23, 1984.

396
"There have been a lot"
Akron Beacon-Journal, August 30, 1984.

"They agreed that"
Hughes FBI file, September 2, 1984

"Ted Cozza from"
ALPRO file, Section 9, December 1, 1984.

"When Patriarca heard"
Based on ALPRO file, Section 9, September 12, 1984.

399
Stephen Trott, head
FBI memo, Revell to Webster, June 6, 1985.

"I felt like"
Friedrick statement, January 8, 1986.

399
"Are you sure"
Friedrick statement, January 8, 1986.

400
"Jackie and Tony have been"
Based on five pages of Jigger's notes and one page of Olah's notes of Climaco's presentation. The FBI copied the notes on August 8, 1985, and they were later obtained by the author.

401
Two days later, Friedrick
Friedrick statement, January 8, 1986.

Climaco met at the
The account of this second meeting was reconstructed from fourteen pages of contemporaneous, near-verbatim notes of the meeting taken by Jigger and Olah. The FBI copied these pages on August 8, 1985, and they were later obtained by the author.

402
"McKinnon thanked"
Ibid.

403
"We didn't have"
Friedrick statement, January 8, 1986.

"Marty, Climaco went"
Based on Friedrick statement, January 8, 1986.

Without explicitly
Ibid.

404
"What I was trying"
Friedrick statement, January 8, 1986.

"The message that"
Friedrick statement, January 9, 1986.

405
"keeping Nardi on"
McCann's sworn statement to the Cleveland Strike Force, signed June 26, 1985.

"Subsequent to the merger"
Foran's sworn statement to the Cleveland Strike Force, signed June 26, 1985.

A week later, Revell
FBI memo, 3 pages, Revell to Webster, June 27, 1985.

474

By then, Olah
Author interview with William Beyer, Friedrick's lawyer, who reviewed all relevant documents, many of which are still under court seal.

"Insanity and lies"
Washington Post, July 26, 1985.

407
"He was a little"
Friedrick statement, January 8, 1986.

In a speech
New York Times, August 3, 1985.

"I think I can"
Washington Post, October 27, 1985.

408
Foran, upset
Friedrick statement, January 8, 1986.

Friedrick was tiptoeing
Friedrick statement, January 9, 1986.

409
Some of the information
Based on ALPRO file, Section 12, December 11, 1985.

"Tony Giacolone"
ALPRO file, Section 12, January 9, 1986.

410
Friedrick told the truth
Friedrick statement, January 8, 1986.

413
Reagan, a little
Washington Post, January 15, 1986.

"I hear we're"
FBI memo, Potts to Floyd Clarke, May 13, 1986.

414
"That's our number-one"
A May 14, 1986, internal FBI memo from Floyd Clarke to Revell recounted conversations at the meeting.

415
"You might as well"
Hughes FBI file, May 15, 1986.

415
"As secretary of labor"
Proceedings, 23rd Convention, IBT, May 19–22, 1986.

420
Privately, Jackie didn't
Plain Dealer, September 4, 1987. Meese was not so hands-off in other less publicized decisions. A Justice Department study released only after Reagan left office said Meese violated government ethics codes so seriously when he was attorney general that he should be subjected to presidential discipline.

421
"Our DRIVE organization"
New York Times, October 30, 1987.

After his speech
Locigno interview with the author.

422
"He called me"
Hughes interview with the author.

423
Jackie would never
Letter from Dr. Robert F. Spetzler, Barrow's Neurological Institute, to U.S. District Court Judge George W. White, Northern District of Ohio, who presided over Presser's trial.

On June 28, the
IBT Civil RICO.

28. EPILOGUE

Page
427
Throughout the five years
How local Teamsters leaders felt about Presser and his programs was learned from the results of a confidential questionnaire returned by more than seven hundred delegates at the 1986 convention. Those responding were guaranteed anonymity. Some typical suggestions for improvement: "More organizing"; "More guidance on organizing"; "Nothing, doing a good job"; "Do not back Ronald Reagan"; "More communication with our members, especially to alleviate the current comment that Jackie is a criminal."

428
he had been involved in
Based on a March 5, 1974, memo, from Nick Akerman to Henry S. Ruth, Watergate Special Prosecutor's files, National Archives. The Watergate Special Prosecutor's office

476

examined Colson's involvement in election-law violations in the 1972 campaign. The memo recounts an interview with White House aide William Rhatican, who said Colson told him of an anti-McGovern leaflet he wanted distributed at all defense plants. Colson insisted the leaflet not be identified as paid for by the Republican party or the Committee to Re-Elect the President because to do so would hurt their message. Colson told Rhatican to call Teamster official Weldon Mathis who would distribute the flyers. Rhatican said he believed Colson had already cleared the plan through Mathis and that the leafleting was to take place in all heavily populated states with large numbers of defense plant workers.

"There was a lot of phoney-baloney"
McCarthy's testimony, April 4, 1989, before the Senate Permanent Subcommittee on Investigations.

"He is also regarded"
Boston Globe, July 1, 1989.

429
"I would have to go"
McCarthy quotes in this chapter, unless otherwise noted, are taken from a secret tape recording of a private meeting of union representatives in Chicago on October 28, 1988, at the McCormick Inn. McCarthy had called them there to hear his agenda for the future. For over two hours, McCarthy flitted from topic to topic, without a set program or message. For many union officials from the Midwest and West, this was their first impression of the new president and many grumbled about the poorly outlined program.

At fifteen
McCarthy admitted this at his closed-door October 28 union meeting.

Around this time
Ibid.

430
Winter didn't threaten
McCarthy deposition, IBT Civil RICO, August 15, 1988.

However, according to a 1977
This internal report, not intended for public disclosure, was based on research and analysis by Hope Breiding, intelligence analyst and research coordinator, Department of Justice, and written by Douglas P. Roller, Cleveland Strike Force chief, and Peter F. Vaira, Chicago Strike Force chief.

Raymond L. S. Patriarca, Mafia boss
FBI airtel, June 9, 1965, to the FBI Director from the Boston special agent in charge, regarding Raymond L. S. Patriarca, file no. BS 92-118.

431
McCarthy said he knew
Report of FBI interview of McCarthy, February 26, 1974, case no. BS 92-1955.

431
In 1976, FBI agents
FBI report, October 29, 1976, Boston case no. 9-3045.

In 1982, he was questioned
FBI report, July 14, 1982, by Boston FBI agents Michael L. Manigan and Carl J. Schilling. McCarthy confirmed in this interview that the Teamsters hadn't wanted Donovan as secretary of labor, but instead supported National Labor Relations Board member Betty Murphy.

433
McCarthy awarded a $3-million-a-year
Boston Globe, March 28, 1989.

434
LaPiana's National Labor
ALPRO file, Section 9, September 2, 1984.

In June 1983, LaPiana
ALPRO file, Section 5, July 13, 1983.

Bibliography

BOOKS

Allen, Edward Joseph. *Merchants of Menace*. Thomas Books, 1962.

Brill, Steven. *The Teamsters*. Simon and Schuster, 1978.

Condon, George E. *Cleveland: The Best Kept Secret.* Doubleday and Co., 1967.

Demaris, Ovid. *The Last Mafioso.* Times Books, 1981.

Douglas, Sara U. *Unions and the Mass Media.* Ablex Publishing Corp., 1986.

Friedman, Allen, and Ted Schwarz. *Power and Greed.* Franklin Watts, 1989.

Gartner, Lloyd P. *History of the Jews of Cleveland.* The Western Reserve Historical Society, 1978.

Hoffa, James R. *Hoffa: The Real Story* (as told to Oscar Fraley). Stein and Day, 1975.

Hutchinson, John. *The Imperfect Union.* E. P. Dutton, 1970.

Illman, Harry R. *Unholy Toledo.* Polemio Press Publications, 1985.

James, Ralph C., and Estelle Dinerstein. *James Hoffa and the Teamsters.* D. Van Nostrand Co., 1965.

Josephson, Matthew. *Union House, Union Bar.* Random House, 1956.

Kwitny, Jonathan. *Vicious Circles.* Norton, 1979.

Lukas, J. Anthony. *Nightmare: The Underside of the Nixon Years.* Viking, 1976.

Messick, Hank. *The Silent Syndicate.* The Macmillan Co., 1967.

Moldea, Dan E. *The Hoffa Wars.* Paddington Press Ltd., 1978.

Mollenhoff, Clark R. *Tentacles of Power: The Story of Jimmy Hoffa.* World Publishing Co., 1965.

Naas, Bernard G., and Carmelita S. Sakr. *American Labor Union Periodicals: A Guide to Their Location.* Cornell University Press, 1956.

479

Reid, Ed, and Ovid Demaris. *The Green Felt Jungle.* Trident Press, 1963.

Romer, Sam. *The International Brotherhood of Teamsters: Its Government and Structure.* John Wiley and Sons, 1962.

Schlesinger, Arthur M., Jr. *Robert F. Kennedy and His Times.* Houghton Mifflin Co., 1978.

Sheridan, Walter. *The Fall and Rise of Jimmy Hoffa.* Saturday Review Press, 1972.

Turner, Wallace. *Gamblers' Money.* Houghton Mifflin Co., 1965.

Van Tassel, David D., and John J. Grabowski, eds. *The Encyclopedia of Cleveland History.* Indiana University Press, 1987.

Vincent, Sidney Z. *Personal and Professional: Memoirs of a Life in Community Service.* The Jewish Community Federation of Cleveland, 1982.

Vincent, Sidney Z., and Judah Rubinstein. *Merging Traditions: Jewish Life in Cleveland.* The Western Reserve Historical Society and the Jewish Community Federation of Cleveland, 1978.

Von Hoffman, Nicholas. *Citizen Cohn.* Doubleday and Co., 1988.

GOVERNMENT DOCUMENTS

President's Commission on Organized Crime. *Record of Hearing VI—Labor.* April 22–24, 1985.

———. *The Edge: Appendix.* October 1985.

———. *The Edge: Organized Crime, Business and Labor Unions.* March 1986.

U.S. Congress, House. Joint Subcommittees of the Committee on Education and Labor and the Committee on Government Operations. *Hearings: Investigation of Racketeering in the Detroit Area.* June 1953.

———. *Hearings: Investigation of Racketeering in the Cleveland Area.* September 1954.

U.S. Congress. House. Select Committee on Aging. *Fraud and Abuse in Pensions and Related Employee Benefit Plans.* November 4, 1981, report no. 97-324.

U.S. Congress. House. Subcommittee on Oversight, Committee on Ways and Means. *Hearing: Central States Teamsters Fund.* March 22, 1978.

U.S. Congress. Senate. Committee on Labor and Human Resources. *Hearing: Oversight of the Teamsters Union.* June 7, 1983.

U.S. Congress. Senate. Permanent Subcommittee on Investigations. *Hearings: Teamsters Central States Pension Fund.* July 18 and 21, 1977.

480

————. *Hearings: Labor Management Racketeering.* April 24 and 25, 1978.

————. *Hearings: Oversight of the Labor Department's Investigation of Teamsters Central States Pension Fund.* August 25 and 26 and September 29 and 30, 1980.

————. *Interim Report: Oversight Inquiry of the Labor Department's Investigation of Teamsters Central States Pension Fund.* May 20, 1981.

————. *Oversight Inquiry of the Department of Labor's Investigation of the Teamsters Central States Pension Fund.* July 1981, report no. 97-177.

————. *Record of Hearings: Hotel Employees and Restaurant Employees International Union.* Part 2, September 28, 1982, and Part 5, May 15, 1984.

————. *Hearings: Profile of Organized Crime, Great Lakes Region.* January 25, 26, and 31 and February 1, 1984.

————. *Report: Hotel Employees and Restaurant Employees International Union.* August 27, 1984.

————. *Hearing: Department of Justice's Handling of the Jackie Presser Ghostworkers Case.* May 9, 1986.

————. *Hearings: Organized Crime: Twenty-five Years After Valachi.* April 1988.

U.S. Congress. Senate. Select Committee on Improper Activities in the Labor or Management Field. *Hearings.* 58 vols. February 1957–March 1960.

————. *Reports.* 7 filed, 1957–60.

U.S. General Accounting Office. *Report by the Comptroller General: Investigation to Reform Teamsters Central States Pension Fund Found Inadequate.* April 28, 1982.

————. *Briefing Report to the Permanent Subcommittee on Investigations: Criminal Investigations of Mr. Jackie Presser and Other Teamsters Officials.* December 1986.

COURT RECORDS

Carley's Dry Cleaning Corp. v. International Association of Cleaning and Dye Houseworkers, William Presser, et al. Cuyahoga County Common Pleas Court, case no. 483322.

Renato Cremona v. Teamsters, et al. Cuyahoga County Common Pleas Court, 1977, case no. 966783.

Harry Haler v. Hoover-Gorin & Associates. Superior Court of California, Los Angeles County, no. C191549.

Hotel and Restaurant Workers International v. Jackie Presser, et al. Cuyahoga County Common Pleas Court, case no. 703813.

Marstan Hat Cleaners, Inc., v. William B. Beckerman, William Presser, et al. Cuyahoga Common Pleas Court, case no. 431341.

Ohio v. Thomas Lanci, et al. Cuyahoga County Common Pleas Court, case no. 38130.

Carmen Presser v. Jackie Presser. Cuyahoga County Common Pleas Court, case no. 134641.

Jackie Presser v. Patricia Presser. Cuyahoga County Common Pleas Court, case no. 18657.

William Presser v. Peter J. Brennan, et al. District Court for the Northern District of Ohio, case no. C-75-83.

Public National Bank and Trust v. Leo Dixon and William Presser. Cuyahoga County Common Pleas Court, case no. 25522.

Teamsters Central States Pension Fund v. Eastgate Coliseum, et al. Cuyahoga County Common Pleas Court, 1964, case no. 792985.

James Thomas and George Simmons v. John Climaco. Cuyahoga County Common Pleas Court, case no. CV 67891.

U.S. v. Eugene Boffa, et al. District Court for the Southern District of Delaware, case no. 80 Cr. 36.

U.S. v. Carl Angelo DeLuna, et al. District Court for the Western District of Missouri, case no. 83 Cr. 124.

U.S. v. Allen Dorfman, et al. District Court for the Northern District of Illinois, case no. 81 Cr. 269.

U.S. v. Allen Friedman. District Court for the Northern District of Ohio, case no. Cr. 83-188.

U.S. v. Allen Friedman, et al. Northern District of Ohio, case numbers 19888-91, filed December 27, 1949.

U.S. v. Harold Friedman, et al. District Court for the Northern District of Ohio, case no. Cr. 86-114.

U.S. v. Robert S. Friedrick. District Court for the District of Columbia, case no. CR 86-188.

U.S. v. International Brotherhood of Teamsters, et al. District Court for the Southern District of New York, case no. 88 Civ. 4486.

U.S. v. William Presser. District Court for the Northern District of Ohio, case no. Cr. 23276.

U.S. v. William Presser. District Court for the Northern District of Ohio, case no. CR 71-396.

BIBLIOGRAPHY

U.S. v. William Presser and James Franks. District Court for the Northern District of Ohio, case no. CR 70-393.

U.S. v. Anthony Salerno, et al. District Court for the Southern District of New York, case no. 85 Cr. 139.

U.S. v. Anthony Salerno, et al. District Court for the Southern District of New York, case no. 86 Cr. 245.

U.S. v. Frank Sheeran, et al. District of Delaware, 80 Cr. 36.

U.S. v. Tobacco and Candy Jobbers Association, Inc., William Presser, et al. District Court for the Northern District of Ohio, case no. 20338.

FILES RELEASED UNDER FREEDOM OF INFORMATION ACT AND OTHER DISCLOSURES

FBI
Aratari, Louis
Dalitz, Morris
Dorfman, Allen
Ferrito, Raymond
Fratianno, Jimmy
Haler, Harry
Hughes, Anthony
Lanci, Thomas
Licavoli, James
Lonardo, Angelo
Presser, Jackie
Presser, William
Rabinowitz, Geraldine Linhart
Williams, Roy Lee

Department of Housing and Urban Development
Teamster Housing, Inc.

Department of Labor
Cook United Corporation
Front Row Theater Investigation
Gifts of Bally Stock to the Presser Family
Hoover-Gorin Investigation
Joint Council 41, Misuse of Travel Funds
Local 507 Audit
Local 507 Ghost Employees Investigation
Management of Housing for Teamster Retirees
Ohio Teamster Journal

483

Department of Justice
Friedrick, Robert S.
Hoffa, James R., Pardon Attorney files.
Presser, Jackie
Presser, William, including U.S. Parole Commission and Pardon Attorney files.

National Archives
Papers of Labor Secretary Raymond J. Donovan
Papers of Labor Secretary Ray Marshall
President's Commission on Organized Crime, working papers (partial release)

Index

Glick, Allen R., 203–11, 298; loan from Central States Pension Fund for Las Vegas casinos, 200–03, 205
Glimco, Joey, 96, 235–36
Goeble, Elaine, 77–78, 80–82
Golden, Louis B., 48
Goldman, Rabbi S., 7
Gordon, George, 199
Gordon, Nelson, 360–62
Gorin, Abnor, 176
Grady, James, 431
Gray, Robert, 379, 394
Greco, Frank, 18
Greene, Danny, 257, 260; and John Nardi, 246–51; killed, 263–64
Griffin, Joe, 324, 349, 356, 360, 406, 417
Grotz, George, 316
Groves, Robert R., 231–32

Hackett, Judge, 59
Hagan, Timothy F., 373
Haig, Alexander, 420
Halbin, Peter, 213, 214, 216
Haldeman, H. R., 164–65, 174
Haler, Harry, 183, 241–42, 317, 318, 320, 328–29, 343; and Justice Department connections, 165–67; and Pressers, 167–71; and Hoover-Gorin and Associates, 176–79; and Simmons and Thomas, 322–25
Hall, Paul, 164
Hanley, Edward T., 82, 193, 420
Hatch, Orrin, 369, 374, 376, 424
Hatch, Steve, 350, 352
Hell's Angels, 248–49, 250
Herrington, John, 395
Hoffa, James P., 172, 173
Hoffa, Jimmy, 40, 57, 63, 88, 118, 139, 235–36, 247, 431; and Roy Lee

Williams, 91–95; and Bill Presser, 112–14; imprisoned at Lewisburg Federal Prison, 151–52; and Teamsters power struggle, 170–75, 183; and Fitzsimmons murder contract, 172–73, 184–85; and Central States Pension Fund, 194–98; and adopted son Chuckie, 268–69
Hoffa, Josephine, 40, 172
Hoffman, Clare, 68, 70–74
Holland, Robert, 57–58
Holmes, Bobby, 370
Holohan, Gustava, 88
Hoover, George Arthur "Duke," 176–79, 183, 319, 324–25
Hoover, J. Edgar, 95, 108–09
Hoover-Gorin and Associates, 176–79, 183, 318, 319, 326. See also Haler, Harry
Hopcraft, David, 317–19, 345–47, 350–51
Hope, Bob, 66
Hope, Jack, 66
Hotel and Restaurant Employees Union, 78–80, 82–83, 89; Local 10, 192–93; Local 274, 86–88
HUD (U.S. Department of Housing and Urban Development), 187, 375–76
Hughes, Anthony "Tony," 143, 242, 255–57, 261, 326, 328–29, 331, 355, 375, 381, 395, 401–06 passim, 413–15, 422; friendship with Jackie Presser, 121–23; as FBI informant, 136–37; and Forge restaurant, 186–91; and Robert Friedrick, 392–93
Hughes, Anthony "Happy," 27
Hughes, Robert, 100, 154
Hulligan, Welden E., 248

490

Leo "Lips"; Rockman, Milton
"Maishe"; Scalish, John
Mafia (Kansas City), and Allen Glick,
204–05; in Las Vegas, 205–08. *See
also* Civella, Carl; Civella, Nick
Mafia (Los Angeles), 181
Mafia (Milwaukee), and Allen Glick in
Las Vegas, 202–04
Magee, Robert, 363
Mann, Patrick J., 331
Marchiondo, William, 283
Marciano, Rocky, 134
Marconi, Carmen, 263
Margolis, David, 322, 325, 346, 351,
364, 398, 400–01, 414
Marks, Richard, 432
Marshall, Prentice, 368
Martinico, Vince, 323, 325
Massa, Andrew G., 289, 301
Mastro, Randy, 432
Mathis, Weldon, 370, 396, 415,
422–23, 426–27, 431
Matowitz, George Julius, 66, 67
Maxwell, Moose: *See* Finley, Richard
Mayfield Road Gang, 63–64
McBride, Arthur B. "Mickey," 24, 132
McCann, Marty, 190, 253, 255–56,
345, 393, 401–06, 408–10; as FBI
handler of Tony Hughes, 136–37
McCarthy, William J., 177, 396, 422,
426–34
McClellan committee, 96–101, 197
McCullough, Daniel, 58–59
McGinty, Thomas, 198
McKinnon, Roy, 393, 402
McLean, James J. "Buddy," 420
McSweeney, Bill, 235
McTaggert, Kevin, 248–49
McWeeney, Sean, 386
MDM Investment Company, 134
Meany, George, 96, 175, 215

Meese, Edwin, 302, 304–05, 380, 399,
410, 420
Meir, Golda, 157
Messick, Hank, 23
Metzenbaum, Howard, 84, 86, 374
Meyers, Ray G., 18
Milano, Anthony "Old Man," 23, 45
Milano, Frank, 23, 244–45
Milano, Jerry, 329
Milano, Peter, 181, 199
Milano, John, 258
Miller, Ed, 78–80, 88–89
Miller, Trina, 218
Milstein, Carl, 187
Minor, Paul, 409–10
Mitchell, John, 165
Moceri, Leo "Lips," 243, 246, 250–51
Mock, George, 308
Moffett, Elwood, 164–65
Molinaro, Camillo "Bill," 305
Molnar, Ernest, 24
Montana, John "Curly," 261
Moody, Jim, 339, 393
Moore, William Carlos, 175
Morgan, Joseph, 177, 306, 372, 387,
396, 432
Morrow, Neil, 193
Moss, Robert, 219

NAACP, 111
Nardi, Jack, 381, 394, 402, 404; as
ghost employee of Teamsters Local
507, 327–29, 335–36; and Cleveland
Strike Force, 358–64
Nardi, John, Sr., 243, 256–59, 327–28;
as partner of Bill Presser, 45–46; and
Mob warfare in Cleveland, 245–46;
and Danny Greene, 246–51; killed,
259–60
Nardi, Lillian, 41
Nardi, Nick, 199, 260, 359

493